Religious Leaders and Faith-Based Politics

Ten Profiles

Jo Renee Formicola
and Hubert Morken, Editors

ROWMAN & LITTLEFIELD PUBLISHERS, INC.
Lanham • Boulder • New York • Oxford

ROWMAN & LITTLEFIELD PUBLISHERS, INC.

Published in the United States of America
by Rowman & Littlefield Publishers, Inc.
4720 Boston Way, Lanham, Maryland 20706
www.rowmanlittlefield.com

12 Hid's Copse Road
Cumnor Hill, Oxford OX2 9JJ, England

Copyright © 2001 by Rowman & Littlefield Publishers, Inc.

All rights reserved. No part of this publication may be reproduced, stored in a retrieval system, or transmitted in any form or by any means, electronic, mechanical, photocopying, recording, or otherwise, without the prior permission of the publisher.

British Library Cataloguing-in-Publication Information Available

Library of Congress Cataloging-in-Publication Data

Religious leaders and faith-based politics : ten profiles / edited by Jo Renee Formicola and Hubert Morken.
   p. cm.
   Includes bibliographical references and index.
   ISBN 0-8476-9962-5 (alk. paper) — ISBN 0-8476-9963-3 (pbk. : alk. paper)
   1. Clergy—United States—Political activity—History—20th century. 2. Civil rights workers—United States—History—20th century. 3. Religion and politics—United States—History—20th century. I. Formicola, Jo Renee, 1941– II. Morken, Hubert.

BL65.P7 R45 2001
322'.1'092273—dc21
                                                              2001019883

Printed in the United States of America

∞™ The paper used in this publication meets the minimum requirements of American National Standard for Information Sciences—Permanence of Paper for Printed Library Materials, ANSI/NISO Z39.48-1992.

To those religious leaders in the United States who refuse to be pushed to the margins and out of public life. They awaken spirituality, call for justice, speak up for righteousness, advocate change, motivate individuals, initiate projects, nurture leadership, elevate politics, transform communities, and promote the well-being of the nation.

To Allan and Mary, our spouses, who support us in myriad ways. They respect our work and encourage us to share it with a reading audience far beyond the walls and towers of the academy.

To our friends and colleagues in the Section on Religion and Politics in the American Political Science Association, pioneers all.

Contents

Acknowledgments	vii
Preface	ix
1 The Reverend Floyd Flake: African Methodist Episcopal Church Minister for School Choice *Michael Leo Owens*	1
2 Bishop T. D. Jakes: A Ministry for Empowerment *Hubert Morken*	25
3 The Reverend Al Sharpton: Pentecostal for Racial Justice *Jo Renee Formicola*	53
4 Elder Dallin H. Oaks: The Mormons, Politics, and Family Values *John R. Pottenger*	71
5 Rabbi Daniel Lapin and the Culture Wars *Hubert Morken*	89
6 The Reverend Benjamin Chavis-Muhammed: From Wilmington to Washington, from Chavis to Muhammed *James Lance Taylor*	115

7 The Reverend Michael Farris: Baptist Social Movement
   Organizer   141
   Mark Rozell

8 Dr. Ron Sider: Mennonite Environmentalist
   on the Evangelical Left   159
   Joel Fetzer and Gretchen S. Carnes

9 Sister Maureen Fiedler: A Nun for Gender Equality in Church
   and Society   175
   Mary Segers

10 Father J. Bryan Hehir: Priest, Policy Analyst, and Theologian
   of Dialogue   197
   William J. Gould

Epilogue   225
   Jo Renee Formicola and Hubert Morken

Bibliography   247

Index   261

About the Contributors   27

Acknowledgments

We wish to thank all those who made this book possible. First, we are grateful to those religious leaders and their staffs who gave time in busy schedules to help the authors understand their visions and roles as religious leaders in the United States. We are indebted, second, to all of the authors who took the initiative to interview their subjects, often traveling across the nation. Their efforts brought diverse perspectives and professional acumen to a little-studied phenomenon, growing in importance—the influence of religious leaders in public life. Third, we want to thank Dr. Donald Scruggs, who critiqued some of these chapters that were presented in preliminary form at the Conference of Americanists at the University of Warsaw. His invaluable insights were critical to the final and successful completion of several essays. Fourth, we wish to acknowledge our universities, Seton Hall and Regent, for granting sabbatical support and graduate student assistance, and our faculty colleagues, for their understanding and comments. Finally, we are grateful to our families for supporting us in completing another long, yet fulfilling project.

Preface

One of the first actions of President-Elect George W. Bush was to meet with a small group of influential religious leaders after his election to discuss the possibility of expanding the role of churches in state and federal welfare programs. In reporting the story, the *New York Times* emphasized the division between blacks and Mr. Bush and saw the meeting essentially as an attempt by the new administration to reconcile with African Americans through their religious leaders. This negative spin was offset by the *Washington Post*, which stressed the positive aspects of the meeting. It reported the beginning of a dialogue to focus on AIDS and on remedies for racial discrimination, as well as government support for "charitable choice" programs, which would promote tax credits for contributions to groups that work with the poor. More important than the political interpretation, however, was the fact that neither newspaper reported that Bush's emphasis on a new, "compassionate" social policy—one favoring "faith-based" initiatives—has the potential to bring about a major change in the relationship between government and religion in the United States. Although some decry this and others praise it, evidence indicates that U.S. religious leadership is already well aware that the nation is in the first stages of just such a metamorphosis, as the profiles in this book will show.

Religious Leaders and Faith-Based Politics: Ten Profiles follows our academic and personal interests: the dynamic interplay between religion and politics and their impact on public policy. Individually, we have authored biographies of religious leaders who have had significant influence in this area—the Reverend Pat Robertson and Pope John Paul II. Most recently, we turned our attention to education reform in the United States, publishing *The Politics of School Choice*. For that book, we interviewed numerous activists who worked for change in America's schools, and we found many of them to be members of the clergy. At that time, John Cardinal O'Connor in New York City, the Reverend Floyd Flake in Queens, and local pastors, as well as Catholic, Evangelical, and Jewish activists impressed us with their moral commitment to school choice and their political skills in attempting to advance that public policy.

This led us to take another look at American religious leadership in a broader context and to reconsider the role of the clergy in the U.S. political process today. Simple, yet complex questions arose. Were religious leaders today as active and vocal as the radicals of the turbulent 1960s? Were they still involved in civil rights? Have contentious moral questions such as abortion and social problems such as traditional family values, widely noted and discussed, preempted other issues? Are matters of economic development, education, social justice, human rights, and peace receiving less attention? Were ministers looking primarily to protect their institutional interests? Was a secular America excluding the religious, marginalizing them, keeping them out of politics? Now, in the wake of the 2000 election, as priorities change at the start of a new administration, we asked, *Where might we expect to see greater American religious involvement in the years ahead?*

To get some of these answers, we put out a call for chapter authors in fall 1999. We invited scholars in the field of religion and politics to submit proposals for profiles of religious leaders who have national influence over public life and policy issues. We also asked that emerging leaders be given priority because some, such as the Reverend Billy Graham and the Reverend Jesse Jackson, have already received a great deal of attention. New leaders are rising—some with dramatic speed and much publicity, like Bishop T. D. Jakes, and others gradually with little public notice, like Elder Dallin Oaks. We wanted our book to provide a fresh look at new models and practitioners of religious leadership interacting with the political world. Our one demand was that each writer interview the individual that he or she was going to profile to make our book up to date, vital, and personal, rather than one reliant on secondhand reporting.

The responses we received from scholars of religion and politics reflected an overwhelming interest in articulating the religious leadership of black ministers. This was to be expected as they have steadily become the most visible clerics working to bring equality and equity in the United States. At the start, proposals about Catholic, Evangelical, Jewish, Islamic, Mormon, and female clergy were absent from serious research consideration. This came as a surprise because Catholics and Evangelicals are the largest religious minorities in America. Jewish rabbis are influential with regard to matters of ethnic discrimination and American foreign policy toward Israel and other issues as well. The number of Muslims in America continues to proliferate, and politicians are paying greater attention to them—as both the election and the new administration demonstrate. Mormons, in the west, are the backbone of the family values movement, and their influence is spreading far beyond Utah. Women clergy are increasing by leaps and bounds in many religious denominations, and in all groups, women laity are present and active in political controversies of all kinds. Therefore, to provide as balanced a picture as possible, we began to broaden our search for proposals to reflect a more diverse and accurate portrayal of clergy in U.S. politics. And, after some effort, we are pleased to present essays that give a broad sampling of religious leaders and their public influence in the United States today. Much more could be written about each of them—each deserves a volume—and many other leaders should be studied, but time, space, and access limited our final choices.

This book begins by looking at three Protestant African American ministers who are studies in contrast. The first is the Reverend Floyd Flake. A minister in the African Methodist Episcopal Church, Flake is also a former U.S. congressman. Well-connected politically on the national and state levels, Flake is an activist for school choice in New York and the rest of the United States. Using traditional political tactics, Flake has already won the battle for charter schools in the Empire State. He was also rumored to have been a possible choice for secretary of education within the Bush administration. His establishment leadership style is in sharp contrast with that of Bishop T. D. Jakes and the Reverend Al Sharpton.

Bishop Jakes is in a category of his own. As one scholar puts it, "He can fill a stadium faster than anyone in America." With weekly national and international television programs, satellite outreach into hundreds of prisons, best-selling books published by Putnam, and creative work in music and drama, Jakes is a phenomenon. Able to attract 85,000 women to an annual "Woman, Thou Art Loosed!" Conference and sponsoring large conferences for men and church leaders, Jakes is the pastor of the Potter's House, a 26,000-member congregation in Dallas, Texas. Because of his close ties to Democrats and Republicans and a strong commitment to faith-based local ministry to the poor, some consider him a potential replacement for the Reverend Billy Graham as a national religious spokesperson and minister.

The Reverend Al Sharpton, who is in the news perhaps more than any other religious figure, raising questions and stirring controversy, is a national civil rights leader with Pentecostal roots. An "in-your-face," visible, vocal, and contentious activist, Sharpton has weighed in on every major racial discrimination case in New York City and beyond, from Bernhard Goetz to Abner Louima. He is apt to be on television almost every night, in court regularly, in jail on occasion, and rubbing elbows with the powerful, from U.S. presidents to Fidel Castro. Because of all this attention, Sharpton is well known but less understood than many other religious leaders.

The next three chapters deal with the leaders of significant minority religions in America: the Mormons, Orthodox Jews, and black Muslims. The Church of Jesus Christ of Latter-day Saints (LDS) is quietly involved in American politics today. Motivated by a central religious tenet of the eternity of the family, Mormons are concerned with those social events and political policies that are pressuring and destroying what the church considers to be the essential unit of society. Dallin Oaks, one of the Twelve Apostles of the LDS, was therefore a most welcome subject for one of the chapters. We understand that this is the first time such a high member of the Mormon leadership has consented to an interview for a project of this kind. Therefore, the articulation of his views will add a new dimension to the understanding of the LDS's contributions to public life in the United States.

In this same vein, we are also fortunate to present a profile of Rabbi Daniel Lapin. A soldier in the culture wars, Lapin is an Orthodox Jew who promotes what he calls a religious-based, principled involvement in politics. Because culture wars can divide denominations and even politicians, Lapin's views are contrasted with those of Senator Joseph Lieberman, former candidate for vice president and also an Orthodox Jew. This juxtaposition, we believe, will help the general public understand some of the underlying divisions in American culture and how they affect U.S. politics. Lapin also demonstrates how strategies of cooperation with Evangelicals and others are a distinctive part of coalition building in grassroots American politics. Lapin is an example of how ties with political parties and candidates, specifically with the Republicans and George W. Bush, make it possible for religious leaders to gain access and influence in the policy process.

The growth of Islam in America is also important, and, therefore, we were most anxious to include a chapter on Benjamin Chavis-Muhammed. A member of the "Wilmington Ten" and the National Association for the Advancement of Colored People, he converted to Islam and is now a leader of the Reverend Louis Farrakhan's Nation of Islam. A force behind the Million Man March, Chavis-Muhammed also planned and carried out the Million Family March. We felt that it was incumbent on us to include his views to give as broad a picture as possible of how religion is being used in the political process today by leaders across the entire religious and political spectrum.

Ron Sider and Michael Farris have been included because they are examples of Evangelical activism for the environment and home schooling, two timely issues. Like Lapin and Lieberman, they share the same religious orthodoxy but have little common political ground—one is on the Right, the other, on the Left. Sider is instrumental in getting ecological concerns onto the political agenda and, in the current public debate, promotes more regulation and protection. Farris, on the other hand, works to protect home schooling from what he considers illegal and damaging government regulations. Each, with great vigor, promotes his cause and views it as a sacred calling and obligation. Both are part of the new breed of Christian ministers: educated and influential—one is an author with a Ph.D. from Yale University, and the other, an author and lawyer who has argued before the Supreme Court. Both have created effective organizations and are engaged in the grassroots mobilization of supporters to influence legislation.

This book concludes by looking at two major Catholic religious leaders, the Reverend J. Bryan Hehir and Sister Maureen Fielder. They are contrasts in Catholic leadership styles. Hehir represents the activism of a traditional priest in the public arena. As the editor and author of the Bishop's letter on peace in the early 1980s and the head of the Office of Justice and Peace of the United States Catholic Conference for more than a decade, Hehir served the Catholic Bishops of America as an adviser and developer of public policy on human rights and social justice during the Reagan era and beyond. He was at the center of all major Catholic efforts to influence foreign policy during that time and remains well connected to the Washington power elite because of his current positions at Harvard University. Sister Fielder, on the other hand, has been anything but traditional in her approach to politics. A nun with strong feminist leanings, Fielder has spoken out for women's rights, has led demonstrations, and today hosts a radio show about the current political climate.

The methodology for this book was simple: interview the individuals at hand and then review all the literature available about them. In most cases, there were no biographies or extensive examinations of their ministries and public roles. As a result, these chapters are initial examinations of religious subjects that provide original comments by the leaders themselves about their work and motivation. Significant amounts of new information, therefore, have been examined and interpreted by the authors. The editors provide an in-depth analysis of this data at the end of the book to place the contributors' findings in a broader context and evaluate them. Information is highlighted, in a search for patterns that will help readers understand the varieties and similarities, the strengths and limitations, of present and future American religious leaders.

The editors share one assumption with all the authors—that religious leadership can play a significant role in politics. Internationally, the rise of Islam has had a major impact on the culture and power structure in the Middle East. The pontificate of Pope John Paul II has influenced the demise of communism and post–Cold War politics. Both reinforce the fact that religious leadership has become a major force on the political spectrum in international relations. Domestically as well, the growth of conservative Christianity in America, the emergence of religious diversity, and the increasing involvement of denominational groups in the public arena attest to the fact that religious leaders are able to play a part in shaping public policy in the United States. Most significantly, the outreach of President George W. Bush to that leadership is extending an opportunity for clergy to become an even greater force for the delivery of social and charitable services in America today. Scholars who study the interaction of religion and politics know that each institution has the potential to be a force for good or evil in the lives of peoples, communities, and nations. We believe, therefore, that this book will help shed light on religious leaders and political causes, demonstrating their capacities to change lives and influence politics for the future.

1

The Reverend Floyd Flake: African Methodist Episcopal Church Minister for School Choice

Michael Leo Owens

Responsibility for improving the academic performance of students in urban public schools rests with a diverse set of individuals and institutions. As political scientist Jeffrey Henig and his colleagues remarked after studying urban school reform in Atlanta, Baltimore, Detroit, and Washington, D.C., "school reform is a complex multi-actor game."[1] Contestants include elected and appointed policy makers and bureaucrats as well as others. Often collaborating with them in a variety of ways are nongovernmental actors, ranging from academics to activists.[2] Among the latter, Afro-Christian religious leaders are conspicuous,[3] for some are traditional stakeholders in the urban public school system and can be identified as "major players" in the public school reform game.[4] According to Joseph Vitteritti, a political scientist who runs the Program on Education and Civil Society at New York University, Afro-Christian religious leaders, collectively, are "the sleeping giant in the whole urban school-reform movement."[5]

One of the most important Afro-Christian religious leaders trying to reform urban public schools is the Reverend Dr. Floyd H. Flake. Flake is pastor of the Allen African Methodist Episcopal (AME) Church in New York City. He identifies the need for quality urban public schools as the primary political cause for religious leaders and civil rights organizations in the twenty-first century. Referring to the New Testament, the Reverend Flake speaks to why Afro-Christian religious leaders should champion improvements in the quality of education that children receive from urban public schools as a political cause: "In the Gospels, we learn that Jesus called to a woman who appeared outside [a] synagogue bent over. He touched her. Then he sent her from that place straightened up. I think the business of Jesus, which animates my actions, is to try to straighten up bent-over situations. Right now, the most bent-over situation I see is public schooling in our inner cities. It's part of our job to straighten it up."[6]

The Reverend Flake knows of the problem of urban public schools. In 1999, in the public school district where Allen AME Church is located, 66 percent and 68 percent of fourth grade students and eighth grade students, respectively, in the public schools did not meet the standards for English language arts (reading, writing, and comprehension) set by the New York State Board of Education.[7] While the school district is 87 percent black and Latino, it is not poor. Rather, it, like southeast Queens generally, is largely middle class, with black median household incomes being among the highest in the country.[8] For the Reverend Flake, if public schools can fail to teach the children in a relatively affluent urban neighborhood like his, then the situation facing black and Latino children in less prosperous communities is dire.[9]

Public opinion is on the side of the reverend. In New York, 71 percent of African American respondents and 54 percent of Latino respondents to a statewide survey rated the quality of public education in the state as "not so good" or "poor."[10] As for the quality of public education in poor and minority neighborhoods, 60 percent of whites and 72 percent of both blacks and Latinos consider it to be worsening.[11]

As a religious leader, the Reverend Flake believes that his mandate, especially as a pastor from a minority community, is to speak publicly about the injustice of public schools that fail to prepare students from inner cities to assume productive roles in society. His mission is to reform how public school students learn by changing where they learn. A few years ago, public-funded vouchers for use at public, parochial, and private schools were the chief policy alternative the Reverend Flake promoted to accomplish this goal. Under school voucher programs, authority over the use of a portion of government funds earmarked for public education would transfer from bureaucrats to parents, who then might use the monies to send their children to public or private schools, whichever they believed would offer them the best education. Vouchers, Flake thought initially, could expand the educational choices of parents, albeit some, not all. However, his support for vouchers has waned because of their potentially limited effect in improving the performance of a critical mass of public school students.[12] Consequently, he has reoriented his focus to charter schools.[13] These are public-funded schools administered by nongovernmental agents and operating free of traditional regulations concerning administration, curriculums, and hiring.[14] Proponents like Flake hail charter schools for their regulatory freedom, pedagogical experimentation, greater parental involvement, smaller student-teacher ratios, higher expectations, and use of teacher incentives to improve student performance. Again, surveys suggest that he has the support of much of the public.[15] In championing charter schools, the Reverend Flake still makes use of vouchers, but they remain his "gorilla in the closet," which he releases whenever he wants to frighten anti–school choice advocates and encourage them to soften their opposition to the use of charter schools in urban school districts.[16]

The Reverend Flake's commitment to charter schools, along with his acceptance of other reforms like scholarships and vouchers, makes him a leader in the American school choice movement, that political network of individuals and institutions that support the incorporation of free market elements such as competition to achieve greater accountability, innovation, and excellence from urban public schools.[17] However, it is the visibility and authority gained from his multiple positions of public influence that he uses to speak on the issue of charter schools that permit him recognition as one of the leaders of the movement.[18] These positions include pastor of a nationally known megachurch and retired congressman. He is also senior fellow at the Manhattan Institute for Policy Research, a neoconservative think tank,[19] and opinion columnist for the *New York Post*, a politically conservative daily newspaper. He also serves as president of Edison Charter Schools, a for-profit education management enterprise, and as a member of numerous boards of directors of public and private institutions. Because of the influence that comes from these positions, the Reverend Flake does not have to limit himself to what he describes as "sounding brass and tingling cymbal"; he can do more than just publicly lament the situation of urban public schools. As he says, "Words don't build; it takes really the involvement of people to make political changes."[20] Consequently, the Reverend Flake takes political action to draw attention to the problem of poor student performance in urban public schools. By his political action, he encourages policy makers, teachers, and parents to accept charter schools as the best means of educating students in urban public school systems.

Generally, the types of political action that the Reverend Flake relies on are common to many policy advocates. He practices traditional pressure tactics to get policy makers and the public to consider the merits of charter schools. This chapter focuses on those political means used to advance charter schools in New York State and the nation.

NEO-PENTECOSTAL PREACHER AND ACTIVIST PASTOR

Born in Los Angeles, California, in 1945, Floyd Flake grew up in Houston, Texas, in a Christian family that had deep working-class roots but was sometimes impoverished. Throughout his adolescence, Flake, eight of his thirteen siblings, and his parents shared a small two-bedroom house that lacked running water.[21] To escape poverty, Flake's parents, who lacked even an elementary education, encouraged him to go to college. To them, education was the primary path out of the Houston ghetto for a young black man. Heeding them, Flake would later graduate from Wilberforce University, a historically black university affiliated with the AME denomination in Ohio. After earning his degree, Flake later became an associate dean of students at Lincoln University in Pennsylvania (1970–73). Subsequently, he moved to Boston, where he served as director of the Martin Luther King Jr. Afro-American Center, dean of students, and university chaplain at Boston University (1973–76). Eventually, he would receive a Doctorate of Ministry from United Theological Seminary in Dayton, Ohio (1994).

During his tenure as a college administrator, Flake, who began preaching at age thirteen, sermonized on Sundays at local AME churches. Until the mid-1970s, Flake had only led others in prayer and worship as a visiting minister; he never led his own congregation. That changed in 1976, when AME Bishop Richard Allen Hildebrand installed Flake as senior pastor of Allen AME Church in Jamaica, Queens, one of the boroughs of New York City. Although Flake lacked the experience to lead a congregation, his reputation as a superior preacher and minister committed to community outreach earned him his appointment to head the 140-year-old Afro-Christian church. He assumed his pulpit at age thirty-one. Now approaching his twenty-fifth year at Allen AME, the Reverend Flake shepherds a flock of 11,000, up from his initial 1,400.[22]

As a preacher, the Reverend Flake is what sociologists of the black church describe as a neo-Pentecostal, one who combines "the letter and the spirit [of the Bible], transcending the sheer emotionalism" of traditional Pentecostals by incorporating spirit-filled services with biblical exegesis and instruction.[23] While maintaining elements of the formality of traditional AME worship, what C. Eric Lincoln and Lawrence Mamiya refer to as "order and decorum," Flake livens his worship services with emotive preaching, praising, and proclaiming.[24] Whereas Flake's predecessor at Allen AME was content to preach from behind the pulpit, Flake is different. During services, he is physical. He steps, even dances, from behind the rostrum into the aisles of the church. Reaching out to his congregants, he touches them. He also encourages them to express their passion for their God through song, dance, and speaking in tongues.

Floyd Flake may be a neo-Pentecostal preacher whose services are often reminiscent of revivals or camp meetings, but he is not an otherworldly pastor. He does not maintain the "pie-in-the-sky attitude toward everyday social and political problems" that sociologists Lincoln and Mamiya encountered among many black clergy in conducting their research on black churches in the African American experience.[25] That is, the Reverend Flake attends to the earthly needs and values of his congregants. He speaks to the temporal difficulties of black folk, inclusive of individual sin, neighborhood problems, and community deficits. Flake is a minister who expresses publicly and demonstrates tangibly his Savior's deep care for black people and wishes for them to be free of poverty and pathology while they are among the living. As he notes, "Heaven is found not merely in the reward of the afterlife but in the heavenly environment that [we] create in this life."[26] Consequently, he seconds the statement of the Reverend Gardner C. Taylor (former pastor of Brooklyn's Concord Baptist Church of Christ) that black Christians sometimes "must get out of the Bible and into people's lives."[27] In tandem with the Methodist tradition of concern for the underprivileged and black liberation theology, Flake accepts the charge to address social problems, like failing students in urban public schools, though a moral perspective.[28] As he explained, "Black liberation theology plays a major role in my seeing the African American church being the vehicle for the energizing of people to bring about positive political and social change. It also allows me to see that the black church has the potential to be more than just a once a week emotional cathartic experience but, rather, an empowering and liberating force if utilized properly."[29] For the Reverend Flake, Afro-Christian churches can best "make the Word flesh" by seeking to better temporal conditions for blacks in cities.[30]

Unlike some adherents of black liberation theology, Flake is more reformer than revolutionary. He is devoted, to use the words of religion sociologists Baer and Singer, "to a reformist strategy of social activism that will enable African Americans to become better integrated into the political, economic, and social institutions of the larger society . . . [and] share in the benefits of the American Dream."[31] Nevertheless, as an adherent of black liberation theology, the Reverend Flake believes that God directs him to use his prophetic voice as a preacher to advocate the interests of the black poor and those living between the poles of poverty and prosperity. He agrees with black liberation theologian Gayraud Wilmore that the black pulpit should practice "more a theology of the people than an academic, professional theology. Its overarching interest [should be] in making contact with the masses and reeducating them for taking and wielding power."[32] To this end, Flake preaches and practices a Christianity that seeks to alleviate poor conditions that a large proportion of black people continue to face by bettering the social and economic opportunity structures in their communities. Although the Reverend Flake appreciates the power of black electoral and protest mobilization to secure government redress of social problems, he understands that they alone are insufficient means for changing the state of the black working class and unemployed in America. Personal initiative and enterprise, he advocates, are also necessary, and he believes that the church can be a catalyst for helping people pick themselves up by their bootstraps and rebuild urban black communities, starting with the education of their children and the economics of their neighborhoods.[33] For the Reverend Flake, his church is more than an institution for spiritual transcendence. He considers it "God's institution for energizing, empowering, and inspiring God's people to find the best that is within themselves[;] then [they are able] to utilize what God has given them to empower others through what we call the development of a witness which is physical and emotional and gives hope to the dreams and aspirations of people."[34]

To manifest his concern for the sacred and secular needs of his congregants and residents of the community where his church stands, the Reverend Flake amalgamates the three historic types of activist Afro-Christian religious leaders:[35] community developer, social reformer, and political leader. Like a "church-based programmatic activist," Flake immerses himself in church-driven community development, "focus[ing] essentially on organization through the church structure to achieve certain goals mainly of an economic nature, such as jobs, better housing, better health care, and better educational facilities."[36] He expends the resources of his congregation, particularly the 11 million dollars it contributes annually to Allen AME Church, for his church to develop programs that provide community residents with neighborhood-based programs of social, physical, and financial uplift. Since 1976, for example, Allen AME Church has used its operating budget to leverage public and private assistance for the development of approximately 200 units of affordable housing and the creation of almost 1,000 jobs for the residents of southeast Queens. The church also, according to the reverend, has catalyzed the investment of more than 100 million dollars of public and private funds in the neighborhoods surrounding the church.[37] As a result, Allen AME Church has become a model of effective Afro-Christian church-based community development. Presently, with eleven corporate (for-profit and not-for-profit) enterprises with combined assets of approximately 25 million dollars, the church is addressing a range of community needs.

Following the pattern of the "church-based local activist," the Reverend Flake involves himself in social reform campaigns. In contrast to some other Afro-Christian religious leaders in New York, such as Al Sharpton (National Action Network), Herbert Daughtry (House of the Lord), or Calvin Butts (Abyssinian Baptist Church), Floyd Flake rarely participates in mass action or public agitation. For instance, with the exception of the killing of an unarmed African immigrant by the New York Police Department in 1999, the Reverend Flake has joined few of the notable protest demonstrations in New York City. His absence from the frontlines of protest in New York City is not due to a lack of concern. Rather, boycotts and demonstrations for social reform are not his methods. He prefers individual action on civic issues:

I think my responsibility is to call attention to problems, and clergy's responsibility is to call attention to problems and not necessarily accept the status quo. I think that's what Jesus' ministry was all about. But there are various ways to go about that. You can do it the way Jesse Jackson and Al Sharpton do it—with protest. I don't stand opposed to their method, but you also have to have someone who is the builder and the processor. I think those two roles of clergy, the protester on the one, the protest leader and the activist, and then the processor, the person who takes the time to really process the arguments that they make and bring about some visible evidence that what they speak about is a possibility.[38]

As "processor," Flake functions as a political insider, one who attempts to influence privately the decisions and actions of policy makers. The reverend may not take to the streets, but he makes telephone calls to, and meets behind closed doors with, influential allies to negotiate political change or manage conflict. He also is quick to voice his views through established organs such as the opinion pages of the press and participate in political processes like public hearings. Because he limits his participation in direct protest action, political and economic elites view him as a respectable man and responsible black leader; they do not consider him militant or radical. Consequently, public officials and corporate executives invite him to sit on influential boards, call on him to give them policy advice, and sometimes seek from him political cover for actions that have negative consequences. In return, Flake increases his access to policy makers and receives a broader hearing of his claims for particular political reforms.

Similar to the "community-based local activist," the Reverend Flake uses politics, especially electoral politics, to advance his theology. Describing himself as a "moderate with a basic conservative economic philosophy and a moderate to liberal social philosophy,"[39] Flake readily exchanges his political support for elected officials for patronage to his church and community. For example, during the late 1970s and early 1980s, Flake backed Democratic and Republican incumbents, including New York City Mayor Edward I. Koch and U.S. Senator Alfonse D'Amato, for reelection, which yielded government contracts, grants, and land to Allen AME Church and its subsidiary corporations. For instance, the political support of Flake enabled Allen AME Church to secure a loan from the U.S. Department of Housing and Urban Development to build a $10 million affordable housing complex for senior citizens. Flake's pattern of bartering political support for patronage and privilege continued during his eleven-year stint in the U.S. House of Representatives, where Flake was a maverick partisan.[40] Generally, Flake voted the party line of congressional Democrats on issues like Medicare and Medicaid, housing subsidies, and public transportation. On some economic and moral issues like privatization and abortion, however, Flake sided with Republicans. His alliances with, and political endorsements of, Republicans—both moderate and archconservative—vexed Democrats. The Reverend Flake, however, continued to "vote for power, not party."[41] During his later years in Congress, remaining responsive to those with the political authority to address his concerns translated into Flake allying himself more with Republicans on a number of other issues, ranging from bank lending, to affordable housing, to school vouchers. The logic underlying his dalliances with the Right was political; Flake would not let political differences stand in the way of bringing public resources (e.g., federal agency buildings, public jobs, and housing development loans and grants) to his and other black communities.[42] Since retiring from Congress in 1997, Flake has continued to seek alliances with right-leaning political, as well as economic, elites to advance his political causes. No cause has benefited more from his alliances with the Right than the reform of urban public schooling through charter schools.

CHARTER SCHOOLS: TAKING UP THE CAUSE AND SEEKING ALLIES

On 18 December 1998, New York became the thirty-fifth state to legalize charter schools. The New York Charter Schools Act expresses the hope held by the state's legislators and the governor that this form of school choice will improve the performance of public school students, particularly those from urban school districts. The act provides a framework for the creation, operation, and financing of 100 charter schools.

Eight months before the enactment of charter schools in New York, Governor George Pataki held a press conference to announce the legislation for the Charter Schools Act. A phalanx of proponents stood with the governor, but the Reverend Flake was one of the few he permitted to speak in support of his legislation. Few observers were surprised to see the reverend there. Fewer were surprised that the governor allowed him to speak, for the involvement of the Reverend Flake in the politics of school choice and his support for charter schools began in the 1980s.

Responding to reports of low student performance on reading and arithmetic tests in the public schools that dot the neighborhoods around Allen AME Church, Flake led his congregation in protest. However, instead of protesting through confrontation, the Reverend Flake and his congregants protested through competition. The church developed and funded a model school, the Allen Christian School (Allen School), to compete with the local public schools for students. The purpose was twofold: (1) to better educate neighborhood children and (2) to demonstrate that low student performance in public schools was the fault of rigid bureaucratic practices concerning administration and teaching. The Reverend Flake recounted the logic behind the creation of the Allen School:

> Where public education fails is not just in the area of not having small classrooms, or not having certified teachers, or not having buildings that are in the best state of repair; but where they fail is low expectations and the lowering of standards for minority students, which then mitigates against the possibility of them being able to score well on tests and mitigates against the possibility that they will be better to get into the better institutions. So I got us involved by trying to build a model, in building the Allen Christian School, that I felt could show that kids from these communities and communities like southeast Queens could be educated if the expectations were high and if they had an environment in which they had an ability to develop the kind of self-esteem and self-worth that I think is still necessary for many African American young people.

The Allen School was a success from its inception. Founded in 1982, the Allen School is a private academy that combines Christian teaching with traditional elementary pedagogy and curriculum, emphasizing reading and arithmetic. Within a few years, the school went from offering prekindergarten through third grade instruction to include classes through the eighth grade. It also moved from the basement of the church to a $3.8 million four-story complex owned by the church. It has seventeen instruction and resource rooms, a computer lab, a library–media resource center, and a music room, cafeteria, gymnasium, chapel, and play area. The church financed the building through the tithes and pledges of its congregants, along with commercial loans. The church continues to subsidize the school, which keeps tuition relatively low ($3,400) and offers scholarships to needy students. According to the Reverend Flake, some of the best high schools in the city recruit its graduates, and 99 percent of its graduates receive college degrees. He also claims that, minus its sectarian aspects, the Allen School functions much like a charter school. It is small, admitting fewer than 600 students annually, and it is resource rich. Furthermore, it requires, unlike public schools in the district, that the parents of its students be involved in the operation of the school. Finally, the school keeps administrative costs to a minimum, allowing for a lean bureaucracy and more direct use of funds for teaching and supplies. Beyond providing students with a quality education, the Allen School provides parents in southeast Queens, as well as other parts of the city, with an expanded choice for educating their children.

The Allen School became the working charter school model for the Reverend Flake of how a small school, as well as private scholarships, could make a difference in the performance of students from urban neighborhoods. In the late 1980s, Flake, supported by the successes of the Allen School, began to promote charter schools, along with scholarships and vouchers, to policy makers and the public, especially leaders in urban black communities. He contended that charter schools could be an effective method for addressing some of the problems of urban public schools in of New York and elsewhere. Flake received positive responses from the Republicans and centrist Democrats. Liberals in the Democratic Party, however, attacked the reverend as a neoconservative dupe of the Right. Claiming to represent best the interests and values held by urban blacks, his critics, including many members of the Congressional Black Caucus and the National Association for the Advancement of Colored People, charged that Flake opposed public education and minority teachers. His defense was that public schools were not his enemy rather that bad administrators, unqualified teachers, and public schools were.

> My argument is that the system of public education as we know it needs challenge and without any challenge will continue to promise reforms but will not feel a need to deliver on them because they do not have to be accountable for the fodder they produce in order to get their constant flow of per capitation dollars from the state budgets. Until you find a way to force them to have to compete for those dollars, I just don't think you're going to see a change in the schools in the most terrible urban communities. I'm not against public education; I'm against inferior education. If it is not delivered at a quality where every parent believes their child has an opportunity to learn and be competitive with other children, then I must fight for them.[43]

In carrying his fight forward into the national and subnational legislatures and administrative agencies, the Reverend Flake courted allies to lobby for the expansion of governmental support for the authorization of charter schools, along with other policy alternatives such as vouchers, private scholarships, and magnet schools, even if only as pilot programs.

Most of the allies of the Reverend Flake in the fight to bring charter schools to New York and the rest of the county came out of the school choice movement. Included among them were neoconservative education experts such as former U.S. Secretary of Education William Bennett. Affluent Wall Street and Madison Avenue executives like Steven Klinsky, the founder and chief executive officer of the for-profit education management firm Victory Schools, and Peter Flanigan, founder of the School Choice Scholarship Program, also joined with the Reverend Flake on the charter schools campaign. Likewise, philanthropists such as Ted Forstman and John Walton, who founded the Children's Scholarship Fund, threw their support behind Flake.[44] So too did activists like Jeanne Allen, founder of the Center for Education Reform.[45] Initially, few members of the activist wing of Afro-Christian religious leadership supported Flake. There were black ministers and pastors who were unaware of the charter school movement, particularly black involvement in it. Partisan Democrats among them, who opposed vouchers, assumed that charters were a veiled attempt by conservative Republicans to reduce funding for public schools. Then, too, there were black pastors who saw charter schools as a threat to the finances of their churches; public school teachers and administrators occupy more than a few pews in black churches. Eventually, however, a number of black pastors backed Flake's appeals to expand school choice in urban public school districts through charter schools. Among them were the Reverend Dr. Wyatt Tee Walker of Canaan Baptist Church of Christ in Harlem, New York, and the Reverend Marlon Moss of Greater Northeast Baptist Church in Indianapolis. As for legislators, Republicans like Congressman J. C. Watts and former Ohio Secretary of State Kenneth Blackwell welcomed the appeals of Flake, but few Democrats were receptive. Like some pastors, they identified charter schools with vouchers and feared cuts in funding to schools in their districts. In 1997, New York State Senator Lawrence Seabrook remarked of his colleagues in the state legislature, "The idea is just not understood. Most of my colleagues think that charter schools have something to do with vouchers, and this confusion has generated a lot of resistance."[46] They also questioned the general lack of blacks among the leadership of the school choice movement. Furthermore, some who had been public school teachers, or at least received campaign and reelection support from teachers' unions, favored reforms that might improve schools without transferring authority to nongovernmental entities. Such reforms included merit pay for teachers, construction of new classrooms to reduce class sizes, and equalized financing of school districts. But, like the black pastors, eventually a few black elected officials such as State Senator Seabrook and New York State Assemblyman Roger Green allied themselves with the Reverend Flake on the charter schools issue. With this diverse group of allies, Flake engaged in political action both inside and outside the formal channels of education policy making to bias the support of policy makers, and their constituents, for charter schools.

POLITICAL ACTION ON BEHALF OF THE CAUSE

The ways of accessing and influencing the decisions and actions of policy makers are varied. The use of one form of political action by an activist seeking policy changes does not preclude the use of another.[47] Accordingly, before passage of the 1998 New York Charter Schools Act, the Reverend Flake carried out three types of political strategies to legalize charter schools in New York: activities to impact the legislature, tactics to affect elections, and efforts to educate and energize the public about the public school reform issue.

Lobbying the Legislature

Legislative lobbying was a common political act of the Reverend Flake. That is, he engaged in continuous discussions and advisement with state legislators about education policy alternatives. The efforts of the Reverend Flake to influence state legislators in New York involved direct methods of communication. The telephone call was the chief means of communicating his views about charter schools to legislators. Unlike many, perhaps most, education activists in the charter school debate, Flake was a former elected congressman and a well-connected politician, who had endorsed, stumped, and assisted in raising campaign funds for others. He also represented an 11,000-member church known for electoral mobilization. Thus, Flake had the clout to call on state legislators such as Steven Sanders, chair of the New York State Assembly Education Committee, or Assembly Speaker Sheldon Silver to express his opinions about pending legislation, to offer proposals for future legislation, or to get answers regarding the progress of bills. Still, Flake also relied on office visits. He, alone or as part of a delegation, had enough influence to ensure meetings with powerful legislators to discuss the problem of low student performance in the state's public schools and the range of options available to address it. Beyond placing calls and meeting with legislators, the Reverend Flake testified at legislative hearings on the state of public education as well. By his estimate, in the two years leading up to the enactment of the New York Charter Schools Law, he testified on behalf of charter schools and other school choice initiatives at more than one dozen hearings.[48]

During his consultations with legislators and in his expert testimony before legislative committees, Flake emphasized the poor state of academic achievement in urban public schools and the success of the Allen School in turning around the grades of low-performing students. He supported evaluations concerning the prospects of charter schools and other reforms, updated what other states had done or planned to do on the issue, and outlined the steps legislators could take to ease charter schools into the public school system.[49] Legislators, even those sympathetic to charter schools, often answered the Reverend Flake with statements to the effect that union opposition was too strong for charter schools to become law in New York. As a result, the reverend would instinctively raise the issue of vouchers. Flake's introduction of vouchers into his consultations and testimony was particularly effective in pragmatic politics, rather than an attempt at rational policy making. For Flake, vouchers represent a fulcrum of fear. As the Reverend Flake has commented,

> I have used the voucher [issue] as sort of my hammer to get attention to the issue of urban education or the problems of education. Vouchers cannot solve the problems

because most of the people who are most severely impacted by public education today are in the lower tier economically. Unless you were giving vouchers that were equal to the public per capitation per student, they would not be nearly as effective. But one of the things the public bureaucracy understands is if you had a major voucher movement, supported in part by the business elites that began to pour massive dollars into [it], you could bleed numerous kids out of the current system if they could ever get enough dollars to support every child.[50]

The fear of vouchers among the legislators, as well as the traditional stakeholders in the public school system, namely, unionized administrators and teachers, strengthened Flake's appeals for the legislature to authorize less drastic policy changes in public education in New York. Specifically, he used their fear of vouchers to leverage the introduction and expansion of charter schools, which he knew were more acceptable to the anti-choice lobby in Albany.

Although all members of the legislature were important to any vote on charter schools, the Reverend Flake focused his appeals on a core group of swing voters in the state legislature. In particular, he targeted the black and Latino caucuses, comprised of Democrats from the Assembly and the Senate. In approaching this group of legislators, the Reverend Flake relied on moral and ethical appeals, along with shame, in his attempts to pierce their perceptual screen concerning charter schools. Generally, black and Latino legislators opposed charter schools as a Republican attempt to decrease public investment in public schools and a step toward the legalization of vouchers. Blacks and Latinos in the leadership of the Assembly and those who were key recipients of contributions from the New York State United Teachers voiced this view most often. Whether they believed their statements is debatable. Knowing that most black and Latino legislators were Christians and relied on the backing of Afro-Christian churches for their electoral success, the Reverend Flake made a case to them for charter schools, sometimes even in the pulpits of their own churches, by incorporating Scripture and references to the Gospels. His message was moral as well as political:

> I think as we look at the crisis of education, we are looking at a necessity for straightening, and healing, and bringing about a new sense of self-worth. That's what Jesus did at every turn. That's what he did when he told the man, "Take up your bed. You have been palsied and on this bed too long. So take up your bed and walk." I think that is the challenge of black leadership on charter schools. They need to look within themselves and find their greater strengths. Though they have believed they would be lying down until their deaths, they must become empowered to pick themselves up and go do for their communities what they can do, as opposed to waiting for others to serve their communities while they just lie there.[51]

Also, as he did when he was a member of the Congressional Black Caucus in the U.S. House of Representatives, Flake highlighted the ethical problems of opposition to charter schools by black and Latino legislators. Specifically, he argued that there was nothing wrong with legislators educating their children at parochial and private schools, which most did. But he maintained that it was unfair of them to oppose legislation that would extend the same privilege to their constituents, most of whom could only send their children to public schools with poor reputations for student achievement: "I told them, you cannot sit there and not let other kids be educated. You will not put your own kids in public schools. So my reaction was if it ain't good enough for their kids, then it ain't good enough for the other kids, and they had a responsibility to change it to make it good for everybody."[52]

Additionally, Flake challenged publicly the reputations and records of legislators, albeit not by name. Echoing a common critique of black and Latino electoral incorporation, the Reverend Flake asserted that the legislators were of little effect to their constituents, especially when it came to education policy. To him, black faces in elected positions had made little difference in the educational opportunities and performance of black and Latino children. His evidence was that the schools with the worst student performance were in the districts of black and Latino legislators.

Of course, an unspoken reality was if moral-ethical appeals and shaming failed to influence legislators, Flake could, if he wanted to, exploit their self-interest. The reputation of the Reverend Flake in New York is that he can broker benefits from the city and state of New York, as well as the private sector. While guarantees were impossible, some legislators believed that if they had difficulty getting a project or funding for their district, or if an appointment of a supporter to a board that was important to him or her stalled, the backing of Flake could play a role in biasing the outcome. After all, Flake was comfortable working with the Republican administrations in New York City and Albany, and his patrons on the Right were often amenable to his suggestions. Furthermore, Flake was known to have friends with deep pockets, whose campaign giving he could possibly sway. All of these factors probably encouraged some legislators to side eventually with him and his allies on the charter school issue.

Electioneering

Beyond lobbying the legislature, the Reverend Flake made conscious attempts to influence the selection and decisions of public policy makers. Influencing who holds elected office and their appointments of administrative departments that oversee the implementation of their decisions is critical to determining the quality and degree of government responsiveness to public issues, particularly one as contentious as urban public school reform. Therefore, an important, but small, part of the efforts of the Reverend Flake to bring charter schools to New York included electioneering. Foremost among his electoral activities were endorsements. Flake made key endorsements of candidates supporting charter schools legislation in New York in the 1997 New York City mayoral reelection campaign of Rudolph Giuliani and the 1998 gubernatorial reelection campaign of George Pataki. Giuliani was a strong advocate for radically changing public education in New York, particularly in New York City. Along with charter schools, the mayor favored private-funded scholarships and public-funded vouchers, along with the use of parochial schools to educate a segment of the city's public school students. As for Pataki, Flake had been working with him for months on the charter schools legislation, as well as a number of other issues related to inner-city economic development and the Allen AME Church.

Detractors of the minister contended that his endorsements were quid pro quos for his church to continue receiving patronage dispensed from the Republican administrations and for Flake to remain silent during racially polarizing events related to police brutality. Alternatively, they argued that Flake's endorsements were attempts to build a base of support for a future bid for mayor of New York City. If predictions come true and Flake runs for mayor of New York City in 2001, it is plausible that he could receive the endorsement of Governor Pataki, Mayor Giuliani, and the rest of the Republican Party, along with a Democratic Party nod if he wins its primary, which is possible. The cynics may be correct, but there are other reasons why Flake endorsed Republicans. First, and most important, Flake's support for Pataki and Giuliani increased the likelihood that his pathways for accessing the powerful remained open to him so that he could influence the attentiveness and responsiveness of policy makers to the problems of urban public education. The Reverend Flake agrees: "I've endorsed across what African Americans would see as our party line, the Democratic line, but it gave me access to be able to be in constant dialogue on the whole question of educational reform with charters."[53] Understanding that the true power of endorsing someone comes from reminding the recipient of the support, the Reverend Flake, after endorsing candidates, would routinely contact them to learn what policy makers were thinking and share with them his own policy views and proposals. Second, his endorsements demonstrated to his GOP allies that his support for them, at least on education issues, was sincere and unimpeachable. Third, he telegraphed his requirement to Democrats that his future support for them, especially in the 2001 and 2002 races, for mayor of New York City and governor, respectively, would necessitate that they support school choice experimentation. Fourth, Flake signaled to other Afro-Christian religious leaders, in New York and around the country, that they and their communities could benefit by voting for those with power rather than those seeking power.

Educating the Public

When he was not lobbying or electioneering, much of Flake's work on behalf of charter schools involved civic education. Through public appearances and mass media, he instructed the broader public about charter schools and appealed for its support. The Reverend Flake took advantage of nearly every opportunity possible for him to communicate his opinions about reforming public education, particularly to minority groups. Among the venues where the Reverend Flake spread the gospel of choice and charter schools were Afro-Christian churches. Because of his superior preaching ability, national name recognition, fund-raising skills, and the success of the community development organizations affiliated with Allen AME, other pastors regularly invited Flake to stand in their own pulpits and sermonize. According to the reverend, in every sermon he gave as a guest preacher, which was more than 100 times, he inserted a school choice message. Aside from churches, however, cable television and talk radio gave the Reverend Flake platforms from which he could broadcast his views. Included among the most important venues was C-Span, the twenty-four-hour public affairs network on cable television. Every couple of months, C-Span would show one-on-one interviews with the Reverend Flake or his public addresses at think tanks and panel presentations at conferences. Beyond C-Span, electronic media targeted to black communities also gave the Reverend Flake opportunities to make direct appeals to black citizens to support charter schools. Among the shows he appeared on were *The Tom Joyner Show*, a popular nationally syndicated black talk radio program, and *BET Tonight with Travis Smiley*, a public affairs and entertainment program on the Black Entertainment Television network.

When he was not before an audience or on the airwaves, the Reverend Flake appealed to the broader public through mainstream and targeted publications. Unlike many of his allies in the school choice movement, Flake had regular access to major newspapers. For example, when Flake retired from Congress in 1997, one of his new jobs was editorial columnist for the *New York Post*. Although it had, and continues to have, a reputation among some blacks as a racist paper, the *Post* has a relatively large circulation in the New York metropolitan area. Common citizens and policy makers alike read it, especially blue-collar white ethnic voters, who appreciate its conservative bent and coverage of local and state politics. Understanding this fact, Flake readily agreed to write a weekly opinion piece for the paper. His published opinions cover a range of issues, but the core of his essays focuses on charter schools and the need for greater school choice. So too do his op-ed pieces that the *New York Times* and *Wall Street Journal* published. He also increased his visibility and spread his message of school choice by commenting on public education issues or by being the subject of a number of published interviews and articles in popular magazines such as *Time*, *U.S. News and World Report*, and *Emerge*.

Through his televised and public appearances and public writings, the Reverend Flake attempted to foster civic education about the problem of low student performance in urban public schools and the potential of charter schools to make a difference. An expectation of Flake and his allies was that citizens would feel capable to advocate on their own behalf for public education policy changes from the government and private-sector elites. Another was that the disengaged would mobilize and engage themselves in the politics of school reform. They hoped that the potential politicization of a larger segment of the public could assist Flake and his supporters, either independently or collectively, in lobbying for the redistribution of governmental authority over where students were educated. Whether the Reverend Flake fostered civic empowerment and subsequently affected the votes of legislators is uncertain. It is likely, however, that his efforts influenced the perceptions of many ordinary citizens.

UPDATE AND ASSESSMENT

Since the enactment of the New York charter schools law, the Reverend Flake has continued to use lobbying, electoral endorsements, and civic education in a campaign to expand the number of charter schools in and beyond New York. Concerning his endorsements, during the New York Democratic presidential primary, Flake endorsed former U.S. Senator Bill Bradley over Vice President Al Gore. Flake chose the former over the latter primarily because Bradley had voiced support for experimenting with various school choice policies. In addition, while falling short of a full endorsement, the Reverend Flake ostensibly threw some of his support behind the bid by Republican Governor George Bush of Texas for U.S. president. At an autumn 1999 campaign speech by Bush at the Manhattan Institute, the Reverend Flake introduced the governor as his "home boy" or compatriot in the politics to change public education in the United States.

As for civic education, Flake is trying hard to increase the involvement of more Afro-Christian, as well as Latino, religious leaders in the school choice movement and local politics. Believing that pastors leading urban churches should be education activists in support of school choice, Flake is traveling the country to raise the school choice issue with as many pastors as will listen. A point he emphasizes to the pastors is that they have the resources to become active and influential players in the urban public school reform game. Many have politicized congregants, growing church operating budgets, and community support. They also own property, both land and buildings. Consequently, the Reverend Flake contends that "where you have churches like in Durham, where they have twenty-five classrooms that sit all week long, major capital investment that brings no return because it does nothing but wait for either some evening meetings or Sunday morning Sunday school, you can have a charter school." Many pastors are heeding Flake's call, especially in New York. For example, among the first charter schools to open in New York was the Sisulu Children's Charter School in central Harlem. The school, which offers instruction for kindergarten through second grade, leases space in a four million dollar building from the Center for Community Enrichment, a subsidiary of the Canaan Baptist Church of Christ where the Reverend Wyatt Tee Walker is pastor. However, Flake is not stopping at getting more churches to host charter schools. Instead, he is trying to animate pastors to get involved directly in local school boards. The Reverend Flake is very clear on this point:

> I see my role as educating pastors about running for their school boards. I also have to educate lay people about a pastor doing more than one thing. This historical thing that all a pastor can do is bury the dead and marry folk—that model is really getting blown away. Because of the work of pastors like myself, you're going to see more and more pastors, I think, becoming involved in this whole educational process, either by their involvement in school boards, or by building schools, or by becoming more vocal voices, because I've been in enough sessions to tell you it is a major concern now. We ought in the year 2000 to be bringing about the kind of equality that was guaranteed by *Brown vs. Board of Education* because we have not seen that guarantee fulfilled in this generation of our children.[54]

In spring 2000, the Reverend Flake became the president of Edison Charter Schools (ECS), which manages charter schools in more than one dozen states.[55] In this position, Flake is responsible for identifying new markets for the consulting and management services that Edison offers to school districts and organizations wanting to start charter schools. Additionally, he oversees the structuring of management agreements among Edison, school districts, and the boards of charter schools. Consequently, he has added a new category of political action to his repertoire: regulatory affairs. He is now involved in consultations with administrative heads and their appointees in departments of education and urban school districts about creating new charter schools or converting traditional public schools into charter schools. The Reverend Flake now has more influence with politicians and charter schools in more states than New York. He admitted,

> I was on the phone Thursday with Tom Ridge, who is the governor of Pennsylvania, who worked with me in Congress, where they are taking over the schools and may

be taking over the Philadelphia schools. So I'll be meeting with [Philadelphia] Mayor Street on Wednesday morning. I've already had telephone conversations with the secretary of state of New Jersey where they are taking over schools in Camden and Jersey City. I'm all over the country right now. I'm on way to San Diego, too, to assist in trying to get some charter schools started. We'll be in North Carolina in the next few weeks.[56]

As the leader of ECS, Flake has also been reprising his role as lobbyist, lobbying both the legislature and the executive branches to address problems arising from the introduction of charter schools into the system of public education and finance. New York's charter school law, for example, authorizes the creation of a state fund to cover some of the costs borne by the organizations approved to operate charter schools and those preparing charter school proposals. In May 2000, Governor Pataki announced the implementation of the New York State Charter School Stimulus Fund. The fund has a budget of three million dollars, culled from state taxes and the federal Public Charter School Program, which provides seed money for application costs. The Reverend Flake has been lobbying the governor and the legislature to increase the budget for the fund, along with increased allocations for charter schools from the budgets of public school districts, to cover the purchase, leasing, or construction of school buildings. His argument is that, even with the fund, the cost of acquiring space for a charter school is still prohibitive for many organizations wishing to apply to open a charter school. It also yields delays in the opening of charter schools that the state has approved. Furthermore, the Reverend Flake argues that, because charter schools are public schools, they should have the full financial backing of the state in terms of the construction of school buildings. The debate for increased funding of charter schools is unsettled.

The possibilities available for the Reverend Flake to take control of the school choice movement in America and to shape it are limitless. At ECS, Flake has new opportunities to make inroads regarding charter schools with more politicians from around the country. Furthermore, he can now directly foster the creation of charter schools and shape their success at educating low-performing students from urban school districts—which is something that few school choice activists can claim. Through ECS, Flake can also solidify his role and enhance his legitimacy as a national spokesperson for the school choice movement. Furthermore, if he chose to do so, the Reverend Flake could tap his network of financiers and pastors favoring charter schools and other school choice ideals and establish a formal means of educating the public about changing how and where students can learn better and perform at higher levels. This would require the reverend, however, to place a greater emphasis on deliberate collective action over his traditional individual action on public affairs. He could also establish a network of citizens' policy academies to train ordinary citizens about the public policy process and how to influence it, particularly regarding the financing of public schools. Additionally, beyond encouraging ministers to entertain charter schools on church property, he could formally spearhead a campaign to mobilize church congregations to press their legislators for more changes on the school choice front, which is something that few black churches ever do.[57] The Reverend Flake sees one of his roles as "educating pastors, particularly, to the reality that a part of the solution for academically weak kids and bad schools rests with them." Perhaps he will also see his role as the catalyst for a formal alliance of mainline and Pentecostal preachers from the pulpits of megachurches and storefronts to institutionalize their commitment to school choice as ministry, mission, and mandate and lobby for the placement of school choice initiatives on ballots in states and localities where they are legal.[58] Finally, while the Reverend Flake continues to advocate for charter schools, he may call again for vouchers, particularly for use at sectarian schools. Political attitudes and public policy may influence his call. Observing the times, Flake has detected a window opening for the formal inclusion of Christian schools in public education reform:

> The language that we hear now clearly has opened the door for it. In almost every other arena, whether it's housing, delivery of services for domestic abuse, or welfare to work, we see public interest in faith-based solutions growing and charitable choice expanding. It's interesting that the only area where there has been an exclusion of faith-based institutions has been in education, and that's in part because that bureaucracy is so much in control and ... politically positioned through its PACs and so forth and through the unions that it is difficult to open up the possibility for competition with parochial and religious institutions. Yet I foresee parochial schools as major players in the future of public education—and not just as sites to put and teach kids from overcrowded public schools.

If he is as good a soothsayer as he is a preacher and advocate, schools like the Allen Christian School may become a real choice available to black and Latino parents in inner-city neighborhoods, regardless of their ability to pay or the brightness of their children.

CONCLUSION

Passage of the New York Charter Schools Act of 1998 by the state legislature and the governor was the culmination of more than a decade of lobbying by school choice proponents to create a parallel system of public education in New York. Currently, under this parallel system, the New York State Education Department mixes traditional public schools run by local school districts with new public-funded schools managed by nongovernmental agents and operating free of traditional regulations concerning administration, curriculums, and hiring.[59] Up from three in 2000, approximately thirty charter schools may be, by autumn 2001, in operation across the state, managed largely by for-profit education management companies like Edison Charter Schools, Victory Schools, and Advantage Schools. Conservative and liberal activists used political pressure to influence policy makers in New York to accept the charter school model. Among the most prominent and influential activists was the Reverend Flake.

Often heard above the din of other activists, clergy and lay alike, Flake continues to spreads his gospel of charter schools on city streets, at press conferences, on college campuses during debates, and in corporate suites during luncheons and annual meetings. For him, "the hope of America is that it gets a dual public [school] system. The dual public school system would have, on one hand, what we know as the traditional schools because they do well in most suburban communities and charter schools that are publicly financed where you have a different kind of accountability model; and I think if those schools succeed that they will force the necessary reform in the traditional educational sphere." By combining the legitimacy and authority of his multiple positions in religious, policy, and civic circles, the Reverend Flake has propelled himself into the forefront of the school choice movement. However, it is his political action, along with connections to political and economic elites, that permits him to maintain an incomparable presence as an activist in the politics of urban public school reform, both in New York and across the country.

NOTES

1. Jeffrey Henig, Richard Hula, Marion Orr, and Desiree Pedescleaux, *The Color of School Reform* (Princeton: Princeton University Press, 1999), 152.

2. For a fuller explanation, see Hubert Morken and Jo Renee Formicola, *The Politics of School Choice* (Lanham, Md.: Rowman & Littlefield, 1999).

3. Afro-Christian religious leaders are those who head churches belonging to Christian denominations founded by African Americans that are administratively independent of white control and authority. Presently, there are eight such denominations: African Methodist Episcopal; African Methodist Episcopal Zion; Christian Methodist Episcopal; National Baptist Convention of America, Inc.; National Missionary Baptist Convention of America; National Baptist Convention, USA, Inc.; Progressive National Baptist Convention, Inc.; and Church of God in Christ. Diverse Afro-Christian religious leaders are involved in urban public school reform. Some side with union leaders and teachers in emphasizing increased school budgets, such as the Reverend Frank Reid of Bethel African Methodist Episcopal Church in Baltimore. Others align themselves with right-leaning re-

formers from the school choice movement such as the Reverend Marlon Moss of Greater Northeast Baptist Church in Indianapolis. See Harold McDougall, *Black Baltimore* (Philadelphia: Temple University Press, 1993), 124–26; and Morken and Formicola, *The Politics of School Choice*, 212–20.

4. Henig et al., *The Color of School Reform*, 142.

5. Anemona Hartocollis, "Religious Leaders Plan Schools with Public Funds in New York," *New York Times*, 29 December 1998: A1.

6. The Reverend Floyd Flake, interview by the author, Queens, New York, 5 June 2000. Herein referred to as "the Flake interview."

7. New York State Education Department, "New York City Public Schools 1998–1999 Annual District Report for District 29," available at http://www.emsc.nysed.gov/repcrd2000.

8. Richard P. Nathan, Julian Chow, and Michael L. Owens, "The Flipside of the Underclass," *Rockefeller Institute Bulletin* (1995): 14–22.

9. The Flake interview.

10. The Empire Foundation and the Lehrman Institute, *Students at Risk: New Yorkers on Education* (New Rochelle, N.Y.: Lehrman Institute, 1995), 83.

11. The Empire Foundation and the Lehrman Institute, *Students at Risk*, 83.

12. The Flake interview.

13. Actually, the Reverend Flake identifies vouchers and tuition tax credits as the reforms least likely to increase educational attainment and achievement among public school students. The most able reforms, he believes, in order of decreasing potential effect, are religious schools, charter schools, magnet schools, private scholarships, and merit pay for teachers. With the exception of religious schools, all of the other reforms are possible through public policy and political action.

14. Charter schools involve what education policy scholars Lorraine McDonnell and Richard Elmore term *system-change*. They define it as transfers of responsibility, authority, and/or resources from one set of individuals and institutions involved in public education to another set of individuals and institutions on the assumption that the latter will perform better than the former. Under charter schools, policy makers transfer responsibility for the education of a group of students from the traditional public schools to new public schools, which often offer experimental teaching and greater resources in an attempt to raise the academic performance of students. For a discussion of system-change policies and other policy instruments in the education field, see Lorraine M. McDonnell and Richard F. Elmore, *Alternative Policy Instruments* (Santa Monica: Center for Policy Research in Education, the Rand Corporation, 1987).

15. Public Agenda, a nonpartisan survey research and citizen education group in New York City, found that 57 percent of respondents to a national telephone survey favored vouchers, whereas 68 percent favored charter schools. See Public Agenda, *On Thin Ice: How Advocates and Opponents Could Misread the Public's Views on Vouchers and Charter Schools* (New York: Public Agenda, 1999).

16. The Flake interview.

17. For a useful discussion of the permutations of school choice, see Morken and Formicola, *The Politics of School Choice*.

18. One survey of the school choice community found that the Reverend Flake is among its most influential representatives. See Morken and Formicola, *The Politics of School Choice*, 281.

19. The Manhattan Institute describes itself as a "think tank whose mission is to develop and disseminate new ideas that foster greater economic choice and individual re-

sponsibility." For more on the organization, see http://www.manhattan-institute.org.

20. The Flake interview.

21. Floyd Flake and Donna Marie Williams, *The Way of the Bootstrapper: Nine Action Steps for Achieving Your Dreams* (New York: HarperCollins, 1999).

22. The members of Allen AME Church come mainly from the ranks of middle-class and upper-working-class blacks. White-collar workers sit in the pews and sing in the choir on Sundays. Many are professionals and entrepreneurs. Most members, however, hold less prestigious positions that pay well, afford them opportunities to own homes, and send their children to private schools. Civil servants, especially postal workers, police officers, and emergency medical technicians, are in abundance.

23. C. Eric Lincoln and Lawrence H. Mamiya, *The Black Church in the African American Experience* (Durham: Duke University Press, 1990), 387.

24. Lincoln and Mamiya, *The Black Church in the African American Experience*, 387.

25. Lincoln and Mamiya, *The Black Church in the African American Experience*, 213.

26. Flake and Williams, *The Way of the Bootstrapper*, 78.

27. Cited in Pamela Ann Toussaint, "Concord Baptist Church: Taking Care of Business in Bed-Stuy," in *Signs of Hope in the City: Ministries of Community Renewal*, ed. Robert D. Carle and Louis A. DeCaro Jr. (Valley Forge, Pa.: Judson Press, 1999), 68.

28. For a treatise on this theology, see James Cone, *Black Theology and Black Power* (New York: Seabury, 1969).

29. The Flake interview.

30. The Flake interview.

31. Hans Baer and Merrill Singer, *African-American Religion in the Twentieth Century: Varieties of Protest and Accommodation* (Knoxville: University of Tennessee Press, 1992), 58–59.

32. Gayraud Wilmore, *Black Religion and Black Radicalism* (Maryknoll, N.Y.: Orbis, 1995), 234.

33. Wilmore, *Black Religion and Black Radicalism*, 234.

34. Wilmore, *Black Religion and Black Radicalism*, 234.

35. Charles V. Hamilton, *The Black Preacher* (New York: William Morrow, 1972), 126–32.

36. Hamilton, *The Black Preacher*, 132.

37. The Flake interview.

38. The Flake interview.

39. The Flake interview.

40. For more on his campaign, see Michael Leo Owens, "Local Party Failure and Alternative, Black Church-Based Nonparty Organizations," *Western Journal of Black Studies* 21, no. 3 (1997): 162–72.

41. The Flake interview.

42. Flake and Williams, *The Way of the Bootstrapper*, 33.

43. The Flake interview.

44. The Children's Scholarship Fund provides tuition grants to help low-income families educate their children at private or parochial schools in New York and Washington, D.C. The Reverend Flake serves on the board of directors of the organization.

45. The Center for Education Reform is a Washington-based, nonpartisan education policy research and advocacy organization that tracks changes in school choice legislation and publishes opinion and research pieces on school reform.

46. The Honorable Lawrence Seabrook, New York State Senate, testimony given at the

Citicorp Foundation on Public Charter Schools, New York, 20 November 1997.

47. Jack Walker, *Mobilizing Interest Groups in America* (Ann Arbor: University of Michigan Press, 1991).

48. The Flake interview.

49. Scholar-activist allies in the school choice movement provided much of the empirical data that Flake relied on when appealing to legislators to support charter schools, as well as vouchers and scholarships. Chief among them were political scientists Paul Peterson and Jay Greene. Peterson directs the Program on Education Policy and Governance at Harvard University. Green, a former student of Peterson, is a senior fellow, like Flake, at the Manhattan Institute.

50. The Flake interview.

51. The Flake interview.

52. The Flake interview.

53. The Flake interview.

54. The Flake interview.

55. Edison Charter Schools is an affiliate of the Edison Project. Entrepreneur Chris Whittle, chairman of Whittle Communications and creator of Channel One, founded the Edison Project as a for-profit education enterprise to manage a network of schools across the country.

56. The Flake interview.

57. Henig et al., *The Color of School Reform*, especially 142–52.

58. Henig et al., *The Color of School Reform*, especially 142–52.

59. For more on charter schools in New York, visit the homepages of the Charter Schools Institute of the State University of New York (www.newyorkcharters.org), the New York State Education Department (www.emsc.nysed.gov), and the New York Charter School Resource Center (www.nycharterschools.org).

2

Bishop T. D. Jakes: A Ministry for Empowerment

Hubert Morken

The week that 271 electors secured the presidency for George W. Bush, the *Washington Post* reported that the Reverend T. D. Jakes was on vacation. Why was this black minister's whereabouts a newsworthy event? It was because Bush was about to meet with a group of influential religious leaders, and Jakes would be missing. Fewer African Americans had voted Republican than at any time since 1964—less than 9 percent. Keenly aware of the racial divide and feeling himself misunderstood on race, President-Elect Bush wanted Jakes included in his effort to build bridges to the one segment of the electorate that gave him so little support.[1]

Bishop Jakes is already a widely recognized religious force and is very likely to become a key figure in the public life of the nation as well. He knows Bush; he knows Gore. He is one of the leaders of the next generation that will speak for the African American community. Reeling after the defeat of Vice President Al Gore, the African American leaders who supported him most vehemently will have little access to the Bush White House. With harsh rhetoric, Jesse Jackson and his supporters burned their political bridges with Republicans before and after the election. Not so Jakes. He is poised to be a long-term influence with both Democrats and Republicans, and this leverage comes at a critical time with a national house divided. Jakes is not political in the partisan sense. He is independent and will not be easy to manipulate. Yet he is an emerging power to be courted in the political world and a religious leader who will have influence. He has the potential to stand for the national conscience or at least the substantial part of it that remains religious, filling a void left by the passing from center stage of Dr. Billy Graham, John Cardinal O'Connor, the Reverend Martin Luther King Jr., and other notable twentieth-century American spiritual figures.

Historically, religious leaders with large influence in society come in different colors, shapes, and sizes. Some were involved in politics, some were not. What they have in common is an understanding of the times and an ability to reach out to ordinary people, and to leaders, and be heard. Sooner or later, political figures and public officials listen, seek their counsel, or try to silence them.

Jakes is about to be heard. For several years Bush built ties to Jakes and his staff in Texas. Democrats also reached out to him. Thus we can expect that his role as a national reconciler will grow, pushed by the momentum of events that Jakes himself never anticipated or promoted. Bishop Jakes is being propelled onto a national stage as a religious figure with a public vision. How well this new role fits him and the likelihood of his success depend heavily on the foundations of his thought and ministry, already secured. Now is the time to examine T. D. Jakes, his person, history, thinking, motivation, ministry, organization, and goals.

Until recently, Jakes was a total unknown—a pastor in the hills of West Virginia, with an average congregation. Suddenly his was a national ministry. Now there is no time for him to prepare for the next step. He must, he says, "Maximize the moment." Jakes has no idea what that moment will bring or how it will end. But it is here.[2]

INTRODUCING BISHOP T. D. JAKES

High up in the press box of the Atlanta Georgia Dome this observer watched as over 65,000 women sang, clapped, and danced the praises of God on the first night of the year 2000 at the "Woman, Thou Art Loosed!" Conference sponsored by Bishop T. D. Jakes.[3] In 1999 Jakes set the all-time attendance record for the Dome, and any indoor arena, with over 85,000 attendees, breaking a mark held by Dr. Billy Graham. A year later, as I was sitting next to a staff member of the firm that represents both Graham and Jakes, the staffer commented to me that Jakes defies stereotypes—that he was no ordinary preacher, that he breaks the mold. Confirming her statement, women in 200-plus prisons watched Jakes live via satellite hookup, and cameras in three of these prisons allowed the women in Atlanta to see prisoners share in the meeting.

That night in the Dome, Jakes preached from the book of Romans, taking as his text "If God is for us, who can be against us?" Instead of simply affirming God's love, Jakes asked the huge crowd the tough question: In the face of all they had suffered, past, present, and future, how did they know that God is for them? We need solid assurances from the Scripture, he said, on which to base our confidence in God when circumstances go up and down.

What followed was a cogent message reviewing the teachings of the New Testament book of Romans chapter by chapter, culminating in a close examination of chapter 8 when Jakes listed five reasons why Christians can be confident of the Lord's favor and assistance no matter what happens, good or bad.[4]

Jakes is one of the fastest rising religious stars in the United States. Both spiritual and secular people know of him. He believes and teaches traditional ideas, for example, that men are to be the heads of their households, protecting and providing for the needs of their families, a position he defends on both biblical and practical grounds. But he is also known for his creativity and innovations, for work in prisons, and for the fact that no one else in America can fill a stadium faster than him.[5]

In Atlanta, Jakes sponsored two other events that illustrate the quality and breadth of his ministry, still very much in the early stages of its development. First, he put on a two-day seminar for 9,000 women, mostly African Americans, teaching them entrepreneurial start-up skills with the help of successful Christian businesspeople and major corporations. Second, Jakes premiered his second major play, "Behind Closed Doors," at the Atlanta Civic Center, working with themes from the Abraham, Sarah, and Hagar story in Genesis—and the reputed relationship of Thomas Jefferson and Sally Hemings—addressing the issues of breast cancer, race, sexuality, wealth, relationships, and spirituality in a modern setting. This gospel play tours in major cities and is sponsored by T. D. Jakes Enterprises, a for-profit arm of Jakes's ministry that also helps to manage his books, plays, and music activities.[6]

A few weeks later, in South Dallas, Texas, the Potter's House, the 26,000-member church (and growing) that Jakes founded in 1996, moved into its new facility. Governor George W. Bush presided over the groundbreaking of "Project 2000" for Jakes, and Vice President Al Gore and the Reverend Pat Robertson, among other civic and religious notables, celebrated the official church dedication in late October. So much had happened so fast that the world sat up and took notice. This could be seen at the ceremony in the brief comments of Dallas Mayor Ron Kirk. New buildings were not something new or unusual in Dallas, the mayor said: What he came to celebrate was not bricks and mortar but the leadership that Bishop Jakes modeled, which encouraged him to be an effective leader in his civic duties. Shortly after Jakes arrived in the city, Kirk related, he rented the Dallas Convention Center to host an all-day all-city resources gathering for the homeless. Thousands came to receive help. Putting this together as a newcomer took courage and demonstrated true leadership, Kirk observed.[7]

This chapter is to be a snapshot, a brief introduction to Bishop Jakes and his leadership in South Dallas, in the nation, and overseas. It is an effort to understand his motivation, his thinking, his activities, his multiple organizations, and his vision for the dispossessed and the lost—for those who need him most. There is a personal side to this story, although Jakes may not want a biography written on him just yet. He thinks that would be premature. There is nevertheless much to write about, just dealing with the different dimensions of his present ministry, which includes a local church, television, prison ministry, community and civic development, major conferences, church relations with other churches, consulting with public officials, and for-profit enterprises that include publications, music, and the arts. Jakes has a keen sense that life is short, and he is packing as much as he can into a twenty-four-hour day and a seven-day week. But even more important is how he is instructing and empowering religious leaders of his generation—encouraging and equipping them to fulfill their callings, far beyond church walls.[8]

THE LAUNCHPAD: SETTING A TRAJECTORY

> I sought solace and answers in the Bible. I can never forget where I came from. The sense of time and life ticking away is an undercurrent of my message.[9]

Thomas D. Jakes was born in 1957 in Charleston, West Virginia, the son of Ernest, the owner of a janitorial service, and Odith, a teacher. At the age of ten he saw his father struck down with a kidney disease that slowly killed him. Instead of rejecting God because of his father's suffering, Jakes pursued the Lord. Raised a Baptist, he became a Pentecostal, a member first of the Apostolic Church and later of the Higher Ground Always Abounding Assemblies. From the age of twenty-two he began to pastor small storefront churches, and by 1990 he moved to South Charleston, West Virginia, where his church grew from 100 to 300 members. Pastoring in obscurity, which is where Jakes came from, how did his star rise after 1993, when both the Trinity Broadcasting Network (TBN) and Black Entertainment Television (BET) made room for his weekly teaching and sermons?[10]

In 1992 Jakes gave a teaching entitled "Woman, Thou Art Loosed!" to a Sunday school class in his own church. This was a one-week commitment. He expected to be rejected for bringing up painful subjects such as child and spousal abuse. Instead, the women in the class asked for more. In a short time Jakes was traveling to other churches and auditoriums around the country with this message. In 1993 he spoke at the Azusa Conference in Tulsa, Oklahoma, sponsored by Bishop Carlton Pearson, and from there he launched it on TBN at the invitation of its founder, Paul Crouch. Swiftly outgrowing his home base in West Virginia—his staff remembers that people coming to his conferences had to be housed in four states—Jakes moved to Dallas, Texas, in May 1996, with his family and fifty members of his ministry team, to found the Potter's House, a church that in four years grew to 26,000 members.[11]

Today Bishop Jakes has a substantial television ministry in Europe and in Africa. After a recent meeting in Soweto, South Africa, he made a commitment to enlarge this ministry overseas. He travels about a dozen times a year to hold meetings and get to his speaking engagements. In the year 2000 this included trips to London, England, and Lagos, Nigeria.[12]

Meanwhile, Jakes has moved aggressively to expand his home base of operations in South Dallas, dedicating a new $32 million church building seating over 8,200 people (there is an overflow room in the older facility seating over 2,000) and starting a major community development initiative valued at $135.2 million called "Project 2000." The latter is expected to include a K–12 school, an education/recreation facility, a performing arts center, a business incubator, an executive retreat center, a golf course, office buildings, a mall, and more, all designed to enhance the quality of life in a part of the city suffering from underdevelopment. Jakes wants to be actively involved in helping to plan the future for this part of Dallas.[13]

Much more can be said about Jakes—he has published twenty-five books, the most recent, on sound Christian living and budget practices, titled *The Great Investment: Faith, Family, and Finance*, and has widely marketed a tape series. Three times a year T. D. Jakes Ministries puts on large conferences on the themes of empowerment: "Woman, Thou Art Loosed!" and "Manpower," as well as a pastors' "Leadership Conference." Jakes also mentors a group of pastors, from 231 churches in thirteen denominations, called the Pater Alliance, providing oversight and encouragement.

Politically Jakes is totally nonpartisan, though he did go to the Clinton White House and knows the former Texas governor, President George W. Bush. This is somewhat unusual for African American preachers who commonly endorse political candidates. However, this political firewall has not stopped Bishop Jakes from being a speaker at a Congressional Black Caucus prayer breakfast, as he was this year, or from relating to Republicans.[14]

What does the future hold for Bishop Jakes? A few years ago at an Oral Roberts University commencement, evangelist Oral Roberts predicted that God was going to raise up a new generation of African American Christian leaders, and to the faithful, Jakes is a confirmation of the prediction's truth. However, potentially he is far more than a religious leader or merely the representative of one ethnic community.[15]

Jakes reminds the public that people of all races and economic conditions hurt. According to him, the Gospel and the God he serves are bent on restoration—on helping those most destroyed by the Devil and by adverse circumstances. Jakes remembers, "The poor heard him gladly," and, "Those forgiven much, love much." He celebrates returning prodigals, like the famous football player Deion Sanders, even as he calls for the proper care of little ones not yet scarred by sin and suffering.[16]

As the famous preachers of the twentieth century pass from the scene, people speculate on their successors. Even the *New York Times* published an article listing Bishop Jakes as a candidate for the role of national spiritual leader for the new century. Time will tell what the reach of his ministry will be. He bases much of his message on four principles: the importance of the Bible, the need for unity within and among groups, the imperative to balance the ideal with the real in all of life, and the universal theme of profitability. His message is universal, and his heart reaches out to those most in need. But is America ready for a national pastor who stands not just for racial reconciliation but for a full-orbed gospel with religious and social dimensions that many find compelling but others reject?[17]

A FULL-ORBED GOSPEL: THE T. D. JAKES MESSAGE OF RESTORATION

Finding the Answers in the Bible

During two interviews Jakes stressed the criticality of the Word of God: "You know the Bible. I know a lot of preachers who do not know the Bible."[18] It is his concern that writers, journalists, and even pastors may have difficulty understanding him, if they do not know the Scriptures. For example, after one writer listening to tapes of his sermons got it wrong a few years back, Jakes responded by self-publishing his first book, selling out the 5,000 copies, he recalls, in two weeks. Appalled at the ignorance of the educated, not wanting to have other people misrepresent him, and hardly knowing how to type, Jakes launched his career as a successful author. Millions now read him, but not all, he knows, fully understand him.[19]

Jakes prides himself on delivering clear, easy-to-understand, theologically sound sermons or teachings, designed to instruct and deliver hearers from ignorance, false ideas, and personal bondage. He is a powerful motivational speaker, often using visual or dramatic illustrations with actors to make his point. He also communicates with creative word play and vivid language to make sure that what he says is easy to remember. An example of this is a T. D. Jakes sermon given to thousands of pastors. He stuttered severely for over half an hour in a dramatic ruse to make the point that human weakness can be a great asset to a preacher, keeping him or her humble and useable by

God. Jakes is frequently on the edge, taking risks and appealing to those who can to walk with him, to see and to understand the deeper meanings and harsher truth that require spiritual and intellectual maturity, and also personal honesty, to comprehend. He will ask in so many words, "Do you hear what I am saying?" from time to time, not because he looks down on his audience, something he does not do, but because, even as he works to make sure that everyone understands the main points, he says many other things, quickly or subtly, that hearers miss if they are not alert and sensitive. Let the first-time listener beware: Much is going on in a T. D. Jakes sermon that never registers to the untutored ear.[20]

A favorite book of Bishop Jakes is Romans, written by the Apostle Paul. Even in his own time Paul was hard to understand, as the Apostle Peter observed. Yet Jakes delights in the mind of Paul, not just the message of the apostle. Jakes studies his logic, and his thought processes, as Paul makes his theological case—and strives to copy him in his own work.[21]

During his interview, Jakes studied the questions asked of him and comments made to him, intent on honing his own skills. This makes a fundamental point. For Jakes, the Bible and people living today are not far apart, not utterly different, because he thinks that both have a human voice and both come from God. He learns from both. Giving respect to the divine authority and inspiration of the Bible as he does, even defending it fiercely, Jakes also finds it accessible and applicable to himself and to issues of his day. Biblical writings and the characters they describe are not just distant authorities; they are his peers and his friends in absentia, reaching across space, culture, and time to direct, to empower, and to legitimate his ministry. To put it simply, Jakes not only studies the Bible in its divine and human dimensions but sees himself like a biblical character, much like anyone else in the Bible (apart from Christ), capable of doing great and foolish things and, with all his limitations, able to preach. Even without the Damascus road experience, Jakes is a modern Paul. He is intense, sees Jesus as the Truth, and is severe in focusing on the Gospel.[22]

Jakes reminds his listeners that when Paul got into trouble, "he didn't hire an attorney." Instead, he wrote letters to churches and to friends, letters that resonate to this day. Long-term influence, Jakes reasons, flows more from the written word than from visible demonstrations of power. His own life is transformed by reading, so he spends considerable time writing, with the hope that others will benefit from his insights, now and later.[23]

Jakes feels humanized by the Bible, by the written word, contrary to the experience and prejudices of many people both inside and outside the church who either ignore the Bible or are alienated by it. He sees the book, and the God behind it, putting him in touch with all that is human—the good, the bad, and even the trivial. On the tangible grounds of daily experience he feels sorry for people who are out of touch with faith. They find solace in false comforts, like money and fame, or pursue illusory dreams through drugs and alcohol, he suggests, and miss out on the wisdom and teaching that enhances all that is good in life. More than that, Jakes says that they are unprepared for disasters that come to all people, sooner or later. They are vulnerable. When they are sick, broke, betrayed, and alone, Jakes asks, where will they turn for help, and what will give them a reason to live and the reserves to fight on? Jakes is blunt on this point. He asserts that African Americans could never have survived slavery, let alone have thrived as they often did, without the power, the faith, and the assistance of the black church. For Jakes there can be no argument here. African Americans, he contends, may disagree with him and reject Jesus Christ, but they would not even have the breath to disagree if it were not for the survival power of the Gospel and the good news of salvation by grace through faith. The Gospel may be false, as the nonbeliever claims, but in the here and now it sure worked to keep people alive, Jakes asserts. To him, that fact is unassailable, distinct from the issue of eternity.[24]

Discovering the Power of Unity

This leads to a further point central to all that Jakes believes and teaches, namely, that unity is as necessary for everyone today as it was for African Americans under slavery. He rejects, root and branch, the idea that individuals can make it alone on their own merits without the help of family, friends, and colleagues. This has many applications, and it serves as a strong check on the pride of those who are successful. Furthermore, he teaches that the Gospel of Jesus requires unity—for the church, for families, for humanity.

What follows is a condensed list of issues that Jakes addresses. He rebukes the affluent person for abandoning the old neighborhood and warns against envy and jealousy that tempt the poor to fight success, separating them from those who make it. He blasts bright people who divide a church because they think they know more than the pastor does and want to replace that vision with their own. He tramples on the arrogance of racism that breeds hatred between groups, rebuking not just the extremes of cross burning but even more the insidious and veiled conceits that undermine relationships, especially between blacks and whites. He assaults antimarriage teachings that pit men against women or lead to domination and oppression of one by the other. He grieves over the separation of Africa from African Americans, leaving the latter without roots and the former without the help that he says only the Americans who crossed the Atlantic in chains can now give. He opposes those who would separate the young from the old. He makes short shrift of those who would pit church against state, religious against civil authorities. He denounces any effort to imprison the church in a nonprofit and otherworldly ghetto, where it has no ties with private corporations. He abhors a negative definition of *holiness* that cuts people of faith off from the creative arts, including drama, music, and film. He mocks the polarization so common today in politics. Last, Jakes cannot conceive of a church life with any integrity that ignores those in prison or on the streets. In short, Jakes presses for unity based on respect for differences and distinctions and the need to help one another.[25]

To state this in a more positive way, here is a brief and partial synopsis of Jakes's unity teachings:

- Powerful churches, large and small, must connect the rich to the poor, making it possible to lift the poor out of poverty. No other solution will work, especially in cities where it will take a whole community pulling together to end cultural devastation.
- Everyone must cheer the accomplishments of individuals and strive with patience to fulfill their own dreams, seeing each person's success reflecting positively on all.
- Church pastors must lead, with the full support of elders and parishioners, or nothing will get done either inside the local church or by the church in the community.
- Christians, united as a people of every ethnicity, must work together to maximize the strength that each racial group brings to the table.
- Families, as the cultural generators of strength, must respect and encourage husbands and wives to play complementary roles, faithful to each other and to their extended family, that equip children for life.
- African Americans, like Joseph of old, must reach out to their African brothers to help them overcome their colonial past and meet modern challenges.
- Churches must embrace the songs and the culture of young and old, teaching each group to participate in the full richness contributed by each.
- Government must learn to welcome local churches into their councils for purposes of city planning; and together they can release resources for the positive development of cities and states.
- Churches and families are natural business incubators, where believers must be encouraged to own and operate businesses, independent of church control, that build ties with existing businesses and work for the good of the city.
- Christians must be encouraged to exercise their God-given talents in drama, music, and film and form companies to promote their participation in the arts.

- The two political parties, Democratic and Republican, are less than perfect, but both have something to offer, and both must be held accountable to work for our good.
- God's word commands that Christians visit those in prison and care for the homeless, and this must be done to offer them the truth, hope, skills, and relationships needed for genuine rehabilitation and restoration to the community.

Historically, one institution that understands deeply the power of unity is the black church, Jakes believes. Today, Jakes maintains, Christians and secular people both tend to be too individualistic, diminishing their strength, each going his or her own way. It is time not only to recover unity among groups, built on the strength that each has, but to build unified churches with broad community-wide and culturally sophisticated visions.[26]

Embracing the Tension between the Real and the Ideal

The third principle, notably embraced by Jakes, is that the ideal and the real must both be embraced. Jakes teaches and models this idea, by word and deed, confident that it has an enormous potential spiritual and cultural impact, as yet not understood. This is a lesson he learned almost by accident. Jakes always knew the basics of Christian doctrine: that people were made in the image of God and hence are of enormous value; that sin was a consequence of free choice gone bad that left humanity in need of salvation; that people are capable of great good and great evil. These elementary teachings are unquestioned in the churches that Jakes has pastored. What was missing was reality—not the abstract teaching but the practice of it, according to Jakes, that must be placed in dynamic tension with biblical ideals.[27]

What prevails in churches, he relates, is a conspiracy of silence, a refusal to acknowledge the pain and breakdown in the lives of parishioners and in churches. "Get real," Jakes says, remembering his own reluctance to address the issues lying just below the surface of religious respectability. The breakthrough he was not even seeking occurred in the early 1990s when the ladies of his church asked him to present a teaching for women in a Sunday school class, as already noted. In his own words, before a large audience of men, Jakes recalled the moment:

> "How can you preach this stuff, bishop?" I don't know. I don't know. I never wanted to lay it on the line. When I started, people were not even talking about it. They are going to think I am crazy. They are going to laugh at me. They are going to dig into my life. I don't even want to talk about it. Everyone is going to run away from me—

instead they ran to me. Because the church has had its hand over its mouth for years and never talked about issues. That is why men left the church.[28]

According to Jakes, it is also why women in the church have failed to prosper, especially in their relationships. The "Woman, Thou Art Loosed!" message catapulted Jakes into a worldwide ministry with a yet unmeasured trajectory. After this recollection, Jakes then asked the men for an "offering" of honesty. He called on everyone in the crowd who was abused as a child or a youth or had been an abuser to come forward for prayer and ministry. Men flocked forward. To deny reality, namely, ignoring the hurt and pain suffered in the past or perpetrated in the present, cuts one off from healing, in Jakes view. All progress toward the goal of wholeness, he says, begins by facing the facts. But it does not end there.[29]

Owning the Principle of Profitability

Perhaps the one controlling teaching for the entire Jakes ministry he summarizes in the word *profitability*, a word easily misunderstood if taken out of the context of his larger work. Jakes does not mean "getting rich," in the crude terms of the prosperity gospel preached widely in the past few years. In fact, Jakes criticizes prosperity teachings that do not grasp the elementary principles of sound personal economics, that is, living within one's means, saving, and investing. Nor is he simply talking about money—a big bank account does not mean that one is profitable, it just means that one is rich. Jakes endorses economic empowerment for all and prosperity for the poor, but profitability is the more elemental and foundational teaching.[30]

Jakes asserts that profitability means adding something of value to the Kingdom of God, to oneself, to one's family, and to all humanity. "You have breath, what are you doing with it?" Jakes asks. He tells of visiting with a terminally ill AIDS patient who was holed up in a bedroom waiting to die. The sun was shinning outside. Jakes asked the man, "What do you want to do? Where do you want to go? What do you want to see? Who do you want to visit?" He was appalled at the passivity of the victim. Lying down at death's door, merely existing in the shadows, when one can still walk and talk, sing and pray, is being "unprofitable." Living life to the last drop is a command, not an option to Jakes because God expects it, and with encouragement we can do it.[31]

Jakes grudgingly accepts sleep and vacations. "What is profitable about sleep?" he asks. "The dead sleep." To be profitable takes discipline; but Jakes also acknowledges that there are internal and external chains that keep people from living life to the fullest. These are the issues—the ignorance, the passivity, the unbelief, the old, the obstacles, the silence—he addresses with such intensity and boldness. Breaking the silence is the masterstroke, the starting point for profitability, provided by the Jakes ministry.[32]

Jakes is convinced that silence about suffering and sin inevitably breeds cynicism and prolongs weakness. On the other hand, honesty about personal brokenness, without anything else being said or done, leaves the weak in despair. Here Jakes comes forward with a prescription of rich and varied remedies that distinguish his ministry. For women, Jakes prescribes a close study of the women in the Bible, who, though misunderstood or even opposed by men, persevered and obtained what they sought. He hails the examples of Ruth, Esther, Mary, and Elizabeth, for example, applying their experiences to modern problems. He holds up Proverbs 31 as a template for the virtuous woman, defined as someone with strength in her family relationships, in her integrity, in her generosity, and in her business. His own life radically changed, Jakes relates,[33] when he first captured the meaning of Psalms 1:1–3, which reads, "Blessed is the man who does not walk in the counsel of the wicked or stand in the way of sinners or sit in the seat of mockers. But his delight is in the law of the Lord, and on his law he meditates day and night. He is like a tree planted by streams of water, which yields fruit in season and whose leaf does not wither. Whatever he does prospers."

Jakes was amazed. "'Whatever he does prospers'? Does this mean in every area of life?" If so, well then, Jakes says to his listeners, just "do it!" That is, after obeying what this Scripture says—which means inventorying and discarding false ideas and maxims that one has been taught by family and friends and replacing them with Godly wisdom found in the Bible and taught by the church—seize the moment and do the one thing that one enjoys most and does best. "What is that one thing," Jakes asks, "that God has put in you and that makes space for you to succeed?"[34]—find it and "work it!" Breaking generational curses is part of the deliverance process that Jakes speaks about. For centuries, under slavery, African American men were encouraged to produce babies but not to father them. This must end. After slavery, for generations, the emancipated were encouraged to spend what little money they made to enjoy life; but children were not taught to save, to invest, to own, or to defer gratification for a greater purpose down the road. That too must end, Jakes teaches. We all need a vision for foundations that will benefit the next four generations, he advises.[35]

Recognizing a Sign of God's Favor

Finding the answers in the Bible, discovering the power of unity, embracing the tension between the real and the ideal, and owning the principle of profitability are important T. D. Jakes essentials. But they are not enough for the down and out or the rich and spiritually blind. By experience and from studying ancient Israel in Egypt, Jakes knows that too many people are so personally destroyed and distracted that they have no hope, not even enough to pray for help, and they simply groan, unable to hear Jakes, no matter how powerfully he preaches. As for the alienated rich, they have dismissed the church as irrelevant and see religion as another scam. Their comfortable lives may insulate them from any need to find God or the struggles of faith. Hence, the most carefully laid out teaching is difficult for many of the poor or the affluent to receive. Jakes, however, has an answer for this problem, namely, "If you do not believe what I say, believe what I do," my paraphrase of the words of Jesus.

Standing before thousands of church leaders in the newly opened state-of-the-art facility of the Potter's House in Dallas, Jakes announced, "This is not a building, a church, or a sanctuary. This is a sign!"[36] Signs, biblically, are meant to authenticate the truth of a message—reassuring doubters. But if it is a sign, then what does it signify? The answer is found in the strong exhortation delivered by Jakes to the assembled clergy when he said, "Your church has to be friendly to broken families."[37] At the same time, he asserted, "Intelligent people want to be in an intelligent ministry." The Potter's House brings together those with the greatest need and those with great resources, where together they can "move mountains." The sign is the mountain moved, in the form of a facility that houses effective Kingdom-centered programs. It is also the best, if not the only, way to communicate to the discouraged and the disinterested, to those who cannot hear mere words. Modern technology, like miracles of old, are a demonstration of power. For Jakes, the positive fruits of faith and initiative embodied in such a facility are a testimony, pointing to God's presence and favor.

Jakes is convinced that when people come together with faith and in unity, focusing on the needs and dreams of ordinary people, they release creative energy—they are profitable. The Potter's House is something new, not only for predominately African American churches but also for all local congregations. In short, it is meant to be a prototype church for the twenty-first century. Buildings are a significant part of this vision, but renewed leadership is far more important. Jakes comments, "Whenever it comes to redemption and restoration, God will always use someone who can relate to you, somebody who understands you. But he will always use somebody who was not held down like you were held down, so you can prepare to go to the next level."[38]

This is the Jakes role, the one he models, and the one he hopes that effective pastors will emulate. Pastors, like Moses, he comments, must be enough like the flock of parishioners to understand them and yet not have the crushing limitations of the dispossessed. As he preached this particular sermon,

Jakes sat hidden in the crowd, speaking into his mike, pleading with fellow clergy to look for the hurting people in their pews like they were looking for him. Find them, he said, and minister to their needs, and when you do, never forget that you too have weaknesses. In another related sermon, titled "The Staff and the Stutter," based on Moses, Jakes concentrated on the internal leadership dynamics of churches and the inner world of the pastor. Trust your staff, he urged the pastors, delegate duties to them, and set them free to be innovative under your direction. Do not micromanage them, unless you want a small and feeble church, he warned. As for the stutter, this image (taken from Moses, who stuttered) was not a trivial point, he argued. Moses must have thought, Jakes commented, "How can I deliver the message that delivers people when I cannot deliver my own tongue?" Similarly, every preacher has disabilities, for example, "I can rebuke cancer, but I cannot balance my checkbook." To be effective, some limitations must be overcome, but others, like the stutter, are there for a reason—to keep one approachable and to protect one from arrogance and pride. "Some of you are too eloquent to be blessed," concluded Jakes.[39]

When I get to heaven, Jakes said, I have one question: "Why did you call me?" He asked himself, "How can I do it—given my tensions and conflicts?" Jakes stuttered out his message because in no sense did he consider himself sufficient for this responsibility. Self-awareness, call it humility if you will, helped to prepare him—like Moses—for his task.[40]

African Americans identify with Moses and the Children of Israel because of slavery. Jakes may identify even more with Joshua because he is preparing to enter the promised land. Here are a few of his quotes: "You are the generation chosen to cross over"; "This is the launching of a dream"; "We are leading a multitude into a global revolution"; "The church is meant to be the pivot point for social change"; "God wants us to enter the worldwide economic conversation"; "The local church is the gateway to the local community." These pithy maxims express Jakes's desire for Christians to break free from old ideas, old sins, old limits, to get into the providential flow of blessing that step by step will take losers and make them winners, to become "the head and not the tail." It is one thing to talk about this, and it is another to do it, and that is why Jakes works so hard to stay focused—to keep his multifaceted ministry on line with his vision of restoration.[41]

What is restoration? Biblically and prophetically this is a concept rich in meaning and application. It is more than just getting back what was lost. It is that. However, it is also what happens, Jakes says, when "God moves into a mess."[42] Jakes is not just about social redemption, which is the repair of family and civic fabric, torn and shredded. He sees restoration happening only in the context of faith and hard work. The church matters. He also sees it happening with much greater speed and deeper effect than incremental natural processes. Yes, full restoration will take time and even generations, but it is also accompanied with bursts of energy. If demons contributed to one's destruction, the Holy Spirit, angels, and favor from unexpected human sources can help to put it right faster than one could ever imagine. Jakes anticipates just such assistance. He is issuing a wake-up call to "Get ready!" to receive it. As the prophet Amos wrote of restoration in Israel, "The days are coming, declares the Lord, when the reaper will be overtaken by the plowman and the planter by the treading of grapes. New wine will drip from the mountains and flow from all the hills."[43] This is Jakes's full-orbed gospel.

A COMPREHENSIVE MINISTRY: THE T. D. JAKES OPERATIONS

Introducing a Master Plan

T. D. Jakes is unique. But Oprah Winfrey is perhaps the closest person to his profile. Jakes holds Oprah up as a positive example of leadership, first, because she started by doing one thing well—television entertainment. But unlike other talk show hosts she did not stop there. Her work encouraging literacy and reading, her magazine, and her assistance to suffering families have launched Oprah into uncharted territory, addressing issues of need nationally. Jakes senses rightly that this is a new leadership model that leverages success in one area into a wide-ranging career while maintaining the original role.[44]

Jakes was and is a pastor of a local church. However, he says, "I feel called to talk to leaders more than laity. . . . My ministry is more apostolic than pastoral."[45] This blending of responsibilities with shifting emphasis was confirmed by direct interviews with his senior staff. A primary means of communication between Jakes and heads of the various entities is e-mail. Face-to-face communication occurs when needed, but even senior administrators do not have frequent direct access to him. Jakes moves from task to task, allocating time carefully to what requires his attention, delegating duties to subordinates. Keeping these distinct organizations coordinated is his sole responsibility, not shared with anyone.[46]

Jakes has always been a businessman, inheriting this interest, he says, from his father. He descends, Jakes relates, from four generations of entrepreneurs. When his ministry outgrew his parish, initially he held large meetings in auditoriums in different cities. This outreach was greatly expanded by television shows on TBN and BET. Immediately there was a huge demand for T. D. Jakes tapes and videos that are now marketed by T. D. Jakes Ministries, a nonprofit entity that also manages conferences, overseas trips, relations with other churches, and television appearances. When Jakes outgrew West Virginia, where there was not room in its limited facilities to house large conferences, Jakes seized the opportunity to move to Dallas when a large facility of a bankrupt ministry was put on the market. This move was not part of a long-term plan. It happened quickly when Jakes understood that he could not divide his forces between Dallas and West Virginia—commuting between states made no sense. With Dallas as his base, Jakes immediately started the Potter's House. Then, to meet the needs of the local community, Jakes set up a separate nonprofit (501C3) organization, the Metroplex Economic Development Corporation, which is devoted to alleviating poverty in southwest Dallas through real estate development, cooperative programs, and regional planning. Meanwhile, publishing books became the source of expanded influence and his primary source of personal income, as Jakes transitioned from self-publishing, to small Christian publishers, to large Christian publishers, to a large secular publisher, G. P. Putnam's Sons. Today, T. D. Jakes Enterprises is a for-profit corporation that markets the books Jakes writes and also produces and promotes the plays, records, and movies that Jakes directly or indirectly creates.[47]

It is no wonder that when Jakes teaches about success he describes it in biblical terms as a "weight of glory." Poverty and failure weigh something, he notes, but his present fields of service and commercial activity far outweigh, as a burden, his struggling "storefront church" days. Even as he encouraged preachers to dream and to expand, he warned them to prepare for a heavy load of responsibility. It takes, he says, a passionately committed, loyal, qualified, and experienced staff to carry this weight. Even then Jakes fully expects some to transition out to other ministries and callings and others to fall out of step, in disagreement or even betrayal. Setting high standards, what Jakes calls the ideal, is matched by his realistic expectations about human frailty, sin, and differences. Jakes says, it takes three to five years to be fully confident of the loyalty and competence of staff.[48]

The Potter's House: A Church for the Twenty-first Century

In his West Virginia ministry, well before the "Woman, Thou Art Loosed!" explosion, Jakes traveled out of state to participate in conferences and meetings. Often he took church staff with him to broaden their horizons. The Reverend Lawrence Robinson, senior associate pastor, related, "Bishop always knew the one advantage of having good people around: he could travel, evangelize, and knew that the homes were taken care of. He didn't have to worry about the church going under and church in-fighting."[49] In short, Jakes had no reason to fear that things would fall apart when he was gone. Today, as the senior associate minister under Bishop Jakes, Robinson plays this role in the Potter's House, standing in for him. He has known the bishop for twenty-three years and served under him for sixteen years. Identifying with the armor bearer of Jonathan, the son of King Saul in the Bible, Robinson tells Bishop Jakes, "Do all that's in your heart." He is able then to follow Jakes, taking risks:

> Our church back in West Virginia could only fit 500. We had 1,000 before we got here, so coming here to this is trial and error—we haven't done this before—we're here by the grace of God. We didn't know that on the first Sunday [in Dallas], 1,500 people joined at one time—more than we ever had in our life. It just catapulted. We were running around saying, "Wait! Slow down! Don't y'all come over here—we're not ready!" God evidently saw that we were ready. . . . Then if he [Jakes] says he wants to jump on this 8,000-capacity building in four years, we can have all of the human questioning, reasoning, doubting, etc. . . . but he likes the challenge. Tell him it's impossible, tell him he can't do it—he says, "OK, watch." Tell him it's not feasible, man has never done this before, Christendom has never done this—"What else is new? What else can I overcome?" He's not thinking of doing it by himself, but "I can do all things through Christ. God is for me. I can do it if it's for me to do."[50]

Robinson's temperament, that is, "laid back," contrasts with the relentless and active Jakes—they balance each other. Robinson supervises a huge church with an unusual number of programs with the help of a management team. In addition to the thirty-eight full-time ministers that are part of the church, the Potter's House is educating and training over 300 future pastors and evangelists, who eventually will be ordained and commissioned to start related churches and ministries. There is a vigorous Christian Education Program, with five weeknight and Saturday classes offered six times a year.[51] New church members have their curriculum. There is a volunteer program of over 1,000 members, coordinated by a young staff member who left corporate America to pursue this opportunity. In addition, "First Lady" Mrs. Serita Jakes plays a major role especially in women's programs in the church. As the various needs in the congregation are addressed, Jakes continues to show his concern for outsiders. Robinson remembered,

> God gave Bishop [Jakes] a vision: he was looking out of the back door of a restaurant where someone threw out all of the half-eaten meat out in the back. He saw the meat and said, "Wow, this meat is still good—why would you throw it away?" God spoke to him that those were the kind of people He was calling him to, people who have been discarded and don't believe they are any good anymore. Bishop [Jakes] sees the good in those people. He can relate to the places where people are.[52]

The pastor at the Potter's House responsible for the homeless ministry, Raven's Refuge, is Elder Pat Martin, an energetic fireplug of a man whose wife runs the church bookstore.[53] On weekend evenings Martin is in the streets (with a bodyguard) rendering assistance and ministering the Gospel. Under his supervision, a busload or more of homeless men and women arrive at the church each Sunday. They take showers, receive a haircut or beauty treatment, have breakfast, get new clothes, and then go the service, sitting scattered throughout the congregation. Martin, calling the homeless "VIPs," takes seriously the biblical admonition not to treat anyone as a second-class person. In fall 2000 he inaugurated Masters Commission, a one-year internship for college credit that will infuse his programs with youthful enthusiasm:

> They will go spend an hour of prayer in the morning, an hour of Bible study, an hour of Scripture memory, and the rest of the morning is in class teaching. In the afternoon they spend on-hands training in every facet of the ministry of the Potter's House. So they'll learn mime, drama, children's ministry, youth ministry, street ministry, bookstore ministry, maintenance and housekeeping ministry, hospital visitation, convalescent home visitation, television ministry, audio-visual ministry, and the prayer center ministry. Outside the Potter's House, we'll partner with Metro Kids Church that has the panel vans that go into all the projects. The volunteer will be able to support other ministries with fifty interns this next year. . . . In the next five years, you will literally see dozens of Masters Commissions pop up in the black churches across the country because we crossed the barrier here.[54]

Starting in March, Martin began to plan for the main event of the year for the homeless, called "Novemberfest," to be held on 1 December 2000. Jakes partners with the City of Dallas and the Department of Veteran Affairs to hold a medical and job fair. Martin commented,

> We have a host of companies from UPS to Kentucky Fried Chicken that come in as service providers. We also provide a nice meal, not just sandwiches—we're talking chicken, turkey, and the fixings. We purposely do it in between Thanksgiving and Christmas because everybody does a lot for Thanksgiving and Christmas, but it's the in-between time where there's a lull. We have toys for the children and the Metro Kids Church ministers to the kids that come. We provide clothes, a meal, and medical services for everyone as well as a job fair where people can interview and get jobs on the spot.[55]

Martin is proud that this effort rallies the resources of the whole community, uniting Christians, Jews, businesses, and government in a dramatic and effective way.

To convey the atmosphere of the Potter's House to a first-time visitor and to members, that it is a positive place where people will be treated right, a superb cadre of ushers, formally dressed, answer questions, seat people, and generally smooth the flow throughout the service. I was amazed at the professionalism and courtesy with which these well-organized ushers executed this supposedly mundane task. Jakes wants every aspect of the operation to convey his message that people count and that one of the most exciting things to do in the whole world is to go to church. Large numbers of men attend (45 percent), most of the congregation is African American (77 percent), and there are significant numbers that are white (13 percent) or Hispanic (7 percent). Jakes desires a multiplicity of cultures in the Potter's House. He says that the church is its own ethnicity. And the preaching and music can be seen on videos to be purchased at most bookstores.[56]

The T. D. Jakes Ministries: Communicating beyond the Four Walls

Elder Silas Wheeler, also from West Virginia and a longtime friend and associate of Jakes, is the administrator and vice president of T. D. Jakes Ministries, responsible for television programs, domestic and international conferences, the Pater Alliance of affiliated pastors, external speaking engagements, and the videos and other materials present for sale in bookstores across the country. The magnitude of the logistical effort to orchestrate all these programs is immense. For just one conference in Atlanta, Georgia, or St. Petersburg, Florida, for example, hundreds of Potter's House volunteers fly to the conference for several days to help put the conference on. Every effort is made to use the latest marketing techniques in advertising events and products—consistent with the Jakes message and image.[57]

Besides his U.S. television presence, Jakes is televised weekly in Europe and in Africa and occasionally in Central and South America as well. At one time Jakes put on many conferences a year. Now he concentrates on a few megaconferences that take less of his time without reducing broader impact. One thing to be reminded of is that this is a ministry in motion, increasing not only in size and reach but also in its goals and purposes. Initially, Jakes refused to ordain ministers or to start a new denomination. That decision is under review, and there is every indication that the Pater Alliance, headed by the Reverend William Blue, which provides weekly communication among pastors in different denominations with ties to Jakes, may be supplemented by a new organization of Jakes-related churches—in effect, if not in name, a fledgling denomination. If this occurs, Jakes's influence, especially in the African American church world but also outside of it, may increase dramatically.[58]

Economic Development: Targeting South Dallas and Business Start-Ups

Nathaniel L. Tate heads the Metroplex Economic Development Corporation (MEDC), a nonprofit corporation formed in 1998 to create a public/private partnership to reverse poverty and release economic and social initiatives in

South Dallas. Tate, originally from New York, is a relative newcomer to the Jakes team. He is a communications engineer with great experience in international television, including responsibility for audio transmissions of the Atlanta Olympics and setting up a television operation in the Middle East. He is also the Jakes go-to man for behind-the-scenes program development and supervision and the author of a recent book on church administration.[59]

Tate watched over the recent construction of the Potter's House sanctuary. Taking me on a tour of the building, he delighted in pointing out the superb television, audio, computer, electrical power, and video systems in the auditorium and other rooms. But his true field of dreams is a mile or so away, located on low hills and farmland where MEDC owns land it is in the process of developing. Driving along the perimeters of the property, Tate related that he was shocked that Dallas had no real plan to guide the process of urban expansion in the area. He not only wanted that rectified but also wanted MEDC and the other Jakes entities to have leadership (not a mere voice) in any future planning. Tate enjoys negotiating, forming alliances, partnering, and leveraging the presence of Jakes to benefit the whole community—something he is busy doing—and when necessary, he is ready to play good old-fashioned, clean hardball in this local government arena.[60]

One of Bishop Jakes's biggest complaints is that one billion dollars or more, he says, flows out of South Dallas every year into rich areas of the city with better shopping malls, offices, and specialty stores. He wants this reversed, for the good of African Americans concentrated in that part of the city and for the betterment of the whole metro area. This is not negotiable. Jakes fully intends, systematically, to create space for new ideas, now taking root in the shadow of the Potter's House.[61] Initial MEDC plans under way include

- a major drug and alcohol rehabilitation outpatient center for individuals and groups;
- an adult education GED completion program;
- a business resource network targeting minority businesses for consultant support;
- a youth entrepreneurship, skills, and mentoring program;
- a business empowerment initiative for women with corporate support;
- a private Christian preschool and elementary school—Clay Academy;
- a national prison initiative to provide distance education to inmates by satellite;
- a intergenerational community center—including an executive retreat facility;
- a golf course, shopping center, office buildings, independent living center, and more.

Working with the zoning commission, which voted its unanimous approval in 1999, and corporate allies, Jakes is pushing ahead with these plans in a ten-year time frame. This is an unusual and creative moment for a religious ministry working through a nonprofit entity to promote urban recovery on such a large scale. This is a bold stroke for a newcomer to Dallas.[62]

T. D. Jakes Enterprises: Books, Plays, Music, and Movies

T. D. Jakes, by precept and example, engages in business. His recent *New York Times* business best-seller, *Maximize the Moment*, banks on his recent experience, giving practical advice and biblical insight on how to live to those inside and outside the church. "Time," Jakes tells us, is priceless because you cannot buy more of it. Learn to use your time wisely. This book is a crossover title, designed to appeal to those who might never buy a religious book or enter a Christian bookstore. Similarly, his more recent release, *The Great Investment: Faith, Family, and Finance*, explores the interconnections among dimensions of living. Bringing things together to make everything work better is another sign, says Jakes, that God's principles do govern in each area of life whether we admit it or not. We all need help in learning how to manage our gifts, time, relationships, and resources. Faith keeps wealth from controlling us, argues Jakes, and it promotes gratitude, contentment, and generosity. Family keeps people connected to one another, "functioning as a team," ready to sacrifice for the common good. Living within one's means, and learning the life-and-death power of exponential interest, prevents long-term poverty and promotes wealth. These are a few of the core ideas presented by Jakes in his teaching and books.[63]

Curtis Wallace, a young Dallas attorney, heads up T. D. Jakes Enterprises, which promotes the for-profit books, plays, music, and movie side of the house. The books are a sure thing—they sell in the hundreds of thousands, like those of any other best-selling author who has secured a loyal following. Marketing Jakes's writings to his supporters and to the public in Wal-Mart and Barnes & Noble guarantees success. This, however, is not true for the creative arts side of the house—Touchdown Concepts and Dexterity Sounds. Jakes takes risks when he produces the play "Behind Closed Doors" and sends it on the road. Who will respond and pay the ticket price? Who will buy the music CDs he creates? How many will attend the movie *Woman, Thou Art Loosed!*? Will Jakes recover production costs and make a substantial profit? He could reduce risk by only promoting and selling to his loyal constituency, but this would be to give up his larger vision. If Jakes wants to "add value to the quality of human life," a phrase from the T. D. Jakes Enterprises Mission Statement, then he has to succeed in the market against all comers, embracing competition. Jakes welcomes this challenge, ready to fail, because that is the only way to accomplish his dream—and to instruct by example.[64]

THE PUBLIC AND POLITICAL INFLUENCE OF T. D. JAKES

The 2000 election changed and accelerated the public role of Bishop Jakes. First, with the bitterness of this election and with the racial divide, there is a call for healing and for unity to face common tasks. Religious leaders will be part of this national discussion, and no one is better positioned than Bishop Jakes to facilitate understanding. Second, President Bush wants to be known as a uniter, not a divider. He has ties to Jakes, and in the earliest days after the election he worked to enlist the minister's support. Other African American leaders, such as the Reverend Jesse Jackson and the Reverend Al Sharpton, are entrenched in their own interests and cannot rise above Washington's political battles. They are party players who exacerbate conflicts, who initiated opposition to Bush, and who seek to create opportunities to advance their own personal or racial agendas. They are not willing or able to pour oil on troubled waters; nor is that their chosen role.[65]

Bishop Jakes will never leave his ministry to go into politics. He will not run for public office. In the presidential election race of 2000 he endorsed no one, nor is he likely to in the future. Leveraging this independence allows Jakes to develop close ties to whomever is in power or likely to be in power. George Bush and Al Gore both visited the Potter's House, and when Bush listed Jakes as a spiritual adviser, Larry King, the talk show host, put him on the show the next night. Jakes does not court this exposure. Larry King asked Jakes questions of little relevance to him, like who would be the Bush vice president nominee, rather than questions that concern African Americans, their place in the nation, and the political process. This disappointed Jakes. The press is not interested in what the church brings to the table, he said. Nor is he confident that either political party fully understands how best to help the poor. But by remaining independent, and by persevering in his communications with them, he hopes to influence government leaders of both parties.[66]

Jakes has observed that both Republicans and Democrats now support the concept of government partnering with faith-based organizations for the delivery of goods and services. He applauds this change and is prepared to cooperate in Dallas with local, state, and federal efforts to help the region. As the new president and Congress consider legislation that connects governments to churches, sharing resources and responsibility, Jakes will be consulted.[67]

Potentially these cooperative efforts will break some new ground in church–state relations. One experienced city administrator and scholar, James Oliver, has commented,

> Jakes is on the cutting edge of re-defining (or perhaps returning) the concept of church to fit the times. The Church that Jakes describes is an entrepreneurial church "accepting" even "gladly" the retreat of government from running social and human programs. It's not just going back to "Catholic Charities" or the version of "charities" that were founded in the pre and post Depression era. It is more of a public–private partnership with various "equities" (including sweat as well as money) being introduced. There is something "new" here. And, in Jakes' case, it's really big, bigger than earlier church versions of programs. There is something "transformational" here rather than incremental or just shifting burdens (from government or society to church). There is a real re-defining going on here. And Jakes may be a precursor that others will follow.[68]

In the future, Jakes is hopeful that Christians will commonly be in positions of influence in government. He is confident that the Potter's House and churches like it will produce faith-filled leaders with a positive view of government service. He sees a day when the church will no longer be preoccupied with pulling people out of the gutter: "I want to see Godly men rise to power. . . . I want to see some Godly mayors, governors, presidents, lawyers, businessmen, and saints of God, coming to the altar."[69]

These three political roles for Jakes, influencing the powerful, partnering with government, and producing leaders, are not the whole story. His greatest public impact, long term, is related to Jakes's spiritual and cultural impact—some call it "cultural lift"—that is prepolitical. Jakes knows that as long as Christians as a group are weak and divided they will have almost no public responsibility. This changes, predictably, when Christians, or any group, are numerous, strong, united, and motivated, with interests to promote and with precise goals to achieve. That day is coming, Jakes is confident, today in South Dallas and tomorrow in the nation. A people dispossessed, without influence, is vulnerable. For most of his people that vulnerability is the legacy of slavery and segregation. However, there is no spiritual and economic restoration without political restoration. It is all one package, Jakes knows, but the spiritual, social, and economic recovery precedes the political, and this will take time to achieve.

By maintaining a separation between his ministry and the maelstrom of politics, Jakes constructs a safe harbor for people learning to deal with the basics of faith, family, and work. Public responsibilities inevitably will come when they are ready for them—perhaps in the next generation, after Jakes passes on his mantle. Meanwhile, Bishop Jakes can serve as a reconciler in the nation, boldly pressuring people to get along, to strive to work together, to bridge differences. He will do this by his example, relating to partisans on both sides, and will call for good sense and good faith efforts. With the aid of politicians and the media, Jakes will have a prominent platform from which to speak. The times call for a reconciler to stand forward.

There is one last comment to make regarding his contributions to public peace and wholeness. Jakes's four principal teachings noted above—on the relevance of the Bible, unity, the tension between the real and the ideal, and profitability—all have political applications. Exploring these connections may not yet be on the formal Jakes agenda. However, as far as human frailty permits, predictably, Bishop Jakes will think and act in ways consistent with these principles in his new public role. For example, Jakes is sensitive to human weakness and offers people assistance, yet he stands against a victim mentality that refuses to accept responsibility and passively awaits deliverance. This tension in his thought helps him to avoid the extremes that polarize everyday public discussion of policy issues.

CONCLUSION: THE T. D. JAKES PHENOMENON

T. D. Jakes is riding the wind, moving more swiftly than a simple snapshot like this one can capture or keep in focus. Jakes is a phenomenon, and each aspect of his ministry—such as the prison ministry alone, hardly dealt with here—is a story unto itself. Grasping the meaning of it all is difficult too, for the Jakes story is just beginning. Will it keep its present speed and trajectory? Other leaders have risen just as fast, Martin Luther King Jr., Billy Graham, and Oral Roberts come to mind. Each had his own trajectory—King cut short, Graham preaching into his old age, and Roberts losing much of his influence in his latter years. Jakes himself is ready to die tomorrow, content with being faithful. However, he has a destiny that he wants to complete. What might that be?

First and foremost, T. D. Jakes wants to restore individuals to full and productive lives. That is an endless task, for as Jesus said, "The poor you have with you always." What is distinctive about Jakes is his desire to restore the Invisible One to the central place in the lives of all people, high and low, rich and poor. That is the true meaning of the Potter's House, which Jakes says is a sign, not a building, a church, or a sanctuary.

Second, Jakes is in the early stages of creating a fellowship of churches, which may or may not become a denomination someday, and raising up a new generation of church leaders who will take his innovations to the next level. Many of these preachers are younger than he is. They are responding to his example—dreaming new dreams, thinking outside the narrow confines of tradition. Other churches, of varied ethnicity and doctrinal persuasion, are also learning from him.

Third, Jakes is ready for the next challenge, the impossible task. He is always moving on, ready to accept risks in a true pioneering spirit. So far this boldness—he calls it obedience coupled with commitment—takes him into a variety of spheres, for-profit and nonprofit, where he spends his talent and energies on an amazing range of projects. This too must change, as Jakes walks onto a wider stage. Soon he will narrow his focus, reducing the number of his tasks, as the demands of national counselor to those in power weigh in. Jakes adjusts priorities well, as opportunities and duties warrant. Will this be a temporary phase in his life or a permanent role? That depends on his limits, his capacity to be a burden bearer in times that may turn rough.

Jakes draws a line between worldly success—fame, wealth, and power—and profitability defined as adding value to humanity and to the Kingdom of God. There can be no profitability, in this definition, without faith and obedience to God. God comes first. If the church loses this message, Jakes tells us, no one else will preach it:

> Come, all you who are thirsty, come to the waters;
>   and you who have no money, come, buy and eat!
> Come buy wine and milk without money and without cost. . . .
> Whoever is thirsty, let him come; and whoever wishes, let him take the free gift of the water of life.[70]

Does this ancient biblical message preached by Bishop T. D. Jakes have social and political implications? The best answer is to look back in history and see how often those who were the least partisan had the greatest long-term political impact because of their concern for justice and the total well-being of people. Jakes is just such a man, and the foolishness of preaching, not public service, is his calling. That is what makes him so attractive to those who have spent lifetimes in pursuit of transitory success.

When Jakes finished his vacation in December 2000, he was back at work as a minister to the nation. He will join the Bush outreach to partner with churches for social and charitable causes. He will oppose racial bigotry. The church, Bishop Jakes asserts, has its own ethnicity, and it is color-blind.

NOTES

1. Dana Milbank, "Bush to Host Black Ministers," *Washington Post*, Federal Page, The Transition, 19 December 2000: A1.

2. *Maximize the Moment* (New York: G. P. Putnam's Sons, 1999) is a recent book by T. D. Jakes. There is no biography of Bishop Jakes or book written on his ministry. This essay is based on three trips to interview and observe Jakes, one to Atlanta in summer 2000 and two to Dallas shortly thereafter. In addition, I interviewed his senior staff, attended

conferences and services, and researched the books, articles, and videos of his teaching. Professor Vinson Synan, a distinguished scholar of Pentecostal and Charismatic church movements, was most helpful in assisting this effort. Elder Shawn Paul Wood, the public relations coordinator of the Potter's House, was a master of scheduling and provider of sources.

3. I attended the "Woman, Thou Art Loosed!" Conference in Atlanta on 27 July 2000.

4. "Woman, Thou Art Loosed!" Conference; T. D. Jakes Ministries, videotape, *WTAL 2000*, 27 July 2000.

5. Comments made by a panel of scholars at the American Political Science Association meeting I attended in Atlanta in 1999; T. D. Jakes, *The Great Investment: Faith, Family, and Finance* (New York: G. P. Putnam's Sons, 2000).

6. I attended the "Woman, Thou Art Loosed—Plus" economic empowerment conference and the premier of "Behind Closed Doors" in Atlanta on 26–27 July 2000.

7. I attended the dedication of the Potter's House in Dallas on 22 October 2000.

8. A sample of clippings from the national press on Jakes includes Gustav Niebuhr and Laurie Goodstein, "New Wave of Evangelists Vying for National Pulpit," *New York Times*, 1 January 1999; Lisa Miller, "Grammy Nomination, Book Deal, TV Spots—A Holy Empire Is Born," *Wall Street Journal*, 21 August 1998; Hanna Rosin, "Force for Change: Preaching Phenom Stops by Washington," *Washington Post*, 11 September 1999; John Blake, "Amazing Jakes," *Atlanta Journal-Constitution*, 31 July 1999.

9. T. D. Jakes Ministries, information brochure.

10. Biographical information provided by T. D. Jakes Ministries.

11. Interviews by the author with T. D. Jakes's staff—Pastor Lawrence Robinson; Elders Silas Wheeler, William Blue, Stephen Sledge, Pat Martin, Nathaniel Tate, David Yeazell, and Shawn Wood; and Mr. Curtis Wallace, Esq.—Dallas, 10–11 August 2000; in addition, materials provided by T. D. Jakes Ministries.

12. Interviews with T. D. Jakes's staff, Dallas, 10–11 August 2000; T. D. Jakes Ministries, *Video 1-3*, Soweto, South Africa, 19 March 2000.

13. Interviews with Executive Director Nathaniel Tate, Dallas, 10–11 August 2000; and brochures of the Metroplex Economic Development Corporation, "Project 2000."

14. Information materials from T. D. Jakes Ministries.

15. I was present at the commencement, Tulsa, Oklahoma; information from a representative of the public relations firm representing T. D. Jakes on his vision for the ministry and marketing.

16. Deion Sanders, *Power, Money and Sex* (Dallas: Word Books, 1998).

17. Niebuhr and Goodstein, "New Wave of Evangelists Vying for National Pulpit."

18. Interview with T. D. Jakes, Atlanta, 25 July 2000.

19. T. D. Jakes Video, *Video #3: Money*, Power, Money and Sex Series. For comments by Bishop Jakes on his theology, see *Christianity Today*, available at http://www.christianitytoday.com/ct/current/0221/0221c.html.

20. Interview with Jakes, Atlanta, 25 July 2000; and Dallas Pastors and Leadership Conference, Dallas, October 2000.

21. Interview with Jakes, Atlanta, 25 July 2000; and Dallas Pastors and Leadership Conference.

22. Interview with Jakes, Atlanta, 25 July 2000; and Dallas Pastors and Leadership Conference.

23. Interview with Jakes, Atlanta, 25 July 2000; and Dallas Pastors and Leadership Conference.
24. T. D. Jakes Video, *Video #3: Money*, Power, Money and Sex Series; T. D. Jakes Ministries, *Video 1-3*, Soweto, South Africa, 19 March 2000.
25. This is a compilation from Jakes's sermons I heard, his books, and his videos.
26. This is a compilation from Jakes's sermons I heard, his books, and his videos.
27. T. D. Jakes, sermon, Dallas Pastors and Leadership Conference.
28. T. D. Jakes Video, *Video #4: Sex*, Power, Money and Sex Series.
29. T. D. Jakes Video, *Video #4: Sex*, Power, Money and Sex Series.
30. Jakes, *Maximize the Moment* and *The Great Investment*.
31. T. D. Jakes, sermon.
32. T. D. Jakes Video, *Videos #2 and #3: Money*, Power, Money and Sex Series.
33. T. D. Jakes Video, *Videos #2 and #3: Money*, Power, Money and Sex Series.
34. T. D. Jakes Video, *Videos #2 and #3: Money*, Power, Money and Sex Series.
35. T. D. Jakes Video, *Videos #2 and #3: Money*, Power, Money and Sex Series. "Seize the Moment" was the theme of the "Woman, Thou Art Loosed!" 2000 conference.
36. Jakes, sermon, Dallas Pastors and Leadership Conference.
37. Jakes, sermon, Dallas Pastors and Leadership Conference.
38. T. D. Jakes Ministries, *Video 1-3*, Soweto, South Africa, 19 March 2000.
39. Jakes, sermon, Dallas Pastors and Leadership Conference.
40. Jakes, sermon, Dallas Pastors and Leadership Conference.
41. This is a compilation from Jakes's sermons I heard, his books, and his videos.
42. T. D. Jakes, sermon.
43. Amos 9:13, New International Version.
44. T. D. Jakes Video, *Video #2: Money*, Power, Money and Sex Series.
45. Jakes, sermon, Dallas Pastors and Leadership Conference.
46. Interviews with T. D. Jakes's staff, Dallas, 10–11 August 2000.
47. Interviews with T. D. Jakes's staff, Dallas, 10–11 August 2000.
48. Jakes, sermon, Dallas Pastors and Leadership Conference.
49. Interview with Pastor Lawrence Robinson, Dallas, 10–11 August 2000.
50. Interview with Pastor Lawrence Robinson, Dallas, 10–11 August 2000.
51. Interview with Elder David Yeazell, Dallas, 10–11 August 2000.
52. Interview with Pastor Lawrence Robinson, Dallas, 10–11 August 2000.
53. Interview with Elder Pat Martin, Dallas, 10–11 August 2000.
54. Interview with Elder Pat Martin, Dallas, 10–11 August 2000.
55. Interview with Elder Pat Martin, Dallas, 10–11 August 2000.
56. Observations made and heard at the Dallas Pastors and Leadership Conference. Documentation provided by Elder Shawn Wood.
57. Interviews with Elders Silas Wheeler, William Blue, and Stephen Sledge, Dallas, 10–11 August 2000.
58. Interviews with Elders Silas Wheeler, William Blue, and Stephen Sledge, and other pastoral staff, Dallas, 10–11 August 2000.
59. Interview with Elder Nathaniel Tate, Dallas, 10–11 August 2000.
60. Interview with Elder Nathaniel Tate, Dallas, 10–11 August 2000.
61. T. D. Jakes, sermons.
62. Metroplex Economic Development Corporation brochure and information packet.

63. See T. D. Jakes's books and sermons, including *Maximize the Moment* and *The Great Investment*.

64. Interview with Mr. Curtis Wallace, Esq., and T. D. Jakes Enterprises power point presentation, Dallas, 10–11 August 2000.

65. For more information on the Reverend Al Sharpton, see chapter 3.

66. Interview with Jakes, Atlanta, 25 July 2000; and Dallas Pastors and Leadership Conference.

67. T. D. Jakes press conferences in Atlanta and in Dallas.

68. Professor James Oliver, Regent University, note to the author, December 2000.

69. T. D. Jakes Video, *Video #2: Money*, Power, Money and Sex Series.

70. Isaiah 55:1 and Revelations 22:17, New International Version.

3

The Reverend Al Sharpton: Pentecostal for Racial Justice

Jo Renee Formicola

He seems to be everywhere—on radio talk shows and the nightly news. Leading noisy, chaotic demonstrations as well as silent, passive prayer vigils, he's in Detroit demanding jobs for blacks at Burger King or supporting efforts to penalize Coca Cola for its hiring practices. There's no corporation that scares him.

He's debating with politicians, and he's marching with ministers. He's in jail. He's with grieving families. He's in court. He's at the White House. He's outside the Supreme Court demonstrating to recount ballots in Florida. He's opposing the new president's cabinet appointments. He's in Israel. He's calling for the cancellation of African debt by the World Bank. He's having lunch with Fidel Castro.

Marginalized blacks seek his counsel and support, candidates for public office want his endorsement, and yet most people agree: he is offensive, in your face, and trouble. This is the popular perception of the public Al Sharpton, a product and opponent of a New York City that he believes is racist. But this is also the façade of the Reverend Al Sharpton, a very different, compassionate, committed, pastoral, and multidimensional person in private; a minister who once said, "A preacher is part religious leader, social leader, social worker, and entertainer."[1]

Al Sharpton was born in Brooklyn, New York, in 1954. The son of religious parents, he was brought to church from the time he was an infant; and according to him, he knew that he wanted to be a preacher by the time he was three years old. Becoming a junior usher in the black Pentecostal church and then a protégé of Bishop Washington of the Washington Temple, Sharpton was preaching to a congregation of several thousand by the time he was four.

The "Wonderboy," as he was nicknamed, was soon evangelizing all over the New York area while he was still a child. He was certified as a minister in the Pentecostal Church at the age of ten, one of the youngest ministers on record.

Adam Clayton Powell was one of the earliest influences on Al Sharpton. The pastor of the largest religious institution in Harlem, Powell was a U.S. congressman as well as the leader of the 10,000-member Abyssinian Baptist Church. He became a hero as well as a mentor to the young Sharpton, who as a child admired Powell because he defied limitations and taboos; because he was independent, self-assured, and arrogant; and because whites saw him as a troublemaker.[2] As a teenager, Sharpton joined the Southern Christian Leadership Conference, and when Jesse Jackson came from Chicago to recruit young people to work for his Operation Breadbasket, Sharpton was quick to join, to go on protests, and to participate in demonstrations for civil rights. In 1969, at the age of fifteen, the teenager was appointed director of Operation Breadbasket for New York City.

Through these kinds of contacts, activities, and weekly preaching, Sharpton quickly came to know the influential blacks within the emerging national power structure as well as those with major influence in the Big Apple. But, increasingly, he came to recognize that there was no identifiable black leadership in New York City that either emulated the civil rights model in the rest of the country or advanced the racial cause. He blamed this lack of political direction and social progress on the fact that the black power establishment in New York had been in a comfortable alliance with white politicians for a long time. Sharpton believed that because the black leadership came to have money, power, and prestige, it was content to go along in order to get along. He asserted, and continues to maintain, that New York is still ruled by a black elite, that is, by important black politicians who do not want to antagonize their white friends.[3] He says that many of them have made peace with their service to the white establishment at the expense of the community.[4] And he also insists that New York is still controlled by the same racists who run Wall Street, the media, and Broadway.

Radicalized by a teachers' strike in New York City during the 1960s, Sharpton as a teenager took part in a major protest against the largest food store chain in the United States, the A&P. Encouraged by the success of the sit-in, he founded the National Youth Movement in 1971 to target other major corporations with discriminatory hiring and business practices. He was able to get entertainer James Brown to do a benefit concert for the organization and as a result spent some time touring with him as a bodyguard and a musical promoter. This gave Sharpton the opportunity to see the state of civil rights in America and to move in celebrity circles. He worked with Michael Jackson to get jobs for blacks in the entertainment industry and with Don

King to promote boxing matches. And, by maintaining his relationship with James Brown, he was later able to accompany the singer to meet President Ronald Reagan at the White House.

But even after his travels and a variety of jobs, Sharpton returned to his true vocation, the ministry. Addressing worshippers at a variety of different churches on Sundays, rather than affiliating with just one institution, Sharpton found that he was in a position to see what was going on all over New York. Racial injustice in many forms and in many places was still rampant. During the 1980s he became a more independent minister, attacking both the blacks and the whites for doing nothing to eliminate discrimination in the largest, wealthiest, most liberal city in the world.

SHARPTON'S PERSONAL JOURNEY

Repression and religion have always been at the core of the American democratic experience for blacks. During the 200-year history of slavery in the United States, whites often used the theology and culture of their Christian churches to subdue and inculcate the Africans into the Anglo-Saxon way of life and its Protestant religion. But, after the Civil War and the freeing of the slaves, a different, black Christianity emerged in America. Taking on new forms of worship and organization, it reflected the growing autonomy of its members. Some scholars contend, however, that even the changed Christianity subverted black resistance to the social plight of its members during the Jim Crow period. They maintain that the post–Civil War black churches emphasized spiritual solace as a balm for political rejection, a phenomenon that resulted in African American political apathy and quietism.[5]

Another school of thought, however, stresses that blacks used the Christian faith to survive and to protect their interests during their period of slavery. These same scholars contend that after the Civil War the separate and decentralized houses of worship inspired the development of competent, religiously committed blacks—individuals who learned organizational skills and resource management within their religious institutions. They claim that the use of diverse formats for religious services encouraged and underscored black culture, changing the social role of the church and fostering a training ground for political liberation and activism in the future.[6]

By end of World War I, a booming, industrialized northern economy motivated many blacks, who were seeking greater opportunities, to migrate from the agricultural, rural areas of the South. Local black churches increasingly served more than just a religious purpose; they became instrumental in helping the newly arrived migrants to acclimate to life in the teeming cities. More importantly, the black churches, alone, dealt with the varied problems of segregation in places that still did not accept racial equality. Some scholars, such as Frederick Harris,[7] argue that as a result of this multidimensional function, the churches became sources of refuge, culture, community, and advancement. They became institutions where individuals could develop themselves personally and professionally by participating in the governance and business of the church—often the most significant and most powerful organization in their neighborhoods.

By the 1960s, black churches became even more critical in black communities. As the focal points of African American moral resistance to racial injustice, they also became the structural underpinnings for the political movement for civil rights in the United States. And, because black ministers were, in most cases, the most educated persons in their churches, they became the social, religious, and *political* leaders of their congregations as well. Often, black ministers also became the link between their communities and the white political establishments in most cities, thrusting the men of the cloth into positions of social, economic, and political leadership, asserting a power never before experienced by their race in America. Adam Clayton Powell, Martin Luther King Jr., Jesse Jackson, Ralph David Abernathy, and T. J. Jamison immediately come to mind as powerful black religious and political leaders. But today other names such as Calvin Butts, T. D. Jakes, Floyd Flake, and Al Sharpton are also demanding, and receiving, political attention for the problems that still exist in the black communities in America.

THE RELIGIOUS VIEWS OF THE REVEREND AL SHARPTON

Sharpton uses his pulpit to decry the racial injustice that he sees everywhere in the black community. This, he contends, is a natural reaction—his political behavior is impelled by his Christian religious beliefs.

Most blacks in America are, indeed, Christian. About 50 percent of African Americans worship in the Baptist Church and are affiliated with national organizations such as the National Baptist Convention USA and the Progressive National Convention. Another 10 percent participate in the Methodist Church and are tied to the American Methodist Episcopal (AME) Church, the AME Zion Church, or the Pentecostal Church of God in Christ. The remaining American black population belongs to other independent, "storefront" Evangelical, or Muslim houses of worship.[8]

The Reverend Al Sharpton is an ordained Pentecostal minister. This religious denomination is considered a part of the Protestant body, but it does not have its roots in either the European or the English Reformation. It is known as being "Holiness" or "Pentecostal" in nature because of the importance the church ascribes to the Day of Pentecost, the fiftieth day after Easter. It is also believed that the gifts of the Holy Spirit, which included a "sound from heaven," "tongues of fire," and the "power to speak in languages," were manifested to the followers of Christ on that day, making the church more abundant and powerful.

The Pentecostal Church of God in Christ, Sharpton's church, is a branch of the larger Pentecostal body. Charles Harrison Mason of Memphis, Tennessee, founded the church by forming a militant cadre of Baptist preachers,[9] who together conducted a revival in Jackson, Mississippi, in 1896. They claimed that their evangelizing brought about conversions, sanctification, and faith healing, assertions that led them to be ostracized from their more conservative Baptist association. In response they established a church of their own in 1897, with Mason eventually breaking away from the others after claiming to have received the Holy Ghost. His religious experience led to the founding of the Pentecostal Church of God in Christ, which is now the second-largest Pentecostal group in America.[10] It has over four million members in over ten thousand congregations.[11]

The theology of the Pentecostal Church of God in Christ is based on seven critical tenets. It is focused on the Bible, which is considered to be the inspired and infallible written word of God, and it is based on the belief in one God, who exists as a trinity of the Father, the Son, and the Holy Spirit. The Pentecostal faith rests on the notion of Blessed Hope, that is, a belief in the Second Coming of Christ, and is predicated on the doctrine that man was born in sin and needs to be born again, sanctified, and cleansed from sin. This regeneration, it is believed, comes though the Holy Ghost and is absolutely essential for salvation. It holds that Christ redeemed man by his death on the Cross and maintains that Baptism should be given to those who ask for it. Finally, it is based on the belief that the sanctifying power of the Holy Spirit enables the Christian to live a holy and separated life in the present world.

The Pentecostal Church is essentially conservative in its theology but progressive in its social agenda and politics. And it is based very closely on the Old Testament model of religion, in which the paths of the temporal and the spiritual often crossed. Pentecostal religious tenets have been translated into social and political action for black liberation, empowerment, justice, and equality. While conflicts, schisms, and personality rifts are often visible in some churches, the Pentecostal Church of God in Christ functions as a hierarchical organization giving national direction but allowing local autonomy. Each congregation is tied to a central, elected governing board of bishops and has a defined mission; but each hires its own pastor and pursues its own social agenda.[12]

THE REVEREND AL SHARPTON'S
POLITICAL CAUSE: RACIAL JUSTICE

Race is the "American Dilemma" according to the Reverend Al Sharpton. To him it is central to most political, social, and economic problems in the United States. So although Sharpton had set out originally to be a minister, his religious convictions as well as his personal experiences impelled him into social activism and political involvement to advance racial justice. He is a personal work in progress, a major actor in New York committed to social and political change. He firmly believes that "the Christian walk [is] to help the needy . . . [and] protect the weak" and that social activism is a "calling" that comes from one's interior life as a Christian.[13]

In his autobiography, Sharpton talks about himself as a child, growing up and acting out of instinct and anger. As a young man he believed that he also behaved out of emotion, and he paid the price for his quick reactions to racial injustice by being stabbed in the chest by a white man in 1991. This, he believes, was one of the defining moments of his life. At that time, he says, "I realized that confronting American racism at its base [was] a very dangerous thing and not to be undertaken without serious spiritual and mental preparation."[14] It was then that he claimed to realize the full import of being a Christian activist and set about to change his life.

His Christianity makes him different from others, he says, because his values are central to his activity. Sharpton has claimed that his values are "not on the side."[15] Now he is happy with himself and sees himself as a proactive adult. He considers himself a religious person committed to change socioeconomic conditions for blacks, to make needed changes in the body politic, to educate people about racism, and to form alliances with those who can make meaningful change in society.

In 1985, Al Sharpton plunged headlong into the chaos of the New York racial scene when several young black men were shot by a white subway rider, Bernhard Goetz. Fearing that they were muggers rather than panhandlers, Goetz fired at the teenagers and permanently paralyzed one of them. He became a folk hero among Big Apple whites, an urban legend of the New York press. He had not been indicted; nor had a gun charge even been brought against him. And no one in the black power structure in New York stood up for the teenagers. Sharpton admitted that he was "shook up" by the incident and called a news conference to denounce what he believed to be vigilantism. He organized demonstrations and prayer vigils at Goetz's apartment house and went to the court proceedings. He gave interviews. And soon, in his own words, he became an "activist in the media age."[16] As a result, Goetz was indicted, convicted of carrying a concealed weapon, and sentenced to spend a year in jail on the gun violation.

Other high-profile cases followed. In 1986, a distraught family called for help to deal with a racial killing in Howard Beach. There, Michael Griffith, a young black man who went into a pizzeria with two friends, was killed by a car after being taunted and chased onto a highway by a group of white teenagers. At the family's home listening to the two witnesses to the incident, Sharpton knew that he was going to do something and that *from now on* he would do *something*, in every situation where possible, to counter the racial injustice in New York. In this case he challenged the press and labeled the situation a racial murder. He offered a reward for information; he held a rally in Howard Beach at the pizza restaurant—and he purchased pizza for all the protestors who were with him. Now he was leading marches of thousands of people and being accompanied by leaders of the black political establishment as well. He also came to know and work with C. Vernon Mason and Alton Maddox, two attorneys who, together with Sharpton, became a team dedicated to protecting the rights of blacks in New York. As a result of this case, Sharpton contends that he "had arrived as an activist, and [that] even the most respected members of the community were standing with me"; at the same time however, he also realized that he was also becoming a symbol of hate and derision among whites.[17]

The opportunity to "put him in his place" seemed to come in 1987. At that time, a young black woman named Tawana Brawley contended that she had been abducted by a group of white men in Newburgh, New York. She accused them of holding her captive for several days; tormenting, raping, and sodomizing her; and then letting her go. An assistant district attorney in the county, Steven Pagones, was rumored to be a participant in the alleged incident. Sharpton and his two lawyer associates, Maddox and Mason, publicly named Pagones as being one of Brawley's attackers on a New York television station. The sordidness of the case and the possibility that a public official could be involved caused then Governor of the State of New York, Mario Cuomo, to appoint a special prosecutor to deal with the matter. But, when the case went to the grand jury, its members refused to indict anyone, concluding that there was no rape. The attorney general then maintained that all the allegations were a hoax and threw out the case. Sharpton, nevertheless, stood by Brawley and her family. As a result, Steven Pagones sued him and the lawyers in the case for $395 million for defamation of character. The Pagones case dragged on for another ten years and ended with an eight-month trial. A jury finally found Sharpton and his lawyers guilty of slander, with Sharpton personally being fined $65,000.

As a result of the Brawley case, Sharpton was pilloried in the press. Very soon after the original charges were thrown out, Sharpton was also accused of being an FBI informant, of tax evasion and embezzlement, of attempting to make contacts with wanted felons, and of wiretapping his associates. Acquitted of all the charges, but required to pay damages to Pagones, Sharpton has dealt with these attacks philosophically. It has been his contention that "if everybody's after you, it must be that you have the ball. Nobody's chasing anybody that doesn't have the ball."[18]

In 1989, he was in the forefront of another major racial incident, the Yousif Hawkins case. The black teenager and three of his friends went to Bensonhurst, a section of Brooklyn, to look at a used car but got off at the wrong subway stop. They had to walk though the neighborhood and were chased by a group of white boys who eventually shot Hawkins twice in the heart. The murdered boy's family asked for Sharpton's help, which resulted in advice, a series of marches, and keeping the pressure on the justice system. A jury found one of the white boys guilty of murder and sentenced him to thirty-two years to life for the crime. In the longer term, however, Sharpton felt that the publicity he brought to the case underscored the sad fact that black life was cheap in the New York area.[19]

In 1991, Sharpton became involved in one of the most volatile cases in New York history, the death of Gavin Cato. Tragically, the car of the grand rebbe of the Lubavitcher, a Hasidic Jewish sect, swerved to miss an oncoming car and hit two black children, killing one of them, Gavin Cato. Word of the accident spread through the neighborhood, people poured out onto the streets, and a young rabbinical student, Yankel Rosenbaum, was stabbed to death allegedly by a black youth, Limerick Nelson. The situation ignited a racial confrontation between the Hasidic Jews and the blacks who had long lived together in the community. The driver of the car fled to Israel, to be followed later by Sharpton and others demanding justice. Again, marches and pressure were brought to bear on the justice system, and a jury acquitted Nelson. It created a major cleavage between the blacks and the Jews, a natural coalition of oppressed peoples who had worked together in New York City against the mainstream world of American, white, Anglo-Saxon Protestants. It has taken time to heal this split, but Sharpton and community leaders are attempting to rebuild the relationship that existed before this unfortunate incident occurred.

Just this past year, two major bias incidents involving the New York City police again propelled Sharpton into the public arena. In 1999, Abner Louima, a Haitian immigrant, was arrested and sodomized by three police officers. Bringing pressure to bear by rallying politicians, entertainers, and members of the community, Sharpton was instrumental in making sure that Justin Volpe, the arresting officer, was convicted of the horrendous crime. Very soon thereafter, another case of police brutality was in the news. Amadou Diallo, a Guinean immigrant, was shot forty-one times by an elite police unit that mistook him for a rape suspect. In this case, Sharpton and his followers were not able to influence the judicial system, which allowed a change of venue in the case. All four of the police officers were acquitted. Currently, Sharpton and his followers are working on the Patrick Dorismond case, another situation in which a young black man was shot to death after being offered and refusing drugs from the New York City police.

Sharpton believes that the Crown Heights situation was the one that essentially turned him around, the one that convinced him that the best way to attain racial justice was by empowering the black community politically. After that, he began to turn his attention more to *political*, rather than social, activism. He maintains that in order to "make a real impact" an individual must be engaged in the political process, that it is the only way to institute social policy. He knows that people can try to influence elections by backing certain candidates, but ultimately he believes that someone like himself must try to gain office in order to make serious social change.[20] At the time, he knew he could organize. He knew he could lead. He knew he had the support of the marginalized. He knew the time was coming for him to take a political stand of his own.

THE REVEREND SHARPTON'S POLITICAL STRATEGY AND TACTICS

Philosophically, some black scholars view the social movements of the 1960s and 1970s as a period of "creedal passion,"[21] that is, as a time of liberal political action sustained by religious fervor. But they also argue that such activism drained the black religious community and resulted in conservative political backlashes in the 1980s. That decade saw the political pendulum swing to the right, reversing black social, economic, and political progress previously advanced by church groups in the United States. Moving back to the center during the 1990s, however, politicians on both the Left and the Right worked to reform much of the black social agenda,[22] particularly in terms of welfare policy and affirmative action. In its new state, these priorities are being re-embraced not only by liberals but also by members of the center of both political parties.

Historically, there has been an affinity between blacks and the Democratic Party, but in the very recent past there has been a jolt to the New York political establishment by the changed nature of the coalition. The "disturbance in the force" has come as a result of the courting of Al Sharpton by political candidates Bill Bradley, Al Gore, and Hillary Rodham Clinton. Their express recognition of the independent minister as a political force within New York shocked and continues to stagger those who see Sharpton's political currency on the rise and his legitimacy as a new part of the state's political equation.

How has the brash preacher gone from loudmouth to legitimate? from power broker to potential serious political candidate himself? How did he go from being ripe for exploitation by the political pros, both black and white, to being a competent political actor in his own right? He believes that if individuals want to be taken seriously, then they must take themselves seriously.[23] He says he is a changed person, both internally and externally, a rational, proactive leader.

Sharpton's new political strategy is based on the premise that the black polity in New York has been taken for granted by both its own and the white political establishment. As a result, he believes that he must be the person to articulate the African American agenda for the millennium. His tactics, therefore, are designed to empower the black voter through media pressure, organization, and participation in the political process.

Sharpton spends a major part of his time getting the attention of the press, the radio, and the TV media to dramatize issues that are important to the black community. This is how he goes about educating the public. Indeed, the day we met he was in the process of meeting with the New York media to provide a platform for, and to give credence to, a claim by two young black women of sexual molestation in a gang frenzy in Central Park. As in all cases, the young women contacted Sharpton for help. His staff maintains that he does not reach out or impose himself in controversial situations simply because he does not want to look like a media hound. Instead, he is willing to act as an advocate and a support. He provided attorneys who would do pro bono work for the young women and has a number of lawyers he can call on in these types of situations. He allowed the victims to use his offices for a press conference. He stood behind them, both figuratively and literally.

Sharpton says that it is critical to identify important discriminatory events and keep them before the eye of the public. He maintains that it is essential to keep community pressure on the perpetrators of racial injustice by participating in marches and demonstrations and even going to jail if necessary. He takes it one step further, however, because he likes to startle the public by being where racial injustice is practiced. He says, "I'm on their block,"[24] and indeed, he has been known to demonstrate, sit in, and hold prayer vigils outside the homes of CEOs and others for jobs, equal opportunities for the poor, and racial justice. He has also been arrested on numerous occasions as well, the longest being a ninety-day sentence for demonstrating against U.S. bombing practices in Vieques, Puerto Rico.

Sharpton has been educating the public while also working to organize the black community politically in New York City for the last decade. He has done this specifically by mobilizing the grassroots, getting out new voters, and involving the community's businesspeople in the politics of their neighborhoods. Speaking about himself and other ministers in the same situation, he says, "We've gone from preachers to politicians, and we need businessmen so that we don't have to be at the financial mercy of others."[25]

Sharpton has been successful in organizing the black community because of the force of his personality, the relevance of his message, and the establishment of a permanent organization, known as the National Action Network (NAN). Its mission is to combat racism in the criminal justice system, the political arena, and the business world while supporting progressive people-based social policies and protecting human services. Founded by Sharpton in 1991, the same year as the Crown Heights incident, its purpose is to empower people politically, to educate and register the black polity, and to support small community businesses. NAN, however, also gives Sharpton's actions and causes a sense of credibility, that is, a legitimacy that comes from also interacting with other influential, sometimes larger, and more diverse black organizations such as Jesse Jackson's Rainbow/Push Coalition.

NAN has a number ongoing departments that deal with the needs and issues that are important to members of the black community. A prisoners' rights committee, a black business and finance division, and a section for the disabled are part of NAN. Crisis management, a neighborhood patrol, a court patrol, and a law enforcement section are also critical. A scholars, drama, photography, and book club, a youth division, a choir, a women's and men's auxiliary, a sports program, and a children's services committee round out the organization.

A major program that has emerged from NAN is the Madison Avenue Initiative. Its mission is to advocate the use of minority media and advertising agencies; to work with federal, state, and local governments to influence public policy; and to interpret, improve, and strengthen relations between the minority media and advertisers and the corporate and government agencies engaged in the same activities. In this way, NAN is intimately involved in educating and organizing the public. Its executive committee is a veritable who's who of black and Hispanic CEOs, corporate presidents, and leaders in the minority communities. Thus, NAN and the Madison Avenue Initiative have become the portals through which Sharpton can enter into the world of the minority establishment that he has doubted for so long. And they also serve as a conduit to legitimize a political agenda more synonymous with his own and that of the impoverished black community.

NAN also conducts weekly community forums called "Action Rallies" at its Harlem auditorium, known as the House of Justice, and it broadcasts over two radio stations that reach thousands of black listeners weekly in the New York area. NAN has chapters in Atlanta, Dallas, Miami, and Philadelphia, as well as New York.

Its organization has served to give further credence and support to the activities of Al Sharpton in the areas of local, national, and international racial justice. In 1991, NAN led the fight to restore train and bus passes to several hundred thousand students in New York City. In 1995, it led a march to Albany, New York, and a rally of over 30,000 people to stop proposed budget cuts that would harm the poor. It convened the first statewide black political convention in New York State. Nationally, NAN led a vigil at the home of Supreme Court Justice Clarence Thomas because of his positions against affirmative action, protecting minority voters, prisoner rights, and civil rights. It opposed Proposition 187 in California, assisted the Rainbow Coalition of the Reverend Jesse Jackson to begin prison ministries, and protested against radio talk shows that promote hate. Internationally, NAN became the vehicle through which Sharpton and other members of the clergy served as observers in the election of Nelson Mandela in South Africa. It also supported a delegation, led by Al Sharpton, to stop the genocide in Rwanda and to bring pressure to bear to deliver supplies to refugees in Zaire. Most recently, Sharpton met with Fidel Castro in Cuba to discuss ways to end the U.S. embargo on Cuban trade.

While he believes in nonviolence, Sharpton also insists on a "pan-African" approach to communal and global problems, that is, a black commitment to social, economic, and political progress. To paraphrase him, every single black person must do whatever he or she can do to advance the cause, for who will save the blacks if they do not do it themselves?[26]

Sharpton practices what he preaches. He ran for state political office in New York in 1978, and even without a political base or significant financing, he garnered nearly 70 percent of the black vote. By 1992, with more expertise, money, and name recognition, he participated in the Democratic primary for senator from the State of New York and made a credible showing. He calls this campaign the second defining moment of his life. He also ran for the Democratic mayoral primary of New York City in 1997, garnering a surprising 32 percent of the vote,[27] almost forcing a runoff. And reportedly he is considering a run for president of the United States in 2004.

In campaigns that he contends became crusades, Sharpton attempted to create a political dialogue with those whom he considers the true leadership in many of the poor communities in New York.[28] And he has attempted to open up the Big Apple political process by coordinating a clerical group known as the Rainbow/Push Coalition (RPC), as mentioned earlier.

Jesse Jackson, whom Sharpton has known since his teenage years, is the founder and head of the RPC. Self-described as a "multiracial, multi-issue, international membership organization," the RPC has been founded to move the world toward greater social, racial, and economic justice.[29] It is through his coordinating position with Jackson's organization that Sharpton has been able to participate and play a role in a myriad of efforts to advance these causes more broadly and to move in major power circles. For example, Sharpton recently participated, along with his mentor and friend, Jesse Jackson, in bringing together the New York Stock Exchange and over 4,000 ministers to learn about the opportunities of the market through the RPC's "One Thousand Churches Connected" program.[30] Sharpton is now moving to a new level of social, economic, and political activism, having already established a grassroots organization of his own. Now he is beginning to work in meaningful coalition with other religious and social groups to expand his base, its causes, and its influence.

THE FUTURE

This maverick minister has been unique in New York City and New York State politics because he has attempted to do two critical things. First, he has struggled to underscore the problems of racial injustice that plague the impoverished black community there. No one has taken such an active and vocal stand for the marginalized people that he has come to represent. And second, he is trying, increasingly, to take the higher ground now in seeking solutions to the discrimination that has gone on for so long in black neighborhoods. As a religious leader, it is important to Sharpton that he raises the moral imperative in politics,[31] criticizing and even attacking those who would perpetrate injustice on African Americans for no reason other than the color of their skin. To him, the social and political reference point must always start with the morality of the issue. He believes that his activism in both arenas must go beyond "might," that questions like killing demand a moral response that must ultimately be played out it the justice system.[32]

There are those, however, within the white, conservative political establishment in New York and the wider United States who see Sharpton as a threat. They fear and oppose him, believing that he is a brash egomaniac hiding behind a pulpit, a racist in the guise of a civil rights leader, and an opportunist who will exploit any racial situation to advance himself. During the Republican primary for the American presidency in 2000, Senator John McCain of Arizona called Sharpton a religious leader on "the outer reaches of American politics" and an "agent of intolerance" to whom neither party should pander.[33] His attack was followed by another, more vicious one from Jim Nicholson, the chairman of the Republican National Committee, who wrote a letter to the *Washington Post* accusing Sharpton of inciting riots and protests that led to deaths in Crown Heights in 1991 and in Harlem in 1995. He characterized

Sharpton as a "hatemonger, an anti-Semite, and a racist."[34] Sharpton immediately retaliated by filing a $30 million dollar lawsuit against the Republican National Committee for slander.

Some black political leaders are wary of Sharpton as well. And he has openly lost patience with many of them.[35] He is tired of their cozy relationships with the white political establishment. While some people realize that he has the ability to reawaken the black pride of the 1960s, some of his African American adversaries, that is, middle-class professionals, would prefer him to embrace religious reconciliation. They want him to become more mainstream and to put aside the radical ideas that have catapulted him to his current prominence.

Sharpton, however, is his own man. He respects the role of the individual church, the independent minister, and the special place of each in the black community. He has often said, "The power of the black church is real. It's important to make this point at the turn of the century."[36] But it is becoming obvious that the traditional roles of the black church and its ministers in the United States are being eroded as agendas and coalitions blur. A new wave of highly educated African American government officials and business leaders is emerging, causing some to believe that there might be a willingness on the new leaders' parts to compromise the black civil rights program for greater political credibility, opportunity, and integration. Could they dilute black advocacy politics and simply make it a thing of the past?[37] Sharpton will not let this happen. When questioned about the relevance of *his* ministry, he claimed that it was critical that he and other black ministers continue their work as long as the Diallos and the poor exist. His work, he said, is still important even as young Afro-American professionals get pulled over by white policemen. No one, he said, is immune to racial prejudice.[38]

Sharpton is clearly an anomaly—a throwback to the militant, religious civil rights leadership of the 1960s and an astute politician of the millennium. He is a man in the middle of the old and the new black politics. He is also feared and despised by many white politicians who are still standing in his way. He is alone—except for his constituency of the alienated, impoverished poor. Asked about his legacy, he said he simply wanted to be remembered as a man who continued the tradition of black ministers in social service.[39]

Most observers believe that Sharpton will have a difficult time achieving elected political office, a position that he now understands as the means to advance the African American social, economic, and racial cause. The Brawley case continues to loom large in the minds of most white New Yorkers. With Sharpton's friends now having paid the financial judgment awarded to Steven Pagones for slander, but without a public apology to him, Sharpton may still be treated as a political pariah, a divider rather than a unifier—as a racist himself.

Ironically, the Pagones case has also recently served to shed light on the murky financial base that supports Sharpton's ministry. During the attempt to collect the $65,000 awarded by the court to Pagones in the Brawley case, Sharpton was deposed about his finances. The reverend claimed that he could not pay the judgment because he has no assets. He asserted that he earns his money through his position as the head of the National Action Network, for which he is paid $72,000 a year, which is garnished at a rate of 10 percent for Pagones already. He claimed that he is also paid for his Sunday evening radio program, which provides him with $600 a month; and he admitted to receiving donations from preaching at various churches.[40] But it is virtually impossible to track the path of this money or how it pays for his lifestyle. He says that his salary from NAN is placed into his "Rev. Als Productions," an organization that Sharpton claims is incorporated but that in reality is not recorded in the State of New York or with Dun and Bradstreet. No one understands how he pays the rent or maintenance on his home in Brooklyn or the $30,000 in tuition that it costs to send both his daughters to Poly Prep Country Day School. He has claimed under oath that he owns no suits; that he has no cars, airplanes, or boats and no pianos, stereos, radios, televisions, or diamonds; and that he does not have any income from trust funds. He does admit to owning a $300 watch and a wedding ring.[41]

Surprisingly though, even with the Brawley hoax in his past and the financial cloud over his present, Sharpton is still a powerful political broker. He leveraged the black vote in New York City for both Al Gore and Hillary Clinton. During the volatile presidential election in 2000, Sharpton led a contingent of black voters to protest their disenfranchisement outside the U.S. Supreme Court, and he joined with the Reverend Jesse Jackson to protest civil and voters' rights violations in Florida. He was also active in trying to stop the nominations of both Linda Chavez and John Ashcroft to the Bush cabinet. Should Sharpton choose to endorse candidates for political office in the future, he could still emerge as a force with which to be reckoned. As a result, he could just end up being an appointed maverick instead of an elected one.

And it also cannot be forgotten that Sharpton is weighing his options to run for president of the United States in 2004. In order to be considered a serious contender, however, he will have to clear up his past mistakes and finances. He will have to make amends with Pagones, disavow his support of Tawana Brawley and her family, and do outreach to "establishment blacks," whom he has antagonized in the past. He will have to seek funds from them and liberal whites, many of whom are Jewish and still unforgiving about the Crown Heights situation, in order to secure the financial resources to mount a major political campaign. These are formidable tasks, ones that are currently being put on the back burner as Sharpton chooses, instead, to participate in national politics to discredit the legitimacy and agenda of George W. Bush. Sharpton can only emerge as a serious potential contender for the leadership position of the United States if he begins now to make major changes in his message and tactics—two things that are becoming more and more important within the national political context. He garnered a significant portion of the black vote when he ran for mayor in 1997 and made a respectable showing when he ran in the Democratic primary for the New York Senate. But only Sharpton himself can take his religious commitment to the marginalized to a higher moral and political level, a phenomenon yet to be seen.

NOTES

1. Al Sharpton and Anthony Walton, *Go Tell Pharaoh* (New York: Doubleday, 1996), 25.
2. Sharpton and Walton, *Go Tell Pharaoh*, 40–41.
3. Sharpton and Walton, *Go Tell Pharaoh*, 111.
4. The Reverend Al Sharpton, interview by the author, New York, 14 June 2000. Herein referred to as "the Sharpton interview."
5. See, for example, Eugene Gordon, "A New Religion for the Negro," in *A Documentary History of the Negro People in the United States*, vol. 3, ed. Herbert Aptheker (New York: Citadel Press, 1972), 572–79.
6. See, for example, Eugene Genovese, *Roll, Jordan, Roll* (New York: Vintage Books, 1974); and Albert Raboteau, *Slave Religion: The "Invisible Institution" in the Antebellum South* (New York: Oxford University Press, 1978).
7. Frederick Harris, *Something Within: Religion in Afro-American Political Activism* (New York: Oxford University Press, 1999).
8. Robert Booth Fowler and Allen D. Hertzke, *Religion and Politics in America* (New York: Westview Press, 1995), chapter 7.
9. These ministers included C. P. Jones of Jackson, Mississippi, J. E. Jeter of Little Rock, Arkansas, and W. S. Pleasant of Hazelhurst, Mississippi.
10. See the Church of God in Christ, "The Story of Our Church," available at http://www.cogic.org.
11. Harris, *Something Within*, 32.
12. The church is run nationally by a board of directors of bishops, ministers who are elected to their positions by the laity and the clergy.
13. Sharpton and Walton, *Go Tell Pharaoh*, 168.
14. Sharpton and Walton, *Go Tell Pharaoh*, 188–89.
15. The Sharpton interview.
16. Sharpton and Walton, *Go Tell Pharaoh*, 89.
17. Sharpton and Walton, *Go Tell Pharaoh*, 104.
18. Sharpton and Walton, *Go Tell Pharaoh*, 141.
19. Sharpton and Walton, *Go Tell Pharaoh*, 165.
20. The Sharpton interview.
21. Georgia Persons, *Dilemmas of Black Politics* (New York: HarperCollins, 1993), 1.
22. See, for example, cases of welfare reform and affirmative action.

23. The Sharpton interview.
24. Sharpton and Walton, *Go Tell Pharaoh*, 117.
25. Sharpton and Walton, *Go Tell Pharaoh*, 266.
26. Sharpton and Walton, *Go Tell Pharaoh*, 188.
27. See HYPERLINK http://www.africana.com.
28. Sharpton and Walton, *Go Tell Pharaoh*, 238.
29. See http://www.rainbowpush.org/aboutrpc.
30. See http://www.nyse.com.
31. Sharpton and Walton, *Go Tell Pharaoh*, 214.
32. The Sharpton interview.
33. David Barstow, "The 2000 Campaign: The Arizona Senator; McCain Denounces Political Tactics of Christian Right," *New York Times*, 29 February 2000: A1. Sharpton was included along with the Reverend Jerry Falwell, the Reverend Pat Robertson of the Christian Coalition, and Minister Louis Farrakhan of the Nation of Islam.
34. See "Al Sharpton Sues RNC for $30 Million," available at http://www.courttv.com.
35. He was particularly at odds with David Dinkins, the black mayor of New York City. They clashed over the Crown Heights incident. Now that Dinkins is no longer mayor, they appear to be working together in a closer and more effective way.
36. Harris, *Something Within*, 28.
37. See Persons, *Dilemmas of Black Politics*, introduction.
38. The Sharpton interview.
39. The Sharpton interview.
40. Alan Feuer, "Asking How Sharpton Pays for Those Suits," *New York Times*, 21 December 2000: B1.
41. Feuer, "Asking How Sharpton Pays for Those Suits," B1, B6.

4

Elder Dallin H. Oaks:
The Mormons, Politics, and Family Values

John R. Pottenger

Since its founding by Joseph Smith and five others during the tumultuous Second Great Awakening in western New York in 1830, the Church of Jesus Christ of Latter-day Saints, also known as the LDS Church or the Mormons, has grown exponentially. At the dawn of the twenty-first century, Mormons number nearly 11 million worldwide.[1] Their beliefs in continuing revelation and an acceptance of an open canon have provided the LDS Church with the flexibility and vitality to attract adherents across cultures and continents.[2] Recognizing the phenomenal growth and universal appeal of the LDS Church, non-Mormon historian Jan Shipps argues that Mormonism, the fifth-largest denomination in the United States, is on the verge of becoming a major world religion.[3]

Yet, since its inception, conflict has existed between Mormons and others in society. Early criticism from Americans with more traditional Christian beliefs as well as from the U.S. government focused on the Mormon practices of communal economics and "plural marriage" or polygamy. Today, Mormons feel threatened by secular society itself. Despite a century of having abandoned polygamy, Mormon teachings have continually emphasized the importance of the family as well as the imperative of protecting religious liberty. To defend their faith, the LDS Church and individual Mormons have been politically active in resisting perceived threats to religion and family unity and have directed their activism toward electoral politics, legislative lobbying, and judicial challenges.

DALLIN H. OAKS: DISCIPLE-SCHOLAR

One of the more articulate defenders of the Mormon faith and LDS Church activism is also one of its more prominent ecclesiastical leaders: Dallin H.

Oaks, an elder in the LDS Church and a member of the Quorum of Twelve Apostles. This quorum serves as an advisory body to the president of the church as well as oversees the church's worldwide operations. On 7 April 1984, Elder Oaks was presented before a general conference of the worldwide membership of the LDS Church and "sustained" or approved by a vote of the entire membership to become a member of the Quorum of the Twelve. The leaders of the church then ordained him an apostle on 3 May 1984, at age fifty-one.[4] Given the historical precedence of apostolic succession to leadership in the LDS Church, Elder Oaks may be considered eighth in the line of succession to the church presidency itself.

Elder Oaks is considered an eminent constitutional scholar, focusing on contemporary as well as historical issues of church–state relations, judicial activism, and individual rights.[5] In addition, he is considered an inspiring religious leader who has managed to combine both discipleship and scholarship. "Though the scholarly focus is on knowledge," Elder Oaks explains, "the process of scholarship and teaching obviously contemplates that the learner will act upon the knowledge acquired."[6] Elder Oaks's academic training has served him well in advancing the cause of the LDS Church's proselytizing efforts and religious practices as they promote and defend family unity.[7]

Dallin H. Oaks graduated in 1954 with high honors from Brigham Young University (BYU) and then entered the Law School of the University of Chicago. He edited the school's law review in 1956–57 and received his juris doctorate degree, graduating cum laude, in 1957. After graduation, Oaks served for a year as a law clerk to Chief Justice of the U.S. Supreme Court Earl Warren. From 1958 to 1961, after moving back to Chicago, Oaks began his career in private practice with a strong commitment to serving those in need. According to historian Lavina Fielding Anderson, Oaks was the first in his law firm to represent an indigent before the Illinois Supreme Court.[8] Indeed, his active commitment to the welfare of the community included various public service activities. After accepting a teaching position at the University of Chicago (1961–71), Oaks organized law students to work on criminal defense and in neighborhood legal clinics. During this time, Oaks was admitted to practice law before the bars in Illinois (1957) and Utah (1971) and before the U.S. Supreme Court (1970). In addition, he served as the executive director of the American Bar Foundation in Chicago, an assistant states attorney for Cook County, and a consultant on legal services for the Office of Economic Opportunity. Oaks also taught as a visiting professor of law at the University of Michigan Law School, conducted a study on the Criminal Justice Act for the U.S. Department of Justice, and served as legal counsel to the Bill of Rights Committee of the Illinois Constitutional Convention.

In 1971, Oaks returned to Utah as president of BYU, serving in this position for nine years before being confirmed as a justice on the Utah Supreme Court (1981–84). From the window of his administrative office at BYU, Oaks could see the Missionary Training Center of the worldwide proselytizing efforts of the LDS Church and the church's Provo Temple, both powerful symbols of Mormon teachings and practices. Anderson quotes Oaks as saying, "I tell visitors who share this sight that these three institutions—university, mission, and temple—are three of the most powerful institutions on the face of the earth."[9] For the LDS Church and Oaks, these institutions are clearly interrelated in the promotion of family values. But a necessary condition for sustaining the integrity of the family, according to Oaks, is religious liberty.

MORMONISM: A NEW RELIGION IN AMERICA

In its relatively short existence, the LDS Church has captured the attention of many observers,[10] including contemporary social critic Harold Bloom, who asserts that the imagination of Joseph Smith, free from dependence on and control by European religious beliefs and institutions, led to the creation of a uniquely American religious tradition.[11] Among his many religious views, Smith made startling claims about the relationship between God and man. In particular, he asserted that God, after centuries of silence precipitated by Christian apostasy from the basic doctrines and authority of the Gospel of Jesus, had once again begun to reveal his divine will via a prophet. Being the first in modern times to be so chosen, Smith asserted that he and all successive LDS prophets would continue to receive and reveal God's will.[12] Furthermore, as the first prophet to receive and thus restore the true Gospel of Jesus Christ to humankind, Smith proposed the acceptance of new, divinely inspired Scripture. This included the Book of Mormon, to be used with the Bible. In addition, the possibility of man becoming like God and even a god had led Smith to consider the purpose of human relationships in this life.[13] He perceived a seamless whole between mortal existence and the Kingdom of God, teaching that human relationships are imperfect yet perfectible images of relationships in the hereafter and for eternity. And the place where these proper relationships are to be found, he maintained, is in the family. Indeed, the individual cannot achieve "exaltation" or the highest state of salvation without family unity, with the husband and wife "sealed" to each other in one of the LDS Church's sacred temples. This belief in the eternal nature of the family goes to the heart of Mormon theology, social behavior, and political activity.

Smith initiated controversial social practices based on his religious beliefs such as economic communalism and plural or polygamous marriages.[14] In addition, he organized his followers within a hierarchical structure to propagate the new religion's beliefs, which immediately produced friction between the Mormons and their non-Mormon neighbors. By 1846 open conflict and even warfare, including the murder of Smith and other church leaders by outraged non-Mormons, ultimately forced the Mormons to emigrate from Ohio, Missouri, Illinois, and other states of the Midwest to the relative obscurity and safety of present-day Utah, then technically under Mexican sovereignty.[15]

At the conclusion of the Mexican–American War in 1848, Mexico ceded nearly 50 percent of its territory, including the Rocky Mountain West, to the United States. Because this territory contained myriad Mormon settlements, conflict intensified between Mormons and the increasing presence of non-Mormon American settlers, with the notoriety of the LDS Church receiving national attention. For example, in the presidential campaign of 1856, the Republican Party's platform denounced slavery and polygamy as the "twin relics of barbarism." The following year President James Buchanan sent the U.S. Army to Utah to subdue and control Mormon settlements. And the Mountain Meadows massacre of 120 members of an openly anti-Mormon wagon train passing through southern Utah at the hands of a Mormon militia further inflamed public opinion.[16]

After scrutinizing the Utah territorial theocracy under Mormon prophet Brigham Young, the U.S. Congress passed, and President Lincoln signed into law, the Anti-Bigamy Act (the Morrill Law) of 1862 banning polygamy. The act was upheld by the U.S. Supreme Court in *Reynolds v. the United States* (1878) and succeeding cases.[17] In subsequent legislation, including the Poland Act (1874), the Edmunds Act (1882), and the Edmunds–Tucker Act (1887), the U.S. government placed additional penalties on those guilty of practicing polygamy, dissolved the corporation of the LDS Church, restricted further Mormon emigration to the Utah territory, placed territorial schools under U.S. government jurisdiction, and abolished women's suffrage in Utah. By the end of the nineteenth century, the LDS Church appeared defeated in public opinion, in Congress, and in the courts. The Mormons' religious liberty was severely restricted, and their polygamous family practices were under assault. In 1890, to regain civil rights for its members and to repossess its property holdings, the LDS Church formally and publicly abandoned its controversial practice of polygamy.[18] Although limited accommodation to secular demands imposed by non-Mormon governments was certainly preferable to physical annihilation that would end the Mormon spiritual mission, the LDS Church, nevertheless, harbored grave suspicions of governmental authority.[19]

According to some observers, it is this continued suspicion of secular government policies and programs that encourages individual Mormons to be active in politics, yet nonpartisan.[20] Although it no longer teaches, practices, or endorses polygamy, the LDS Church continues to emphasize the importance of understanding the nature of the family and defending its role "as the fundamental unit of society."[21] For example, in the late 1970s the church provided financial aid and mobilized local members in certain states to oppose ratification of the proposed Equal Rights Amendment to the U.S. Constitution. The church perceived the amendment as a threat to its religious liberty, a challenge to its patriarchal organizational structure, and a threat to its fundamental teachings about the distinct and divine nature of gender roles.[22] Similarly, in 1996 the LDS Church joined with the Catholic Church in Hawaii to form the political organization "Hawaii's Future Today" to oppose legislation recognizing same-sex marriage.[23] To resist what it considers to be the immoral encroachments of secular society, the LDS Church engages in selective political activism to defend religious liberty as a means to protect its religious beliefs and practices.

THE MORAL IMPERATIVE OF RELIGIOUS LIBERTY

One of the thirteen basic tenets or articles of faith of the LDS Church is the affirmation of religious liberty. The article states, "We claim the privilege of worshipping Almighty God according to the dictates of our conscience, and allow men the same privilege, let them worship how, where, or what they may."[24] Embracing this article, Elder Oaks defends religious liberty as a necessary condition for an individual to exercise moral responsibility for good citizenship as well as personal and family salvation. "This right of choice is the key to happiness," says Elder Oaks, "and it is essential to salvation. Every person has a God-given right to hear and a right to choose. Because of the central importance of these rights to the very purpose of life, no man or government is justified in interfering with them."[25]

To lay the foundation for defending religious liberty, Elder Oaks accepts the revelation received by Joseph Smith that the U.S. Constitution is a divinely inspired document.[26] However, this does not mean that Mormons accept the Constitution as Scripture. As Elder Oaks has pointed out, "Personally, I have never considered it necessary to defend every line of the Constitution as scriptural." For Oaks, the writing of the Constitution included "five great fundamentals" for the success of political and civil society that he believes to be divinely inspired: the doctrine of separation of powers, the division of powers or federalism, popular sovereignty, the rule of law, and a written bill of rights. Specifically with regard to the great fundamental of a written bill of rights and in particular the First Amendment, Elder Oaks asserts the following: "I have always felt that the United States Constitution's closest approach to scriptural stature is in the phrasing of our Bill of Rights. Without the free exercise of religion, America could not have served as the host nation for the restoration of the gospel [through the prophet Joseph Smith], which began just three decades after the Bill of Rights was ratified."[27]

For Elder Oaks, religious liberty must be protected and encouraged for a pluralistic democracy to survive. In fact, he maintains that "religious liberty is the oldest of the internationally recognized 'human rights,' providing motivation, precedent, and support for the growth of other freedoms, such as the freedoms of speech, the press, and assembly."[28] In his public remarks as official signatory for the LDS Church of the interdenominational Williamsburg Charter on religious liberty, Elder Oaks said, "The people called Mormons have known the sting of official repression and the lash of popular fury. We endorse the need and join in this celebration and reaffirmation of religious liberty."[29]

In American society, however, a consensus on the meaning of the First Amendment's reference to religion—"Congress shall make no law respecting an establishment of religion, or prohibiting the free exercise thereof . . ."—has yet to be achieved, according to Elder Oaks: "The prohibition against establishment seems to forbid government support for religion, but the guarantee of free exercise seems to compel the very same support. In the relationship between government and religion, free exercise seems to require accommodation, while non-establishment forbids it."[30] He argues that part of the confusion over the intent of the First Amendment is the common misperception that the amendment contains two religion clauses, when in fact there is only one clause with only one reference to "religion." This misperception has led to conflicting definitions and applications of the word *religion*. The courts have generally interpreted "free exercise" as recognizing virtually any belief system, theistic or nontheistic, to be religious or a religion. By contrast, the traditional definition of *religion* as a theistic belief system has also generally been used to prohibit governmental establishment of religion, thus leading to decisions that have prevented public policy makers from working alongside religious institutions on matters of common interest, such as in education reform efforts:[31] "It is painfully apparent that 'religion' means something quite different for purposes of the protections of free exercise than for the rules against establishment. Curiously, these differences both work against religions based on belief in God, minimizing the unique advantages and maximizing the special disadvantages of traditional theistic religion."[32]

In recent years the effect of the broader definition of *religion* for accommodation purposes has begun to weaken the "wall of separation between church and state." But this increase in accommodation, according to Elder

Oaks, has also resulted in the reclassification of certain religious activities as secular ones for regulatory and tax purposes. These include permitting the use of public facilities for voluntary religious activities and removing churches' traditional exemption from payroll taxes.[33] Ironically, the effect has been to bring church and state closer together as a result of increased government regulation while undermining support for free exercise. He notes, "In this position, constitutional litigation will be a less effective safeguard of free exercise, and churches and religious practices will need to protect their interests more frequently through legislative lobbying."[34] It should be expected, then, that legislative lobbying will increase the likelihood of political activism from religious organizations in the public sphere. After all, government regulations generally include various prohibitions of discriminatory practices that may have an adverse impact on religious practices. Even if the prohibitions are resisted as restrictions on religious liberty, they are likely nonetheless to be upheld by judicial courts. Thus, religious organizations will have to participate in the public sector by emphasizing legislative lobbying over judicial challenges to have the laws changed.

RELIGIOUS LIBERTY AND THE PUBLIC SQUARE

Elder Oaks believes that religion and symbols of religion in society have come under increasingly hostile attack in recent decades, with the ultimate aim of removing the presence of religion from the public square. He maintains that this hostility originated with the U.S. Supreme Court school prayer decisions of the 1960s, in which the court maintained that government does not have the power to prescribe an official prayer for public activities. Oaks writes, "When the school prayer cases were decided, I interpreted them to forbid state-authored and state-required prayers. As such, the cases, I thought, were correctly decided."[35] Strict adherence to this interpretation, he believed, would have avoided potential threats to religious liberty; whereas permitting government to compose official prayers could have led to the government prescribing and compelling citizens to adopt a state religious orthodoxy.[36] Yet what Elder Oaks did not foresee at the time was the eventual instrumental use of the school prayer decisions by opponents of religion to construct arguments that exceed the original intent of the Court, such as prohibitions on the observance of a moment of silence in addition to the removal of school prayer: "In short, many understand the law today as being hostile rather than neutral toward religion—as forbidding all public prayers rather than simply prohibiting state-authored and state-required prayers in public schools. Instead of just preventing instances of state-sponsored religion in the public schools, the school prayer cases have unleashed forces that have sometimes been used to prevent the free exercise of religion."[37]

Public schools tend to reinforce a corollary belief now prevalent in society that there is no role for religious leaders and faith-based values in policy debates in the public square. Yet, for Elder Oaks, this belief is contrary to the history of American religious liberty and the intent of public policy making in a democratic polity. In U.S. society, he maintains, a system of law cannot exist without moral absolutes at its foundation: "The moral absolutes are the ones derived from what we refer to as the Judeo-Christian tradition, as set forth in the Bible—Old Testament and New Testament."[38] Because much of public policy is based on this moral foundation, those religious leaders promoting a particular set of religious values have a legitimate right to participate alongside secular leaders in debate and decision making in the public sphere: "No person with values based on religious beliefs should apologize for taking those values into the public square. . . . I believe that questions of right and wrong, whether based on religious principles or any other source of values, are legitimate in any debate over laws or public policy. Is there anything more important to debate than what is right and wrong? And those arguments should be open across the entire political spectrum."[39] Hence, religious leaders and organizations have the same right as any other individual and organization to participate in public policy debates. Indeed, "when religion has a special constitutional right to its free exercise, religious leaders and churches should have more freedom than other persons and organizations, not less."[40]

Elder Oaks recognizes that despite a religious organization's or leader's claims to a higher moral authority, the faith-based arguments must be presented and received on the same basis as any other opinion, evaluated on their merits, and "challenged by and measured against secular-based legislative or political judgments."[41] Furthermore, he advises religious organizations to avoid single-issue politics in favor of seeking broader solutions to general problems faced by society. The LDS Church, too, will participate in the public square "to maintain the freedom of religion . . . to maintain a moral climate in which people are permitted or encouraged to make wise choices consistent with gospel teachings."[42] But the church will also evaluate carefully the moral merits of social issues before it becomes politically involved.

MORAL ISSUES VERSUS POLITICAL ISSUES

The LDS Church has strenuously resisted the politicization of its beliefs and practices. For example, the church refuses to permit the Christian Coalition to distribute voter guides at Mormon chapels on the Sunday before an election. Indeed, the LDS Church also refuses to endorse candidates for public office or allow its buildings to be used by candidates for political purposes. These prohibitions are an attempt to preserve the church's perception of a distinction between "moral issues" and "political issues," a distinction necessary to preserve religious liberty and resist secular threats to the family. In addition, this distinction distances the church from entanglement in myriad provincial disputes, thus allowing it to preserve its universal religious appeal across cultural, ideological, and political divides. Elder Oaks defends the pragmatic value of this distinction while not being able to define precisely the two categories themselves:

> I subscribe to the distinction between "moral issues," on which our church may comment, and "political issues," on which it generally will not comment. The distinction admittedly is not precise because the definitions of these two categories are not precise. However, the lack of precise categories is not disabling when one considers the purpose of our distinction between moral and political. This is not a distinction we need to consider in preaching or in any of our primary activities as a church. It is only a distinction we need to apply to identify those political (i.e., generally legislative) issues on which the church will or will not take a position.[43]

The body politic, however, cannot escape the moral dimension attendant to most matters of public policy. Referring primarily to legislative bills, Elder Oaks conceded that "there are few things in our society that are not tinged with at least some moral overlay"; nevertheless, he noted, given the plethora of state and national issues before legislative bodies, as a practical matter "our church has to have a general characterization that rules out church positions on most legislative issues. The moral versus political distinction is that general characterization. What I understand it to mean is that our church will rarely take a position on any political issue." The imprecision of Elder Oaks's distinction affords the LDS Church great flexibility in assigning specific issues to one category or the other. While scarcely arbitrary in its moral determination, given the centrality of family unity in Mormon teachings, the LDS Church will weigh in on such moral issues as abortion while avoiding such political issues as gun control.

Elder Oaks has frequently spoken on behalf of the LDS Church on select political issues of considerable moral magnitude, primarily those affecting religious liberty. In 1992 he testified before committees of both houses of Congress holding hearings on the proposed Religious Freedom Restoration Act (RFRA).[44] He argued that the act was a good attempt to restore the precedent of the "compelling governmental interest" test as a protection of religious liberty, a precedent that was overturned by the U.S. Supreme Court in *Employment Division v.*

Smith (1990). After the RFRA was signed into law in 1993 and subsequently ruled unconstitutional in 1997, Elder Oaks testified once again before a committee of the U.S. Senate in 1998 in support of the Religious Liberty Protection Act.[45] For Elder Oaks, the issue of religious liberty is not only political but moral as well: "For our purposes, these issues [such as the congressional legislation on religious liberty] are 'moral' because we call them 'moral' — not because they are more 'moral' than someone else's list of moral issues. In other words, these are 'our' list of moral issues, on which our church chooses to go into the public square to debate, as a church, on a public issue."[46]

Elder Oaks's distinction between moral issues and political issues further suggests that all moral issues of any social consequence have a political dimension. It is the political dimension of a moral issue that justifies the LDS Church's presence in the public square. On the other hand, his distinction also suggests that every political issue does not necessarily have a moral dimension, thus precluding political activism by the church. Consequently, the LDS Church must first identify the moral dimension before being heard in the public square. For example, in March 2000 the LDS Church actively supported the successful passage of Proposition 22 in California, which prevents state recognition of same-sex marriages performed in other states. Elder Oaks's defense of the LDS Church's political activism through mobilizing local Mormons to vote in favor of the proposition reveals an important insight into the question of which battles to fight: "The Proposition 22 fight in California was not initiated or even encouraged by our church. But when that issue got on the ballot our church had little choice other than to participate. What brought that issue to the ballot and thus brought our church into the fray were the aggressive efforts of a particular group to establish a new definition of marriage. That controversy was not sought by the church but was placed on its doorstep by others."[47] This example suggests that the LDS Church tends to follow a quiet path of resistance to actual or anticipated social changes it finds morally threatening, rather than seeking out and calling attention to manifestations of social injustice.

While it will condemn social practices it finds immoral, the LDS Church stops short of enlisting radical social critiques to identify the systemic causes of injustice. The church's own tragic experience of a minority religion suffering persecution at the hands of an overwhelming and hostile majority has virtually precluded the development of a revolutionary ethos. Instead, the LDS Church avails itself of only legally legitimate opportunities for political expression and influence to hinder undesirable changes, as well as to advance its own causes and achieve its own objectives. In addition to the LDS Church's involvement in politics of the family, Elder Oaks maintains, the church may also be involved in politics to meet its own organizational needs:

"For example, our church recently sponsored congressional testimony in support of legislation needed to facilitate visas for LDS missionaries from other countries to come to the U.S. for their missionary service."[48]

Individual Mormons, too, are encouraged to act responsibly in the political arena. For example, in the case of *Santa Fe Independent Schools v. Jane Doe* (1999), two families, one Catholic and one Mormon, challenged student-led prayers at public high school football games. On appeal, the U.S. Supreme Court decided in favor of the families. According to Elder Oaks, the LDS Church did not file an *amicus curiae* brief in this case; "the plaintiffs who filed the case did so in their capacity as private citizens and without church encouragement or sponsorship."[49] Indeed, the LDS Church frequently avails itself of legal opportunities to support moral causes. In this particular case, however, Elder Oaks is less supportive of the Mormon family's argument before the Court and the Court's final decision than he is of the decisions in the earlier school prayer cases: "Personally, I believe in public as well as private prayer and, whatever the merits of the decision of the Supreme Court (which are subject to legitimate debate), I felt sympathetic to the dissent of Chief Justice Rehnquist, who objected to 'the tone of the Court's opinion[, which] bristles with hostility to all things religious in public life.'"[50]

Elder Oaks, too, has been politically active both as a Mormon and as a private citizen. During his academic career, he served on a committee appointed by the national board of the American Civil Liberties Union to conduct a study on whether or not an individual has a constitutional right to minimum income. He concluded that there is no such right. Also, on behalf of the presidential campaign of Barry Goldwater and William Miller, Oaks volunteered his services by contacting other professors to sponsor a political advertisement in the *New York Times* under the heading "Scholars for Goldwater–Miller." According to Elder Oaks, "I did this because my basic sympathies were Republican and I thought Goldwater and Miller were getting a bad rap in the campaign. I have never had any other formal political activity or membership and have generally split my ticket in voting."[51] More recently, Elder Oaks called on juvenile and family court judges to avail themselves of the opportunity to use the religious and moral beliefs of the faith community to resolve disputes. He encouraged judges to form interfaith advisory boards to identify potential foster families and adoptive parents from local congregations to the court and to serve as faith-based mentors: "A judge does not need to vault over the wall between church and state to become a preacher of right and wrong."[52]

To resist social policies that undermine family unity and to support policies that promote it, Elder Oaks served for twenty-five years on the board of directors of the Howard Center for Family, Religion, and Society. A private research and information organization based in Rockford, Illinois, the Howard Center defends the traditional family as the source of individual liberty and virtue. In 1996, the Howard Center initiated the World Congress of Families project, holding the first World Congress in Prague, the Czech Republic, in 1997. In 1999, in conjunction with the World Family Policy Center (formerly NGO Family Voice) at BYU and other cosponsors, the Howard Center convened the second World Congress in Geneva, Switzerland. In preparation for the congress, the Howard Center called on world leaders and representatives from diverse cultural, national, and religious backgrounds to affirm the centrality of the "natural human family." Specifically, they were asked to participate legitimately within their respective political systems to defend the family from the ideological agendas of particular pressure groups. Among their concerns were those that "deny the natural origin and status of the family, the equal but complementary roles of men and women, the miracle of human fertility and procreation, the dignity and worth of every human person, and the autonomy of the family itself."[53] Speaking in support of this call for religious members of society to become politically involved, Elder Oaks declared that "Latter-day Saints cannot afford to ignore a worldwide climate that threatens the family."[54]

Echoing LDS Church teachings, Elder Oaks asserts that "the purpose of mortal families is to bring children into the world, to teach them what is right, and to prepare all family members for exaltation in eternal family relationships."[55] But he believes that society is increasingly tolerating social practices that threaten the family's existence, including "same-gender attraction" and "elective abortion for personal or social convenience." According to Elder Oaks, proponents of homosexuality threaten the divine nature of the family. This is through their attempt "to undermine the principle of individual accountability, to persuade us to misuse our sacred powers of procreation, to discourage marriage and childbearing by worthy men and women, and to confuse what it means to be male or female."[56] In resisting social tolerance of homosexuality, he supports the recent U.S. Supreme Court decision in *Boy Scouts of America v. Dale* (2000), in which the LDS Church filed an *amicus curiae* brief, affirming the right of the Boys Scouts to prohibit homosexuals from serving in leadership positions.[57] In this legal victory for the Boy Scouts, Elder Oaks finds both legal and moral support for his declaration that individual accountability or moral responsibility is crucial for the eternal existence of the family.

Similarly, Elder Oaks believes that elective abortion is a flight from moral responsibility if the woman made a free choice to engage in sexual activity resulting in pregnancy.[58] Once she has become pregnant, he argues, the woman has lost her moral right to make a choice on the life or death of the fetus. Conversely, in a pregnancy resulting from rape, the woman's moral responsibility has been taken from her by force. In this case, Elder Oaks admits that possible exceptions may exist to his opposition to abortion: "[LDS Church] leaders have taught that the only possible exceptions are when the pregnancy resulted from rape or incest, or a competent physician has determined that the life or health of the mother is in serious jeopardy, or the fetus has severe defects that will not allow the baby to survive beyond birth. But even these exceptions do not justify abortion automatically."[59] Indeed, according to Oaks, the life and potential property rights of the fetus "must not be extinguished without due process of law."[60]

In defense of family unity, Elder Oaks morally and politically opposes laws and public policies that tend to inhibit public prayer, promote homosexuality, and permit unrestricted abortion. Especially with regard to abortion, his commitment to the family is most revealing. Given Elder Oaks's assertion of possible exceptions permitting elective abortion, particularly with regard to rape or incest, one may conclude that his position can only be justified by accepting the proposition that the life of the fetus is less important than the continuation of family unity. Indeed, given his religious beliefs as developed and propounded by the LDS Church, Elder Oaks believes that the family setting provides optimal possibilities for individuals to develop and exercise moral responsibility. Hence the family must be protected and its values defended in the public square. Mormons, then, are encouraged to take advantage of any legally and lawfully appropriate means to be engaged politically with issues whose moral content deals with family unity and values.

RESISTANCE, NOT REVOLUTION

Mormon leaders in the nineteenth century were highly critical of economic and other social institutions in U.S. society. With their criticisms of liberal individualism, as well as private property and unbridled capitalism, the LDS Church attempted to build a just community or Zion based on economic cooperation and family unity. First settling in Ohio and Missouri, then in Illinois, and finally in present-day Utah, the Mormons instituted alternative social arrangements, such as communal economics and polygamous marriages. The LDS Church's attempt at constructing Zion was secessionist in nature, leading the Mormons to remove themselves from mainstream American practices and then literally to withdraw from America itself. Their ultimate exodus to the Rocky Mountain West was predicated on the assumption that there would be no assistance from the American or any other host society or government.[61]

Today, criticisms of capitalism by LDS Church leaders are rare. Elder Oaks candidly admits that such critiques are beyond his "education and experience." Thus, he has limited his public discourses on such issues to "the morality of certain individual economic decisions."[62] Consequently, the abandonment of economic criticism by the LDS Church has shifted the primary focus of Mormon social critique toward other concerns. In addition, Mormons' preference for resistance over revolution continues. Thus, in contrast with more activist religious denominations that call for radical transformation of social institutions to alleviate such problems as human rights violations and economic poverty, the LDS Church prefers resistance within the established political order to encroachments on religious liberty and threats to family unity.

It appears, then, that the LDS Church has retreated from its heritage of alternative social experimentation based on wide-ranging criticisms of social institutions and has narrowed its contemporary focus to a defense of a single social institution, the family. According to Elder Oaks, "The truth is that the family is far and away the most important social institution under the sun."[63] Yet Elder Oaks's apparent defense of the status quo is not necessarily contrary to Mormon intellectual roots and the intent of early LDS Church social practices. Today, as the presence of Mormons increases throughout the world, the secessionist urge of the LDS Church continues. But this urge has shifted away from the literal building of Zion (by withdrawing from secular society, as in the nineteenth century) to the metaphorical distinction between moral issues and political issues (while remaining in society). A shift in either direction may permit the existence of a relatively independent sphere of religious activity.

The metaphorical distinction, however, does not insulate the LDS Church from cultural and political pressures of unwarranted and undesirable social change. Social engagement by Mormons, either privately or with church support, is unavoidable. Elder Oaks's advocacy of Mormon participation in politics to defend traditional family values and unity suggests that the LDS Church will indeed use its resources in the political arena when necessary—but only to prevent change that it deems morally harmful.

NOTES

1. According to LDS Church official website figures from 31 December 1999, worldwide membership is 10,752,986, and approximate U.S. membership is 5,113,000. See http://www.lds.org, accessed 4 December 2000.

2. Edwin B. Firmage, "Restoring the Church: Zion in the Nineteenth and Twenty-first Centuries," in *The Wilderness of Faith*, ed. John Sillito (Salt Lake City: Signature Books, 1991), 1–13.

3. Jan Shipps, *Mormonism: The Story of a New Religious Tradition* (Urbana: University of Illinois Press, 1985).

4. Dallin H. Oaks was born on 12 August 1932 in Provo, Utah, the son of Dr. Lloyd E. Oaks and Stella Harris Oaks. Elder Oaks has six children, twenty-four grandchildren, and two great-grandchildren. His wife, June Dixon Oaks, died in July 1998; in August 2000, Elder Oaks married Kristen McMain.

5. Elder Oaks has written nine books and over 100 articles on secular and religious topics. For representative academic works, see Dallin H. Oaks, "Judicial Activism," *Harvard Journal of Law and Public Policy* 7, no. 1 (1984): 1–11; Dallin H. Oaks, "Rights and Responsibilities," *Mercer Law Review* 36 (1985): 427–42; and Dallin H. Oaks and Marvin S. Hill, *Carthage Conspiracy: The Trial of the Accused Assassins of Joseph Smith* (Urbana: University of Illinois Press, 1975).

6. Dallin H. Oaks, "On Learning and Becoming," in *On Becoming a Disciple-Scholar*, ed. Henry B. Eyring (Salt Lake City: Bookcraft, 1995), 96–97.

7. The following biographical information has been gleaned from an interview conducted on 14 July 2000 by the author with Elder Oaks, herein referred to as "the Oaks interview"; a "Summary of Biographical Data" supplied by Elder Oaks; and other published interviews.

8. Lavina Fielding Anderson, "Dallin H. Oaks: The Disciplined Edge," *Ensign* 11, no. 4 (April 1981): 32. *Ensign* is an official publication of the LDS Church.

9. Anderson, "Dallin H. Oaks," 35.

10. See, for example, John Stuart Mill, *On Liberty* (1859); Karl Marx, "Letter to Lion Philips" (1864); and Max Weber, *The Protestant Ethic and the Spirit of Capitalism* (1904–05).

11. Harold Bloom, *The American Religion: The Emergence of the Post-Christian Nation* (New York: Simon and Schuster, 1992).

12. Richard L. Bushman, *Joseph Smith and the Beginnings of Mormonism* (Urbana: University of Illinois Press, 1984).

13. Sterling M. McMurrin, *The Theological Foundations of the Mormon Religion* (Salt Lake City: University of Utah Press, 1965).

14. Thomas F. O'Dea, *The Mormons* (Chicago: University of Chicago Press, 1957).

15. Kenneth H. Winn, *Exiles in a Land of Liberty: Mormons in America, 1830–1846* (Chapel Hill: University of North Carolina Press, 1989).

16. Marvin S. Hill, *Quest for Refuge: The Mormon Flight from American Pluralism* (Salt Lake City: Signature Books, 1989); and Leonard J. Arrington and Davis Bitton, *The Mormon Experience: A History of the Latter-day Saints* (New York: Vintage Press, 1980).

17. For a brief overview of the appropriate court cases, see John Witte Jr., *Religion and the American Constitutional Experiment: Essential Rights and Liberties* (Boulder: Westview Press, 2000), 102–04.

18. Richard S. Van Wagoner, *Mormon Polygamy: A History* (Salt Lake City: Signature Books, 1992).

19. John R. Pottenger, "Mormonism and the American Industrial State," *International Journal of Social Economics* 14, no. 2 (1987): 25–38.

20. See, for example, Robert Booth Fowler, Allen D. Hertzke, and Laura R. Olson, *Religion and Politics in America: Faith, Culture, and Strategic Choices*, 2nd ed. (Boulder: Westview Press, 1999), 204–07.

21. Gordon B. Hinckley, "The Family: A Proclamation to the World," *Ensign* 25, no. 11 (November 1995): 102.

22. Church Educational System, *Church History in the Fulness of Times* (Salt Lake City: LDS Church, 1989), 586.

23. Relatedly, the LDS Church filed an amicus curiae brief in the case of *Baehr v. Miike* (1999), in which the Hawaii Supreme Court ultimately found that Hawaii law did not discriminate by defining marriage as only between a man and a woman.

24. The "Articles of Faith," written by Joseph Smith on 1 March 1842 and later canonized in 1880, are found in the Pearl of Great Price, another of four books accepted as inspired scripture by the LDS Church. The four books or "standard works" recognized as scriptural by the LDS Church are the Bible, the Book of Mormon, Doctrine and Covenants, and the Pearl of Great Price.

25. Dallin H. Oaks and Lance B. Wickman, "The Missionary Work of the Church of Jesus Christ of Latter-day Saints," in *Sharing the Book: Perspectives on the Rights and Wrongs of Proselytism*, ed. John Witte Jr. and Richard C. Martin (Maryknoll, N.Y.: Orbis Books, 1999), 252; cf. Dallin H. Oaks, "Free Agency and Freedom," in *The Book of Mormon: Second Nephi, The Doctrinal Structure*, ed. Monte S. Nyman and Charles D. Tate Jr. (Provo: Religious Studies Center, Brigham Young University, 1989), 1–17.

26. Dallin H. Oaks, "The Divinely Inspired Constitution," *Ensign* 22, no. 2 (February 1992): 68–74; cf. a revelation received by Joseph Smith on 16 December 1833, in Doctrine and Covenants, section 101:77, 80.

27. Oaks, "The Divinely Inspired Constitution," 71.

28. Dallin H. Oaks, "Religion in Public Life," *Ensign* 20, no. 7 (July 1990): 7.

29. Oaks, "Religion in Public Life," 7. See the Williamsburg Charter in *Articles of Faith, Articles of Peace, the Religious Liberty Clauses and the American Public Philosophy*, ed. James Davison Hunter and Os Guiness (Washington, D.C.: Brookings Books, 1990), 127–45.

30. Dallin H. Oaks, "Separation, Accommodation, and the Future of Church and State," *DePaul Law Review* 35, no. 1 (Fall 1985): 2.

31. Oaks, "Separation, Accommodation, and the Future of Church and State," 7–9.

32. Dallin H. Oaks, "Religion and Law in the Eighties," in *Belief, Faith and Reason*, ed. John A. Howard (Belfast: Christian Journals, 1981), 115.

33. Oaks, "Separation, Accommodation, and the Future of Church and State," 10–21.

34. Oaks, "Separation, Accommodation, and the Future of Church and State," 21.

35. Oaks, "Religion in Public Life," 8; similarly, Dallin H. Oaks, "Antidotes for the School Prayer Cases," *The Improvement Era* 66 (December 1963): 1050.

36. Dallin H. Oaks, "Introduction," in *The Wall between Church and State*, ed. Dallin H. Oaks (Chicago: University of Chicago Press, 1963), 15.

37. Oaks, "Religion in Public Life," 8.

38. Dallin H. Oaks, "Religious Values and Public Policy," *Ensign* 22, no. 10 (October 1992): 60–61.

39. Oaks, "Religious Values and Public Policy," 62.

40. Oaks, "Religious Values and Public Policy," 63–64.

41. Dallin H. Oaks, "Some Responsibilities of Citizenship," in *The Spirit of America* (Salt Lake City: Bookcraft, 1998), 119–20.

42. The Oaks interview. Indeed, Elder Oaks believes that nothing short of world peace is attainable with such wise choices; see Dallin H. Oaks, "World Peace," *Ensign* 20, no. 5 (May 1990): 71–73.

43. The Oaks interview.

44. Dallin H. Oaks, "Statement on the Religious Freedom Restoration Act," testimony before the Subcommittee on Civil and Constitutional Rights of the Committee on the Judiciary, U.S. House of Representatives, on H.R. 2797 (13 May 1992): 23–32; and Dallin H. Oaks, "Statement on the Religious Freedom Restoration Act," testimony before the Committee on the Judiciary, U.S. Senate, on S. 2969 (18 September 1992): 30–40.

45. Dallin H. Oaks, "Statement on the Religious Liberty Protection Act," testimony before the Committee on the Judiciary, U.S. Senate, on S. 2148 (23 June 1998): 6–17.

46. The Oaks interview.

47. The Oaks interview.

48. The Oaks interview.

49. The Oaks interview.

50. The Oaks interview.

51. The Oaks interview.

52. Hans Camporreales, "Elder Oaks Talks to Judges," *Deseret News*, 17 July 2000, http://www.desnews.com, accessed 19 July 2000.

53. Howard Center, "A Call from the Families of the World," 17–20 May 1998, http://www.worldcongress.org/call99, accessed 8 August 2000.

54. R. Scott Lloyd, "Looking Forward to Congress of Families," *Deseret News*, 28 November 1998, http://www.desnews.com, accessed 8 August 2000.

55. Dallin H. Oaks, "Weightier Matters," devotional address at Brigham Young University, 9 February 1999, http://speeches.byu.edu/devo/98-99/OaksW99.html, accessed 10 July 2000, 2.

56. Dallin H. Oaks, "Same-Gender Attraction," *Ensign* 25, no. 10 (October 1995): 8.

57. The Oaks interview.

58. Oaks, "Weightier Matters," 2–4.

59. Oaks, "Weightier Matters," 3.

60. Dallin H. Oaks, "Abortion and Due Process," *Child and Family* 9, no. 4 (1970): 348.

61. Leonard J. Arrington, *Great Basin Kingdom: An Economic History of the Latter-day Saints, 1830–1900* (Lincoln: University of Nebraska Press, 1958).

62. The Oaks interview.

63. Dallin H. Oaks, "The Family in Today's World," *Utah Parent Teacher* (May–June 1972): 8.

5

Rabbi Daniel Lapin and the Culture Wars

Hubert Morken

Daniel Lapin, an Orthodox rabbi, is the founder of Toward Tradition, an organization dedicated to building close ties between Jews and Christians, many of whom are active in the Republican Party. Lapin was the only rabbi at the meeting of religious leaders that President-Elect George W. Bush convened right after his election was affirmed in December 2000. However, Stephen Goldsmith, former mayor of Indianapolis and a strong supporter of "faith-based action," who is Jewish, was also present at this meeting. Attending were Catholics, including Bishop Joseph Fiorenza of Houston, president of the National Conference of Catholic Bishops, and the Reverend Robert Sirico of the Acton Institute, as well as prominent African American ministers such as the Reverend Eugene Rivers, the Reverend Floyd Flake, the Reverend Charles Blake, the Reverend Carlton Pearson, and the Reverend Cheryl Sanders. Its purpose was to discuss faith-based social programs and to promote racial reconciliation after the bruising election contest.[1]

It is important for the president-elect to reach out to the Jewish electorate, especially because less than one-third voted for him. While it has been widely noted that there are no Jews in the Bush cabinet, it is significant that Rabbi Lapin was invited to the meeting and asked to speak. Lapin is well known for his support of Bush, for his commitment to similar principles, and for being held in high esteem in conservative Republican circles.[2] The Bush transition team asked him to make short opening comments, which included the following words of encouragement for the president-elect and strong support for his new administration:

> Mr. President-Elect, your action in bringing us here today will help to undo the epidemic of secularism that was unleashed in America eight years ago. You have reminded

Americans that faith is not about how many angels can dance on the head of a pin, but it is about families that empower education, that defeat crime, and that create wealth.

You are continuing in the American tradition of George Washington and Abraham Lincoln, who turned again and again to Biblical wisdom, and prayers to the Almighty, to guide our country in difficult times. Furthermore, by placing religious values at the core of your incoming Administration, you will do a great deal to help unify the country after the most contentious election in modern times.[3]

Lapin's thoughts assign to religion an honored place in public and private life, resisting what he calls eight years of secularism. Without naming him, he blames President Bill Clinton for the problem. This perception, that Democratic leaders are irreligious if not antireligious, was a political liability addressed by the party at the top of its ticket in the election. Democratic presidential candidate, Al Gore, named Senator Joseph Lieberman, an Orthodox Jew, to be his nominee for vice president. The appointment of the first man of his faith and ethnicity to receive this honor in American history posed a challenge for Rabbi Daniel Lapin because he disagreed with his politics. Lieberman spoke religiously on the campaign stump. He talked of his faith in God. He spoke as a Jew, without apology, much like Jimmy Carter had done in 1976 as a born-again Christian. Democrats no longer seemed so secular, and Lieberman was of Lapin's religious affiliation. But Lapin, for reasons of principle, disagreed with Lieberman on the issues discussed in the campaign and opposed him.

There was a modicum of common ground between Lieberman and Lapin, a residual of respect that arose when Lieberman defended a Republican from false charges of anti-Semitism—an issue dear to Lapin's heart. It could have been expected, then, that Lapin would have been delighted with the choice of Lieberman for vice president, and that he would have praised Lieberman for his policy statements on school vouchers, which they both support, and on the corrupting influences of Hollywood, which they both abhor. Shouldn't Lapin have commended Lieberman's celebrated public rebuke of President Bill Clinton in the Monica Lewinsky affair? In short, considering that Lapin and Lieberman agreed on many things, why did they find themselves on opposite sides of the 2000 election?

Part of Lapin celebrated the nomination of a fellow Orthodox Jew as an affirmation of his people and a confirmation of America's respect for one and all, much as Catholics affirmed Jack Kennedy in 1960. He also praised Lieberman when they agreed. But another part of him stood in dissent—particularly on substantive issues that trumped his loyalty to kinship or denominational affiliation.

Christians are on both sides of the political aisle—the Reverend Pat Robertson supported George W. Bush and the Reverend Jesse Jackson backed the Gore/Lieberman ticket. No one is surprised at this. In fact, in the great political contests in America, from 1776 when Patriots and Tories opposed each other, to the present, Christians have been both generals and troops in political battles. Muslims and Hindus also divide politically. So should political differences within Orthodox Jewry be expected? The answer is yes: Jews who agree on religion will differ politically, splitting their votes in elections. But it is also true that political and theological conflicts can rupture religious relationships, leading to virtual and even physical civil wars, as evidenced by the splitting of Baptists and Methodists before the Civil War. Are differences between Lieberman and Lapin, the one so liberal and the other so conservative on issues like affirmative action and abortion, manageable, or do they threaten the unity not only of Orthodox Jews but of America? Are internal divisions that put one Jew on the Left and one on the Right harbingers of greater political trauma ahead?[4] It is hard to say.

In the past, disagreements between Orthodox Jews in America were irrelevant to U.S. politics. There have been too few Orthodox Jews in the electorate to make a major impact on public policy, and internal squabbles have rarely been aired in public. Besides, Lieberman has not been particularly divisive within the Jewish community. On the other hand, Rabbi Lapin, an accomplished political and theological debater, does not commonly take on fellow Orthodox Jews; rather, he is known to do battle with those on the Left and secularists. In this election, as Lapin prepared to take on the liberals, it came as a great surprise that his adversary would be Joe Lieberman. Rabbi Lapin is a religious leader worthy of attention. But when Lieberman, an Orthodox Jew, was given a prominent role in national politics, the examination of Lapin's political thinking and activities became even more valuable, illuminating how politically divided America is even within religious communities thought to be unified in their worldview.

It is not uncommon for an Orthodox rabbi to operate outside of politics. But Lapin is involved. To understand Rabbi Lapin and his public role in America, first, it is necessary to study his worldview—his most basic theological and political beliefs that involve him in conflicts commonly called the "culture wars." Second, his early years are important as well. Lapin's work in California was helping nonobservant Jews discover their roots and recover their Jewishness by learning, as he says, to delight in obedience to biblical commandments and the traditions of their ancestors—embracing Orthodoxy as a way of life. Third, Lapin must be understood in terms of his move to Seattle, Washington, and his creation of Toward Tradition. Here he launched the next phase of his career, which is far more political, forming coalitions with conservative Christians, developing media capabilities, and confronting opponents. This segment of his life continues to the present. We can then return to the Lieberman issue, examining it in detail, exploring the interactions of religion and politics in this most recent election. Last, Lapin's involvement with the faith-based initiatives supported by the incoming Bush administration must be articulated in order to understand his future influence in the United States.

One of the difficulties that scholars confront is the way religious people move in and out of politics, active in one period and detached in another. This seems to make no sense. Rabbi Lapin's life illustrates this apparent inconsistency. His early years appear apolitical, in sharp contrast to his present activities. In fact, Lapin sees the stages of his life as the consistent application of the same principles in different arenas. Secularism has always been Lapin's chief foe.

UNDERSTANDING CULTURE WARS

Rabbi Lapin is politically involved in a number of sensitive subjects that some scholars call the culture wars. This intersection of religion, politics, and ideology in the United States shapes and pushes public affairs in new directions and is often the scene of much conflict. It also produces unlikely alliances. Rabbi Lapin, speaking as an Orthodox Jew, is one religious leader who forges such alliances, locally and nationally, making the case for close relations among actively religious people who are willing to oppose a common, largely secular foe.

Lapin wants those who embrace the Bible as God's Word, Jews and Christians particularly but Mormons and others as well, to reclaim what he believes to be the intellectual and political high ground. He would resist the educated elites of the Left found in the media, the universities, and government in a concerted effort to roll back "liberalism." In his view, liberalism, as it is defined and practiced by secular people, what some scholars call radical egalitarians, is hostile to fixed principles, such as the Ten Commandments, historically embraced by Christians in America and by observant Jews.

Orthodox Jews know more about assimilation and its dangers and consequences than any other group of people on earth, having resisted it for 4,000 years. Liberalism, in Lapin's view, is the great assimilator of the day. He says that U.S. intellectual, moral, and constitutional foundations, ranging from common human decency to the rule of law, are at risk. Liberalism tends to be nihilistic, with no fixed standards to live by, he asserts. Thus, the culture wars of the past twenty-five years, Lapin argues, are at root a spiritual conflict about understandings of reality as God made it. These conflicts simply will not go away. Some accept that God is the source of law, and some do not.

Some interpret the will of God one way, and others, a different way. According to Lapin, battles over what is right and wrong, what the government should and should not do, and what God thinks about all this will persist in the United States until one worldview or the other prevails—one that is grounded in revelation and reason or one that rejects such claims.[5]

Examining the culture war phenomenon is a critical scholarly activity. Aaron Wildavsky, a distinguished scholar of U.S. politics, in public lectures delivered in the mid-1980s, commented on the blindness and folly of unlimited culture wars—which leave a permanent scar on peoples and nations and can lead to genocide. Wildavsky was about to fly to Warsaw, Poland, where he was to address the nation's sociologists. Friends advised him not to go because of the Holocaust and its memories. His response was, "I am fighting this war," referring to the last gasps of Marxism-Leninism, "and not the Nazi menace of my father's generation." Poland deserved to be helped in the present, as a victim of communism, no matter what was done to Jews in earlier years. He would go to Poland. In Wildavsky's view, culture wars must out of necessity and with regret be fought, but they are not eternal. Those fighting on the wrong side in one time and place can be on the right side in the next conflict. He also was confident that people, or their children, learn from the past and change.[6]

Culture wars in contemporary America, for Wildavsky and for Lapin, are not conflicts among religious, ethnic, and racial groups like those being fought out in sub-Sahara Africa, Lebanon, or the Balkans. Instead, they incite Christian against Christian and Jew against Jew, leading to the divisions in U.S. politics and culture highlighted by the 2000 election. Wildavsky understood the American culture wars as a conflict between traditional and modern thinking. He once asked a group of religiously observant university students if any of them could articulate reasons for a hierarchical role for husbands and fathers in the home—"Please defend a husband as the head of the house," he said. The students failed to meet his challenge; most could not explain their view. Wildavsky complained that this was common. He could not find Catholic bishops willing to defend hierarchy as a normative principle. All distinctions, in his view, that assign roles on the basis of sex, for example, were suspect in modern thinking, and the religious were rarely prepared to defend what they thought and practiced.[7] Rabbi Lapin agrees.

Wars within groups do accelerate. In effect they become civil wars over how a culture thinks and acts. Social disagreements are politicized. Sexual politics over the issues of equality and differences between men and women, and the legitimacy of gay marriages and the ordination of gay ministers, are examples of these disagreements. Note the current hot disputes within major U.S. religious denominations. In the year 2000, the rapidly growing Southern

Baptist Convention, America's largest Protestant denomination and historically one of the most egalitarian and democratic of denominations in its internal governing structures, announced that it would not ordain women ministers. This is a new rule, and though some claim that fewer than 1 percent of these parishes ordain women, it is not an ancient theoretical tradition like the Roman Catholic refusal to ordain female priests. As they have for over thirty years, traditional Baptists define themselves against the prevailing cultural norms. Explaining and defending his denomination's position on women's ordination in an opinion column in the *New York Times*, R. Albert Mohler Jr., president of the Southern Baptist Theological Seminary, notes,

> Southern Baptists are off the scale of political incorrectness. Why do they insist on traditional roles for women, denounce abortion and homosexuality, and evangelize to people of all religious backgrounds? The answer is that as the culture moves steadily away from a biblical morality, our 16 million members and 41,000 churches are applying the brakes.
>
> Arguments over women in the pastorate and order in the Christian home (two years ago, the convention declared that wives should submit to their husbands) are not well understood by outside observers. For the vast majority of Southern Baptists, these issues are settled by the word of God. . . . In essence, Southern Baptists are engaged in a battle against modernity, earnestly contending for the truth and authority of an ancient faith. To the cultured critics of religion, we are the cantankerous holdouts against the inevitable. But so far as the Southern Baptist Convention is concerned, the future is in God's hands. If faithfulness requires the slings and arrows of outraged opponents, so be it.[8]

At the same time that Southern Baptists are retrenching, building new barriers to the outside, other denominations are discussing the issue of gay marriage and the ordination of gay ministers and rabbis. As Rabbi Lapin notes, some, like the Reformed Jews, have in principle agreed to accommodate such ideas. But the internal tensions even in liberal groups are far from resolved, as one journalist and a pastor have observed:

> [The] debate is growing to a high pitch, invigorated by theological battles inside denominations and the specter of more unofficial "holy union" ceremonies held by defiant clergy. Together with a new Vermont law that after July 1 gives homosexual couples a "civil union" license for financial benefits, it's a recipe for uncivil turmoil in the pews. "The gay groups are quite open about these weddings, but you can see why mainline pastors have to be secretive," says the Rev. Marc G. Benton of Bethlehem Presbyterian Church in Windsor, N.Y. "It's tearing our churches apart. We have very different views on Scripture, different views on God."[9]

Conservative and liberal changes reveal internal divisions within denominations. Exploring the implications of this for relationships, sociologist James

Davison Hunter points out that perceived commonalties tend to draw conservative Christians and Jews together in opposition to liberal Christians and Jews. He calls one group "orthodox" and the other "progressive." Hunter writes,

> I define cultural conflict very simply as political and social hostility rooted in different systems of moral understanding. . . . It is the commitment to different and opposing bases of moral authority and the world views that derive from them that creates the deep cleavages between antagonists in the contemporary culture war. As we will see, this cleavage is so deep that it cuts across the old lines of conflict, making the distinctions that long divided Americans—those between Protestants, Catholics, and Jews—virtually irrelevant.[10]

Rabbi Daniel Lapin embraces this understanding, calling attention to the political common ground shared by religiously conservative Jews and Christians. Other scholars disagree with Hunter and Lapin, noting that religious distinctions are fading as everyone tends to secularize or that some religious groups are withdrawing into protective enclaves that tend to isolate them from the larger culture and from other denominations.[11] In my view, all three of these perspectives—cooperation, assimilation, and marginalization—are correct; they are not mutually exclusive. Each helps to explain part of something real. Look first at cooperation: As pressures increase to erase religious distinctions, denominations do band together across confessional lines against a common foe. For example, the recent conference at Brigham Young University, the Mormon school, celebrated the centennial of the birth of C. S. Lewis, the leading orthodox Christian apologist of the century. Lewis dealt with relativism and atheism in his work and so provides aid and comfort to a different religion with a theology he did not share.[12] Mormons, Catholics, and Evangelicals cooperated recently in a defense of marriage initiative referendum that passed in California. Religious cooperation is continuing to bleed over into politics.

Assimilation and marginalization are also occurring, as Jeremy Rabkin points out in his recent essay, "The Culture War That Isn't." Dealing first with assimilation, Rabkin faults Pat Robertson for not producing distinctively religious television programs:

> When Pat Robertson seized the opportunity presented by cable television to organize his own cable network—the Christian Broadcasting Network—it turned out to fill most of its airtime with recycled Hollywood TV shows and not even from the glorious 1950s but from the troubled 1970s. Perhaps it is a bit cleaner than current fare. But it is not a separate world-view. What does it mean that the same channel has metamorphosed in the past year into the Fox Family Channel without much noticeable change in programming?[13]

There is no culture war in the entertainment programming of the Christian Broadcasting Network, argues Rabkin, because it is simply Hollywood with perhaps a much needed dash of modesty. But Rabkin is harshly critical of "surrender" in the political arena, noting the recent withdrawal of some religiously motivated leaders from politics. This is marginalization—a third response to cultural conflict. He decries the retreat from public life recently advocated by Paul Weyrich, the Catholic conservative activist, and by evangelical columnist Cal Thomas and the Reverend Ed Dobson (not to be confused with Dr. James Dobson of Focus on the Family) in their critique of religious political activism, *Blinded by Might*.[14] Such retreats he calls un-American if not irreligious. If assimilation is going on—and do not be fooled by the labels the religious wear, says Rabkin—then so too is marginalization, whereby those who once fought for change now see such efforts as futile.

A striking example of the tendency toward isolation is the popularity in America of the book series called Left Behind, authored by Tim F. LaHaye and Jerry B. Jenkins. These novels (seven completed out of twelve) are set in the Apocalypse. The latest, *The Indwelling: The Beast Takes Possession* (2000),[15] is number one on the *New York Times* best-sellers list, and the next volume due out in the fall will have a first printing of over three million copies. Set in the seven years following the Rapture of the Church—a doctrine that teaches that believers will ascend to Heaven prior to the bodily return of Christ to this earth in the Second Coming—the novels interpret the Book of Revelation for today's reader. A Christian publisher, Tyndale House, promotes the series, which is sold in secular bookstores. For the purposes of this analysis, it is useful to point out that the Reverend LaHaye was once active in the political cultural wars and is married to Beverly LaHaye, the founder of Concerned Women for America, the largest conservative political issues organization for women. He now is the publishing icon of the Apocalypse, evidently little concerned with the mundane aspects of politics. What is ironic is that a religious "end-time" book has gone mainstream in America.

Today there are crosscurrents and conflicting responses by the faithful to contemporary challenges. In his own work on a cultural theory of politics,[16] Wildavsky describes the essential position of a religion in an alien context as the tension between assimilation into the larger culture versus being marginalized on its boundaries. Each threat is dangerous, he argues, first, because assimilation erases identity, a fate that is permanent and permits no recovery, and second, because marginalization leaves one vulnerable to discrimination, slavery, pogroms, and genocide. Carefully defined and limited cooperation with outsiders is a middle ground in this range of options because it preserves identity and avoids isolation.

Rabbi Lapin and Senator Lieberman as Orthodox Jews make different but similar choices to cooperate. Lapin risks being too closely associated with conservatives, and Lieberman risks being absorbed by liberals. Neither is willing to be isolated and vulnerable—so they cooperate, one with Republicans and the other with Democrats, in the pressure cooker of U.S. politics.

Coalitions are not only a natural way of coping in pluralistic democracies; they are an ancient survival strategy for religious and ethnic minorities. Wildavsky points out crucial issues in culturally based politics in which the existence of a minority is at stake.[17] He claims that for minorities to survive they must avoid the extremes of assimilation or marginalization, although becoming just like one's neighbors is the deadlier temptation of the two. The paramount goal when the term is applied to particular minority groups threatened by outside oppression is always to preserve identity and to survive physically. The objective of a culturally based politics when it is applied to a nation as a whole is to achieve and maintain unity on the basis of common principles. This latter objective is increasingly difficult to do, observes Wildavsky, because radical egalitarians are so strongly represented in certain areas of the culture—such as the universities, the media, and the Democratic Party. The strong presence of radical egalitarians, Wildavsky's term, and secularists, Lapin's label, tends to split America into warring camps.

What makes Rabbi Lapin important is his effort to blend the two senses of culture war into a coherent and workable social and political strategy for Jews and for Christians. First, he wants Jews to survive and to prosper; second, he wants liberty to thrive for all groups and individuals. In his early career Lapin worked tirelessly to help Jews resist the secularizing mainstream of a California culture so focused on individual fulfillment and pleasure and not the commands of God—to avoid assimilation. Now he helps conservative Christians to be active in public life, defend their principles from assaults by opponents, and pass laws consistent with their beliefs. In addition, he forges bonds of trust and cooperation between like-minded Jews and Christians and their organizations to help them work together, multiply their strength, avoid being isolated, and influence public policy and leaders.

What is going on in America, Lapin says, is a debate about its future as a nation "under God." This phrase in the Pledge of Allegiance, spoken daily in public schools and in public gatherings, has more than symbolic meaning, writes Lapin. But what does he mean? In his book, *America's Real War*, Lapin presents the case for what he calls Judeo-Christian values.[18] His argument appeals to those who share his respect for the truth claims of traditional biblical authority. Jews and Christians in America, argues Lapin, need to rethink their politics and their religions in view of basic teachings long espoused in their respective traditions, because of the extreme threat posed by secular beliefs. In short, he argues that liberty, justice, and the rule of law in the United States rest on revealed religion, on a spiritual consensus sincerely and rationally embraced, rather than on simple pluralism or a toleration of diversity. Commenting on this before opening the 106th U.S. Congress with prayer in January 1999, invited to do so by the Republican leadership, Rabbi Lapin asserted,

> We must decide whether we are a nation united by a common love of God and bonded to one another by an embrace of His ideas and values or whether we shall be united by our vigorous rejection of the Almighty and an embrace of the sordid stain of secularism. These two unifying forces are incompatible with one another and our nation must decide which is paramount.
> Both happiness and unity are the inevitable consequences of doing the right thing. Follow God's rules for human society and you can be both happy and unified. Pursue unity and you will surely lose both unity and moral standing. But adhere to principle and you will retain both moral prestige and unity for which you yearn. America's real war is between those who proclaim unreachable utopian unity to be our ambition, and those who recognize unity to be God's ultimate reward for the nation that steadfastly adheres to His values.[19]

Lapin understands culture wars in two ways. First, in the words just noted, the phrase is applied internally to a denomination or a nation that is struggling to understand itself, divided by contrary, if not contradictory, commitments and beliefs. Second, and just as vital for Lapin, culture wars are in one sense a permanent feature of life for minorities at risk of assimilation or persecution and involve adopting strategies of all kinds to survive, ranging from concealment or confrontation to isolation or coalition building.

Early Years

The stages of Lapin's life divide neatly into his early years in South Africa, his education, rabbinical training, teaching, and business (1947–75); his period as a rabbi in Venice, California, at the Pacific Jewish Center (1976–91); and his activism in Seattle as head of Toward Tradition (1992–present).[20] Rabbi Daniel Lapin is the son of an Orthodox rabbi, Abraham Hyam Lapin. His paternal grandfather, Berel Lapin, moved from England to South Africa in 1900. He was a rabbi and a businessman selling ostrich feathers. In 1929 he sent his son A. H., as he was called, to Lithuania to attend a yeshiva for rabbinical education under the tutelage of Rabbi Eliyahu (Elya) Lapin (Lapian), his father's great uncle. Lapin's father traveled on a British passport—when the Nazis came he went to Switzerland and then to England, where he studied philosophy and logic. During the war, young Abraham returned to South Africa. He married shortly after and was active as an Orthodox rabbi in the United Hebrew Congregations of South Africa. In Lapin's early years his father was in charge of Jewish–Christian relations and formed ties with those later in key government positions.[21]

Daniel Lapin was born on 1 January 1947, in Johannesburg, the first of four children. He attended a Jewish grammar and secondary school. Lapin observed that the Jewish community that he was a part of, which he characterized as nominally Orthodox, was suffering from a corrosive lack of discipline. Only a minority was observant, in his estimation. In secondary school, Lapin developed a love for physics—"the Torah of the natural sciences."

Growing up, Lapin developed a distaste for the role of the traditional rabbi modeled by his father. His favorite one-sentence explanation for why he did not follow in his father's footsteps as a congregational rabbi is, "I did not want to have 400 bosses." Later he attended engineering school and a traditional rabbinical training at Gateshead, outside Newcastle, in Great Britain, where he too studied with Rabbi Eliyahu Lapin, his father's great uncle. Subsequently, Lapin received a public ordination as an Orthodox rabbi on three separate occasions, called *Semicha* in Hebrew, at Gateshead Yeshiva in England in 1969, at Yeshiva Kneset Hezekiah in Israel in 1972, and with Rabbi Jacob Ruderman in Baltimore in 1975.

Returning to South Africa, Lapin in his early twenties worked for four years teaching physics and the Bible in the Yeshiva College of South Africa. Learning of the sabbatical concept as it was practiced in the United States, he proposed one for himself to his old school (once he had completed six years of service) to enable him to spend a year in Israel. The school refused, and following his father's advice—"What do you want to do?"—Lapin resigned immediately. Still intent on traveling to Israel to study, he wrote himself a business plan, forming a company, Lapin Marine Enterprises, to manufacture boats. After making enough profit to fund his travel, he sold the company and left for New York in December 1973 with plans to spend a month in America before moving on to Israel.

Lapin had a recurring dream since childhood in which he "saw himself teaching Bible to a group of contemporaries on a beach." He lived in those years nowhere near a beach. Once he arrived in New York Lapin had one of those life-changing experiences, which led him to a beach ministry and eventually to form an organization, Toward Tradition. This vivid experience also illustrates how Lapin learns and thinks, intuitively and imaginatively.

On television Lapin saw pictures of a huge fire in Brooklyn at a telephone exchange. The next day he watched a long line of trucks—about a mile long, he estimated—arriving to help provide temporary telephone service and to begin repair of the facility. He was stunned at the efficiency of the repairs and speed of the recovery. No ordinary culture could do such a thing, in his view.

It required more than money to rebuild an infrastructure. There must be more here than met the eye. Yes, it took a people with a practical can-do capability and vision. But he suspected that America was at bottom a culture anchored quite differently from what he had experienced in South Africa or Great Britain. Lapin had been something of an anglophile, and this discovery came as a complete surprise. Abruptly he set out to understand what made America distinctive, suspecting that it had something to do with the religion of America and the biblical tradition. In this surmise Lapin was following in the tradition of Alexis de Tocqueville without knowing it.

Remaining in the United States, Lapin told his father, in April 1974, that he would never return to South Africa to live. He linked up with Rabbi Matis Weinberg, the son of a Jewish yeshiva leader in Baltimore, and together they planned to start a yeshiva in California for high school and post–high school students. They opened the school, called Kerem College, which means "Vineyard" in Hebrew, in Santa Clara in 1976.

While at Kerem College, Lapin read a book by Michael Medved (who attended Yale law school with Bill and Hillary Clinton) titled *What Really Happened to the Class of '65*. This book chronicles the experimentation indulged in by Medved's high school graduating class—highlighting the disasters and tragedies so commonly met by his classmates. Medved ends his book by saying that he was now going to explore the Jewish beliefs and practices of his ancestors—something he knew little about.[22] Medved's plight, his cultural lostness and that of his generation, resonated with Lapin. He was confident: He could relate his understanding of Torah to these people, who were hungry for meaning and identity as they searched for a better way to live, and could do so without becoming a traditional rabbi.

Resisting Assimilation

Lapin left Kerem College in late 1977, he has said, largely because in Northern California's small Orthodox Jewish population there were too few eligible young Jewish women for a lonely bachelor eager to marry. Needing to find a larger Jewish community, he moved to Southern California and soon linked up with Michael Medved, who two years earlier had already formed a study group of thirty to forty Jews actively studying Torah. Living in the seaside community of Venice, in an old Jewish neighborhood, Medved had a vision of reconstituting the old neighborhood with young Jewish families. They started in a cul-de-sac, buying condominiums where the real estate was cheaper. Medved's group, the Pacific Jewish Center (PJC), was looking for a teaching rabbi. Lapin volunteered for the position but in an unconventional way—he did not want to be paid for his services, choosing instead to support himself through his own business efforts in real estate. He did not want the financial dependency that a traditional rabbi suffers.

Lapin married Susan Friedberg on 15 May 1979, and they now have seven children, six daughters and one son. Eventually the cost of doing "free" ministry and business simultaneously weighed heavily on Lapin personally and on his family. Nevertheless, Lapin served the PJC as an uncompensated rabbi until he left for Seattle in the early 1990s.

Lapin says that over a fifteen-year period he was able to help about 2,000 Jewish family units find their Jewish roots. He did this by teaching—by oral communication—and for many years he refused to be recorded or videotaped. As their teacher, Lapin focused on biblically based wholeness, following "the way," not only obeying the law and staying within its limits in daily observance but stressing the positive reasons for living: "God did not create the beauty in the world for the nonreligious." He taught Torah and paid particular attention to the meaning and glories of the Hebrew language. Distinguishing them from Christians, one belief that all Jews have in common is that Jesus is not the Messiah. But one cannot build an identity on a negative, Lapin reasoned. So he made the Torah look good and studying it as a community desirable. He did this by stressing that the purpose of such study was not to be creative in interpreting the Bible but, rather, to discover its intended meaning by submitting to the text. "There are right answers and wrong answers"—and the right answers he then invited his people to live. "Taste and see that the Lord is Good" is Lapin's prescription for positive Orthodoxy.

The PJC was a community, not a synagogue in a traditional sense. Lapin thinks that the synagogue is not, cannot, and should not be the center of Jewish life. Following a model advocated by Rabbi Samson Raphael Hirsh of Frankfurt in the nineteenth century, Lapin argues that the "synagogue"-centered model is a construct of reform Jews. His model sees the synagogue, the yeshiva, the family, the kosher food store, the free loan society, and so on as all vital to living an observant Jewish life; all are essential, and only the family is in a superior position relative to other Jewish institutions.

PJC is modern in that its members speak English instead of Yiddish, but it made the traditional effort of promoting the development of an Orthodox Jewish neighborhood. Young couples were encouraged to buy homes and to move in. Although the PJC continues to this day, nurturing individuals and families, and Lapin's brother is its rabbi, in the long run this neighborhood dream failed. Medved has noted that crime rates remained high and that it was hard to get young families to pay the price of living in an undesirable part of the city.

A way to understand Lapin's way of assisting in the religious search of young American Jews not brought up to observe the Sabbath, eat kosher, or pray daily is to read David Klinghoffer's recently published autobiography,

The Lord Will Gather Me In: My Journey to Jewish Orthodoxy. Complimenting Lapin for his unique gifts for positive teaching, Klinghoffer writes,

> As much as any rabbi I know, Rabbi Lapin sees Torah as a teaching with implications for every aspect of our lives. Our conversations often focused on hopes or worries I had about my life: my career and ambitions, my relationships with women. He spoke from a deep fund of Torah knowledge and practical experience. At his shul in Venice, he and his wife had made it a specialty of introducing single men to single women. More than a hundred of their matches had led to marriage. He is that kind of rabbi. His advice is invariably on target.[23]

In California, with the help of his close friend Michael Medved, Rabbi Lapin worked tirelessly to recover the lost children of secularized Jews. He carried out this voluntary labor in the social chaos of Southern California. Simultaneously, the Jesus movement and the Christian charismatic movement, both born in California, carried out the same role for confused young Baptists, Methodists, Episcopalians, Roman Catholics, and pure seculars. In prior research, I discovered that by the late 1980s many of these people, the children of the 1960s who had experienced adult religious conversions in the 1970s, were the core of conservative political activism in the 1980s and 1990s. They grew up, got married, had families, started businesses that were successful, and, as their children entered secondary schools, became interested in public life and politics. One such person related, "We knew something was wrong with America in the 1960s, and now we are going to help fix things." These flower children of the 1960s became the grassroots leaders of the new religious Right in U.S. politics.

In a very real sense, securing one's foundations precedes politics. For Lapin, this meant building a Jewish community that was viable and creative. He proved to his own satisfaction that in this most modern of contexts, urban California, the "Word" works for families and daily life. He helped make Medved's experiment with Jewish Orthodoxy succeed. The forces of assimilation could be defeated in the "devil's" backyard. Throughout this process Lapin studied closely the sources of confusion that undercut Jewish identity. Over time he saw that these threats were not only anti-Jewish but also anti-American. At the end of the 1980s Lapin began to transition to a different calling as he saw it, to help non-Jews, nonobservant Jews, and Orthodox Jews wake up politically.

Resisting Marginalization

Theology was the path to politics for Rabbi Lapin. The Bible for him is not just a religious book intended for observant Jews. It is a prescription for living, useful for all human beings and especially for those who embrace the Creator as revealed in Genesis. Fixed rules contained in the covenant with Noah, for example, lay down principles for family life and for government. In his view, any individual, family, or nation that strives to follow these God-given rules will benefit from the positive consequences of this obedience. The United States is such a nation, he says, and needs to be reminded of its origins and the need to recover its biblically derived foundations. He opposes abortion and favors low taxes, private education, restrictions on pornography, welfare reform, and in general the domestic agenda of conservative Christians. Perhaps more critically, he claims that these policies are supported by the Bible and ought to be supported by all observant Jews because they derive ultimately from God's commands and are supported by the Jewish oral tradition. Jews must be motivated by more than support for Israel or rejection of Jesus, according to Lapin. They needed a vision for America and the world, a positive message grounded in the core of historic Jewish teaching and the Torah. He planned to help provide this message to America, connecting Torah teaching to a proper understanding of modern constitutions and relevant political issues.[24]

As long as Rabbi Lapin kept these views mostly to himself and to his small flock, he raised no waves and little opposition. There is nothing unusual about an Orthodox rabbi with conservative political views in America or elsewhere. Other members of the Jewish community could perhaps appreciate the good Lapin did in helping disenchanted youth, but when he left his enclave with this message and called on Jews and Christians to forsake much of the liberal agenda of the Democratic Party, because, as he argued, it was contrary to biblical teaching, he encountered strong, even fierce, resistance.

Lapin sought a larger canvas and more influence, partly out of ambition: he was in his prime, he was tired of speaking many times a week for no compensation, and he was ready to test his principles. In brief, Lapin has said that he wanted to live out as fully as possible the implications of his religious and cultural vision, communicating them to as many people as possible, linking up with people of like mind inside and outside the Jewish community.

Rabbi Lapin formed Toward Tradition in 1991 as a vehicle to help carry his message to a national audience. Toward Tradition sponsors conferences, issues press releases, addresses public issues, and cooperates with conservative Christians and Republicans who share its agenda. Immediately Lapin ran into opposition in the Jewish community, which attempted to discredit and ostracize him. Behind the scenes he was branded as unacceptable. Lapin says that he totally underestimated the vituperative response of Jewish leaders. His opponents were willing to do anything, he says, to discredit him. They did not just fight his ideas or disagree with him—they totally assaulted his person and integrity. These attacks began in late 1991 and preceded his business failure in early 1992. Lapin relates that he went bankrupt, losing all his assets in a dropping real estate market. He recalls this period in 1991–92 as the worst in his life. What preserved his emotional health were prayer, the Psalms, his students of fifteen years, and his family holding him steady.

The two events, his founding Toward Tradition and his business failure, were unrelated, Lapin maintains, but his enemies saw a sinister dimension to his business failure. In the public battle that followed Lapin sued *The Forward*, a Jewish paper, for false statements and won an out-of-court settlement with financial compensation. To this day Lapin is amazed by how he is treated by most establishment Jewish leaders, who consider him the embodiment of evil. To Lapin they are merely ignorant of the truth—to them, he says, he is evil and must be ignored. But he has Jewish supporters: Rabbi Pinchas Stolper, head of the Union of Orthodox Congregations in New York, endorsed his recent book, as did Rabbi Moshe M. Eisemann of Baltimore and Rabbi Avigdor Miller of Brooklyn. He also has published brief comments in *Commentary* magazine.

Lapin moved to Seattle in 1992 prior to the business failure. The move began as a sabbatical—a change of scenery—but it led to a complete shift in his focus. He still refused a traditional rabbi role, unlike his father and two of his brothers. However, he no longer wanted to speak for free—Lapin estimates that he gave 3,500 unpaid speeches over a fifteen-year period. In his first year in Seattle he saw that he could support his family by speaking. He saw Toward Tradition as an alternative voice attempting to reach people. Rising out of the ashes of financial defeat and persecution, he would help Jews to see their commonality with Christians and Christians to see the power of their faith to transform and to preserve culture and politics. Above all he affirmed that biblically grounded religion is good for America, and he was willing to pay the price to get that message heard.

The organization grew rapidly. Toward Tradition holds periodic conferences in Washington, D.C., attracting high-profile conservative speakers. It issues press releases that defend conservative Christians from attacks by their liberal opponents. Lapin speaks to Jewish and to Christian audiences around the nation and reaches out widely on his national radio talk show once a week on Sunday night. Prominent engagements include his address to the national 1996 Republican Party convention and his recent high-profile participation in the ministers meeting of President-Elect Bush. Lapin is also a regular speaker at the annual Christian Coalition conference. When asked about the recent decline in the political activity of religious conservatives, Lapin responded that this is no more than a temporary setback. Most of his work with Toward Tradition puts Lapin in contact with non-Jews such as Dr. James Dobson and Pat Robertson of the Christian Coalition.[25]

Lapin is convinced that many Americans, and especially conservative Christians, are a potential sleeping giant, capable of understanding and supporting his views and providing leadership for an intelligent, biblically grounded conservatism. Helping to awaken that giant is his mission as he conceives it. Asked if he fears Evangelical efforts to convert Jews, Lapin responds that only Jews ignorant of their faith and its teaching are vulnerable. In short, secular Jews are frightened, in his view, and this explains why these Jews oppose Christian evangelism so ferociously; it also explains why they are so ignorant of the variety of Christians and their differences; and it is why they have little contact with pious Christians. Such isolation, grounded in ignorance of Judaism itself, tends to isolate secularized Jews from the religious streams of U.S. culture. This indictment wins Lapin enemies. Secure in his Orthodoxy, unafraid of assimilation or efforts to convert Jews, Lapin calls for strategic partnerships with Christians.

Asked about the potential for a revival of anti-Semitism in the United States, Lapin indicated that he most feared the activities of some leaders in the African American community. He also blamed secular liberal Jews for helping to stir up this black anger by their domination of liberal organizations and liberal politics. Medved has a less sanguine position. He sees ahead the danger of a cultural backlash against Jews by people who call themselves Christians and wonders how Evangelicals and Roman Catholics will respond if this occurs. Lapin answers that conservative Protestants in America do not have a history of pogroms against Jews and today are educated against anti-Semitism. He attributes the positive climate in America toward Jews primarily to this Protestant respect for Jews as God's chosen people.

Lapin also knows that most Orthodox Jews are friendly to America, to democracy, and to republican government. However, there are Jews who see no long-term future for Diaspora Jewry—all Jews, these particular Zionists say, eventually should go to Israel. Lapin disagrees: He argues that a flourishing Jewish religious community outside Israel, in the United States, refutes this position. Medved observes that Lapin has a deeper emotional tie to America than to modern Israel because his love of Torah is greater than his love of Zionism. It is this commitment to a home in America that helps to motivate Lapin to take political action and to form alliances with conservative Christians.

When asked to contrast his views with the neoconservatives of *Commentary* magazine, a leading opinion journal published by the American Jewish Committee, Lapin said that the neoconservatives define themselves by what they reject—socialism and statism—but not by what they stand for. Secular conservatives simply lack theoretical grounding. In his view, they do not go far enough, preferring not to base their ideas on Creation or revelation: "Socialism is a belief system, a religion, and only another religion—biblical

Orthodoxy, Jewish or Christian—will in the end be strong enough to resist it." What is needed, he said, despite all the good work of the neoconservative critique of the Left, is a next step. In this regard, Lapin is much encouraged by recent directions of *Commentary* under its new editor, Neal Kozodoy.

Where is Rabbi Lapin making his greatest impact? Certainly book sales of *America's Real War* are an indicator of who is interested in his ideas. So far the book has sold over 70,000 copies, and he has received some positive Jewish response. However, most Jews do not even know about the book for two reasons. The Jewish press has ignored the book, refusing to review it, and Lapin chose Multnomah Press, a Christian press, as his publisher. Besides impressing the general reader or those who hear his radio broadcasts or speeches, the greatest influence Lapin has is on conservative Evangelical elites, the leaders he defends in public and those whose politics he supports. These leaders not only need some Jewish support to be credible; they need the intellectual armor he provides.

Lapin is totally persuaded that the pre-Christian revelation of the Torah is a master plan for government for gentile nations. There are general principles of law in the Ten Commandments and elsewhere that are not only common sense and rational but also divine prescriptions for the whole human race. Many conservative Christians agree. This is not a prescription for theocracy, but it is a defense of classical American concepts commonly agreed on in the founding era and well into the twentieth century. Christians love to hear their political creed articulated by an Orthodox Jew who rejects Jesus as the Messiah.

Prior to the 2000 Republican National Convention, Lapin and Medved were invited to Philadelphia to address the national Jewish Republican caucus. This is their natural political home at present. It permits some leverage on national issues in the short term. There are good and sound reasons for Jews to resist the secularization of America, they argued in Philadelphia, because it is a religious America that gave Jews a refuge and liberty (not mere toleration) for the past three centuries.

Jews are shockingly ignorant of the Christian world and the differences within it, Lapin maintains. In Philadelphia Lapin reminded his hosts that Orthodox Christians and the Roman Catholics in Europe—but not American Evangelicals—killed Jews. There is some discrimination against Jews in America, Lapin observed—not sanctioned by government or most churches but real. However, he asserted, there is no American history of pogroms against Jews, and if this nation keeps its spiritual base and conservative principles, there never will be. Religious liberty for all prevails because Christians defend it, and a secular America, Lapin predicts, will be the end of liberty and safety for Jews and for Christians as well.[26]

What most alarmed Lapin, he warned those in Philadelphia, was a cycle of hubris in which Jews prospered, became powerful, grew arrogant, and then were rejected. He asked, "Are we safe until the end of time? We had better beware, keep our tradition, and keep peace with the majority." Alienating Christians over abortion made no sense in his view, given the need to forge alliances with allies.[27] This comment betrays some fear that the Christians in the United States may someday turn anti-Semitic if Jews insist on alienating them.

A conservative Orthodox Jew in America has few political choices. There is no room in the Democratic Party or the largely liberal Jewish establishment now that the two major parties have polarized over national issues. One can remain outside of politics as many do. But to do so is to be marginalized. Instead, Lapin chose to ally himself with the conservative wing of the Republican Party.

THE LIEBERMAN NOMINATION

How critical was Lapin of Lieberman the candidate? "Our first reaction is, 'What a country!'" Lapin said, relishing this confirmation that the United States is not anti-Semitic. The nation was more anti-Catholic in 1960 than it was anti-Jewish in 2000, he claims, and he has praised Lieberman for his character and for his rhetorical courage in challenging Hollywood.[28] Later in the campaign, when the Anti-Defamation League (ADL) attacked Lieberman for referring too much to God and to his personal religious beliefs in his speeches and interviews, as though this were un-American, Lapin scoffed:

> Had the ADL been around, it no doubt would have reproached George Washington for his major public addresses, most of which "appealed along religious lines" and "invoked belief in God." And condemned Abraham Lincoln for quoting the 19th Psalm in his Second Inaugural. And criticized the Continental Congress for un-American references to "the Creator" and "Divine Providence" in the Declaration of Independence. Either the greatest, most indispensable leaders in American history were themselves wholly ignorant of "the American ideal," or what the ADL calls "the American ideal" is a product of its own fevered imagination. We think it's the latter.[29]

Lapin concludes that politicians, and not the ADL, were better judges of what constitutes the right use of religious language in elections, and, in fact, Lieberman's professed piety "helped him reconnect with many voters that his party has alienated by being too doggedly secular over the past few decades."[30]

Lapin parted company with Lieberman as a result of his policy shifts on vouchers, for example, and over his vote against a ban on partial-birth abortions after his nomination as vice president. Lapin proposed a deeds test for Lieberman that would examine his actions not his words, faulting him for sounding like an Orthodox Jew but not acting like one. In a newspaper interview he put his objections this way:

> As an Orthodox Jew and as a rabbi, I would be remiss in not pointing out that this is a man who has spoken of family values yet votes against relief for the marriage penalty. He is a man who speaks highly of faith that affirms the value of life but finds no form of abortion sufficiently abhorrent to vote against. He spoke in favor of Clarence Thomas but voted against him. He gave a ringing denunciation on the Senate floor of the president's scandalous behavior but worked and voted to acquit him. These are among the indicators that what is more important than his claim to being an orthodox Jew is that he conducts himself as a standard liberal.[31]

When the Union of Orthodox Rabbis called on Lieberman to refuse to meet with a gay and lesbian organization, Toward Tradition also pled with him to respect the Torah's moral code and to cancel the meeting.[32] Lieberman's use of religion to defend the environmental position of Al Gore also offended Lapin. A more balanced approach that puts human "life and dignity" above the well-being of the earth and not below it is more consistent with a biblical respect for human creativity and wisdom as he saw it. He called Lieberman's position "extremism."[33] In short, Lapin supported George W. Bush's positions on most issues and considered them more consistent with Orthodox theology than Lieberman's views.

COOPERATING WITH GEORGE W. BUSH

A press release of Toward Tradition notes that Lapin was "the only rabbi in a group of fifteen religious leaders" to meet with President-Elect Bush soon after his election. It is not clear what led to this invitation—perhaps the Bush staff knew of Lapin's book. The statement also notes that "Rabbi Lapin was asked by the Bush transition staff to deliver the meeting's opening remarks,"[34] some of which were quoted earlier. Lapin was pleased with the outcome, noting that the meeting was "highly productive and had a positive tone:" "We discussed the President-elect's plans to promote a wide range of faith-based social programs that have performed much better than their secular, bureaucratic counterparts of the welfare state. Judaism believes in—and Toward Tradition has always promoted—an ethic of personal accountability that, in the long run, can only be sustained by religious faith."[35]

Faith and the state should not be at loggerheads—that is what Lapin is saying. But this requires that churches and synagogues be given room to operate without undue restrictions. Some kind of partnership is in order: "It's simply to allow religious organizations to fully participate as the secular organizations do,' Lapin said."[36] Lapin is prepared to work with Bush and to support his efforts to roll back government-run programs that Lapin says undermine personal accountability. How this is to be done is a matter of discussion, and Lapin expects to be part of that process.

What else might Lapin contribute to the Bush presidency? One thing is clear. Lapin will defend Bush against attacks by Jewish and secular organizations. He is offended when a liberal agenda is presumed to be the Jewish position or the intelligent answer, and he will argue on behalf of school choice, tax cuts, and a strong military because he insists that those positions in present circumstances are consistent with Torah and the Jewish tradition. Speaking to a local reporter on Mercer Island after his meeting with Bush, Lapin said,

> For the last 20 years, Jews and Jewish organizations unconditionally support the Democrats, while they will never support Republicans no matter what the party does to benefit Jews. . . . Judaism and the Torah-system, by which Toward Tradition operates, don't uniformly endorse Republican Party politics, but are vehemently at odds with 90 percent of Democratic Party politics. . . . I think the Republican Party has known that, whilst I'm not a moral rubber stamp, I have emphasized the need and legitimacy for claiming the moral ground in politics. . . . My mission is to encourage Jews to abandon the faith and doctrines of secular liberalism and return to the faith of Abraham, Isaac and Jacob. I would like to see Jews confining themselves to kosher food, kosher worship and kosher politics, and that does not mean confining themselves to the secular doctrines of the Democratic Party.[37]

Lapin is a polemicist and is especially offended at elites who "bully" conservatives, trying to intimidate them into silence. The efforts of Toward Tradition are designed to present an alternative Jewish voice in public debates—and to work with conservative Christians. Lapin is confident that Bush has no intention to "Christianize America or impose a theocracy."[38] The rabbi will be active in the media throughout the Bush presidency, and behind the scenes he will be mobilizing help for Bush programs when they are in agreement.

CONCLUSION

It is worth repeating that Rabbi Lapin sees no conflict between his early career teaching Torah to secularized Jews and his recent educational and political activities with conservative Christians like the Reverend Pat Robertson and George W. Bush. Becoming more Jewish in thought and deed is consistent with cooperative politics, in his view, even if that means working with the Christian Coalition.

For Jews facing assimilation Lapin offers a culturally sensitive and modern way to be a fully observant and Orthodox Jew. Medved and Lapin delight in recommending ways for families to resist secularization—neither has a television in the home, though they both watch selected videos. Although Medved is a national movie critic, he is convinced that raising children requires special insulation, if not isolation. Winning the culture war at home and in the synagogue requires vigilance and a healthy local Jewish community. Mercer Island, Washington, where both Lapin and Medved now live, is home to a Jewish enclave of about 5,000 people and sits right across the water from Seattle. But this is not enough. Lapin warns of a growing threat to his people in a larger cultural war being waged in the body politic of the United States.

In this war both Jews and conservative Christians are minorities. What was Lapin to do? His solution, only partially successful at present, is to build a political coalition of Jews and Christians to resist secularization and exercise influence in the nation's leadership councils. So far Lapin has been more successful building relationships with Christians than with Jews. In avoiding being isolated from U.S. politics Lapin found himself marginalized in the American Jewish community. I asked him why he seemed so ready to risk alienation among his own people. His short response was that when the truth was the issue, he would rather speak it for his son's sake, for him to know and follow, than to have more friends today. This is perfectly consistent with Lapin's emphasis on the family over the synagogue. But it weakens his short-term political influence.

The Lieberman candidacy tested Lapin's loyalties. The nomination made him even more proud to be an American, solidifying his commitment to his chosen home, but he spurned what he calls tribalism, that is, voting for a Jew because he or she is a Jew. While praising Lieberman's frequent use of religious rhetoric, he was critical of Lieberman's policy positions as a candidate.

The George W. Bush presidency presents Lapin with unusual opportunities. He has paid his political dues over the past ten years, speaking and writing on behalf of conservatives and conservative causes, defending them from attacks designed to silence them. It is payback time, and the preferred form of payment is access to the Republican corridors of power in Washington. Lapin will walk those corridors, using his influence from time to time, as issues and opportunities present themselves.

Lapin speaks out not just as a conservative, or a concerned citizen, but as a Jew and an Orthodox rabbi. He does not hide his religious identity and speaks as one who has earned the right to be heard. This will lead to more conflict and notoriety for him—with the Left and with other Jews. At the moment, in 2001, Lapin is expanding his radio talk show program to five days a week in the Seattle market and making plans to syndicate it nationally.[39]

Today, about two-thirds of Lapin's time is engaged in business consulting—whereby he teaches the transcendent sources of economic success, drawing especially from the Jewish and the American experience. Is this an abandonment of Toward Tradition, or is it a natural corollary, an economic complement to his political mission? Time will tell. Three things about this are clear, though. First, Rabbi Lapin has always been an entrepreneur. This is nothing new. Second, without money political involvement is impossible. The richer Lapin is, and the richer his supporters are, the more influence he will have. Third, Lapin's principles require that he embrace prosperity as a gift from God and something he earns. Prosperity boosts Lapin's confidence that what he thinks about politics is correct because both his political and his economic principles, he is sure, come from the Bible.

This last point is especially important in political hard times when Lapin's conservative Christian political allies stumble. Lapin is not fazed by these temporary setbacks. They are to be expected as leaders fail and circumstances change. Indeed, the Bush victory over Gore is only one winning battle in a protracted war. What Lapin knows is that the deeper currents of history are not transitory. Culture wars of this magnitude do not end with an election cycle. In fact, the closeness of the 2000 election highlights these divisions. They persist, and Rabbi Lapin wants to lay down precepts for a multigenerational war and eventual victory. This means passing down principles, mobilizing resources, procreating, carefully building alliances, identifying enemies, and living life to the fullest. Lapin's cup is full—though to me he appears far from satisfied.

Orthodox Jews disagree, as expected, dividing much like Christians do over political issues. Rabbi Lapin's presence is one more indication that the deep fissures in U.S. politics are not closing. The culture wars demonstrated so intensely in the election of 2000 go on and on, dividing Orthodox Jews like Lieberman and Lapin and uniting Jews and Christians like Bush and Lapin with a common worldview. In his last interview with CBS anchorman Dan Rather before leaving office, President Bill Clinton was asked how he viewed Special Prosecutor Ken Starr and the Republican-controlled Congress that gave him so much grief. Clinton responded that he had learned to accept them as opponents who were sincere, who thought they were doing the right thing, but who did not share his worldview. Rabbi Lapin would agree.

NOTES

1. Dana Milbank, "Bush to Host Black Ministers," *Washington Post*, 19 December 2000: A1; Dana Milbank and Hamil R. Harris, "Bush, Religious Leaders Meet," *Washington Post*, 21 December 2000: A6.
2. Milbank, "Bush to Host Black Ministers," A1; Milbank and Harris, "Bush, Religious Leaders Meet," A6.
3. Toward Tradition, "President-Elect Bush Seeks Advice from Rabbi Daniel Lapin on Role of Faith in Public Affairs," press release, 20 December 2000.
4. For the Toward Tradition webpages, see http://www.towardtradition.org.
5. Rabbi Daniel Lapin, interview by the author, Mercer Island, Washington, 19 May 2000; herein referred to as "the Lapin interview."
6. Aaron Wildavsky, conversation with the author, Tulsa, Oklahoma, mid-1980s.
7. Aaron Wildavsky, *The Rise of Radical Egalitarianism* (Washington, D.C.: American University Press, 1991), 227–32.
8. R. Albert Mohler Jr., "Against an Immoral Tide," *New York Times*, Opinion, 19 June 2000.
9. Larry Witham, "The Churches Debate Role in Gay Unions," *Washington Times*, 19 June 2000.
10. James Davison Hunter, *Culture Wars: The Struggle to Define America* (New York: Basic Books, 1992), 42–43.
11. Hunter, *Culture Wars*; Jeremy Rabkin, "The Culture War That Isn't," *Policy Review*, August and September 1999: 3–19.
12. Andrew C. Skinner and Robert L. Millet, *C. S. Lewis: The Man and His Message* (Salt Lake City: Bookcraft, 1999).
13. Rabkin, "The Culture War That Isn't."
14. Rabkin, "The Culture War That Isn't"; Cal Thomas and Ed Dobson, *Blinded by Might* (Grand Rapids, Mich.: Zondervan Publishing House, 1999).
15. Tim F. LaHaye and Jerry B. Jenkins, *The Indwelling: The Beast Takes Possession* (Wheaton, Ill.: Tyndale House, 2000).
16. Aaron Wildavsky, *Assimilation versus Separation: Joseph the Administrator and the Politics of Religion in Biblical Israel* (New Brunswick, N.J.: Transaction Books, 1993).
17. Wildavsky, *The Rise of Radical Egalitarianism*.
18. Daniel Lapin, *America's Real War* (Sisters, Oreg.: Multnomah Publishers, 1999).
19. Toward Tradition, "Rabbi Lapin Tells Opening Congressional Bi-Partisan Opening Ceremony, Pray for Unity but Pursue Principle," press release, Mercer Island, Washington, 8 January 1999.
20. Little has been written about Rabbi Lapin. This essay has as its oral sources two interviews with Rabbi Lapin and one interview on 22 May 2000 with his best friend, Michael Medved, a movie critic for *USA Today* and nationally syndicated radio talk show, herein known as "the Medved interview." The book by David Klinghoffer, *The Lord Will Gather Me In: My Journey to Jewish Orthodoxy* (New York: The Free Press,

1999), refers to Rabbi Lapin a number of times and gives insight into his longtime role with young Jewish seekers.

21. The Lapin interview.
22. The Medved interview.
23. Klinghoffer, *The Lord Will Gather Me In*, 200.
24. The Lapin interview; Lapin, *America's Real War*.
25. Again, for the Toward Tradition webpages, see http://www.towardtradition.org.
26. The Medved interview.
27. Daniel Lapin and Michael Medved, address, personal audiotape, Jewish Policy Center Conference, Philadelphia, 9 August 2000.
28. Lapin and Medved, "Thoughts on Senator Lieberman," personal audiotape.
29. Lapin and Medved, "ADL versus Lieberman," personal audiotape.
30. Lapin and Medved, "ADL versus Lieberman," personal audiotape.
31. Lapin, quoted in John Elvin, "Political Faith," Insight on the News, *Washington Times*, 4 September 2000: 10.
32. Adam Pruzan, "Senator Lieberman and Torah Values," Toward Tradition, press release, 6 October 2000.
33. Daniel Lapin, "Does God Command Environmental Extremism?" available at http://www.towardtradition.org.
34. Toward Tradition, "President-Elect Bush Seeks Advice from Rabbi Daniel Lapin on Role of Faith in Public Affairs."
35. Toward Tradition, "President-Elect Bush Seeks Advice from Rabbi Daniel Lapin on Role of Faith in Public Affairs."
36. Stephen Weigand, "Claiming the Moral Ground in Politics—Lapin among Clergy Who Met with President-Elect Bush," *Mercer Island Reporter*, 4 January 2001, available at http://www.mi-reporter.com/sited/story/html/40517.
37. Weigand, "Claiming the Moral Ground in Politics."
38. Weigand, "Claiming the Moral Ground in Politics."
39. Yarden Weidenfeld, national director of Toward Tradition, interview with the author, 10 January 2001.

6

The Reverend Benjamin Chavis-Muhammed: From Wilmington to Washington, from Chavis to Muhammed

James Lance Taylor

The religious conversion of Benjamin F. Chavis Jr.,[1] in February 1997, from black nationalist Christian minister in the United Church of Christ (UCC) to black Muslim minister, came after the development of a five-year relationship with Nation of Islam leader, Louis Farrakhan. This alliance was the result of his work bringing together the National Association for the Advancement of Colored People (NAACP) and the National African American Leadership Summit (NAALS). With the sacred texts of both traditions in his hands, Chavis declared before thousands of Nation of Islam faithful, "I find no theological contradiction between being a Black Christian and a Black Muslim, I am turning to Allah."[2] This transformation came after the relative success of the 1995 "Million Man March/Day of Absence" and the NAALS, so perplexing some observers that it was deemed parcel to "black politics gone haywire" and a general erosion of credibility for Chavis. A more sympathetic commentary contends that after his August 1994 removal from the NAACP amid accusations of mismanagement of association funds, Chavis suffered a "personal tragedy" and "became essentially a client of Farrakhan, financially and politically dependent."[3] Such an organizational conversion as Chavis's, from the helm of the nation's oldest integrationist civil rights organization, the NAACP, to a regional post in the nation's oldest black nationalist-separatist one,[4] the Nation of Islam, is largely unprecedented.[5] Nevertheless, Chavis's conversion should not detract from the very serious political and personal struggles that he has waged over the past several decades.

His work covers many public policy issue areas. These include the environment—in fact, some sources attribute the phrase "environmental racism" to Chavis—workers' rights, health care, voter rights, family values, race discrimination, affirmative action, and economic reparations to Native and African

Americans. But no single issue area threads the life and work of Chavis-Muhammed as does his advocacy for racial justice before the legal and criminal justice systems at both the state and the national levels. One of the common themes of both the 1995 Million Man March and the 16 October 2000 "Million Family March"—for which Chavis-Muhammed served as executive director—reiterated his policy objectives for criminal justice and prison system reform at the state level and personal "atonement" at the individual level.

The political forces that produced Benjamin Chavis stemmed from the social disruptions of the mid-1960s that prompted conflicting demands for "Black Power" and "law and order" after the collapse of the national civil rights movement and the late beginning of North Carolina's quest. The present study focuses on the political and spiritual evolution of one of the civil rights movement's most important and interesting personalities. Before his twenty-fifth birthday, Benjamin Chavis was at the center of the maelstrom that was North Carolina's anachronistic civil rights movement. Being repeatedly charged, jailed, and denied fundamental due process by repressive local, state, and federal law enforcement officials, he was finally sentenced to thirty-four years in prison as a member of the "Wilmington Ten" in the early 1970s. In his own right Chavis-Muhammed has been an uncompromising opponent of racism since his youth, and, according to one biographer, his activism was the epitome of North Carolina's civil rights movement.[6] Chavis's activities in the various communities of North Carolina resulted in ex post facto charges for several crimes including arson, bombing, accessory to murder, conspiracy to commit murder, and so forth.[7] It was in this climate that Chavis developed the radical Christian worldview that informed his personal response to law enforcement and the criminal justice system, a worldview that would later facilitate his transition to the Nation of Islam. Indeed, few of those who have criticized Chavis's embrace of the Nation of Islam have considered this influence, preferring to focus solely on his recent alliance with Farrakhan.

As minister of Muhammad's Mosque Number 7 in Harlem—where Malcolm X, Farrakhan, and Khallid Muhammad preceded him—Chavis-Muhammed has spearheaded the Million Family March's "National Agenda." It includes a litany of policy demands that were distributed to both the Democratic and the Republican National Conventions during the summer of 2000 and to both major presidential candidates. It promises to develop a "third force," that is, a political strategy that Chavis-Muhammed continues to insinuate will be a third political party and will extend to state-level and national elections through the year 2008.

This study begins with a biographical sketch of Chavis, highlighting the familial and ideological influences on his youth activism in Oxford, North Carolina, through his undergraduate college years at the University of North Carolina at Charlotte. It traces his confrontations with law enforcement officials including the Federal Bureau of Investigation's secret Counter Intelligence Program (COINTELPRO); the Treasury Department's Alcohol, Tobacco, and Firearms Division; and the local Rights of White People (ROWP) organizations out of which his radical Christian nationalist worldview formed. Chavis's four-year prison experience in North Carolina's penal system is also covered in order to understand how he developed his policy advocacy for racial justice, vis-à-vis prison reform, police brutality, and fairness in sentencing. Finally, the Chavis–Farrakhan alliance is analyzed within the context of the broader revival of black nationalism in U.S. politics during the last two decades of the twentieth century as evidenced by the events that culminated in the 1995 Million Man March. Analysis of the October 2000 Million Family March National Agenda and its "Public Policy Issues, Analyses, and Programmatic Plan of Action" should prove useful for deciphering Chavis-Muhammed's faith-based motivations and continued commitment to system reform.

SON OF A NORTH CAROLINA CIVIL RIGHTS FAMILY

Benjamin Franklin Chavis Jr. was born in 1948 to an Episcopalian family of educators in the northern border town of Oxford, North Carolina.[8] Amid the turmoil of North Carolina race politics leading up to its late civil rights movement, Chavis, at the age of thirteen, joined the local chapter of the NAACP in 1960. Considered a radical act in view of southern racial hostilities toward civil rights in general and the NAACP in particular, his defiance reflected the "center of consistent resistance" that V. O. Key observed earlier among North Carolina's "Black Belt" counties.[9] The Chavis family traced its roots in social protest to the activities of John Chavis, the man whom historian John Hope Franklin called "the most prominent free Negro in North Carolina," during slavery.[10] Ben Chavis's early political development was informed to a great extent by his family's account of his paternal great-great-grandfather who taught black children to read and write in defiance of the state's antiliteracy laws. In addition to being the first black graduate of what is today Princeton University, John Chavis had a list of prominent white North Carolina students, including the sons of two Supreme Court judges, a future North Carolina governor, and a U.S. senator.[11]

Recalcitrant segregationist social codes, customs, institutions, and political elements ruled and permeated the Oxford of Chavis's youth despite the 1954 Supreme Court *Brown* desegregation ruling. Ironically, at the time of Chavis's birth, Key's *Southern Politics in State and Nation* described North Carolina's "progressive plutocracy" as one of the most racially progressive Southern states of the former Confederacy. It was depicted as a state that had the fewest number of slaves and slave owners of the seven major Confederate states. It was profiled as the state reluctant to join the Confederacy and the only Southern state to support Harry S. Truman in the 1948 split between the national and Southern "Dixiecrat" wings of the Democratic Party. When the southern states engaged in the post-*Brown* reactionary movement known as "Massive Southern Resistance," North Carolina opposed it.[12]

It is apparent that North Carolina's race relations were "two sided," the North Carolina that Key studied was starkly different from the North Carolina that the Chavises and other black North Carolinians experienced.[13] Bass and DeVries argue, "The progressive image the state projected in the late 1940s has evolved into a progressive myth. . . . Although North Carolina has changed with the times, it is perhaps the least changed of the old Confederate states."[14] Pierce contends that the facts behind North Carolina's politics make it a "state of paradoxes" where the term "'repression' is not the right word, but 'progressive' gives North Carolina too much credit."[15] The state's electoral and law enforcement politics iterate these observations. For example, while North Carolina was the only southern state to experience an increase in black voter registration between 1968 and 1970, its 54.8 percent black voting-age population remained the lowest of all eleven.[16] North Carolina was but a microcosm of the vast mobilization of the domestic (and foreign) military/police apparatus that, at the national level, was typified by J. Edgar Hoover's COINTELPRO, directed at "black nationalist-hate groups."[17] Myerson describes the North Carolina prison system as one of the harshest in the nation during the 1970s.[18] There is at least some evidence to support this claim. For example, between 1930 and 1970, North Carolina executed more of its citizens (263) than any state except Georgia (366) and Texas (297); only Georgia executed more of its black citizens (298) than North Carolina (149).[19] Moreover, in 1970, the population of citizens convicted of crimes entering North Carolina prisons (5,969) was double that of neighboring Confederate stronghold South Carolina (2,726). Even controlling for state population differences during the 1970s, North Carolina had the largest per capita prison population in the United States, with the highest number of inmates per 100,000 citizens. It also held the dubious record of jailing more of its citizens and jailing them longer than any other state did. And close to half of its inmates, like Chavis, were less than twenty-five years old. Key certainly provides a useful description of North Carolina's ambidextrous politics at the very end of the 1940s, but within a decade race relations in the region were much more than benign.

By several accounts, the larger civil rights movement ended around 1972, just when North Carolina's movement reached its apex.[20] Upon entering the

University of North Carolina at Charlotte, Chavis organized black student protest activities successfully in demand for a black studies program. A young man at the height of the Black Power movement, roughly between 1966 and 1972, Chavis became increasingly radicalized. Using his position as president of the student body, he invited revolutionary nationalist Stokely Carmichael, later known as Kwame Ture, to speak on campus. He joined the Black Panther Organization, an independent satellite of Oakland's Black Panther Party for Self-Defense, and established a "Black House" on campus and the first of two black Christian nationalist congregations.

BLACK CHRISTIAN NATIONALISM

The various responses of black religionists over the past few centuries have broadly reflected Du Bois's interdependent "double consciousness" corollary: one being essentially militant and nationalistic, the other being essentially liberal-integrationist.[21] In the mid-1960s, this ideological distinction was resuscitated during the advent of "Black Power." The "pie in the sky," "opiate," and "otherworldly" *Negro* church that foundered at the dawn of the civil rights movement had given way to the *black church*,[22] which had been infused with a coherent and radical theology of blackness based in the Black Power movement. The black church needed to speak to the pressing issues that were being addressed by secular forces such as the Student Nonviolent Coordinating Committee and the Congress of Racial Equality (CORE) in order to remain relevant in the black community. Black congregations in the North became increasingly aligned with the nationalist sentiments of the period.

Central to this development among black religionists were several major influences that would largely shape the religio-political worldview of Benjamin Franklin Chavis Jr.: Malcolm X, Martin Luther King Jr., and the racial milieu that conjoined them all simultaneously.[23] Malcolm X's impious criticisms of the Christian church—both white and black—created the theological space that would enable the likes of UCC minister Albert Cleage Jr., of Detroit, to articulate his version of black Christian nationalism. From the outset, this Christian tradition rejected many of the orthodoxies found in European and North American Christian narratives. The publication of Cleage's *The Black Messiah* (in 1968) and *Black Christian Nationalism* (in 1972) delineated the core teachings of the black Christian nationalist movement that Chavis embraced in 1971.[24] Essentially, black Christian nationalism employed a radical anthropomorphic view of the Judeo-Christian godhead,[25] and its great prophets were, with the exception of Marcus Garvey, mostly non-Christian black nationalists such as Elijah Muhammad, Malcolm X, Stokely

Carmichael, and H. Rap Brown of the Black Panther Party. Cleage chiefly developed his iconoclastic interpretation after forming an alliance with Malcolm X in 1963 against mainline black denominations and their ministers such as King and the NAACP-allied churches. The UCC's largely democratic ecumenism and autonomous synod organizational structure also allowed for the unorthodoxy that would reconcile Chavis's Christian faith with his increasing faith in black nationalism.

Chavis's organizing efforts came to the attention of the UCC Commission for Racial Justice, which hired his services as a field organizer. Black communities throughout North Carolina's eastern Black Belt region solicited Chavis's help through the commission.[26] It was also at this juncture that Chavis converted to the UCC and entered its requisite eighteen-month In-Service Ministerial Training Program. By the time that Chavis was beckoned to Wilmington, North Carolina, by a local congregationalist church to help organize student activities there, he had become a minister in the UCC-affiliated Black Christian Pan-Africanist Church established by Cleage in 1967.

The presence of a counter-charismatic such as Martin Luther King Jr. staved the ideological drift among many black Christians who had become frustrated with the NAACP-led coalition of religious gradualists. This is made clear by the multitude of black Christian manifestos, remonstrations, conferences, and individual acts of defiance that emerged especially in the intervening years between "Black Power" and after King's death.[27] Even though King was opposed by important segments of the black and religious communities,[28] his version of social protest ultimately articulated the faith assumptions of the southern black clergy. King's religio-political worldview, which was based in the principles of natural law and biblical texts, provided direction for the eradication of Jim Crow segregation laws and black second-class citizenship. Ben Chavis Jr. first met King face to face in 1967 while serving as the western North Carolina coordinator for the Southern Christian Leadership Conference (SCLC), which he joined one year before attending the 1963 "March on Washington." Chavis explains that "it was in, through, and by the Church, that I was learning how to organize on the community grass-roots level. At this time, I became a devoted follower of Dr. Martin Luther King, Jr. The effective and creative non-violent role the church was playing to bring about social change impressed me to the point that I knew that sooner or later I would devote myself to the church and struggle for justice and humanity."[29]

For a short time after the assassination of Dr. King in 1968, Chavis remained committed to King's protest vision while working as a student organizer for the SCLC. Nevertheless, the same exigencies that prompted the calls for Black Power would soon facilitate Chavis's move from student activist—

finally graduating from the University of North Carolina in 1970 with a chemistry degree—to prison activist.

PSALMS FROM PRISON

The conflicts among black Wilmingtonians, white supremacist organizations, and law enforcement reflected the national "law and order" nadir initiated by President Richard Nixon during both his campaigns and administrations. What emerges from these characterizations, in sum, is the largely unconstitutional usurpation of power that typified and eventually brought scandalous disgrace to the Hoover FBI and Nixon administration. Through COINTELPRO, the state-sponsored reactionary movement that opposed the civil rights movement, declared and carried out nothing short of civil war against its children. Young leaders such as Stokely Carmichael, Angela Davis, Huey P. Newton, Assata Shakur, Fred Hampton, Eldridge Cleaver, and Geronimo Pratt were labeled "Key Black Extremists." In North Carolina, Chavis and close friend Jim Grant were identified by federal authorities as "Known Black Militants."[30] The nation experienced continuous unrest as law enforcement legitimacy eroded. Amid what had quickly become routine "drive-by" shootings in black Wilmington communities by marauding Ku Klux Klan and ROWP members, Chavis was shot in the back just days after seventy people were struck by some 5,000 rounds of ammunition fired into the Gregory Congregational Church there. Black residents, some of them soldiers from nearby Fort Bragg, armed themselves and retaliated by burning down a white-owned grocery store located in the black community—hence, the main charge against the Wilmington Ten.[31] As the situation grew out of control in Wilmington, Chavis and the local Black Youth Building a Black Community, which he established, rented a building, painted it black, and founded the African Congregation of the Black Messiah, replete with its unorthodox nationalist doctrine. In the first four months of 1972, Chavis was indicted or jailed and released more than fifteen times, with at least five of the charges being felonies. Three weeks before President Nixon's defeat of George McGovern in 1972, and after two blatantly predetermined federal and state trials, Chavis and his Wilmington Ten codefendants were sentenced to a sum of 282 years in prison. Chavis's thirty-four years were the lion's share. The UCC paid $400,000 in bond fees for the defendants during the three-year appellate process that went to the U.S. Supreme Court, where Nixon appointee William Rhenquist recommended that the case be set aside without comment. With all judicial appeals denied at the state and federal levels, the Wilmington Ten would enter North Carolina's penal system in 1976.[32]

Chavis extended his activism to the state prison system of North Carolina. On one occasion, for instance, Chavis led the entire inmate population at Central Prison in nonviolent protest after two inmates there had been set afire in their cells. The head of the state's penal system reluctantly made several concessions while present at the Central Prison standoff, including fire extinguishers and legal representation for those who requested it.[33] Moreover, while an inmate at McCain Prison, Chavis held a hunger strike for 131 days in protest against the conditions in the prison. Chavis's *Psalms from Prison*, which was written in five of North Carolina's seventy-seven correctional facilities,[34] declares, "Prisons in the United States are institutions of state terrorism, hatred, violence, cruelty, and dehumanization. The prisons of North Carolina are like the national norm: overcrowding, excessive noise, poor or no lighting, brutality from guards, and decadent, filthy, rat-infested, ten-by-five-foot prison cells or large warehouse cell blocks." Chavis contends that "the prison cell became a place to do theology as a critical function of the ongoing freedom movement. . . . I wanted to extract from that experience whatever lessons were possible for future theory and practice."[35]

One year after Angela Davis was regarded as a "federal fugitive terrorist" by the president of the United States,[36] activists such as current Congressman John Conyers, author James Baldwin, SCLC's the Reverend Ralph Abernathy, the Soledad Brothers, and the Puerto Rican Nationalist Party coalesced and created the National Alliance against Racist and Political Repression, which made North Carolina the focal point of its activities.[37] Eventually the case against the Wilmington Ten disintegrated when three of the principal witnesses recanted their testimony in sworn affidavits proclaiming that they falsified their stories after being pressured by state and local law enforcement authorities. By 1979, the Wilmington Ten defendants had all been paroled. One year later, a federal appellate court reversed their convictions.

MILLION MAN MARCH ANTECEDENTS: BLACK POLITICS IN THE 1990S

Two critical developments with regard to black politics at the end of the twentieth century were the Jesse Jackson presidential primary campaigns in 1984 and 1988 and the 1995 Million Man March/Day of Absence. Chavis's lieutenancy would play an important role in both. These events encapsulate an inchoate, but no less identifiable, political movement that was largely a mobilization against a reactionary conservatism that was epitomized in the "Reagan Revolution" spanning the same period. Indeed, neither the Jackson campaigns nor the Million Man March/Day of Absence developed in political vacuums. Moderate increases in support of black nationalism in the 1990s help explain the Chavis–Farrakhan and Al Sharpton alliance as it was forged within the crux of a recalcitrant racial conservatism. It is also related to what Reed calls "the racial perfidy of American liberalism."[38] Black nationalism tends to incubate in contexts in which structural or political obstacles, whether real or perceived, extend superfluously to different segments of the community vis-à-vis the black middle class and the ghetto poor in a given period. It also thrives when conventional protest channels fail to yield expected "inclusionary" objectives.[39] Jackson's unprecedented primary campaign in 1984 convened around the same socioeconomic, ideological, political, and leadership issues that would resonate a decade later in the Million Man March/Day of Absence.

Prior to 1983, Farrakhan had been embroiled in a power struggle in the Nation of Islam with Elijah's son Wallace Muhammad and others at the Chicago headquarters. Muhammad sought to move the organization toward traditional Islamic beliefs and practices, while Farrakhan sought to resurrect Elijah Muhammad's racialized version. Farrakhan's previous reticence toward politics highlighted his allegiance to Elijah Muhammad's vision of the Nation of Islam as an essentially apolitical force with mostly conservative fundamentalist parochial concerns. This view, factored into the tension between Malcolm X and other Elijah Muhammad loyalists, resulted in Malcolm's assassination. To engage in politics was, to the Nation of Islam under Elijah Muhammad, tantamount to buying stock in the Titanic.

It was in the midst of the 1983 Harold Washington Chicago mayoral campaign and the initial Jackson campaign that Farrakhan first registered to vote. He emerged on the national political scene causing Jackson greater consternation with the Jewish community of New York, which Jackson had already alienated. From this point on, Farrakhan strove to leadership hegemony among the black leadership class. In August 1983 Minister Farrakhan was permitted by Coretta Scott King and the organizers of the twentieth anniversary March on Washington to address a crowd of roughly 300,000 people. There, Farrakhan stood side by side with the likes of Andrew Young, NAACP Executive Secretary Benjamin Hooks, James Farmer of CORE, Dorothy Height of the National Council of Negro Women, and King disciples John Lewis, Ralph Abernathy, and Benjamin Chavis of the UCC Commission for Racial Justice.[40] Farrakhan also joined with feminists such as Bella Abzug and Judy Goldsmith of the National Organization for Women, as well as representatives from the gay and lesbian communities, Jews, and labor.[41] The main target of this assembly was the Reagan-era recession results of high joblessness rates, unprecedented drug abuse, escalating poverty, and family dissolution among black communities in the nation's urban centers. Also present on the podium that day was Jesse Jackson, who used his speech to test the winds of a potential presidential campaign as the crowd cheered, "Run, Jesse, run!"

Farrakhan had been a political novice, and Chavis had very real differences with him. These centered on the question of political activism vis-à-vis the 1972 Gary, Indiana, Black Political Convention and the subsequent National Black Independent Political Party, for which Chavis authored, and Farrakhan opposed, a resolution for the creation of an all-black political party. Chavis's experience as a political activist with ties to both grassroots and the liberal establishment communities would prove, however, to be of great use to Farrakhan. This developed when he sought in the 1990s to moderate his image and to establish stronger ties to many of the civil rights establishment leaders and organizations that he harshly criticized throughout the 1980s.[42] The Chavis–Farrakhan alliance is thus open to the interpretation that this relationship was forged in order to lend a sense of "mainstream" legitimacy to Farrakhan. Much of his credibility had been lost because of the tumultuous conflicts with black elected officials, Jews, gays, and even black Christians who recoiled at his frequent anti-Christian jeremiads of the mid-1980s to the early 1990s. Farrakhan would broker this alliance, however, only after he alienated the fringe cultural and revolutionary nationalist groups that subsequently withdrew from the NAALS in 1996. Thus, Chavis would become even more necessary for Farrakhan in the future.

Chavis emerged in the 1980s as one of the earliest leaders to make accusations of "environmental racism" and bring attention to the grossly inordinate number of toxic sites located near poor and African American communities throughout the nation. Moreover, while serving as its clergy coordinator, Chavis played an important role for the Jackson campaign by forging what was initially a very tenuous interdenominational alliance of black churches that acted as the main institutional base of Jackson's candidacy. After all, support for Jackson as the preferred candidate to test a modern black presidential candidacy did not bode as well with the black establishment leadership class as it did among grassroots supporters. The powerful National Baptist Convention and the Atlanta Coalition of Coretta King, Ralph Abernathy, Joseph Lowery, and Andrew Young initially opposed a Jackson candidacy. Chavis, who had ties to Young through their UCC ministries, proved to be an important coalition builder on behalf of Jackson and the Rainbow Coalition.

Chavis, outcampaigning even Jackson for the position, eventually became the youngest executive director of the NAACP when his predecessor, Benjamin Hooks, retired from the post in 1993. Consistent with his Christian nationalist roots, Chavis immediately sought to move the NAACP away from the irrelevancy and near financial bankruptcy that had taken hold of the organization as early as the middle 1970s by forging a "united black front" of organizations that included Louis Farrakhan's Nation of Islam. Black leaders, both "organic" and elected, sought to forge a united front in response to an increasingly conservative U.S. public and in an attempt to address the conditions that confronted many black Americans. Courting Farrakhan would be the undoing of Chavis's stillborn NAACP administration in 1994, but the "why" of this relationship is best understood by examining the exigencies of the black experience in the 1990s.

Carmines and Stimson, using a Darwinian model, argue that issues such as race compete for political salience. They contend that race bested all other issues in terms of its adaptability and survivability, reaching a near fever pitch in the 1990s.[43] The struggle and subsequent release of African National Congress leader Nelson Mandela (1990), the revival of Malcolm X as a cultural and leadership icon, and the abolishment of apartheid in South Africa (1994) played critical roles in black politics in the final decade of the twentieth century. The Los Angeles–based national uprising (April 1992), the 1993 March on Washington, the June 1994 passage of California's anti-immigration Proposition 187, and the mass media–driven racial divide surrounding the O. J. Simpson trial coverage and verdicts (1994–95) further exacerbated these experiences. The November 1994 conservative congressional electoral mandate, the 1996 passage of California's anti–affirmative action initiative, and the burning of more than fifty black churches throughout the summers of 1996 and 1997 all prompted the White House to call for a "National Dialogue on Race." It signaled that race was still a highly salient concern.

While Jackson's efforts emerged out of an anti-Reagan grassroots mobilization in southern and northern cities in the early 1980s, the Million Man March/Day of Absence alliance emerged as the culmination of this series of widely publicized phenomena. In order to elucidate the most pertinent of these, the various economic, racial, and political factors that informed the black response to them are discussed here, particularly the New York City and Los Angeles civil disturbances and their effects and the attempt at a "sacred covenant" black united front.

One of the most telling developments of the period was black Americans' increasingly militant responses to several racial incidents in the legal and political systems. Extensive treatments of the racial politics in New York and Los Angeles illuminate this proposition. In fact, in many ways, the racial solidarity politics that characterized New York City politics throughout the 1980s and 1990s strengthened Farrakhan's position as an alternative among black leaders. He presented himself as the uncompromised "freest black man in America" because he was not beholden to interests external to the Nation of Islam.[44] Several violent incidents in New York City provided Farrakhan with the opportunity to speak defiantly to the issues of race in a manner that most liberal and moderate black leaders were unable to model.[45] New York was only a subtext to a much larger phenomenon. Indeed, the Los Angeles–centered upheaval that swept across the nation on 29 April 1992 was the most racially and economically taxing domestic uprising in contemporary U.S. life; property losses in billions of dollars, scores of deaths, and thousands of arrests reinforce this point. Latinos made up more than half of all those arrested (2,852); blacks represented 36 percent (2,037); whites/Anglos represented 10 percent (601); Asians and others represented 4 percent (147). Blacks also represented the largest number of casualties. And the political casualties of the unrest/riots of 1992 were manifold.[46] The Los Angeles civil disturbances exposed the undercurrent of high unemployment and social distance that was extant among those who were the primary participants. Cornel West's characterization of the 1992 upheaval allows for a closer linkage between it and the Million Man March. He concludes that "what happened in Los Angeles [and across the nation] in April of 1992 was neither a race riot nor a class rebellion. Rather, this monumental upheaval was a multiracial, trans-class, and largely male display of justified social rage. . . . What we witnessed in Los Angeles was the consequence of a lethal linkage of economic decline, cultural decay, and political lethargy in American life. Race was the visible catalyst, not the underlying cause."[47]

Several political scientists have highlighted the economic and racial corollary that was exacerbated by the events surrounding the Rodney King beating and verdict in Los Angeles in 1991 and 1992.[48] For instance, Pohlmann shows patterns of increased police brutality directed mostly at young Latino and black men that neither began nor ended with the Rodney King videotaped beating.[49] Between the Los Angeles rebellion and the Million Man March/Day of Absence, Chavis and Farrakhan successfully caucused with gang leaders across the nation in an attempt to "stop the killing."[50] But there would be no institutional support forthcoming to redirect the gangs into job training programs, for the truces were projected as an ominous threat to whites and law enforcement.

Marable also notes socioeconomic determinants of the 1992 Los Angeles civil disturbances. Indeed, he argues that the "Battle of Los Angeles" highlighted the general condition of despair in urban America that followed increased class and racial stratification:

> By contrast, since the late 1970s general conditions for most of the African-American community have become worse. . . . Standards in health care for millions within the African-American community have fallen, with the black male life expectancy declining to only 64.7 years in 1993. By 1990 about 12 percent of all Black families now live below the federal government's poverty level, and 46 percent of all black

families are headed by single women. . . . By 1992, 23 percent of all young African-American men between the ages of twenty and twenty-nine were in prison, on probation, parole, or awaiting trial.[51]

The largest total jail and prison populations of black men are in New York City (18,000 inmates) and Los Angeles (21,000 inmates). The intensification of economic hardship has been particularly devastating for the promotion of family life and cohesion for these young men. Sum and Fogg chronicle the real inflation-adjusted annual earnings and employment of American men (ages twenty to sixty-four years old) between 1973 and 1987. They conclude that while young men (twenty to twenty-nine years old) from *all* major subgroups suffered declines in their annual earnings because of a lack of education and manufacturing-based job markets during this period, black men have fared the worst.[52] The U.S. prison population, which has been disproportionately black especially since the Reagan declaration of the "War on Drugs" in light of the U.S. crack cocaine epidemic, more than doubled from 750,000 in 1985 to two million in the year 2000. In the same year of the Million Man March, 150 new U.S. prisons would be built and filled to capacity; young black men would make up the largest cohort in this increase. Indeed, by 1995 black male offenders accounted for nearly two-thirds of all prison admissions (64.1 percent) and two-thirds of the total year-end prison population (65.3 percent).

This is the area where the Nation of Islam has had its greatest impact. Few penal authorities can deny the successes of the Nation's prison rehabilitation programs. Recidivism among Nation of Islam converts tends to be much lower than that of the general population. The Nation's prison ministry stresses reform and knowledge of the individual's latent "divine self," which is based on the teachings of Elijah Muhammad. Further, the Nation of Islam insists on strict moral behavior and discipline, at least among its rank and file.[53] Upon release from incarceration, Nation of Islam members are given a "post," for example, as a distributor of its widely circulated *Final Call* newspaper, which is intended as a first step in their total rehabilitation. One of the long-standing demands of the Nation of Islam has been "the freedom of all Believers of Islam now held in federal prisons." In addition, the rapid increase in Latino and black male prison incarceration and the privatization of the U.S. "prison industrial complex" peaked during the period between the Los Angeles disturbances and the Million Man March.[54] As they were less than four years apart, the nationalist tenor of the Million Man March may have represented the same "largely male display of justified social rage" in different form. An important subtext, however, also concerns the strategic and ideological implosion among the black leadership class in the 1990s that highlighted the resurgence of nationalism among black Americans and, in turn, fostered the Chavis–Farrakhan alliance.

THE CHAVIS–FARRAKHAN–SHARPTON ALLIANCE

McCormick and Franklin confirm that the "racial and economic opposition to the inclusionary efforts by African-Americans has sparked longstanding strategic and tactical debates *within* the African-American community."[55] This political jockeying for leadership and organizational hegemony developed generally between the old-guard civil rights organizations such as the NAACP, the Coretta King–Andrew Young Atlanta Coalition, black elected officials, especially the Congressional Black Caucus, Jesse Jackson's Rainbow Coalition, and Farrakhan's Nation of Islam.[56] The black leadership establishment—which initially rejected Jackson in 1983—viewed Farrakhan as even more of a nuisance. Despite Farrakhan's appeal to various segments of the black community, his often vitriolic jeremiads concerning U.S. and Palestinian Jewry in particular and whites in general made him anathema to the black liberal integrationists. Kurlander and Salit contend that the Farrakhan–Sharpton–Fulani coalition represented a twin development alongside the "mainstream" liberal-integrationist strategies evident in the Jackson campaigns of the same period. They note, "From the experience of 1984 a new political development had taken place. Where once the radical elements of the Black political community had been fragmented and marginal, harried by the police and mired in sectarian strife, a new coalition of forces dedicated to radical Black political independence emerged. At its core was the . . . presidential candidacy of Lenora Fulani, who had articulated her 'Two Roads Are Better than One' campaign."[57]

Farrakhan continued to forge alliances with independent black radical Christian preachers and churches, black fraternal organizations, and fringe leaders. New York's Reverend Al Sharpton and Lenora Fulani and influential local leaders, such as Danny Bakewell of Los Angeles,[58] provided him with the organizational readiness and elite alliances that would prove invaluable as he remained on the periphery of black leadership in America. And this would serve him well because alienation was the experience of large segments of the individuals who tended to support him.

Political tensions manifested when Chavis, national secretary of the NAACP, sought to incorporate Farrakhan and other fringe nationalists into the "mainstream" black establishment class in 1993. Chavis sought through the NAALS to "provide a context for input and access of Pan-Africanists, progressives and nationalists into increased membership and active participation within the NAACP at national and local levels."[59] This effort might have gone unnoticed had Farrakhan not been included. While head of the NAACP, Chavis criticized the anti-Semitic rhetoric of the Nation of Islam's ministers and was the first person to contact Abraham Foxman of the Anti-Defamation

League (ADL) after Khallid Muhammad's vitriolic Kean College speech, which called for the murder of whites in general and Jews especially.[60] This speech would have obliterated the "sacred covenant" black united front that would soon be formed. Farrakhan's obsession with the militant Jewish Defense League, the ADL, and the misfit media identification of him as "the black Hitler" were problematic for Chavis and Kweisi Mfume, then leader of the Congressional Black Caucus. Another point of difference between Farrakhan and Chavis centered on the involvement of fascist Lyndon LaRouche in the NAALS.[61] At this juncture, at least organizationally, Chavis had equal standing with Farrakhan. Further exacerbating these tensions was Mfume's urging for the formation of a "sacred covenant" between black leaders and organizations including the Nation of Islam and Louis Farrakhan in September 1993. However, Mfume's "sacred covenant" was a direct response to the backlash that developed when Farrakhan was excluded from the thirtieth anniversary celebration of the 1963 March on Washington.[62] In turn, Mfume brought together members of the Nation of Islam, Jesse Jackson, Farrakhan, and Ben Chavis. Chavis was subsequently fired from the NAACP in August 1994 amid unsubstantiated charges of sexual improprieties with an NAACP employee.[63] Chavis's replacement in 1995 ironically would be Kweisi Mfume. Thus, the slight of Farrakhan and the firing of Chavis, perhaps more than any other immediate factors, prompted Farrakhan to call for the Million Man March two months later.

Surveys have shown that there was no single cause for the Million Man March. Neither the highly publicized O. J. Simpson criminal murder trial and verdict nor support for Nation of Islam Minister Louis Farrakhan scored high among survey respondents. But the resurgence of black nationalism and a desire for greater racial solidarity among blacks have been found to be primary factors that contributed to the Million Man March/Day of Absence assembly. Note, for example, the results of table 6.1, which identifies the "most important" reasons for attending the Million Man March. Some researchers consider most of these responses to be sufficient indicators of black nationalism.[64]

Table 6.1. Most Important Reasons for Million Man March Attendance.

Reason*	Percentage ($N = 1,046$)
Support for the black community	29
Support for black men	25
Demonstrate black unity	25
Demonstrate black economic strength	7

*Reasons given in response to the question, "[What is] the most important reason you decided to attend the Million Man March[?]"

This might explain why 69 percent of the Million Man Marchers cited the desire to "send a message to white people" as an important reason for attending the assembly. More than nine out of ten Million Man March attendants expressed the feeling that racism is a "big problem" in U.S. society; less than one-half of 1 percent (.4) stated that racism is "not a problem." Add to this the feeling among 74 percent of the Million Man March survey respondents that "over the last ten years [1985–95] racial tensions have increased" and its nationalistic components should come into clearer focus. As well, Tate reports that nearly 70 percent of the 1996 National Black Election Study (NBES) respondents agreed that what happens to black people in the United States has a lot to do with them as individuals—displaying an increase in this "racial solidarity/identity" measure over the 1984 survey responses. This point is partially confirmed by modest increases in certain forms of black nationalism between the 1984 and 1996 NBES,[65] as seen in table 6.2.

Table 6.2. Levels of Support for Black Nationalism in 1984 and 1996.

Statements/Questions	1984 Yes/Agree (%)	N	1996 Yes/Agree (%)	N	+/-
Black people should shop in black-owned stores whenever possible.	56	852	59	1,020	+3
Do you think blacks should form their own political party?	29	1,135	31	1,020	+2
Blacks should always vote for black candidates when they run.	19	852	12	1,020	-7
Blacks should not have anything to do with whites if they can help it.	4	852	3	1,020	-1

At dawn, on 16 October 1995, Benjamin Chavis called the Million Man March to order, chanting, "Long live the spirit of the Million Man March." The nation stood aghast at the specter of the mass of mostly black male humanity, ranging between 850,000 and two million in attendance, outnumbering the 1963 March on Washington fourfold. Data also show that the attendants were more nationalistic, of higher income and educational levels, and less identified with the Democratic Party than black American men in general. Some research even suggests that the Million Man March was the sole reason for the unprecedented increase in black male voter participation during the 1996 presidential election.[66] Exit polls estimated that there was an increase of approximately 1.5 million more black men who voted in 1996 when compared with participation levels in 1992. A follow-up poll conducted by the *Washington Post* revealed that 63 percent of its black respondents believed that the Million Man March/Day of Absence had a positive impact "on the black community as a whole." Within the five-year period following the Million Man March, the Christian "Promise Keepers," the "Million Woman's March," the "Million Youth March," and the 2000 anti-gun "Million Mom March" all held assemblies in the nation's capital. As marches go, the Million Man March was a watershed.

Throughout the summer of 2000 Chavis-Muhammed conducted nationwide meetings with members of the black political elite and workers from the Million Family March Local Organizing Committees. Where the Million Family March did not garner the media spectacle or grassroots response of the Million Man March in terms of numbers, it did demonstrate a political maturity that was absent in the former; especially as it enlisted a comprehensive agenda and follow-up plan. Many of the nationalists who participated in the Million Man March such as cultural nationalists Haki Madhubuti and Ron Maulana Karenga were absent. Noticeably absent, too, was the Reverend Jesse Jackson. The Farrakhan–Lyndon LaRouche alliance that developed within the context of the Million Man March had been supplanted by an equally peculiar alliance with the Reverend Sung Yung Moon and the Unification Church, which cosponsored the event. Farrakhan even presided over a mass wedding in a manner that was characteristic of the Unification Church.

The Million Family March was devoid of the aggregate racial conflicts that produced the response to the call for the Million Man March. But like the 1995 Million Man March, the Million Family March was held amid a presidential election that did include some racial issues. Throughout the year 2000, most blacks were unaware that the Million Family March was even being organized or held. Perhaps the forecast of economic good times limited the more recent march's impact. Several other assemblies held during the election season may also have diminished it. These included the anti–police brutality "Redeem the Dream" March led by Martin Luther King III and the Reverend Al Sharpton and the Black Family Reunion March led by Dorothy Height and the National Council of Negro Women. Data on the Million Family March and its impact on the political and social lives of African Americans remain forthcoming; still, it was apparent that it was less insurgent and reflected a multiracial alliance that had not characterized Farrakhan's work over the past two decades. The 2000 Million Family March National Agenda includes among its many social concerns, prison reform, the release of political prisoners in the United States, the elimination of racial profiling and the death penalty, and the restoration of voting rights to convicted offenders. A promise of the Million Family March National Agenda is to hold quadrennial marches through the year 2008 to coincide with national presidential campaigns and elections. The Million Family March also established a national "Million Family March Economic Development Fund," which is intended to serve as an economic clearinghouse for the national black community. A major criticism of the previous assembly was its slow accounting of a massive cash collection that was gathered. This, along with the Economic Development Fund, is Farrakhan's oft-mentioned "third force." Chavis-Muhammed appears to have given greater shape to this third force. What remains to be seen is whether the relative successes of the Million Man March/Day of Absence and the Million Family March will be sufficient capital for Chavis-Muhammed's possible national leadership succession in the Nation of Islam, an organization, unlike the NAACP, that would enable Chavis-Muhammed to continue his faith-based policy advocacy from a nationalist perspective.

The question remains whether Chavis-Muhammed's political aspirations can remain aligned with that of the largely parochial Nation of Islam when Farrakhan's administration ends. Even after his two-year battle with a debilitating illness, no word has been given as to who will succeed Farrakhan. But Chavis-Muhammed does preside over the nation's second-most visible ministerial post in Harlem, New York. It is also true that no single individual in the Nation of Islam could have organized a still impressive turnout at the Million Family March as did Chavis-Muhammed or is even as recognizable outside of the organization. The Million Man March and its follow-up marches may have accomplished Farrakhan's goal of personal and organizational legitimacy—after all, most blacks held increasingly favorable views of Farrakhan after the march and much of what he says today points more to legacy than to vision. Although there is likely to be the rattling of sabers that has historically plagued the Nation of Islam's leadership succession process, it is certain to remain true to Elijah Muhammad's conservative theology of Islamic black nationalism. Deviating from that vision—a vision that is increasingly out of step with the lived experiences of black Americans in the new century—can be lethal. Whoever succeeds Farrakhan must pass the litmus test of loyalty to that path to the satisfaction of Elijah Muhammad's "royal family," which holds the legal and political reigns of power in the seventy-year-old organization.

What can be said with some degree of confidence is that Chavis-Muhammed is likely to continue his faith-based work in pursuit of economic and racial justice for black Americans and multiracial coalition building to that end. Indeed, the conditions that first moved an adolescent Chavis to join the NAACP in segregated Oxford, North Carolina, remain and in many areas have even worsened. For as long as quality of life issues continue to plague black Americans disproportionately, it is highly unlikely that the same individual who endured gunshot wounds, death threats by supremacist groups, federal and state government misconduct, and political imprisonment will surrender his struggle for justice.

NOTES

1. Both of his names are used independently in order to broadly clarify stages of his pre-Islamic and Islamic leadership career; thus, "Chavis" and "Chavis-Muhammed" are not used interchangeably. Information for this chapter has been gathered from numerous telephone conversations with Benjamin Chavis-Muhammed and personal discussions with him from 1996 to 2000. It also includes data gleaned from attendance at Mosque Number 7 and meetings with local organizing members in Oakland, California, prior to the Million Man March and the Million Family March.

2. Louis A. DeCaro Jr., *Malcolm and the Cross: The Nation of Islam, Malcolm X and Christianity* (New York: New York University Press, 1998), 4.

3. Manning Marable, "Black Fundamentalism and Conservative Black Nationalism," *Race and Class* 39, no. 4 (April–June 1998): 164.

4. Chavis is the East Coast Regional Representative of the Honorable Minister Louis Farrakhan, which gives him pastoral jurisdiction in several East Coast cities including Newark, New Jersey; Boston, Massachusetts; New York City; and parts of Connecticut.

5. W. E. B. Du Bois alternated between various pan-Africanist, Communist, and integrationist organizations such as the NAACP. Chicago's powerful Congressman William L. Dawson and Harlem's flamboyant Minister and Congressman Adam Clayton Powell both switched briefly from the Democratic to the Republican Party during the 1960s. Chavis's switch was even more extraordinary, tantamount to Roy Wilkins joining Marcus Garvey.

6. For an excellent biography of Chavis, see Michael Myerson, *Nothing Could Be Finer* (New York: International Publishers, 1978).

7. Brian Glick, *War at Home: Covert Action against U.S. Activists and What We Can Do About It* (Boston: South End Press, 1989). See also Ward Churchill and Jim Vander Wall, *The COINTELPRO Papers* (Boston: South End Press, 1990); Ward Churchill and Jim Vander Wall, *Agents of Repression* (Boston: South End Press, 1990); and Nelson Blackstock, *COINTELPRO: The FBI's Secret War on Political Freedom* (New York: Vintage Books, 1975).

8. Chavis's mother, Elisabeth Ridley Chavis, was a teacher at the predominately black Central Orphanage School in Oxford and his father, Ben Sr., was a lay minister at the local Episcopalian congregation and a supporter of civil rights.

9. Neal R. Pierce, *The Border South States* (New York: Norton, 1975). Pierce notes that the majority of black North Carolinians resided in the eastern region of the state and made up one-third of the eastern region's total population.

10. The seeds of the abolitionist movement germinated nearly 150 miles south of Oxford in Wilmington, North Carolina, where David Walker was born a slave in 1785. According to

Myerson (*Nothing Could Be Finer*, 15), John Chavis distributed and preached the radical message of David Walker's *Appeal to the Coloured Citizens of the World*, which challenged the ethics of slaveholding Christianity. See Gayraud S. Wilmore, *Black Religion and Black Radicalism: An Examination of the Black Experience in Religion* (Garden City, N.Y.: Anchor Press, 1972), 47. Wilmore does not mention John Chavis by name, but he does note that there was a cadre of individuals who secretly distributed the *Appeal* in slave states. See John Hope Franklin, *The Free Negro in North Carolina 1790–1860* (Chapel Hill: University of North Carolina Press, 1995), for treatment of Chavis as a pre-Washingtonian accommodationist who supported gradual and limited emancipation and spoke strongly against Nat Turner's insurrection. North Carolina's legislature created these laws in response to both Walker and Nat Turner's insurrection in neighboring South Carolina in 1831.

11. Specifically, these were Willie P. Mangum, U.S. senator; Priestly Mangum, his brother; Archibald and John Henderson, sons of Chief Justice Henderson; Charles Manly, governor; and Abram Rencher, minister to Portugal and governor of New Mexico.

12. V. O. Key Jr., *Southern Politics in State and Nation* (New York: Alfred A. Knopf, 1949), 206–07. Key notes that "the state has a reputation for fair dealings with its Negro citizens. Its racial relations have been a two-sided picture, but nowhere has cooperation between white and Negro leadership been more effective, . . . more harmonious" (*Southern Politics in State and Nation*, 206–07). See Francis M. Wilhoit, *The Politics of Southern Resistance* (New York: George Braziller, Inc., 1973). Wilhoit shows how white supremacist groups failed to garner widespread support in the state among the citizenry and its political elite in reaction to *Brown*. Members of North Carolina's congressional delegation, namely, Charles B. Deane, Thurmond D. Chathman, and Harold Cooley, refused to sign the "Southern Manifesto," which denounced the *Brown* ruling (though only the latter survived in office as a result). In 1956, the state legislature, led by moderate Governor Luther Hodges, rejected a resolution in support of interposition against federally imposed desegregation.

13. Key, *Southern Politics in State and Nation*, 209. Key does acknowledge that North Carolina had been bereft of corruption for fifty years from the year of publication of *Southern Politics in State and Nation*, which would seem to be a reference to the 1898 "Wilmington massacre," but he makes no direct mention of it in the text. The Wilmington massacre, which resulted in the deaths of eleven blacks and the injuries of three whites and twenty-five blacks, is covered by John Hope Franklin, *From Slavery to Freedom* (New York: Alfred A. Knopf, 1967), 337, 341. Franklin reports that in 1894 as many as 300 black magistrates were appointed in the eastern Black Belt of North Carolina by its fusion government. Black sheriffs were in most counties, and in Wilmington alone there were fourteen black police officers; all of this changed when the fusion government was displaced. See also Myerson, *Nothing Could Be Finer*, 31, 79.

14. Jack Bass and Walter DeVries (in *The Transformation of Southern Politics* [New York: Basic Books, 1976], 219–21) highlight the 1950 Senate race between University of North Carolina President Frank Graham, a moderate Democrat, and conservative Republican Willis Smith, chairman of the Board of Trustees at Duke University. As Graham maintained a lead through the final weeks of campaigning, hand bills urging "WHITE PEOPLE WAKE UP" were distributed throughout the state; Smith was elected senator against a man who just months earlier held a 53,000-vote lead over him. Bass and DeVries also show that between 1965 and 1974, North Carolina's congressional delegations lagged

only behind South Carolina and Mississippi for having the "most conservative voting record" on civil rights.

15. Pierce, *The Border South States*, 34.

16. Myerson, *Nothing Could Be Finer*, 291. The other percentages of the registered black voting-age population are 64.0 percent in Alabama, 71.6 in Arkansas, 67.0 in Florida, 63.6 in Georgia, 61.8 in Louisiana, 67.5 in Mississippi, 57.3 in South Carolina, 76.5 in Tennessee, 84.7 in Texas, and 60.7 in Virginia.

17. Churchill and Vander Wall, *Agents of Repression*, 92. The original memo, dated 25 August 1967, ordered forty-four agency field offices, including those in Charlotte where Chavis was leading the University of North Carolina campus black activists, "to expose, disrupt, misdirect, discredit, or otherwise neutralize the activities of black nationalist, hate-type organizations and groupings, their leadership, spokesmen, membership and supporters, and to counter their propensity for violence and civil disorder. The activities of all such groups . . . must be followed on a continuous basis."

18. Myerson, *Nothing Could Be Finer*, 169.

19. U.S. Department of Justice, Bureau of Prisons, "National Prisoner Statistics Bulletin Number 46—Capital Punishment 1930–1970."

20. In 1960 the beating of several North Carolina A&T students while they were sitting peacefully at a lunch counter as they ignored Jim Crow signs at a Woolworth's store in Greensboro gained national attention. These student "sit-ins" quickly gained the support of local black churches and the civil rights establishment, including King's Southern Christian Leadership Conference (SCLC). A second major development in the racial politics of North Carolina came about when the younger generation created the radical reformist Student Nonviolent Coordinating Committee (under the direction of Ella Baker) less than 100 miles away in the capital city of Raleigh. See Robert C. Smith, *We Have No Leaders: African Americans in the Post–Civil Rights Era* (Albany: State University of New York Press, 1996). See Doug McAdam, *Political Process and Development of Black Insurgency, 1930–1970* (Chicago: University of Chicago Press, 1982), for a description of how tensions among the NAACP, the National Urban League and younger organizations such as the Congress of Racial Equality, and the SCLC over organizational hegemony increased. See also Stokely Carmichael and Charles V. Hamilton, *Black Power* (New York: Vintage Books, 1967).

21. See C. Eric Lincoln and Lawrence Mamiya, *The Black Church in the African American Experience* (Durham: Duke University Press, 1990). They caution against crude dichotomies that do not account for the amorphous quality of black religious responses to slavery, Jim Crow segregation, and race discrimination. It is logical to suggest, then, that various ideological orientations dominated the political scene and that their understanding depends largely on the broader context of race relations and the structure of political opportunities.

22. C. Eric Lincoln, *The Black Church since Frazier* (New York: Schocken Books, 1974).

23. It would also be appropriate to list Dr. Charles Cobb, executive director of the UCC Commission for Racial Justice as a major influence. He aided Chavis in his efforts, was a signer of the "Black Power" statement of the National Council of Black (formerly Negro) Churchmen, and served as one of its presidents.

24. Albert Cleage Jr., *The Black Messiah* (New York: William Morrow and Co., 1968). Pauline "distortions" usurped the "movement" of the black Messiah/Jesus to restore the

"Black Nation Israel," with an institutional church model centered on "pagan atonement" Christology. Pauline "individualism" supplanted the communal (nation) covenant relationship extant in Jehovah's dealing with his "chosen people" collective. Black Christian nationalism employs a doctrine of separateness and includes specific demands for land to be set aside.

25. Albert Cleage Jr., *Black Christian Nationalism* (New York: William Morrow and Co., Inc., 1972), xviii. According to Cleage, (Jehovah) God and (Jesus) Christ/Messiah were black, as evidenced by pre-Renaissance artistic depictions and "shrines" of a black Madonna and Christ child.

26. Chavis organized (Vance) countywide protests in Henderson and Warrenton, where more than thirty teenaged girls were imprisoned in the Raleigh Women's Prison for fighting. In Bladen County, Chavis responded to the public murders of four students in East Arcadia.

27. See Robert S. Lecky and H. Eliott Wright, eds., *Black Manifesto: Religion, Racism, and Reparations* (New York: Sheed and Ward, 1969).

28. Mary R. Sawyer, *Black Ecumenism* (Valley Forge, Pa.: Trinity Press International, 1994), 59. Most notably King was opposed by Joseph H. Jackson, the president of the powerful National Baptist Convention to which he belonged. See also James H. Cone, *Malcolm, Martin and America: A Dream or a Nightmare?* (Mary Knoll, N.Y.: Orbis Books, 1999), 146.

29. Myerson, *Nothing Could Be Finer*, 89. The congregationalist UCC had historic ties in abolitionism, the education of black clergy at its prominent institutions, and the distinction of being the only predominantly white Christian denomination to concede economic reparations ($1.5 million) for slavery and segregation upon the demands of the *Black Manifesto*. Its history of race progressivism, however, was no substitute for the likes of a Martin Luther King in the eyes of young Chavis. See John Auping, *Religion and Social Justice: The Case of Christianity and the Abolition of Slavery in America* (Mexico: Universidad Iberoamericana, 1994), 59. The American Missionary Association also played an integral role in opposing the largely racist colonization movement. It provided legal and financial aid to the Amistad Africans and allowed blacks to participate and take leadership positions in various societies, such as the Union Missionary Society, well before abolition. The American Missionary Association established and supported the Oneida Institute, Howard University, Berea College, the Hampton Institute, Atlanta University, Fisk, Straight (now Dillard) University, Tougaloo College, Talladega College, Leymone (now Leymone-Owen) College, Tillotson (now Huston-Tillotson) College, and the Avery Institute. The followers of Lewis Tappan, a Presbyterian minister, also created mixed schools for blacks and whites, namely, the Oneida Institute in Whitesboro, Lane Seminary near Cincinnati, and Oberlin College.

30. Well before there was a "Wilmington Ten" there was the "Chicago Eight," the "Panther Twenty-One," the "San Quentin Six," the "Attica Brothers," the "Soledad Brothers," George Jackson, and Dr. Angela Davis. The FBI's agent provocateurs (many of them planted black infiltrators and informants) took Hoover's directives to an extreme of manufactured assassinations, violent rivalries, illegal wiretaps, burglaries, marital breakups, false charges, and imprisonment. During these drastic times, the state predictably resorted to drastic measures.

31. After police killed a young activist, snipers shot and killed a local Klansman while he was attempting to carry out a "drive-by" shooting on the church. Then an unidentified Klansman reportedly shot Clifton Eugene at point blank range after he knocked on the

door of local activist, Molly Hicks. Police subsequently arrested Hicks, her teenaged daughter, and, eight months later, Ben Chavis Jr. for "accessory to murder, after the fact." Together, they made up the "Wilmington Three." Chavis was also charged with conspiracy to commit murder for the Klansman shooting and conspiracy to burn incendiary devices related to the grocery store burning thirteen months earlier.

32. Three of his coworkers, Jim Grant, T. J. Reddy, and Charles Parker, were charged with felonies related to the burning of a facility in Charlotte. In addition, both Chavis and Jim Grant were charged and tried for aiding and abetting federal fugitives Al Hood and Walter Washington, who were actually paid operatives used to incriminate both Chavis and Grant in a combination of five separate trials. Hood and Washington reportedly received up to $70,000 from the Justice Department, the Office of Alcohol, Tobacco, and Firearms, and the State of North Carolina for their services. See Myerson, *Nothing Could Be Finer*, 153. Chavis and Grant faced identical charges, but Chavis was found "not guilty," whereas Grant served two and a half years. Hood and Washington were also principal prosecution witnesses against the "Charlotte Three"; in that instance Grant and Reddy served four years each.

33. Just four years earlier, the same director of prisons, Lee Bounds, ordered guards to open fire on inmates during a disturbance, resulting in six inmate deaths. This may have militated against the use of lethal force on this occasion; it is also possible that Chavis's notoriety prevented violence from guards.

34. These were Central Prison in Raleigh, Caledonia State Prison Farm in Tillery, McCain State Prison in McCain, Asheboro State Prison in Asheboro, and Hillsborough State Prison in Hillsborough.

35. Benjamin Chavis, *Psalms from Prison* (New York: Pilgrim Press, 1983), xv–xviii.

36. This was with regard to weapons charges stemming from Jonathan Jackson's ambush in an attempt to free his brother and codefendants from a courthouse in San Rafael, California.

37. See Chavis, *Psalms from Prison*. Davis was made a chairperson, and Chavis was made vice president, of the National Alliance. A large number of religious organizations supported the Wilmington Three and Wilmington Ten. The National Alliance held an "International Day of Solidarity," securing and delivering 500,000 signatures to the White House demanding their release. Supportive declarations also came from places such as Helsinki, Brussels, Finland, Greece, Denmark, Berlin, and Iraq.

38. Adolph Reed Jr., "Black Politics Gone Haywire," *The Progressive* 59, no. 12: 20–23.

39. Joseph P. McCormick II and Sekou Franklin, "Expressions of Racial Consciousness in the African-American Community: Data from the Million Man March," paper presented at the Annual Meeting of the American Political Science Association, Boston, September 1998, 1–6.

40. During the 1980s, Chavis continued his work with the UCC Commission for Racial Justice, eventually becoming its executive director. Chavis used the notoriety that was engendered through the movement to free young activists in North Carolina to support similar cases throughout the country.

41. Manning Marable, *Black American Politics: From the Washington Marches to Jesse Jackson* (London: Verso, 1985), 118–19.

42. For an extended treatment of the "mainstreaming" of Farrakhan, see Arthur J. Magida, *Prophet of Rage: A Life of Louis Farrakhan* (New York: Basic Books, 1996); and

Mattias Gardell, *In the Name of Elijah Muhammad: Louis Farrakhan and the Nation of Islam* (Durham: Duke University Press, 1996).

43. Edward Carmines and James Stimson, *Issue Evolution* (Princeton: Princeton University Press, 1989).

44. He deliberately alienated white liberals as potential coalition partners while accusing black elected officials and black leadership in general of compromising local and national black interests. Indeed, Farrakhan became a kind of litmus test for black elected officials such as the late Tom Bradley of Los Angeles and New York City's David Dinkins, both of whom were torn between their liberal constituents on the issue of repudiating Farrakhan as a racist and anti-Semite. Subsequently, they both did so, but violent riots ended their historic mayoralties. Young, black, and mostly male street-level activists employed violence as a correction against what were perceived as racial injustices in cities governed by black mayors. As a result, Farrakhan's popularity gained momentum with poor urban-dwelling blacks, the black middle classes, and the young.

45. The lynch mob–style murder of a black man in the Howard Beach section of Queens set off a firestorm of events that eventually ushered in New York's first black mayor, former Manhattan Borough President David Dinkins, in 1989. Packaged as a healer, Dinkins counterbalanced black activist Al Sharpton, who played a critical leadership role during this period. For further information, see the chapter on Sharpton in this book. Later, the Farrakhan–Sharpton–Fulani coalition mobilized black New Yorkers against Jews and other white liberal Democrats—and even Dinkins, to the degree that he was unable to govern. The dissolution of the black–Jewish–liberal alliance in New York City came as violence erupted in the Crown Heights section of Brooklyn, heavily populated by both blacks and Jews. As a result, Dinkins lost his reelection bid against Rudolph Guliani in 1993, receiving only one of every four votes cast by white ethnic New Yorkers. The 95 percent support rate that he received from black New Yorkers was insufficient.

46. Darryl F. Gates eventually resigned his post and was subsequently replaced by two successive African American police chiefs, Willie Williams and Bernard Parks. District Attorney Ira Riener, who moved the trial venue of the four officers charged with beating King from Los Angeles to Simi Valley, and black Mayor Tom Bradley refused to seek reelection. Perhaps less obvious is the effect of the unrest and riot on the 1992 presidential election. At the very least, they heightened Bush's domestic vulnerability along with the economic decline that resurfaced amid the presidential campaign season.

47. Cornel West, *Race Matters* (New York: Beacon Press, 1993), 1–2.

48. Manning Marable, "Black Politics after the March," *New Statesmen and Society* 8, no. 376 (October 1995): 14–17. See also Hanes Walton Jr., *African American Power and Politics: The Political Context Variable* (New York: Columbia University Press, 1997), chapter 6; and Paula D. McClain and Joseph Stewart, *"Can We All Get Along?" Racial and Ethnic Minorities in American Politics* (New York: Westview Press, 1998). McClain and Stewart place the events of April 1992 within a larger racial/ethnic narrative reflecting a two-headed "dilemma" having to do with racial/ethnic "political inequality" and "voting rights" in the U.S. political system.

49. Marcus D. Pohlmann, *Black Politics in Conservative America*, 2nd ed. (New York: Longman, 1999), 146–47.

50. The Los Angeles–based "Crips" and "Bloods" and more than 1,000 other street gangs announced a truce less than one week after the Los Angeles rebellion; the truce

would last for more than one year. Six months later, the Chicago-based "Gangster Disciples" and "El Rookins" gangs brokered a tenuous truce in that city.

51. Marable, "Black Politics after the March," 204.

52. Andrew Sum and Neal Fogg, "The Changing Economic Fortunes of Young Black Men in America," *The Black Scholar* 21, no. 1 (January–March 1990): 48.

53. Drinking alcohol, using drugs, smoking, and premarital and extramarital sex are strictly forbidden and severely punished by the "Captains of the Fruit of Islam" soldiers.

54. Earl Ofari Hutchinson, "The Criminalization of Black Men," in *MultiAmerica*, ed. Ishmael Reed (New York: Penguin Books, 1997), 417–24. Hutchinson notes, for instance, that

> the crime mania nearly doubled America's prison population, from 900,000 in 1987 to 1.4 million in 1994. The prison-industrial complex replaced the nearly defunct military-industrial complex as America's largest growth industry. In California, there would be plenty of new prison cells. State taxpayers would pay $21 billion over the next thirty years to build twenty-five new prisons. . . . The criminalization of black men perpetuated the dangerous cycle of arrests and incarceration. The cycle has trapped thousands. In 1992, one out of four young black men were in jail, or in prison, on parole, or probation. Nearly half of America's 1 million prisoners were black. [This] top heavy number of black men in jail reinforced the public view that [blacks] committed most of the major violent crime in a America." ("The Criminalization of Black Men," 420)

55. McCormick and Franklin, "Expressions of Racial Consciousness in the African-American Community," 10.

56. Harold Cruse, *The Crisis of the Negro Intellectual* (New York: William Morrow, 1967). The bifurcation of black leaders and their organizations in the 1990s reflected the ideological conflicts between the various wings of the nineteenth- and twentieth-century black political elite. Both Robert H. Salisbury, "Political Movements in American Politics: An Essay on Concept and Analysis" (*National Political Science Review* 1 [1989]: 15–30), and Doug McAdam, *Political Process Model and Development of Black Insurgency, 1930–1970* (Chicago: University of Chicago Press, 1982), note the political "friendly fire" that is characteristic of movement entrepreneurs and movement organizations as they vie for charismatic leadership/organizational hegemony.

57. Gabrielle Kurlander and Jacqueline Salit, eds., *Independent Black Leadership in America* (New York: Castillo International Publications, 1990), 6. Farrakhan did endorse and finance some part of Fulani's initial presidential campaign and her 1990 run for the New York governor's seat. He said, "We pledge to work with and for Dr. Lenora Fulani's candidacy because we believe in her, although we may not necessarily support the New Alliance Party and all of the New Alliance Party candidates and positions and whatnot."

58. Danny Bakewell is a prominent businessman in Los Angeles who heads the Brotherhood Crusade, an organization dedicated to black civil rights and economic development. It gained notice in the events surrounding the videotaped slaying of a fifteen-year-old black girl, Natasha Harlins, by Korean grocer Soon Ja Doo. The organization picketed the store until it went out of business and led the campaign against Los Angeles Chief of Police Darryl F. Gates. Along with prominent Los Angeles Minister Cecil "Chip" Murray, Bakewell was Farrakhan's chief ally in the city. After the 1992 civil unrest, California's Republican Governor Pete Wilson, President George Bush, and Democratic presidential candidate Bill Clinton caucused with Murray's First African Methodist Episcopal Church before touring the ashes and ruin of the city.

59. Smith, *We Have No Leaders*, 94.

60. Ironically, Farrakhan's attempt at moderation came when his primary lieutenant Khallid Muhammad's bitterly racist/anti-Semitic diatribe at New Jersey's Kean College in late 1993 was published in a full-page ad in the *New York Times*. Farrakhan eventually rejected the "spirit" and "manner" but not the "substance" of Muhammad's speech.

61. Fulani would eventually distance herself from Farrakhan—as would Karenga and Madhubuti after the Million Man March—over Farrakhan's alliance with Lyndon LaRouche.

62. Gardell, *In the Name of Elijah Muhammad*, 262–63. The King–Young Atlanta Coalition refused to allow Farrakhan's participation, despite his participation ten years earlier, after receiving a letter from a rabbi threatening the withdrawal of Jewish financial support and participation. The "Saperstein letter" was eventually circulated by the Nation of Islam to expose the "uneven alliance" between Jewish interests and the black leadership establishment.

63. In June 1996, a nine-member jury rejected Mary Stansel's claim of sexual harassment and ordered her to reimburse the NAACP $63,500. Stansel had collected $87,200 when the payments stopped in May 1994. However, the presiding judge ruled that Chavis was liable for the remaining $245,200. Chavis was fired four months after the payments ended.

64. Lorenzo Morris, "The Million Man March and Presidential Politics," paper presented at the annual National Conference of Black Political Scientists, Savannah, Ga., March 1996.

65. See Michael C. Dawson, *Behind the Mule: Race and Class in African-American Politics* (Princeton: Princeton University Press), 190–91. The 1984 National Black Election Study (NBES) included an additional survey statement (which is excluded from the 1996 NBES), "Black children should learn an African language," whereas the 1996 NBES included the survey measure, "Black children should attend Afro-centric schools." I have chosen to exclude both because they highlight cultural black nationalism as opposed to the "political" black nationalism that the remaining measures highlight.

66. David A. Bositis, "Blacks and the 1996 Elections: A Preliminary Analysis," paper prepared for the Joint Center for Political and Economic Studies, Washington, D.C., 1996; Theodore Cross and Robert Bruce Slater, "The 1996 Elections: The Real Victor Was Black Voter Apathy," *The Journal of Blacks in Higher Education* (Winter 1996): 120–27; and James Lance Taylor, "Black Politics in Transition: From Protest to Politics to Political Neutrality?" Ph.D. dissertation, University of Southern California, 1999.

7

The Reverend Michael Farris: Baptist Social Movement Organizer

Mark Rozell

Michael Farris is an ordained Baptist minister, an attorney, and head of the national Home School Legal Defense Association. He is also the founder of the nation's first college for home schooled students and the founder and head of the Madison Project (PAC). He served as the director of the Washington State Moral Majority, legal counsel to Concerned Women for America, national treasurer for Pat Robertson's presidential campaign, and the Republican nominee for lieutenant governor of Virginia. He was also the plaintiff's attorney in the famed 1986 "Scopes II" trial, *Mozert v. Hawkins County Board of Education*. He is a prolific lecturer, author, and tireless advocate of Christian conservative causes, appearing frequently in leading news media. He and his wife Vickie are the parents of ten children, all educated at home.

With his extensive public profile, Farris is a controversial political figure. The trajectory of his activism has catapulted Farris from leadership in social movement organizations to a position of substantial influence in GOP politics. His efforts have inspired both intense loyalty among Christian Right supporters and harsh denunciations among his detractors.[1] Farris attracts such a range of feelings because his issues and activities are at the heart of the culture wars in the United States. Ultimately, Farris is most successful as a social movement organizer and legal advocate for home schooling. His one foray into the electoral realm was unsuccessful, in contrast to his other achievements in the public arena.

FARRIS'S POLITICAL ACTIVISM

Farris's initial entrance into the political realm was as the executive director of the Washington State Moral Majority in the early 1980s. He was then in his twenties and a recent law school graduate. His political activities in the Moral Majority suggest that Farris was a dedicated activist who took relatively uncompromising stands and, as a result, was very successful at building a state organization for the Christian Right. One study has reported that the Washington chapter was the largest state organization in the Moral Majority.[2]

During the early 1980s, the Reverend Jerry Falwell and the Moral Majority took positions on a variety of issues, including welfare reform, the minimum wage, and support for the apartheid government in South Africa. Farris objected to this broader agenda, and in 1982 he renamed the Washington State Moral Majority the "Bill of Rights Legal Foundation."[3] The founding document of the new organization, mailed to the former state Moral Majority members, defined the group as "the Christian alternative to the American Civil Liberties Union [ACLU]." The group's leading issues took on a different focus: abortion, prayer in school, and pornography. Among its goals were "removing secular humanism and other anti-Christian religions that have invaded many public schools and seek[ing] a return to true religious neutrality."[4]

Farris has been critical of conservatives who do not share his passion for the social issues. Like many social conservatives, Farris was disappointed when the Reagan administration focused primarily on tax cuts and a defense buildup but made little effort to push the social agenda of the Christian Right. He has characterized Robert Bork as "no friend of Christian principles,"[5] and he criticizes conservatives on the Supreme Court as more attuned to "an economic brand of conservatism" than to the concerns of Christian conservatives.[6] He warns Christian conservatives of "the dangers of close alignment with economic conservatives."[7]

Farris blasted the Reagan and Bush administrations for giving nothing more to Christian conservatives than "a bunch of political trinkets." The Republican presidents provided "very little real progress in terms of advancing our public policy goals or getting our kind of people appointed to positions of real influence."[8] Farris complained in 1991 that "our leaders, including President Bush and many other Republicans, are calling for reforms which are straight out of the playbook of the communist notion of planned economies."[9]

When Farris later sought public office, these statements caused him great difficulties. Farris's GOP critics charged that he was not a loyal Republican but merely a movement leader using the party to promote a narrow social agenda. Indeed, Farris advised Christian activists that voting by party affiliation should "not override . . . a candidate's view on abortion."[10] In 1984, Farris claimed that Republicans and Democrats were not very different. He derided both equally: "One wears Hush Puppies and the other wingtips. One is into big government; the other into big business."[11] Consequently, many of Farris's harshest critics today are fellow Republicans.

Nonetheless, Farris has always been a skilled movement leader. In the context of the early 1980s, he was not extreme among Moral Majority executive directors, nor was his rhetoric unusual. Indeed, in a number of respects Farris was thinking well ahead of other Christian Right leaders who would later learn the importance of engaging in broader political outreach and grassroots politics. Whereas other Moral Majority chapters floundered because of a lack of grassroots networks, Farris built an organization based at least as much on its activist base as on its letterhead and publicity. Whereas the other chapters were hampered by religious particularism, Farris appointed a broadly ecumenical board of directors to his organization. The very fact that he renamed the group signifies the mature political judgment that the "Moral Majority" name had become a liability and that he could more effectively promote his goals through a more neutral-sounding organization.

To mobilize a social movement, leaders frequently seek to attract publicity by issuing extreme statements, engaging in public forums, and demonstrating. As a young man in a highly visible role, Farris did the same. He relished the limelight and a good debate. He appeared in forums with ideological opponents, including drug guru Timothy Leary, oftentimes on college campuses. The events were spirited, and Farris did not flinch from heated exchange.

In one forum with a public school teacher who was an ACLU member, Farris fumed, "as a Unitarian my opponent practices transcendental meditation which is also practiced in schools. He should resign from teaching."[12] In another debate, an ACLU official objected to Farris's assertion that God ordained the husband always to be the head of the family. Farris angrily replied, "I take serious offense. . . . This is one of the most unbelievable things I've ever heard. I don't appreciate your slander against the word of God."[13] In one debate, in response to a question about abortion, Farris railed against declining moral standards and maintained that tolerance of such a social ill as abortion may result in future situations in which "we kill off old people to save money for sex education films."[14]

Years later, Farris expressed regret at some of his earlier controversial statements. When he ran for public office in Virginia, Farris's past record became the focus of both his nomination and then general election campaigns. He unsuccessfully tried to shed the past and pleaded, in effect, that he had matured. Yet Farris's controversial record defined the general election campaign, and he lost, running fully twelve percentage points behind the GOP's gubernatorial nominee.

FARRIS AS MORAL CENSOR

To understand why Farris was a controversial candidate for statewide office and remains a focus of some contention today, it is necessary to look at what his critics say about him. Some charge that Farris wants to ban books from public schools and libraries, as well as movies that he believes are offensive. They ground these charges primarily on Farris's legal briefs and arguments and on his early social movement activism.

In the early 1980s, Farris proposed a boycott of a Tacoma, Washington, television station for airing the film *The Deer Hunter* because of that film's often gritty language.[15] He also sought to control the lending of sexually oriented films at public libraries. He tried to get the Washington State Library to release to him the circulation records of a sex education film, *Achieving Sexual Maturity*, and unsuccessfully sued when denied that request on privacy grounds.[16] Farris apparently sought to determine if teenaged children were viewing the film. In 1989, Farris sued the Northern Virginia Community College to stop it from publicly showing the movie *The Last Temptation of Christ*.

Farris represented a parent's efforts to remove the book *The Learning Tree* from the Mead, Washington, high school curriculum. The book, which won an award from the National Conference of Christians and Jews, includes a character who refers to Jesus as a "long-legged, white son of a bitch." The plaintiff's daughter was not actually reading the book; instead, she had been assigned an alternative book by the school in response to the mother's objections. Yet Farris pushed for banning the book from the school curriculum and declared that the school had violated the First Amendment by establishing the religion of humanism as the officially sanctioned religion of the school. A federal judge dismissed Farris's claim.[17]

Farris earned his public profile as an attorney for the defense in the controversial 1986 case *Mozert v. Hawkins County Board of Education* in Church Hill, Tennessee. The case became known as the "Scopes II" trial, as Farris defended parents who had removed their children from public school classes that required what they considered religiously objectionable materials. According to the parents, the textbooks were anti-Christian and taught secular humanism. The parents objected to their children reading *The Wizard of Oz* because of anti-Christian teachings such as the description of a "good witch." Other books that the parents considered objectionable were *Cinderella* and *Rumpelstiltskin*, as well as a play based on *The Diary of Anne Frank*.

Farris's public statements about the case made him a lightning rod for controversy. He declared that a verdict against his clients would cause "the most stringent, strident political upheaval that this country has known since the Civil War" and would mean that "blacks in South Africa will have more rights" than Christians in the United States.[18] Although the federal district court ruled for the parents, a federal appeals court unanimously reversed the decision in August 1987, and on 22 February 1988, the Supreme Court turned down Farris's appeal. Farris famously fumed, "It is time for every born-again Christian to get their children out of public schools."[19]

Because of his roles in *The Learning Tree* controversy and the *Mozert* case, Farris's critics labeled him a book-banning extremist. Farris rejects the label and maintains that he defends the religious rights of parents to educate children as they see fit, even when he personally does not agree with the parents' decision. Farris has said that he has no objections to his own children reading the books in question and explained that his daughter attended a Christian college that assigned to students *The Diary of Anne Frank*.[20] Farris argued that he had never sought to ban the books from the classroom. Instead, he requested separate instruction and separate readings for the plaintiffs' children. Furthermore, he maintained that the plaintiffs objected to the fact that the class text substituted a play based on the book *The Diary of Anne Frank* for the real thing.

Nonetheless, in a 13 January 1986 letter to a potential expert witness in the case, Farris states that the classic children's books were religiously offensive and that a victory in the suit would set a precedent for removing such textbooks from public schools:

> The books teach witchcraft and other forms of magic and occult activities. The Bible teaches that witchcraft, magic, and the like are of Satanic origin and are to be avoided by Christians. Textbooks which teach the religion of Secular Humanism cannot be forced onto children. Although this finding will not directly require the judge to throw the textbooks out of the public schools, *it will be a major building block in the effort to force the public schools to remove such books and practices*. Such a finding could be widely publicized to demonstrate that a federal court made a finding that an ordinary textbook was teaching the religion of Secular Humanism.[21]

Farris argued that the school curriculum forced Christian children "to participate in witchcraft and Eastern religious activities in class."[22] Referring to the "Scopes II" trial label, Farris said that "in Scopes, the Christians chased the evolutionists out, but in this case, the evolutionist-humanists are chasing the Christians out. It's Scopes in reverse."[23]

Once again, rhetoric and actions that are useful in building a social movement and in mobilizing resources for legal struggles later proved damaging to Farris when he sought to run for public office. Farris's political opponents would one day focus their tactics on a number of the above statements and activities.

FARRIS ON THE PUBLIC SCHOOLS

Farris has argued that the public schools teach the religion of secular humanism. His critics charge that Farris wants to undermine public education, primarily because he advocated private tuition and home schooling tax breaks that would allow parents to purchase private education or to acquire the materials needed for a home school curriculum. In one interview, Farris declared an "intellectual war" between Christians and humanists. He has said that humanists are "destroying continuing generations of children" and were responsible for rampant sexually transmitted diseases, incest, and a faltering economy caused by a declining work ethic. He laments the impact of humanism on education: "The vast majority of public school teachers don't even know what's going on. They have been taught in their teacher colleges the religion of humanism without ever knowing what's going on."[24]

Farris accuses the public schools of conforming to "the state's program of values indoctrination."[25] He decries "the vindictive godlessness rampant in our modern school systems" and labels the public school system "a godless monstrosity."[26] He accuses the public schools of having "prescribed orthodox views of politics" such as the belief that "racial integration is good," when such views are "matters of opinion." Consequently, he contends that "the public schools are a multi-billion dollar inculcation machine" and "a far more dangerous propaganda machine" than that which existed in the former Soviet Union.[27]

In a 1987 speech, Farris declared public schools unconstitutional: "I believe . . . that public schools are per se unconstitutional. You can't run a school system without inculcating values. . . . Since inculcation of values is inherently a religious act, what the public schools are doing is indoctrinating your children in religion, no matter what."[28] In perhaps his best known statement about public education, Farris writes, "I would respectfully suggest that those who argue that public education is necessary for the preservation of our democracy are wrong."[29] He advises home schooling fathers that it is acceptable to refuse to abide by state educational standards that conflict with the family's religious views: "Mystical messages from God are every bit as constitutionally protected as solidly based scriptural convictions. If, for instance, you believe you have received a mystical communication from God telling you not to use the Standard Achievement Test, then your belief is entitled to constitutional protection."[30]

Farris also suggests that home schooling families should be exempt from local property taxes for the public schools. He calls an ideal home school law one in which the state refunds to home schooling parents all of the taxes they have paid for the public school system. This position has led critics to charge that Farris favors dismantling the public schools.[31]

FARRIS ON WOMEN AND THE FAMILY

Farris's writings on family relations and the role of women also became the focus of criticism. He advises that the father must, as head of the household, handle any legal conflicts that might arise over home schooling. If they are handled instead by the mother, "there is a tendency for her to become overly fearful and sometimes unnecessarily hysterical."[32] Furthermore, "a mother forced to be the family's 'protector' sometimes overreacts to an explanation of the legal possibilities."[33] Consequently, "you cannot and should not expect your wife to interface with government authorities for the protection of your home school."[34] Regarding his daughters, Farris writes,

> I don't want them chasing the feminist dream of the two-career marriage (or shall we say 'living arrangement'). They can't have it all. . . . Proverbs 31 teaches a godly balance: A woman who possesses work skills and financial resources, but who uses the skills in a way that keeps her home with her children and husband.[35]
>
> Furthermore, Your sons have at least three practical areas in which they need to be prepared for marriage: career and finances, home maintenance, and fatherhood.
>
> Your daughters have at least three areas in which they need practical preparation as well: teaching, homemaking, and motherhood.[36]

Farris writes that his children were not permitted to date until they were ready for marriage. He argues that "boy–girl relationships" are harmful and create "sexual temptation" and "sexual trouble."[37] Farris has admitted that his own harmful vice as a teenager was "chasing girls," a mistake that he wants his sons to avoid.[38] He blames this vice on an upbringing in which young boys in as early as the first grade were encouraged to have girlfriends and vice versa: "Vickie and I have raised our children with different expectations. Any discussion of a boy–girl relationship is always in the context of a possible marriage partner."[39]

FARRIS ON THE BIBLE AND AMERICAN LAW

Much of the controversy over Farris's constitutional interpretations revolves around his belief that the Constitution is founded on "God's moral laws." In his textbook *Constitutional Law for Christian Students*, Farris argues that the Declaration of Independence and the Constitution are like the "articles of incorporation" and the "bylaws" of a corporation. For a corporation, the articles of incorporation provide "the most essential rules" and the bylaws provide the "day-to-day rules for running the business." Consequently, for the U.S. government, the Declaration of Independence provides the overall guidance, and the Constitution, the day-to-day rules. Farris reasons that because the Declaration of Independence maintains that the nation should be bound by the laws of nature—or, "nature's God"—then "constitutional disputes should take into account the law of God . . . when there are constitutional disputes with moral implications"; he adds that "when faced with difficult questions—'Is pornography free speech within the meaning of the First Amendment?' or 'When does human life begin?'—the Supreme Court should be looking to the Declaration for guidance. The Declaration will, in turn, point the Court to the laws of God."[40]

This passage, among others, leads Farris's critics to argue that he is a proponent of theocratic government. They cite as support for that charge Farris's alleged former membership in a controversial group called the Coalition on Revival. Farris's name appears among ninety-seven Christian intellectuals who signed the group's 1986 "manifesto."[41] According to the manifesto, "We believe America can be turned around and once again function as a Christian nation as it did in its earlier years."[42] They also point to a document entitled *The Christian World View of the Law*, by Farris and political scientist Virginia C. Armstrong, which states, "We affirm that a society must inevitably choose between conflicting legal foundations and views of law and should choose Christian views and a Christian foundation because the Christian system is vastly superior to all alternatives."[43]

Farris denies ever signing the manifesto or cowriting the piece on a Christian view of the law. He says that he joined the group in 1984 and soon quit over philosophical differences. The founder of the coalition, Jay Grimstead, once said that he was "certain" that Farris had signed the 1986 document and quit at a later time. Armstrong recalls that she and Farris wrote different parts of the piece on a Christian view of the law and that "he certainly seemed to be in general agreement" with the completed version.[44] Farris's name is listed on the letterhead of a 1990 coalition publication. According to Farris, "They put my name on stuff. I can't help their print shop."[45] Whether it is true or not that Farris had anything to do with this group, his critics have made an issue of his alleged role to further the impression that he is an extremist.

HOME SCHOOLING LEADERSHIP

Farris may be best known today for his leadership role in the home schooling movement. He founded and is chairman of the Home School Legal Defense

Association (HSLDA), a nonprofit advocacy organization that promotes the interests of home schooling families. That organization in part is a defensive one: providing legal assistance to protect the home schools of members. It is also a proactive organization: engaging in issue advocacy at the state and federal levels. The HSLDA has a division called the National Center for Home Education. The center operates a Congressional Action Program to lobby the federal government through a grassroots network of HSLDA members throughout the country.

Farris rejects the common media label of him as a home schooling "advocate." He insists that he is not advocating home schooling for others so much as he is promoting the interests of those who choose to home school. This distinction seems lost on many who write about Farris, but he considers it an important one. He wants to get out the message that the rights and values of home schooling families must be protected and respected but that he is not actively trying to recruit others to join the home schooling movement.

In any case, his success is undeniable. *Education Week* anointed Farris as one of the 100 "Faces of a Century," and home schooling is now the fastest growing segment of the education community in the United States. Farris is widely recognized as a major force in moving home schooling into the mainstream as a respectable educational alternative. Farris explained to me, "When I started in this movement and was sitting on an airplane and people found out I home schooled, they would say, 'Is that legal?' Now when they find out I work for Home School Legal Defense Association, they ask, 'Why do home schoolers need defending? It's legal, right?'" Indeed, when HSLDA was founded, home schooling was either illegal or not recognized in most states. "Its fundamental legality is no longer an issue," Farris noted.[46]

The HSLDA frequently emphasizes the educational achievements of home schooled children, such as a recent national spelling bee champion, as well as competitive and even superior standardized test scores. As Farris has put it,

> Home schooling has sold its academic effectiveness to the American public by excelling. Not only have we won national spelling and geography bees, the vast majority of people now know a home schooling family and uniformly believe that their friends are also producing sharp kids. Home schooling is the comic strips, radio ads for cookware (the overachiever product line), the dictionary, and the NFL. (The Miami Dolphins' defensive end was home schooled. I got his NCAA scholarship reinstated after having been pulled because he had been home schooled.) Comic strips, commercials, and football define our pop culture. We are mainstream.[47]

Farris's recognition from *Education Week* and many others is largely because of his successes in lobbying and litigating on behalf of home schooling. Achieving legitimacy for home schooling required years of active legal activity spearheaded by HSLDA. Farris lists a number of his significant political and legal victories that helped to either protect home schooling or pave the way for the movement eventually to grow. Among these are the following:

1. A February 1994 lobbying campaign to defeat a bill in Congress that would have been detrimental to the interests of home schooling families. Farris helped mobilize over one million phone calls and letters to Congress in an eight-day period, turning a bill favorably reported out of committee into a 422-1 defeat on the floor of the House.
2. Successful efforts to have laws that effectively banned home schooling in Pennsylvania and Michigan overturned as unconstitutional; and additional successful efforts to reverse similar laws through political pressure in North Dakota and Iowa. Farris noted that in New York he was able to achieve laws more lenient toward home schooling.
3. Successfully litigating before the Supreme Court of South Carolina to halt state efforts to require home school parents to be tested with exams required of public school teachers.

Indeed, Farris has maintained that "we have done more than any other organization to hold social workers to the requirements of the Fourth Amendment. There is no child abuse exception to the Fourth Amendment largely as a result of our work. I personally litigated the key cases in this effort."[48]

Finally, Farris noted that home schoolers tend to have a high level of political activity because "the education establishment made the tactical mistake of attacking our fundamental freedoms. In so doing, they turned us into defenders of our liberty." Furthermore, he noted that once these activists experienced success through such efforts, they remained committed to political engagement on an even broader array of issues.

Farris sees little limitation to what the home schooling movement can achieve over the long term. It may seem hyperbolic, but it is nonetheless an earnest expression of Farris's hopes and expectations when he states that "the home schooling movement is well on its way to become the equivalent force within the GOP that the National Education Association is within the Democratic Party."[49]

RUNNING FOR PUBLIC OFFICE

Farris's success in the electoral arena is not so encouraging. He was elected as a delegate to the 1992 Republican National Convention from Virginia. As he explained, a number of the convention speeches appealed to his values, and he felt increasingly comfortable belonging to the Republican Party.[50] In

1993 Farris launched his campaign for the GOP nomination for lieutenant governor of Virginia. He ran against attorney Bobbie Kilberg. Although Kilberg too had never held elective office, she clearly was the GOP "establishment" candidate for her long service in Republican administrations.

The contrast between the two candidates could not have been more stark. Kilberg was pro-choice, a former member of Common Cause, a native New Yorker, and a "Rockefeller Republican." Despite her long record of public service and activism in GOP politics, Farris characterized her as the one in the race who was lacking true Republican credentials because of what he called her political liberalism.

The nomination contest and ultimately the general election were primarily struggles to define Farris. In order to broaden his base, Farris faced the difficult task of defending before the larger public earlier rhetoric that had been intended to mobilize a social movement. Farris's success as a social movement organizer proved a liability to running for office. His statements were generally unacceptable to the average voter, forcing him to justify and qualify his previous views.

Farris ran for the GOP nomination as a mainstream conservative and resisted his opponents' attempts to identify him as a candidate of the Christian Right. He said that he was running on a platform of legal reform, education reform, reducing government debt, and cutting taxes. Although his campaign tried to move the debate away from social issues and Farris's ties to the Christian Right, his opponents forced him to defend his past activism and his written and legal record.

Farris denied some past statements and claimed that others had been taken out of context. When asked to defend his statement that public education is not necessary to the survival of democracy, he claimed what he really meant was that "the public school monopoly is dangerous to democracy." He protested, "At the end of the chapter, when I've talked about public school monopoly for pages and pages and pages, I shorten it up and just say the public schools."[51] Regarding his proposal that home schooling parents get their public school taxes refunded, Farris first claimed that he only offered the idea as a joke. When that explanation met resistance, he responded, "If I made a mistake in writing that, it's a mistake. But it's not what I believe."[52]

During the 1993 campaign, Farris dismissed criticisms of some of his comments and writings as based on "8-, 10-, 12-year-old stories."[53] He did admit to overstatements when he called public schools "a godless monstrosity" characterized by "vindictive godlessness." When challenged about these assertions, Farris said that he just reacted with frustration to a public school teacher having ripped up a Christian art project completed by a client's child.⁵⁴ He expressed regret at having called for all Christians to remove their children from the public schools and explained that he really did not believe what he had said: "It violates my own philosophy to tell other parents how to raise their kids."⁵⁵

Farris's defense of his role in the *Mozert* case was spirited and attracted the most attention. He noted that the case had not sought to ban the books but merely to require the school to offer children an alternative curriculum if their parents believed that the books violated their religious beliefs. When confronted with the text of his letter to Phil Suiter described above, Farris claimed that the controversial passage had nothing to do with book banning. He said that his goal had been "that the books will be voluntarily improved," although he had in fact written of "the effort to force the public schools to remove such books and passages."⁵⁶

Farris claimed that those books were not "even mentioned in either the decision of the United States District Court or the U.S. Court of Appeal."⁵⁷ Nonetheless, the district court decision referred to the part of *The Diary of Anne Frank* that the plaintiffs claim proved "that the books, as a whole, tend to instill in the readers a tolerance for man's diversity."⁵⁸ Farris's court filings referred to the books that his clients considered controversial.

Kilberg's campaign had some success in defining Farris as a radical Christian Right candidate. Even the archconservative editorial page of the *Richmond Times-Dispatch* labeled Farris out of the mainstream. In a scalding reference to Farris, an editorial stated, "Never underestimate the GOP's ability to nominate a flake who turns voters against the entire ticket."⁵⁹ Several moderate and traditional GOP organizations in Virginia unsuccessfully tried to mobilize moderate Republican opposition to Farris.

Farris won the nomination not because he persuaded moderates that he was a mainstream candidate but because he mobilized his base. His supporters attended the convention in large numbers and heavily outnumbered GOP moderates. Farris mobilized home school parents in large numbers, most of whom had never attended party conventions.⁶⁰

Farris lost the general election to incumbent Lieutenant Governor Donald Beyer. The GOP otherwise had a banner year in Virginia, easily winning the gubernatorial and attorney general races by large margins. The unusually high percentage of ticket splitters made it clear that attacks on Farris as a Christian Right extremist had worked.

Farris seriously considered running for the GOP nomination for the U.S. Senate in 1996 against incumbent John Warner but ultimately backed out and instead signed on as a comanager for the losing challenger, James Miller. Farris also worked as the Virginia director of Patrick Buchanan's 1996 presidential campaign. He remains active in Virginia politics in various capacities but has ended all discussion of seeking elective office. Though defeated for public office, Farris successfully mobilized large numbers of new activists into the GOP, and a good many of them have moved on to positions of influence within local GOP organizations in Virginia.

After losing the election, Farris established a political fund-raising organization, the Madison Project, modeled after Emily's List. Using the technique of bundling contributions, the Madison Project supports a number of conservative candidates at the state and congressional levels in each election year. Farris explained that the major criterion for support was that the candidates must be both pro-life and economic conservatives dedicated to limited government and free markets.[61]

THE EVOLUTION OF A SOCIAL MOVEMENT ACTIVIST

Farris attracted national attention once again in 1999 with his plans to found the first college for home schooled students. The uniqueness of the concept and Farris's goals for Patrick Henry College attracted both attention and controversy. Farris promulgated rules that banned alcohol and required students to wear uniforms and go to chapel daily. Students were prohibited from dating on their own and were expected to inform their parents of any "potential romance." They were also expected to get parental approval and to socialize together only when in groups of other students.[62] According to one school pamphlet, students must "show evidence of a personal relationship with Jesus Christ." They must abide by a seven-point statement of faith, including the belief in the literal resurrection of Christ. The application for admission required that prospective students "please describe your personal relationship with Jesus Christ." The college's policy of nondiscrimination says, "The college shall maintain its constitutional and statutory right to discriminate on the basis of religion in order to accomplish the religious mission of the college."[63] The college's literature makes it clear that a major goal of the educational philosophy is to "transform America" by training students for careers in government and ultimately elective office. All students enrolled at the college will be government majors, and all will work in some form of public policy internship. College promotional literature states, "Eventually, these highly qualified public servants will themselves begin to run for elective office and will have the opportunity to lead our nation back to its constitutional roots." Furthermore, "In the future, we believe that many of our graduates will join the ranks of 84 former [congressional] staffers who are now members of Congress." Farris pointed out that currently one-fourth of the Patrick Henry College student body is on the Debate Team: "I am confident that no other college in America has such a great number of people preparing for leadership. Home schoolers are disproportionately interested in politics because they have seen what it is like to live in a nation that attacks our freedoms. They want to change it.[64]

Farris's latest endeavor appears to be a sensible and potentially fruitful alternative to his seeking public office again to promote certain values in the political process. He is a very skilled and effective social movement organizer, but it is highly unlikely that he can ever achieve the kind of broad-based acceptance in the secular world of politics necessary to win meaningful elective office. His past record has generated the kind of "paper trail" that makes him an easy target for partisan attacks. Yet that same paper trail wins him plaudits from fellow Christian social conservatives who regard his past activities and statements as based on the courageous convictions of a man willing to openly profess his religious values in a hostile secular culture.

Farris once tried in vain to redefine himself as a mainstream conservative acceptable to an electorate in a largely conservative state. After that failure, he soon began to gear up for another long-shot campaign only to decide against running. He thus made a realistic decision that his policy goals could best be achieved through other endeavors than elective office. For this reason, it is hard to accept criticism of Farris as motivated by personal power or recognition. He certainly is not shy about recognition, but it is difficult to come to any conclusion other than that he sees publicity as a useful vehicle for promoting his goals.

For example, once Farris broke ground for his home schoolers' college in 1999, he achieved the kind of national and international publicity that established colleges with large public relations offices can only dream about. Granted, not all of the publicity was positive, and much of it carried criticism of the very idea that home schooled persons would, upon reaching adulthood, attend a college only with other people educated at home, thus creating a limited and insular learning environment. Nonetheless, the free media coverage provided extensive publicity that helped Farris reach his intended audience of people inclined to view such an institution favorably.

As long as Farris remains actively involved in politics by promoting his goals through social conservative–based organizations, he will be an effective leader and a major positive force for the Christian Right. Perhaps one day he will again feel the call to run for public office, but it is hard to imagine that, without a dramatic transformation of the culture, the result would be any different than his 1993 defeat. But right now Farris is doing what he does best: fostering a social movement and working on behalf of home schooling.

NOTES

1. Strictly speaking, I do not consider Farris a "religious leader" as opposed to a social movement activist and leader who attracts the support of conservative, religiously motivated people.
2. Jeffrey K. Hadden, Anson Shupe, James Hawdon, and Kenneth Martin, "Why Jerry Falwell Killed the Moral Majority," in *The God Pumpers: Religion in the Electronic Age*, eds. Marshall W. Fishwick and Ray B. Browne (Bowling Green, Ohio: Bowling Green State University Popular Press, 1987), 101–15.
3. Dave Workman, "Moral Majority Changes Name, Methods," *Spokesman-Review*, 8 September 1982.
4. Bill of Rights Legal Foundation, mailing, 1982.
5. Michael P. Farris, *Where Do I Draw the Line?* (Minneapolis: Bethany House Publishers, 1992), 41.
6. Michael P. Farris, *The Home School Court Report*, November 1991.
7. Michael P. Farris, *Home Schooling and the Law* (Paeonian Springs, Va.: Home School Legal Defense Association, 1990), 68.
8. Farris, *Where Do I Draw the Line?* 43.
9. Farris, *The Home School Court Report*.
10. Farris, *Where Do I Draw the Line?* 159.
11. Stephen Bates, "Christian Crossover," *Washington City Paper*, 30 July 1993: 22.
12. *Yakima (Washington) Herald Republic*, 5 April 1981.
13. Jason Vest, "Mike Farris, for God's Sake," *Washington Post*, 5 August 1993: C6. See also Stephen Bates, *Battleground* (New York: Henry Holt and Co., 1994), 116.
14. Timothy Egan, "Timothy Leary Meets the Moral Majority," *Seattle Post-Intelligencer*, 16 April 1981: A2.
15. Vest, "Mike Farris, for God's Sake," C1, C6.
16. Mike Layton, "State Moral Majority Chief Talks about Sex," *Seattle Post-Intelligencer*, 15 February 1981: A2.
17. Vest, "Mike Farris, for God's Sake," C1, C6. See also Bates, *Battleground*, 114.
18. Vest, "Mike Farris, for God's Sake," C6; and Bates, *Battleground*, 116.
19. Michael Farris, "People and Events," *Church and State* (April 1988): 14.
20. Michael Farris, interview by the author, 12 August 1994. Herein referred to as "the 1994 Farris interview."
21. Letter from Michael P. Farris to Dr. Phil Suiter, 13 January 1986, emphasis added.
22. Michael Farris, "Fundamentalists Often Targets of Bigotry," *USA Today*, 11 August 1986: A8.
23. Michael Farris, *Michael Farris in His Own Words* (Washington, D.C.: People for the American Way, 1993), 3.
24. Carol M. Ostrom, "Conservative Christians Fear 'Humanist Takeover,'" *Seattle Times*, 9 April 1983.
25. Farris, *Home Schooling and the Law*, 10.
26. Farris, *Home Schooling and the Law*, 53.
27. Farris, *Home Schooling and the Law*, 59–60.
28. Bates, "Christian Crossover," 22. Farris said more recently, "I would refine my view of that a little. Public schools do indoctrinate kids in values, and when there's a financial

monopoly in values indoctrination, that's unconstitutional" (quoted in Bates, "Christian Crossover," 24).

29. Farris, *Home Schooling and the Law*, 64.
30. Farris, *Home Schooling and the Law*, 128–29.
31. Farris, *Home Schooling and the Law*, 71–72.
32. Michael P. Farris, *The Home Schooling Father* (Hamilton, Va.: Michael P. Farris, 1992), 28.
33. Farris, *The Home Schooling Father*, 29.
34. Farris, *The Home Schooling Father*, 33.
35. Farris, *The Home Schooling Father*, 58.
36. Farris, *The Home Schooling Father*, 66.
37. Farris, *The Home Schooling Father*, 63–65.
38. Layton, "State Moral Majority Chief Talks about Sex," A2.
39. Farris, *The Home Schooling Father*, 63–65.
40. Michael P. Farris, *Constitutional Law for Christian Students* (Paeonian Springs, Va.: Home School Legal Defense Association, 1990), 15.
41. Coalition on Revival, *A Manifesto for the Christian Church* (Sunnyvale, Calif.: Coalition on Revival, Inc., 4 July 1986).
42. Coalition on Revival, *A Manifesto for the Christian Church*, 19.
43. Virginia C. Armstrong and Michael Farris, *The Christian World View of Law* (Sunnyvale, Calif.: Coalition on Revival, Inc., 1986).
44. Warren Fiske, "Lt. Governor Hopeful Distances Himself from 'Hyperbole' of the Past," *Virginian Pilot and Ledger-Star*, 5 September 1993: A3.
45. Peter Baker, "Farris Asserts His Religious Tolerance," *Washington Post*, 18 October 1993: B3.
46. Michael Farris, interview by the author, 29 November 2000. Herein referred to as the 2000 Farris interview.
47. The 2000 Farris interview.
48. The 2000 Farris interview.
49. The 2000 Farris interview.
50. The 1994 Farris interview.
51. Michael P. Farris, "Remarks to the Virginia Beach City Republican Committee Meeting," 12 April 1993.
52. Farris, "Remarks to the Virginia Beach City Republican Committee Meeting."
53. Mike Allen, "An 'Unscary Mike' Offered to Voters," *Richmond Times-Dispatch*, 29 August 1993: B1.
54. Allen, "An 'Unscary Mike' Offered to Voters," B1.
55. Mike Allen, "Farris Positions: Extremist or in Sync?" *Richmond Times-Dispatch*, 29 August 1993: B5.
56. Michael Farris, "Conservative Forum," *Human Events*, 22 April 1994: 2.
57. Fenton Communications, "The Truth about the Textbook Controversy," "Farris for Lt. Governor" press release, 1 May 1993.
58. *Mozert v. Hawkins County Board of Education*, 582 F. Supp. 201, 202, E.D. Tenn. 1984.
59. "Ticket to Ride," *Richmond Times-Dispatch*, 28 February 1993: F6.

60. For the delegate survey findings, see Mark J. Rozell and Clyde Wilcox, *Second Coming: The New Christian Right in Virginia Politics* (Baltimore: Johns Hopkins University Press, 1996), chapter 4.

61. The 1994 Farris interview.

62. See http://www.phc.edu.

63. This information comes from the Patrick Henry College promotional literature and website (http://www.phc.edu). For the college's statement of nondiscrimination, see http://www.phc.edu/DOCS/Application.asp.

64. The 2000 Farris interview.

8

Dr. Ron Sider: Mennonite Environmentalist on the Evangelical Left

Joel Fetzer and Gretchen S. Carnes

For the last twenty-five years, Ron Sider has been one of the most outspoken Evangelical proponents of economic justice and nonviolence.[1] As a Mennonite with long experience working with InterVarsity Christian Fellowship, Sider bridges traditional Anabaptism and the progressive elements of mainstream Evangelical Protestantism.[2] With his classic book *Rich Christians in an Age of Hunger*, he challenges the materialistic values of some American Evangelicals and provides an alternative political perspective for many young, theologically orthodox Christians. Sider is also the founder and president of Evangelicals for Social Action (ESA), a major educational and political organization.[3] In this chapter, the experiential and theological underpinnings of Sider's political thought are examined in order to explore the effectiveness of his efforts to achieve economic justice and environmental protection.

THE MAKING OF RON SIDER

Much of Sider's religious and political perspective is rooted in his upbringing as a Mennonite farm boy.[4] Born to Brethren in Christ parents who farmed and pastored in rural southern Ontario, Canada,[5] Sider adopted their "Anabaptist concern for peace and justice and for the poor." His parents' relatively limited economic resources further motivated Sider's commitment to economic justice. Marrying during the Great Depression, his mother and father "certainly didn't have a lot of money. I didn't start out in life seeing the world from the windows of a Cadillac but, rather, it was the other side." Sider's parents also demonstrated Christian generosity and compassion in their personal lives, adopting an "older sister after all the rest of us were born." Sider maintains that being born a Canadian Anabaptist saved him from "imbib[ing] the kind of God and Country stuff" common to mainstream U.S. evangelicalism, that it gave him a "distance from the culture that . . . has been a real blessing."[6]

EARLY POLITICAL ACTIVISM

Despite this ideological background, Sider did not originally plan a career in political activism. A first-generation college student, he began his undergraduate work at Waterloo Lutheran University intending to become a high school teacher. Because he "liked school," Sider continued on to Yale University for his M.Div. in theology and Ph.D. in Reformation history.[7] Midway through his graduate studies, Sider planned on teaching history at a secular university and advising the local chapter of InterVarsity Christian Fellowship.[8] Living in inner-city New Haven, Connecticut, during the 1960s, however, gradually led him to focus more on problems of economic injustice and racial oppression because he and his wife, Arbutus, resided "at the edge of and then in the center of the black community." They sat with their African American landlords the night Martin Luther King Jr. was assassinated and "got to know the couple's son, who was an angry young man open enough to talk to a white person." Such experiences, he says, "got me so concerned with the racial issues that I felt I could not just go on reading Latin and German for my dissertation. So finally in 1967 I joined the NAACP . . . and did a voter registration drive in '67–'68."[9]

By now acting director of Messiah College's Philadelphia campus,[10] Sider organized "Evangelicals for McGovern" four years later.[11] Together with John Alexander, of *The Other Side* magazine, and a few other left-of-center Evangelicals,[12] the group hoped to win support and contributions from the "rising tide of theologically orthodox Christians who are not chained to conservative politics." The association raised almost $6,000 for McGovern.[13] And it enlisted such Evangelical leaders as political scientist and later Michigan State Representative Stephen Monsma, sociologist and inspirational speaker Tony Campolo, and Fuller Seminary Professor Lewis Smedes.[14] Sider now views the effort as something of a failure because of McGovern's poor showing at the polls.[15] Nonetheless, Sider's work as secretary of "Evangelicals for McGovern" started him thinking about whether "we need some organized structure for evangelical political action . . . say Evangelicals for Justice in Society."[16]

Evangelicals for Social Action

Sider's dream of an Evangelical political organization became a reality with the founding of ESA in 1973. In February of that year, Sider, Wallis, Smedes, African American ministries specialist William Pannell, political scientist and later U.S. Representative from Michigan Paul Henry, and five other Evangelical leaders met at Calvin College to plan a "Thanksgiving Workshop on Evangelicals and Social Concern." Two of Sider's major goals for this workshop were to create a "national organization" for "Evangelical social activists" and to decide whether "such an organization should regularly endorse political candidates . . . or . . . limit itself to taking stands on particular issues."[17] At the 1973 Thanksgiving Workshop itself, fifty prominent Evangelicals discussed such questions and issued the "Chicago Declaration of Evangelical Social Concern," the founding document of ESA.[18] In this declaration, theologically conservative Christians such as theologian and founding editor of *Christianity Today* Carl F. H. Henry, U.S. Senator from Oregon Mark Hatfield, children's advocate Eunice Schatz, and Canadian Director of InterVarsity Christian Fellowship Samuel Escobar lamented that American Evangelicals "have mostly remained silent" in the face of violations of the "social and economic rights of the poor and oppressed." The signers further called on "our fellow evangelical Christians to demonstrate repentance in a Christian discipleship that confronts" such "social and political injustice[s]" as "materialism," the "maldistribution of wealth and services," and the "national pathology of war and violence."[19]

The mainstream Evangelical establishment appears to have approved of the Chicago Declaration and the creation of ESA. *Christianity Today*, for example, reported respectfully on the Thanksgiving Workshop. "Perhaps [the declaration's] most remarkable aspect," the magazine opines, "is that so much could be agreed upon by so many with such a broad range of viewpoints (from Anabaptists . . . to Calvinists . . . and even some whose socio-economic philosophy approximates neo-Marxist economics)."[20]

A few fundamentalists such as Bob Jones, however, opposed the establishment of ESA. In a 1974 editorial in his magazine *Faith for the Family*, he labeled ESA's founders "supporters of . . . socialis[m] and fellow-travelers with the avowed 'Liberals' on political, economic, and social questions." Jones further claimed that the Chicago Declaration "follows the socialist-communist line, . . . decr[ies] old-fashioned American patriotism[,] . . . [and] disregard[s] completely what the Bible has to say about . . . woman's true place in society." ESA-style "New Evangelicalism," he concluded, "is not a 'position' but a half-way house between Biblical orthodoxy and apostasy."[21]

Defying such criticism, ESA sponsored the second in its series of annual conferences in 1974, this time focusing on ways to implement the Chicago

Declaration. Participants agreed, for example, to produce literature on both the social and the personal implications of the Gospel. They also decided to hold fifteen regional workshops on Evangelical social action to encourage "pastoral-prophetic" ministries to state and local politicians, to help promote women's studies programs at Evangelical colleges, and to help fund civil rights activist John Perkins's training of African American community developers.[22] ESA primarily focused on such conferences until 1978, when it expanded its operations to include more educational efforts as well. In 1987 ESA expanded again to include more staff and launch more publications and affiliated organizations.[23] ESA itself currently has a membership of approximately 5,000.[24] About one-third of ESA's annual budget of as much as $1 million originates from its donor base of members and friends. Over the years, the other two-thirds has come from such foundations as the Pew Charitable Trusts, the Luce Foundation, and the Bauman Foundation.[25]

Activism for Economic Justice

Sider draws on a wide range of biblical sources to justify his activism on behalf of the poor. First, he notes that God works through history to empower the economically disadvantaged: "Because the poor are despoiled, because the needy groan, [the Lord] will now rise up" (Ps. 12:5). Second, he contends that God sometimes actually opposes the rich: "Now listen, you rich people, weep and wail because of the misery that is coming upon you" (James 5:1). Sider also cites scriptures that predict punishment for rich people who "do not defend the rights of the poor" (Jer. 5:26–29) or who fail to share their abundance with the needy (Luke 16:19–31). Third, he uses the parable of the sheep and the goats to show that by serving the poor we are actually serving Jesus (Matt. 25:40). Fourth, Sider argues that if we do not stand up for the poor, "we are not really God's people." For example, because "Israel failed to correct oppression and defend poor widows, Isaiah insisted that Israel was really [a] pagan people" (Isa. 1:10–17).[26]

Sider's religious commitment to the poor manifests itself in his writing of *Rich Christians in an Age of Hunger*, which he still sees as one of the "best, most effective thing[s he has] done for the poor."[27] The idea for the book originated with a sermon Sider gave to a small Baptist church in Connecticut in 1967. After comparing global poverty with what the Bible has to say about the subject, Sider concluded by proposing his now famous "graduated tithe," that is, a commitment to donate a larger proportion of one's income to the poor as one's income rises. He and his wife practiced this while he was still a graduate student, and in the early 1970s he published a version of the sermon as an article in InterVarsity Christian Fellowship's *HIS* magazine. Inter-

Varsity Press then offered to publish a short book version of the article, but by the time Sider was finished with the manuscript, the first edition of *Rich Christians in an Age of Hunger* (1977) was the result.[28]

At its core, the book contrasts the desperate poverty of much of the world with the wasteful, affluent lifestyles of most Americans. It sets out a theological case for economic justice for the poor and attacks evil, poverty-producing social structures. Finally, *Rich Christians in an Age of Hunger* proposes specific steps that individuals and groups can take to better the lives of the world's poor. This final section includes not only the graduated tithe but also such proposals as living communally, making microloans to the poor, and canceling the debts of poor nations.[29]

Now in its fourth edition, *Rich Christians in an Age of Hunger* has become an influential Christian classic. *Christianity Today* listed it among the 100 most important religious books of the twentieth century,[30] and it has been translated into eight different languages.[31] When Sider wrote the book, however, he thought that "if it sold 2,000 copies, that would be great. But it really took off." At its peak the text was selling at 23,000 to 24,000 copies a year, and total sales now amount to "well over 350,000."[32] So powerful has been the impact of the book that it even appears to have inspired part of a Billy Graham Evangelical Association film.[33]

Rich Christians in an Age of Hunger has also provoked numerous critical articles and books,[34] the most vehement being David Chilton's self-published work,[35] *Productive Christians in an Age of Guilt Manipulators*. Sporting a cover illustration of a Sider-like figure hanging himself, *Productive Christians in an Age of Guilt Manipulators* attacks Sider for "serving the cause of totalitarianism" and suggests that he is a "calculating propagandist" trying to "convince us that we need a bigger Big Brother."[36] Chilton likewise characterizes Sider's advocacy on behalf of the poor as "encouraging covetousness, envy, and theft against the rich."[37] Another, more thoughtful, critic is John Schneider, who argues in *Godly Materialism* that "to whatever extent we become poorer we create degrees of poverty and . . . foster the powerlessness that comes with being poor. Oddly, by so identifying with weakness, we reduce our power to liberate, and we thus lose our capacity to identify ourselves with the liberating power of God."[38]

Advocacy for the Environment

It is important to understand the theological foundations of political advocacy by ESA and its affiliate, the Evangelical Environmental Network (EEN), on behalf of the environment. Unlike many secular environmental groups, Sider and EEN are concerned about the responsible treatment of nature—what

Sider calls "creation." Sider believes that the Scriptures articulate clearly that human beings have a responsibility as stewards to God to care for God's creation. He emphasizes that "human beings alone are created in the image of God" and that as a result they "alone have a special 'dominion' or stewardship." According to Sider, human beings are "free to use the resources of the earth for human purposes." However, "at the same time, our dominion must be the gentle care of a loving gardener, not the callous exploitation of a self-centered lord." Sider elaborates this point when he writes, "Only a careful, stewardly use of God's plants and animals is legitimate for human beings who worship the Creator."[39] Sider sums up this point by writing, "Our use of the nonhuman creation must [always] be a thoughtful stewardship that honors the creation's dignity and worth in the eyes of the Creator."[40]

Sider also points out that there is an innate goodness to all creation. He cites Job 39:1–2, highlighting that "God watches over the doe in the mountains. No human being may ever see her. But God counts the months of her pregnancy and gently watches over her when she gives birth!"[41] Thus, the doe "has an importance quite apart from any human being."[42]

Sider further directs us to the Old Testament because it offers "explicit commands designed to prevent exploitation of the earth. Every seventh year, for instance, the Israelites' land was to lie fallow because 'the land is to have a year of rest' (Lev. 25:4)." Sider notes that when the Israelites failed to obey this command, God sent them into captivity in Babylon partly to give the land an enforced rest (Lev. 26:34, 42–43).[43] There is a plethora of similar examples from the Bible that Evangelical environmentalists use to argue their case.

These religious ideas have been translated by Sider into the Evangelical Environmental Network. EEN was established in 1993 as a joint project of ESA and the Christian development agency World Vision. Initially funded largely by foundations such as the Pew Charitable Trusts, EEN currently has an annual operating budget of $200,000–$300,000. ESA and EEN now have a combined membership of approximately 9,000.[44]

At base, EEN is a Christian environmental group that focuses on educating Evangelicals about the public and individual "care of creation." The organization's statement of principles reads, "As followers of Jesus Christ, committed to the full authority of the Scriptures, and aware of the ways we have degraded creation, we believe that biblical faith is essential to the solution of our ecological problems." The group uses the term *creation*, rather than *nature*, for two reasons. First, it highlights its belief that a Creator created the Universe (or "the heavens and the earth" [Gen. 1:1]). Second, it emphasizes the relationship between humanity and nature, as both are part of creation, with human beings as fellow creatures with the other creatures God created. EEN laments and tries to publicize several major abuses of creation: (1) land degradation, (2) deforestation, (3) species extinction, (4) water degradation,

(5) global toxification, (6) the alteration of the atmosphere, and (7) human and cultural degradation.[45]

EEN's philosophy is that humans must live with limits in their lives, no matter how uncomfortable this concept is for their accustomed affluent lifestyles. EEN's leaders, therefore, see a strong link between materialism and environmental degradation. Stan LeQuire, former executive director of EEN, voices this idea when he writes, "I believe that the care of creation strikes a deadly blow to the notion of personal sovereignty, freedom, and convenience. It is part of the human condition to want, and to crave a world of our own making."[46] Sider also addresses this connection when he writes, "Biblical faith provides a framework for dealing with the destructive rat race of unbridled consumption . . . . [W]e are created in such a way that human wholeness and fulfillment come not only from material things, but also from right relationships with neighbor and God"; he further adds that "the call to care for the neighbor and the summons to sabbatical worship of God both place limits on more material things."[47] Sider points out an interesting change regarding the politics of materialism. He has stated, "It's absolutely striking to me that in the '70s and in the '80s when I was first talking about living more simply, . . . the driving force was lowering poverty and freeing up resources . . . whereas in the '90s the drive to talk about materialism and living more simply was coming more from the environmental movement, including secular sources."[48] Nonetheless, the adverse consequences of a societal emphasis on material things remain an important issue in alleviating both poverty and environmental degradation.

According to Sider, LeQuire, and the current executive director of EEN, Jim Ball, EEN's primary focus is education rather than public policy. Sider stated that the initial goal is to "help a large number of Evangelicals to really understand creation care—that caring for the environment is something any faithful Evangelical needs to do."[49] EEN's distribution of pro-environmental pamphlets, information packets, and sermon-writing kits are designed to advance this goal.[50] Sider has also claimed that education is the most important mechanism because "in order to implement concern for creation, one must have a much larger group of people who understand the issues. By starting at the individual and congregational level, we can eventually change" national policy.[51] Education, then, is the first step in a national push for a change in environmental policy.

THE EVANGELICAL ENVIRONMENTAL NETWORK AND THE ENDANGERED SPECIES ACT

Although EEN is primarily about educating Evangelicals about "creation," occasionally the group lobbies on vitally important bills before Congress.[52]

Perhaps the greatest policy success of EEN was its involvement with the Endangered Species Act legislation that was debated in 1996. The act was originally signed into law in 1973 by Richard M. Nixon and "extended protection to fish, wildlife and plants that were likely to become either extinct as well as those in immediate danger. [The act] has been credited with saving hundreds of species."[53] The bill under consideration in 1996, Young–Pombo H.R. 2275 (sponsored by Don Young [R-Fla.] and Richard Pombo [R-Calif.]) would have weakened the act's provisions concerning the scope of activities prohibited, recovery plans, authority over federal agencies, and permits for incidental takes.[54]

EEN wanted not only to prevent the Young–Pombo bill from being enacted but also to strengthen the Endangered Species Act even further. EEN therefore eventually supported the Endangered Species Recovery Act as well.[55] This proposed legislation focused more on habitat protection than specific species, which EEN believed would do a better job at caring for creation because it protects all species living in certain areas, not just the endangered or threatened ones. Thus, rather than waiting for a crisis, EEN hoped to help protect animals' habitats and so prevent particular species from ever becoming endangered or threatened.

To initiate the campaign against the Young–Pombo bill, EEN first wrote a "Resolution of the Christian Environmental Council of the Evangelical Environmental Network on the Care and Keeping of Creation and Its Living Species."[56] Next, the group announced a $1 million campaign to educate the public about the Young–Pombo bill's likely effect on endangered species and about some better ways to protect threatened wildlife. EEN then "built an evangelicals' response to Congress on the Endangered Species Act," with approximately 2,000 signers. It also introduced *Green Cross* as an environmental magazine, Green Cross as "the Christian-based activist organization," and itself, ENN, as a "key spokesperson-sponsoring organization for evangelicals on creation care." EEN's strategy also included coalition building and recruiting a small group of spokespersons to "take a stand on the Endangered Species Act and speak on behalf of the Endangered Species Act." This group was made up of influential Evangelical leaders, and all physically lobbied members of Congress on the same day in Washington. They met with as many legislators as possible and distributed EEN's literature all over the Hill. Furthermore, eighteen states were selected as target states for the endangered species cause because EEN already had a "core of people for press conferences and public events" there. A number of editorials and letters to the editor were sent out to all of the targeted states, as well as a series of advertisements telling the public about the Endangered Species Act and about EEN's care for creation and support for "God's gorgeous garden." An issue of EEN's

Green Cross magazine was dedicated to the Endangered Species Act and was "handed out at all press conferences and events" and also "receive[d] general distribution."[57]

One of the most interesting aspects of EEN's success on the Endangered Species Act is that the group was able to show both legislators and the public that not all Evangelicals belong to the Christian Right. The political climate at the time was also intriguing because Republicans had just taken over Congress and were not very enthusiastic about stricter environmental protection. LeQuire described his memories of that time: "We went to Washington, D.C., with [a] message that not all Evangelical voters were in the hip pocket of the new Republican majority" and that "some of us are Evangelical Christians and Republicans, and we just don't agree."[58] EEN came along and showed politicians and constituents alike that a lot of Christians do care about creation (nature) and are willing to show their support for the Endangered Species Act. EEN worked with a number of secular environmental groups on the campaign but was able to reach out to a far greater audience because of its religious perspective. LeQuire has emphasized EEN's particular religious message: "Other groups had been working on the Endangered Species Act for a very long time, and we owe a lot to them . . . [for example,] the Audubon Society, the Wilderness Society, and the Sierra Club; but ours was a distinctly religious message, and at times we take exception with some of the [secularly motivated] environmental groups." Although EEN was not "in the hip pocket of the Audubon Society or any other groups whatsoever," LeQuire also added that "we [EEN] really owe them a debt of gratitude for what they've done, from different motivations perhaps."[59] People who would not normally listen to environmentalists were listening because their fellow Christians were telling them to. Sider stated that EEN "was called to action to counter the perception that [theologically] conservative Christians are often at odds with environmentalists."[60] When Sider was asked whether he thought that his being a religious leader, as opposed to a purely secular political activist, has made him more effective or less effective, he answered, "Taking the whole Bible seriously . . . has enabled me to cross all kinds of lines."[61]

EEN was able to take advantage of what other secular and religious environmental groups had already accomplished concerning the Endangered Species Act and to add the group's own sources of mobilization. Because of the highly public nature of the act, EEN and its coalition partners knew that they had to mobilize the masses in order to obtain the constituent support necessary to defeat the Young–Pombo bill. By recruiting along with many environmental and religious organizations, EEN was able to attract large-scale, mass political support. EEN distributed over 30,000 "Creation Care" packets to churches across the country, for example, and also created a nationwide network of "Noah Congregations." Both the packets and the network of congregations were designed to help mobilize popular Evangelical opinion in favor of the Endangered Species Act.[62] This appeal to Evangelicals was critical to defeating the Young–Pombo bill. And this targeting of Evangelicals made the influence of the environmental coalitions stronger by showing that some Christians do care for the environment, thereby creating a rather strange political coalition that in the end was extremely successful.

Sider indicated that he believes the Endangered Species Act to be ESA's (and correspondingly EEN's) "most visible, specific, effective political activity."[63] It is important to keep in mind, however, that influencing public policy is not the most important goal of ESA or of EEN. Sider, LeQuire, and Ball all emphasize that education is the number one priority of EEN. EEN wishes to educate both decision makers and the public at large, hoping to influence policy decisions indirectly through its educational campaigns.

The timing and political climate when the Endangered Species Act was up for renewal had a lot to do with EEN's success in obtaining its policy goal. However, EEN also hired a media consultant and strategically planned physical lobbying activities in Washington, D.C. Sider described the political environment at the time: "It was just a coming together of the right situation. The Republican majority had gotten elected in November '94, and there was a lot of talk about them rewriting the Endangered Species Act in a way that would greatly weaken it." Sider did not hesitate to suggest that EEN played a crucial role in the renewal of the Endangered Species Act: "To this day the environmental movement would say that we won that round because of the Evangelicals."[64]

Other Environmental Issues Treated by the Evangelical Environmental Network

According to LeQuire, there are four other major environmental issues about which EEN has lobbied occasionally: (1) global warming, (2) deforestation, (3) "takings" legislation, and (4) environmental justice. Most recently EEN has been including clean air and water in its campaign. On the first issue, Sider cites many scientific sources who say that global warming has already begun. Since the beginning of the Industrial Revolution, humans (mostly from affluent countries) have spewed an incredible amount of carbon into the air, thereby instigating global warming. Thus, the link between materialism and environmental degradation is clear. The Industrial Revolution resulted in a grandiose emphasis on material items as a way to make humans happy and fulfilled, but, as Sider points out, this concept is inherently flawed. Sider writes, "People persist in the fruitless effort to quench their thirst for meaning and fulfillment with an ever-rising river of possessions . . . the personal result is agonizing distress and undefined dissatisfaction."[65] His solution regarding this problem is to educate people so that they realize that "our deepest joy comes from right relationships—with God, neighbor, and the earth."[66]

Sider's emphasis on such character transformation (at a personal level to place less emphasis on material happiness and goals and more emphasis on right relationships) is a unique attribute to his goals as a leader. As opposed to secular leaders, who focus strictly on the political aspects of their issues, Sider also concentrates at the personal level on character transformation. This ingredient seems to help both his religious/nonpolitical goals and his political agenda.

EEN's second current focus, rapid deforestation, "increases flooding, deprives us of potential new medicines, and contributes to increasing levels of atmospheric carbon."[67] "Takings" legislation, EEN's third concern, "would force taxpayers to reimburse property owners when laws reduce potential income from the unrestricted use of their property."[68] EEN argues that taxpayers need not compensate private landowners who are obliged by environmental laws to forgo certain profitable activities in order to protect an endangered or threatened species living on their property.

Environmental justice, EEN's fourth lobbying area, has two elements: domestic and international. There is some commonality between the two, however. For example, both domestically and internationally the poor suffer the most as a result of environmental degradation. Sider explains that the poor are most affected in two ways: first, the poor "suffer from reduced food production, unproductive land, polluted rivers, and toxic wastes that the rich do not want in their backyards"; second, "unless we can redirect economic life in a way that dramatically reduces environmental decay, it will be impossible to expand economic growth enough in poor nations to enable them to enjoy a decent standard of living."[69] Sider blames this problem on structural injustice.

Sider sees a clear relationship between poverty and environmental degradation. He notes, for example, that the affluent from rich, industrialized countries produce much more atmospheric pollution as a result of the burning of fossil fuels than do poor countries. The poor, however, also damage the environment: "Developing nations often use less sophisticated technology and consequently consume fossil fuels less efficiently." Sider further argues that "desperately poor people try to farm marginal land and [consequently] destroy tropical forests."[70] He also notes that "in the Third World, forests are cleared to provide for cropland, fuelwood, cattle ranching, and tropical hardwood for industrial countries." The reason that many people in poor countries farm marginal land is because "inequitable land distribution, population growth, and expansion by large, export-cropping corporations have left them little land on which to grow food for their families."[71] Poor countries export crops while their own populations do not have enough to eat because their own peoples cannot afford to purchase the crops. Thus, the crops are exported abroad to rich countries and sold at low prices for American standards. According to Sider, the link between poverty and environmental degradation is thus abundantly clear.

CONCLUSION

Ron Sider has achieved three major successes in his career as a politically active religious leader. The first is the publication of *Rich Christians in an Age of Hunger*, which has sold hundreds of thousands of copies in nine different languages. Sider has noted that when the book was first published he had no idea that it would become so successful. His goal was to share his views and ideas about poverty, the environment, and social justice, and 350,000 copies later it is easy to see that he has accomplished this goal. In addition, Sider has written a plethora of books, book chapters, and articles in which he has been able to share his ideas. However, none has equaled the impact of *Rich Christians in an Age of Hunger*.

Second, Sider's founding of Evangelicals for Social Action has also had an impact on economic policy. The group began with a few people writing the "Chicago Declaration of Evangelical Social Concern" and grew into a significant educational and lobbying organization. The emphasis on action, particularly political action, is certainly one of the reasons why ESA has been able to accomplish what it has and why it has been able to survive as long as it has on limited funding.

Sider's third great accomplishment as a politically engaged religious leader has been his success in influencing the passage of the Endangered Species Act. After launching a $1 million campaign focused on eighteen states, Sider must have realized the potential of his political influence. The timing and political climate at the time certainly contributed to the success of the Endangered Species Act, but Sider's role as an Evangelical leader was also crucial. Newspaper articles appeared in virtually all major cities in the country. Advertisements ran in magazines, in newspapers, and on television. A letter writing campaign further publicized EEN's message. And some of the most influential Evangelical leaders stormed Washington on the same day to have their voices heard regarding the endangered species legislation.[72] Ultimately, after a tremendous amount of work and spent energy, not only was the Young–Pombo bill defeated but EEN and its allies were able to come up with a better version of the act. The Endangered Species Recovery Act emerged, which contains an emphasis on habitat protection so that species can be saved before a crisis occurs.

Sider's career as a religious-political leader has been focused and successful. He admits that an overwhelming amount of work still needs to be done before economic and environmental justice will become a reality for all people. Perhaps his greatest contribution, then, is that Sider also recognizes that his efforts have helped American Evangelicals, in particular, to recognize a new dimension of their religion and to increase their commitment to this goal.

NOTES

1. Although Sider is probably known almost as much for his advocacy of nonviolence as for his antipoverty activism, this chapter does not cover his pacifistic activities extensively. For more on his opposition to war and other forms of violence, see Ronald J. Sider, *Christ and Violence* (Scottdale, Pa.: Herald Press, 1979); Ronald J. Sider and Richard K. Taylor, *Nuclear Holocaust and Christian Hope* (Downers Grove, Ill.: InterVarsity Press, 1982); Ronald J. Sider, *Completely Pro-Life* (Downers Grove, Ill.: InterVarsity Press, 1987); and James R. Lynch, "Christian Peacemaking Teams: Opportunities for Active Peacemaking," in *Sustaining Peace Witness in the Twenty-first Century: Papers from the 1997 Quaker Peace Roundtable*, ed. Chuck Fager (Wallingford, Pa.: Pendle Hill Issues Program, 1997), 263–304.

2. Jeffrey McClain Jones, "Ronald Sider and Radical Evangelical Political Theology," Ph.D. dissertation, Northwestern University and Garrett-Evangelical Theological Seminary, 1990.

3. Evangelicals for Social Action, "Dr. Ron Sider: President and Founder of Evangelicals for Social Action," 1999, http://www.esa-online.org/esa/staff.html, accessed 2 October 1999; Evangelicals for Social Action, "Dr. Ron Sider—President and Founder of ESA," 2000, http://www.esa-online.org/about/staff/sider.html, accessed 23 February 2000.

4. Ronald J. Sider, discussion at meeting of the Muskegon County Cooperating Churches, Grand Rapids, Mich., 25 June 2000, notes by Gretchen Carnes.

5. The Brethren in Christ make up a small, "peace-church" denomination similar to the Mennonites. Besides their Anabaptist heritage, the Brethren in Christ draw on historical links to German Pietism and the Wesleyan Holiness tradition. They belong to the National Association of Evangelicals as well as inter-Mennonite agencies such as the Mennonite Central Committee. Sider is currently an ordained minister in both the Brethren in Christ and Mennonite Church denominations. See James E. Horsch, ed., *Mennonite Directory 1999* (Scottdale, Pa.: Herald Press, 1999), 196; Ronald J. Sider, interview by Joel Fetzer, Germantown, Pa., 28 May 2000—herein referred to as "the first Sider interview"; Ronald J. Sider, "Curriculum Vitae, Ronald J. Sider," photocopy (Eastern Baptist Theological Seminary, Wynnewood, Pa., 2000), 6.

6. Quotes in this paragraph are from the first Sider interview.

7. The first Sider interview.

8. Jones, "Ronald Sider and Radical Evangelical Political Theology," 406–07.

9. Jones, "Ronald Sider and Radical Evangelical Political Theology," 406.

10. Sider, "Curriculum Vitae, Ronald J. Sider"; Ronald J. Sider, letter to "Dear Friend," n.d. [September 1972?], Evangelicals for Social Action Papers, collection 37, box 1, folder 4, Billy Graham Center Archives, Wheaton College (Ill.).

11. Jones, "Ronald Sider and Radical Evangelical Political Theology," 407. Sider himself, however, could not yet vote because he did not become a U.S. citizen until 1974.

12. Michael McIntyre, "Religionists on the Campaign Trail," *The Christian Century*, 27 December 1972: 1319–22; Ronald J. Sider, letter to Joel Fetzer, 30 August 2000, personal files of Joel Fetzer, Central Michigan University.

13. Ronald J. Sider, letter to Stephen Charles Mott, 14 November 1972, Evangelicals for Social Action Papers, collection 37, box 1, folder 4, Billy Graham Center Archives, Wheaton College (Ill.).

14. Sider, letter to "Dear Friend."

15. The first Sider interview.

16. Sider, letter to Mott.

17. Ronald J. Sider, letter to David Moberg, 19 February 1973, Evangelicals for Social Action Papers, collection 37, box 1, folder 12, Billy Graham Center Archives, Wheaton College (Ill.); Ronald J. Sider, letter to Richard Pierard, 18 June 1973, Evangelicals for Social Action Papers, collection 37, box 1, folder 11, Billy Graham Center Archives, Wheaton College (Ill.).

18. Ronald J. Sider, "News Release," 27 November 1973, Evangelicals for Social Action Papers, collection 37, box 1, folder 17, Billy Graham Center Archives, Wheaton College (Ill.); Evangelicals for Social Action, "History," 2000, http://www.esa-online.org/about/history.html, accessed 23 February 2000; Robert Booth Fowler, *A New Engagement: Evangelical Political Thought, 1966–1976* (Grand Rapids, Mich.: Eerdmans, 1982), 96.

19. Ronald Sider et al., "Chicago Declaration of Evangelical Social Concern," 25 November 1973, Evangelicals for Social Action Papers, collection 37, box 1, folder 9, Billy Graham Center Archives, Wheaton College (Ill.).

20. "Evangelicals on Justice: Socially Speaking . . . ," *Christianity Today*, 21 December 1973: 38–39.

21. Bob Jones, "Editorial," *Faith for the Family* (published by Bob Jones University) 2, no. 4 (September–October 1974): 2; located in Evangelicals for Social Action Papers, collection 37, box 3, folder 10, Billy Graham Center Archives, Wheaton College (Ill.).

22. Evangelicals for Social Action, "News Release," 3 December 1974, Evangelicals for Social Action Papers, collection 37, box 3, folder 7, Billy Graham Center Archives, Wheaton College (Ill.).

23. Evangelicals for Social Action, "Evangelicals for Social Action," 2000, http://www.esa-online.org, accessed 23 February 2000.

24. Sider, letter to Fetzer.

25. Ronald J. Sider, telephone interview by Joel Fetzer, Wynnewood, Pa., 9 November 2000; herein referred to as "the Sider telephone interview." See also Evangelicals for Social Action, "What Is Evangelicals for Social Action," 1999, http://www.esa-online.org, accessed 2 October 1999.

26. Ronald J. Sider, *Just Generosity: A New Vision for Overcoming Poverty in America* (Grand Rapids, Mich.: Baker Books, 1999), 56–58.

27. The first Sider interview.

28. Ronald J. Sider, "They're Still Hungry; We're Still Rich," *Prism* (published by Evangelicals for Social Action) (May–June 1997): 34.

29. Ronald J. Sider, *Rich Christians in an Age of Hunger*, 4th ed. (Dallas: Word Publishing, 1997).

30. Evangelicals for Social Action, "Ron Sider's Opinion Editorials," 1999, http://www.esa-online.org/sider.html, accessed 10 May 2000.

31. Sider, "They're Still Hungry."

32. The first Sider interview.

33. In the film *The Prodigal*, two middle-class, Evangelical seminary students choose to live in inner-city "Factory Town" and defend the poor from slumlords as a way to "live out" their faith à la *Rich Christians in an Age of Hunger*. See Billy Graham Evangelical Association, *The Prodigal* (Minneapolis, Minn.: World Wide Pictures, 1983), archived at Billy Graham Center Archives, Wheaton College (Ill.).

34. The first Sider interview. See also Ronald J. Sider, "*Rich Christians in an Age of Hunger*—Revisited," *Christian Scholar's Review* 26, no. 3 (Spring 1997): 322–35.

35. Dwight Ozard, "*Rich Christians in an Age of Hunger*: An Introduction," *Prism* (May–June 1997): 8–9.

36. David Chilton, *Productive Christians in an Age of Guilt Manipulators: A Biblical Response to Ronald J. Sider* (Tyler, Texas: Institute for Christian Economics, 1985), 205.

37. Chilton, *Productive Christians in an Age of Guilt Manipulators*, 83.

38. John Schneider, *Godly Materialism: Rethinking Money and Possessions* (Downers Grove, Ill.: InterVarsity Press, 1994), 173. Other critiques of Sider include Lloyd Billingsley, *The Generation That Knew Not Josef* (Portland, Oreg.: Multnomah Press, 1985); and Ronald H. Nash, *Why the Left Is Not Right: The Religious Left—Who They Are and What They Believe* (Grand Rapids, Mich.: Zondervan, 1996). See also Craig M. Gay, *With Liberty and Justice for Whom? The Recent Evangelical Debate over Capitalism* (Grand Rapids, Mich.: Eerdmans, 1991).

39. Ronald J. Sider, *Living like Jesus: Eleven Essentials for Growing a Genuine Faith* (Grand Rapids, Mich.: Baker Books, 1999), 159.

40. Ronald J. Sider, "Redeeming the Environmentalists," *Christianity Today*, 21 June 1993: 26–29.

41. Sider, *Living like Jesus*, 160.

42. Ronald J. Sider, interview by Gretchen Carnes, Grand Rapids, Mich., 24 June 2000; herein referred to as "the second Sider interview."

43. Sider, "Redeeming the Environmentalists."

44. Sider, letter to Fetzer; the Sider telephone interview. See Jim Ball, telephone interview by Joel Fetzer, Washington, D.C., 15 November 2000; herein referred to as "the Ball interview." See also Robert Booth Fowler, *The Greening of Protestant Thought* (Chapel Hill: University of North Carolina Press, 1995), 17–18.

45. Evangelical Environmental Network, "Evangelical Declaration on the Care of Creation," 1996, http://www.esa-online.org/een/Resources/Declaration/declaration.html, accessed 23 February 2000.

46. Stan LeQuire, "A Ministry of Madness," unpublished manuscript, Eastern Baptist Theological Seminary, Wynnewood, Pa., 2000.

47. Ronald J. Sider, "Message from an Evangelical—The Place of Humans in the Garden of God," *Amicus Journal* (published by the National Resource Defense Council) (Spring 1995): 14.

48. The second Sider interview. Sider is conscious of and approves of sometimes using secular sources to justify his views on the environment. "All truth is God's truth," he has argued. "One doesn't have to be a Christian to understand lots of things about the natural

world." Sider is therefore "happy to learn from anyone who has been studying the world carefully" (the Sider telephone interview).

49. The second Sider interview.

50. Evangelical Environmental Network, "Resources from EEN," 2000, http://www.creationcare.org/Resources/resources.html, accessed 15 November 2000.

51. Sider, letter to Fetzer.

52. The Ball interview.

53. Bill Broadway, "Tending God's Garden—Evangelical Group Embraces Environment," *Washington Post*, 17 February 1996: C8.

54. Evangelical Environmental Network, "Comparison of Current Endangered Species Act with Proposed Legislation as of January 1996," January 1996, internal memorandum, private files of Evangelical Environmental Network, Wynnewood, Pa. "Incidental takes" means that some allowance of injury to an endangered or threatened species can occur, so long as adequate mitigation efforts take place once a project is completed.

55. Endangered Species Coalition, letter to Stan LeQuire, n.d. [1996?], private files of Evangelical Environmental Network, Wynnewood, Pa.

56. Evangelical Environmental Network, "Resolution of the Christian Environmental Council of the Evangelical Environmental Network on the Care and Keeping of Creation and Its Living Species," 21 October 1995, private files of Evangelical Environmental Network, Wynnewood, Pa.

57. Evangelical Environmental Network, "Endangered Species Act (ESA) Strategy," n.d. [1996?], internal memorandum, private files of Evangelical Environmental Network, Wynnewood, Pa.; Religious News Service, "Evangelicals Back Up Endangered Species," *Cleveland Plain Dealer*, 5 February 1996; the Sider telephone interview.

58. Stan LeQuire, telephone interview by Gretchen Carnes, Wynnewood, Pa., 8 August 2000; herein referred to as "the LeQuire interview."

59. The LeQuire interview.

60. D'Jamila Salem, "Stronger Endangered Species Law Urged—Coalition of Evangelicals Opens Campaign to Keep Congress from Weakening Statute. Ads Will Highlight Biblical Teachings," *Los Angeles Times*, 1 February 1996.

61. The first Sider interview.

62. Fenton Communications, "Evangelicals Kick Off Million-Dollar Campaign to Protect Endangered Species," press release, 31 January 1996.

63. The first Sider interview.

64. The first Sider interview.

65. Sider, *Rich Christians in an Age of Hunger*, 24.

66. Sider, *Rich Christians in an Age of Hunger*, 24.

67. Sider, *Rich Christians in an Age of Hunger*, 161.

68. Sider, *Rich Christians in an Age of Hunger*, 240.

69. Sider, *Rich Christians in an Age of Hunger*, 157–58; Sider, letter to Fetzer.

70. Sider, *Rich Christians in an Age of Hunger*, 158.

71. Sider, *Rich Christians in an Age of Hunger*, 161.

72. The LeQuire interview; Evangelical Environmental Network, "Endangered Species Act (ESA) Strategy"; Fenton Communications, "Evangelicals Kick Off Million-Dollar Campaign to Protect Endangered Species."

9

Sister Maureen Fiedler:
A Nun for Gender Equality in Church and Society

Mary Segers

Maureen Fiedler is a feminist nun who has spent a good part of the last thirty-five years campaigning for gender equality and social justice in church and society. A progressive Catholic and political activist, Fiedler is a Sister of Loretto with decades of experience working from a faith perspective on women's issues, race relations, U.S. foreign policy in Central America and Haiti, and issues of reform within the Roman Catholic Church. In the 1980s and early 1990s, she codirected Quest for Peace, a program of humanitarian aid for the people of Nicaragua. From 1977 to 1982, she cofounded and codirected Catholics Act for ERA. In 1982, she was one of seven women who fasted for thirty-seven days for Equal Rights Amendment (ERA) ratification at the state capitol in Springfield, Illinois. Fiedler's radical political activism is no surprise to those who know her. As she likes to say, it is no accident that she was born on Halloween (31 October 1942) because she has been spooking people ever since!

Fiedler holds a Ph.D. in government from Georgetown University and has long been interested in the ways in which religious beliefs intersect with public policy. She has used her expertise in public opinion polling to construct and analyze numerous surveys of the Gallup Organization. She is also a writer and journalist, working in both print and broadcast media. Fiedler has been a commentator for both National Public Radio (NPR) and WAMU-FM, a local NPR affiliate in the Washington, D.C., area. In addition, she has made guest appearances on CNN, CNBC, public television, and numerous talk radio shows throughout the United States.

Indeed, her work in broadcast journalism has led to a major radio project. Fiedler is talk show host for *Faith Matters*, a weekly interfaith radio program.

On Sunday, 21 November 1999, *Faith Matters* made its debut on the nation's airwaves. It is heard in four markets: Boulder, Colorado; Portland, Oregon; St. Louis, Missouri; and southern Illinois (on WCBW). It is also featured nationwide on the Internet.

Faith Matters is a live, call-in talk radio show intended to broaden religious programming and to serve as an alternative to Mother Angelica's Eternal Word Television Network and to such Religious Right broadcasters as Pat Robertson, Jerry Falwell, and James Dobson. Fiedler stresses that the show is designed to provide lively and informative discussions of contemporary religious issues in a manner that is dialogic rather than preachy or dogmatic. The purpose of *Faith Matters* is to make interreligious dialogue productive of respect, tolerance, and genuine acceptance of other faith traditions.

Given space limitations, it is impossible to do justice to Maureen Fiedler's many projects and accomplishments. Accordingly, this essay will focus on the work she has done to promote gender justice and on her broadcast journalism. Fiedler's work is impelled by Gospel principles and Catholic social justice teachings. Her work on behalf of women's rights and her religious broadcasting illustrate well how religious belief, theological reflection, and secular learning can be used to promote reform of church and society.

HISTORICAL BACKGROUND:
AMERICAN CATHOLIC SISTERS AND POLITICAL ACTIVITY

Fiedler exemplifies a tradition of social leadership in Catholic sisterhoods. Political activism and lobbying have a long, though relatively little known, history among congregations of U.S. Catholic women. From their early beginnings—the arrival of the Ursulines in New Orleans in 1727—American sisters have interacted with political figures in order to protect their institutional projects and their work in education, nursing, and social services on behalf of immigrants, the poor, and Native Americans. Despite canonical rules of enclosure designed to keep religious sisterhoods sheltered from secular culture and worldly corruption, the administration of hospitals, schools, and orphanages made sisters aware of social problems and brought them into contact with public officials to seek remedies.

In 1874 and 1884, the Little Sisters of the Poor in Washington, D.C., had bills introduced in Congress that resulted in grants of money for the construction of a home for the elderly poor.[1] The Sisters of the Holy Names of Jesus and Mary successfully challenged an Oregon law requiring all children between the ages of eight and sixteen to attend public schools. In its 1925 decision in *Pierce v. Society of Sisters*, the U.S. Supreme Court ruled in the sisters' favor and upheld the constitutionality of separate Catholic parochial schools.[2]

Individual American sisters also exerted influence in the political arena. Sister Blandina Segale (1850–1941) built schools and hospitals in Colorado and New Mexico and lobbied legislators to obtain support for her hospitals. She championed the rights of Native Americans and Mexicans and single-handedly put an end to lynch law in Trinidad, Colorado. Mother Katharine Drexel, recently canonized a saint by Pope John Paul II, came from the wealthy Drexel family in Philadelphia and used her money to found the Sisters of the Blessed Sacrament in 1891, an order devoted to work among blacks and Native Americans. She founded Xavier University in New Orleans, lobbied actively for an antilynching bill before Congress in 1934, and monitored government contracts with schools on Indian reservations.[3]

Many Catholic sisters, leaders of their congregations, exerted indirect political influence through the large network of Catholic women's colleges they established at the end of the nineteenth and beginning of the twentieth centuries. These colleges were important in fostering an awareness of national and international affairs and in promoting the study of social problems. Ewens notes that many of the women in top political positions in the 1980s (and 1990s) were graduates of these Catholic women's colleges.[4]

The Second Vatican Council, meeting in Rome from 1962 to 1965, had a major impact on the political activism of U.S. sisters. This council of the world's Roman Catholic bishops states, in its *Pastoral Constitution on the Church in the Modern World (Gaudium et Spes)*, that Catholics worldwide have a responsibility to promote the values of human dignity and human rights and to build up the human community. At the same time, the council asked religious congregations to reexamine their lives in the light of the Gospel and the needs of the contemporary world. This call for Church renewal led to the development of the idea of political ministry for sisters. In the decade following the Vatican Council, sisters participated in civil rights marches and voter registration drives. They protested the Vietnam War, boycotted grapes and Nestle products, campaigned for better housing for the poor, and organized the Grey Panthers to lobby for more benefits for the elderly. In 1971, forty-seven Catholic sisters met in Washington, D.C., to found NETWORK, the first registered Catholic social justice lobby. In the 1970s and 1980s, sisters involved in political ministry not only organized the poor but even stood for public office in order to shape more equitable social policies.[5]

This historical background provides the context in which to place Maureen Fiedler's work. The Second Vatican Council had the same dramatic impact on her life and work as it did on the activities of these sisters. It moved her in the direction of working for the rights of the poor and for improvement of the status of women in church and society.

BIOGRAPHY: RELIGIOUS COMMITMENT, POLITICAL AWARENESS, FEMINIST CONSCIOUSNESS

Fiedler is codirector of the Quixote Center, an international justice and peace center headquartered in Brentwood, Maryland, near Washington, D.C. Founded in 1976, the Quixote Center houses some eight different projects. These range from opposition to the death penalty, the development of inclusive language texts in liturgy and Scripture, reforestation and literacy in Haiti, humanitarian assistance to Nicaragua, mobilization for church reform, and political action on behalf of the poor and the homeless. It also houses the Nicaraguan Cultural Alliance, an artistic cooperative that provides an outlet for Nicaraguan poets, painters, and craftspeople.

Quixote is a faith- and conscience-based nonprofit social justice center that "strives to make our world, our nation, and our church more just, peaceful and equitable in [its] policies and practices." Like Don (and Dona) Quixote, these activists dare to dream impossible dreams. But they are not naive utopians tilting at windmills. These folks are analysts, organizers, activists, and fundraisers. As a nonprofit organization, Quixote must raise the money necessary to carry on its work. Its various projects are dependent on private funding sources, and the staff does frequent mailings to individual supporters across the country. Group supports include many religious communities (mostly women's religious orders plus one or two men's congregations). The annual report for 1999 shows revenues and expenditures of $1,740,136 and net assets of $542,124.[6]

Within the Quixote Center, Fiedler is currently associated with two projects. She is an adviser to Catholics Speak Out (CSO) (she had been, until recently, national coordinator). Also, as mentioned earlier, she is the host for the center's newest project, *Faith Matters*. Founded in 1986, CSO encourages reform in the Roman Catholic Church and adult responsibility for faith. Its purpose, according to Fiedler, is to help Catholics take responsibility for their church and their faith by speaking out on issues they care about. CSO has sponsored several full-page signature ads in major publications and commissioned a nationwide Gallup survey of U.S. Catholic opinion. It has also defended theologians and church leaders under attack by the Vatican and has published the book *Rome Has Spoken*, a compendium of papal and conciliar statements that reveal changes in church teaching over the centuries.[7] Fiedler is also the U.S. representative to the International We Are Church Movement, which advocates reform within the church on a global scale.

Fiedler has spent the last twenty-four years working at the Quixote Center on these various social justice projects. Earlier she taught high school for six years in Erie and Pittsburgh, Pennsylvania. She then left teaching to earn a doctorate in political science at Georgetown in 1977. In 1977, she joined the Quixote Center and began working on women's ordination and the ERA. When the center took on a project in gay and lesbian ministry, her religious superiors basically ordered her to leave the center, "which must have seemed like wild, unknown territory to them." As Fiedler has stated, "You notice what effect this had—I'm still here!"[8] But the incident led her to search out a new congregation.

Fiedler has belonged to two religious congregations, the Sisters of Mercy from 1962 to 1984 and the Sisters of Loretto from 1984 to the present.[9] What impelled this bright, articulate, humorous, personable woman to, first, join a religious community of sisters and, second, devote the bulk of her work to political ministry? How did she develop political awareness and feminist consciousness? What, for her, are the connections between religious beliefs and political action?

Fiedler attended Catholic elementary and secondary schools in Lockport, New York, then Mercyhurst College in Erie. After two years of college, she entered the Sisters of Mercy. There is a classic saying among nuns: "It doesn't matter why you entered the convent, it's why you stay." Fiedler's answer was simple:

> I entered because—this is going to sound classical, but it's true—I felt a call from God. It was not a call to go do social justice. I didn't even know that phrase in those days. It was a call to lead a more deeply spiritual and dedicated life. That doesn't go away. It deepens and it changes. So why did I stick it out? Because I felt that religious life gave me more freedom to follow that call to do social justice than had I gone off by myself. It gave me both freedom and a support system. It allowed me to follow what I believe was a genuine call. I still do!

Fiedler has innate political instincts that have been honed through years of activism. She has attributed her fascination with politics to "an innate interest and a realization that this was the stuff that could change society. I wasn't interested in changing it yet. I was just interested in what was going on and understanding it. After all, the 1950s were the deadest time in recent memory. If there were social movements around, I didn't know about them; I was pretty isolated from change makers. At the same time, I was interested in all those things."

If political interests were innate, feminist consciousness developed more gradually and was influenced by several different factors. Fiedler mentioned the formative influence of her father, who urged her to take physics, chemistry, biology, and trigonometry courses in her high school years: "He was encouraging me to 'think outside the box' as a female." When she expressed interest in nursing as a future career, he said, "Oh, no! If you go into medicine, you will be a doctor."

During her high school years, the Catholic girls' school she attended merged with a nearby Catholic boys high school. At the conclusion of senior year, she had achieved the highest grade point average and was therefore slated to be class valedictorian. But this was the first time since the schools merged that a girl had the highest average. Fiedler related what happened next:

> The school principal, who of course was a priest, called me into his office and told me I could not give the valedictory speech at graduation (which was a big deal)—because I was a girl. This was *blatant* sex discrimination by anybody's standards. But it was 1960. The women's movement had not been heard from since Susan B. Anthony practically. I was stunned. I knew this was wrong. Just innately, I knew this was wrong. So I went home and talked to my mother about it. And her major advice was, "Don't get into a fight with a priest."
>
> At first, I had no idea what to do. Here I was only seventeen years old. But I knew I had to do something. And I thought, "Well, you expose what you think is wrong." So I went back the next day. And to this day, I don't know where this came from. But I said to the priest, "This is wrong, this is unjust, I have earned this, and it will look perfectly terrible on the front page of our local newspaper!" Within twenty-four hours, he agreed that I would give the speech!

Apart from these early experiences, Fiedler mentioned other sources of feminist awareness. At Georgetown, she did her dissertation on women and U.S. politics, which exposed her to a wide range of feminist literature. She read women theologians, Catholic and Protestant, as well as the writings of Martin Luther King Jr. on racial equality. She began to apply arguments about racial equality and civil rights to issues of gender equality and women's rights. At bottom, however, Fiedler's feminism draws inspiration from her religious tradition. When asked whether the ideas that motivate her feminism and political action came from both the Church and the women's movement, she replied,

> I would not say Church, but Gospel. The message of the Gospel at its bedrock is a call to love one another. That's not just an individual thing but a call to try to develop structures in society that will implement and facilitate people's being able to love one another. I don't see how that is possible if we seek to dominate or cling to submissiveness. If we don't accord one another equal dignity, equal status, equal respect, that is an abridgment of loving one another. What feminist theory and literature did was get me to explore what equality means in the gender sense.

When asked whether she was influenced by Catholic social justice teachings, Fiedler mentioned several papal encyclicals, *Pacem in Terris* by Pope John XXIII and *Populorum Progressio* by Pope Paul VI. But after the Gospel, the most influential document for her was the Second Vatican Council's *Pastoral Constitution on the Church in the Modern World (Gaudium et Spes)*:

> I remember reading and rereading that many times when I was in the novitiate. I still go back to it. I was particularly struck by the teachings on economics and on peace. But it also says, in paragraph 29, "Every type of discrimination based on sex is to be overcome and eradicated as contrary to God's intent." I was really inspired by that. And it fit with the Gospel. I thought, "Yes! Obviously, we should ordain women. Not to do so is discrimination. I don't understand why these men with miters don't get it."
>
> The other thing I have done over the years is to study a lot of women theologians and the ways in which they have interpreted the Scriptures—not just Catholics either. I've read Virginia Ramey Mollenkott as well as Elisabeth Schussler-Fiorenza. I came to understand that Jesus treated women equally; he was not a sexist. Gradually, all the arguments against women's ordination fall away when you understand that he didn't ordain *anybody*, male or female; he simply called people to ministry. We laid an "ordination" interpretation on the Last Supper much later in history. Feminist theologians helped me read the Jesus story with a feminist lens.

Fiedler is clearly an egalitarian who takes Gospel notions of human dignity and equality very seriously. Her decision in 1969 to remove the nun's traditional veil and habit illustrates her deep commitment to equality and her opposition to clerical privilege. She has never been comfortable with the enforced separation of religious and laity, the division between secular and sacred that places nuns on a higher plane. She explained her decision this way:

> In the beginning it wasn't feminist consciousness. It had more to do with not wanting to separate from people and not wanting to project the cultural stereotypes that went with "nun." What went with "nun" was naïveté, not using certain words because she would be offended, the idea that she didn't know much about life and certainly nothing about sex, or men, or whatever. Probably she ought to be playing ball, eating cotton candy, and swinging on swings. There were common stereotypes around, and I didn't want to be part of them. They removed me from real life.
>
> There was also a specific incident. When I taught in Pittsburgh, I wore the full habit. I got on a city bus one day. I was a young strapping nun, healthy and vigorous. An older woman, who had a bag of groceries, got up and gave me her seat—or tried to. I didn't let her, of course. Now if I hadn't worn a habit, she would never have known and would never have done that. The habit clashed with my notion of vocation. I was there to serve people like this woman and let her have a seat, not get undue adulation and deference. I had a sense of the equality of the faithful and the equality of all people, and I did not want to be different, especially different in a way that projected negative, naive, stupid stereotypes.

These citations from an interview with Fiedler provide insight into the links between religious belief and political action in her case. The Christian

Gospels are fundamental as a source of inspiration. In addition, the documents of Vatican II, papal encyclicals, the writings of women theologians and religious feminists, and secular feminist thought—all were formative in her thinking. But the basic source of inspiration for Fiedler is the Gospel.

POLITICAL ACTION FOR GENDER EQUITY AND EQUALITY

Fiedler's political activity illustrates what Katzenstein has called *discursive politics*. Discursive politics has to do with knowledge and consciousness; it is a politics of reflection and reformulation. Much of this politics involves words and images. According to Katzenstein,

> Practitioners of discursive politics speak, write and publish, talk, hold workshops . . . produce newsletters, write memoranda, pamphlets, news releases, and books. Within the Catholic community, the feminist women and men who do this intensely political work are engaged in the construction of a knowledge community whose view of the institutional church and of society is self-consciously at odds with the present-day Catholic hierarchy. In its vision and in much of its lived reality, this is an explicitly radical politics. Feminist activists in the U.S. Catholic Church call for nothing less than a restructuring of both church and society.[10]

Fiedler's activism on behalf of gender equality and church reform exemplifies discursive politics. Much of her activity involves writing, speaking, brainstorming at conferences, and publishing newsletters and books. But she is no stranger to political protest and political mobilization either. Demonstrations, protests, news releases, marches, strikes, job actions, sit-ins, pickets, and rallies are classic forms of protest politics; and Fiedler's feminist work has included many of these political tactics and strategies.

Demonstration and protest characterized one of the earlier political initiatives Fiedler took, helping to organize the "Stand Up for Women" demonstration on the occasion of Pope John Paul II's first visit to the United States in October 1979. The setting for this protest was the pope's address to women religious at the Shrine of the Immaculate Conception in Washington, D.C. Fifty-three sisters wore blue armbands and stood throughout the pope's address to call attention to the lack of equality in church and society. Fiedler distributed a press release in advance that explained the reasons for this silent witness. Basically, it stated, "We stand in solidarity with all women out of love and concern for the church, to call the church to repentance for the injustice of sexism, and because we believe the church can change."[11]

The pope's address was also the occasion for a short welcoming speech by Sister Theresa Kane, president of the Leadership Conference of Women Religious and then head of the Sisters of Mercy. Before a television audience of millions and the assembled group of women religious, she made Church history by asking the pope to open up all ministries of the Church to women. She urged him "to be mindful of the intense suffering and pain of many women in the United States . . . who are desirous of serving in and through the Church as fully participating members." Judging from the TV image, the pope was surprised to hear her remarks.[12]

Kane and the fifty-three sisters who "stood up for women" made history that day. The story was on the front page of the *New York Times* the next morning, and millions of Americans had seen Kane's statement on television. But if she made history, the American Catholic Church hierarchy has in effect treated this pivotal moment as nonhistory. In April 2000, on a visit to the nation's capital, I stopped by the Shrine of the Immaculate Conception. In the basement crypt was a photo exhibit celebrating the pope's first visit in October 1979. In the narrative displayed alongside the photographs, there was absolutely no mention of Kane or of the other sisters who stood in silent witness.[13]

THE WOMEN'S ORDINATION CONFERENCE AND THE ERA

Fiedler was completing her doctorate at Georgetown when two opportunities arose for her to pursue her interests in religious feminism and gender politics. In 1975, she attended the first national women's ordination meeting in Detroit. Twelve hundred attended this major assembly of Catholics committed to an inclusive priesthood (600 had to be turned away). This meeting grew into the organization called the Women's Ordination Conference (WOC).[14] Fiedler was heavily involved in WOC from the beginning, eventually serving on the board and as an officer. In subsequent meetings she has been a shrewd political strategist and articulate spokesperson for women's equality. In 1995, at the twentieth anniversary of WOC's founding, Fiedler commented on a proposal to abandon the goal of ordination as too reformist and limited. Her political good sense is evident in her remarks: "If I were a bishop and I heard that this group no longer wanted the ordination of women, I would say, 'Thank God, they are off our backs.' Every institution in this country is patriarchal. . . . Am I going to tell women not to run for Congress, not to take tenured positions in universities? No, I am going to tell them to take that chisel and chisel from inside . . . even as we need people outside the walls blowing the trumpet."[15]

The Quixote Center afforded Fiedler a second opportunity to pursue her commitment to gender equality. Once she joined the center, she immediately began work on an extensive polling project, designed to assess whether Catholics were ready to accept ordained women within the Church. Here Fiedler was able to use the survey skills acquired in the course of her doctoral studies. The result was the publication *Are Catholics Ready?* coauthored with Dolly Pomerleau, which analyzes data from an October 1976 survey of forty-three worshipping communities in nineteen states and the District of Columbia.[16]

The study concludes that Vatican II Catholics, or "emerging Catholics," to use the language of the survey, were ready for women priests whereas more traditional Catholics were part of a gradual trend toward greater receptivity. Given these trends, the study predicts that "Catholic opinion is moving steadily in a direction supportive of full equality for men and women in ministry." Fielder and Quixote Center associates have done periodic polling on the ordination question to follow up on this initial study. Using as a benchmark Andrew Greeley's 1974 survey showing that 29 percent of American Catholics favored women's ordination, Fiedler's polling showed that, by 1992, that figure had risen to 67 percent. As Fiedler predicted, there has been steady growth.

THE ERA CAMPAIGN AND THE FAST FOR RATIFICATION

The Quixote Center offered Fiedler yet another opportunity to pursue gender equality with the campaign to ratify the Equal Rights Amendment. Because ERA work meant lobbying, Fiedler started a new corporation, called "Windmills," to do that work legally. The critical provision of the ERA simply declares that "equality of rights under the law shall not be denied or abridged by the United States or by any State on account of sex." In March 1972 this amendment to the U.S. Constitution passed the Senate of the United States by a vote of 84-8. In the ensuing ten years—from 1972 to 1982—a majority of Americans consistently told interviewers that they favored the ERA. Yet, on 30 June 1982, the deadline for ratifying the amendment passed with only thirty-five of the required thirty-eight states having ratified it.

Fiedler was part of the struggle to secure ERA ratification. From 1977 to 1982, she cofounded and codirected Catholics Act for ERA, an advocacy group intended to mobilize support for the ERA and to counter developing opposition among Catholic bishops to the amendment. She worked hard to neutralize the bishops' opposition and to organize supporters in Illinois, Oklahoma, Nevada, Missouri, and Florida. And she has credited the ERA campaign for her knowledge of basic political skills:

That was a fascinating four years. I worked full-time from 1978 to 1982 on the ERA. I met all the players: Molly Yard, Ellie Smeal, Patricia Ireland, and all kinds of people in the feminist movement, which was very valuable. I learned fund-raising; I learned how to be an effective political stump speaker because I was doing that everywhere. I would go any place I was invited to go, including major demonstrations, talking to 3,000 to 4,000 people. I learned how to do radio and TV interviews and political lobbying, particularly in Illinois. I was living in Chicago and would frequently go to Springfield and lobby directly as well as do grassroots organizing. We also met one on one with bishops in Illinois to talk with them about the ERA.

The Republican Party withdrew its endorsement of the ERA from the 1980 party platform, despite the fact that every GOP platform since 1940 had supported the amendment. In protest, twelve women, including Maureen Fiedler and Sonia Johnson, chained themselves to the doorway of the Republican National Committee in Washington, D.C., on 26 August 1980, the anniversary of the 19th Amendment granting women the right to vote.[17] Fiedler was organizing, writing, and lobbying as well as engaging in direct action to promote ratification.

The most impressive direct action Fiedler undertook was a thirty-seven-day fast in 1982 at the state capitol in Springfield, Illinois. On Tuesday, 18 May 1982, a group of seven women announced the beginning of a solemn fast (water only) for ratification of the ERA.[18] Invoking the memory of the suffragists who marched and demonstrated for women's right to vote, these members of the "Women's Fast for Justice" resorted to this dramatic action in the closing days of the ERA campaign in order to get the only remaining northern state (Illinois) to ratify the amendment. But Illinois had a supermajority rule requiring a three-fifths vote to approve constitutional amendments. That proved an insuperable obstacle.

Fiedler acted as press liaison for the fasters, arranging press conferences and writing all press releases. She also became a de facto facilitator at group meetings of the fasters, surfacing agenda items, moving discussion through thorny issues, and pushing for decisions. When asked if there was any training or preparation for a lengthy fast, she said no but indicated that the fasters were monitored by a physician and by the nurse on duty at the state capitol. They knew they had to drink plenty of water and watch electrolyte balance: "We were very clear that we were not fasting to the death, although we didn't say that publicly. We knew that among ourselves. Eventually, we did say that when people asked us; we were not trying to kill ourselves."

Religious motivation impelled the fasters. They made a real effort to distinguish their fast, which clearly had political implications (trying to get the ERA ratified) from what IRA prisoners were doing in Northern Ireland (fasting to death). The fasters saw themselves as witnesses to the truth of equality for all Americans and to the seriousness and sacredness of women's cause—that women hunger for justice. According to Fiedler, religious reasons provided the principal motivation: "It was very deep. Sonia Johnson [one of the fasters] certainly believed [that the campaign for gender justice was a religious cause]. The Mormon tradition calls for a lot of fasting, the Catholic tradition does; Mary Ann Beall [another faster] is a Quaker and a very religious woman." Not everybody on the fast was religious, but they were using a practice associated with many religious traditions.

Near the end of the fast, Fiedler announced at a press conference that twenty-three Catholic bishops had come out in support of the ERA. This had a deterrent effect—that is, the effect of the bishops' statement was to prevent the larger, official body, the National Conference of Catholic Bishops (NCCB), from taking the opposite position. According to Fiedler, there were plenty of bishops who would have liked to oppose the ERA. But because the NCCB prefers to be unanimous, the ERA endorsement by twenty-three of their members made it very difficult for the entire conference to take a position against it. When I asked Fiedler why the NCCB officially refused to endorse the ERA, she mentioned two factors: First, some bishops linked the ERA with the Supreme Court's legalization of abortion and "thought the ERA would bring wholesale abortions if it were ratified." Second, many bishops feared that the ERA would raise anew the issue of gender equality in ministry and pressure them to ordain women.[19]

By 23 June 1982, it was clear that the Illinois legislature was not going to reach the 60 percent vote necessary to ratify the ERA. And so the fast ended after thirty-seven days. Several of the women had been hospitalized, and Fiedler herself was taken to the emergency room to have an EKG on 22 June (the day before). At a final press conference in the capitol rotunda, they drank grape juice and vowed to carry on the struggle for justice—to the applause of many spectators.

Asked why, in her judgment, the ERA failed to gain the thirty-eight states necessary to ratify it, Fielder maintained that several factors contributed to the defeat of the amendment. These included economic interests, a growing conservative political movement, cultural conservatism, and the fact that statutory laws and court rulings during the 1970s, which promoted gender equality, made it seem that the ERA was unnecessary. According to Fielder, the tale of the ERA defeat lies in who was funding the opposition, and she mentioned, in particular, insurance companies that feared that equal insurance rates would really hurt them financially. She also said that the conservative Right wing that organized in the mid- to late 1970s used the anti-ERA drive as a test of its political strength. This political conservatism was able to draw on a cultural conservatism represented by Phyllis Schlafly and others: women who benefited from traditional family role arrangements and who felt threatened by feminism. Speaking of Schlafly and her Eagle Forum women who came to see the "Women's Fast for Justice," Fiedler noted,

> These women came and made fun [of the fasters], ate candy bars, and wore their little red "STOP ERA" buttons. They probably led protected lives and didn't think deeply about issues. If somebody told them that there would be unisex bathrooms, they were horrified, and they would lobby their legislators about it. Or they might say that the ERA meant women could be drafted into the military, but they didn't seem to consider the justice of equal-gender jeopardy or the fact that women could then resist war equally with men!

The Supreme Court's decision in *Roe v. Wade* in 1973 also led some to link the ERA with legalized abortion and conclude that an activist Court would use the equal rights constitutional amendment to further expand its judicial power in ways that would undermine traditional American values. Although Fiedler and others argued that the two issues were separate and that the ERA had no obvious direct bearing on whether "abortion is murder," the two issues nonetheless became politically linked. As Mansbridge has noted, "Unable to overturn the Roe decision directly, many conservatives sought to turn the ERA into a referendum on that decision. To a significant degree, they succeeded."[20]

THE *NEW YORK TIMES* AD AND THE "VATICAN 24"

The abortion issue continued to be a thorn in the side of U.S. Catholics throughout the 1980s. The debate became particularly contentious during the 1984 presidential election campaign when Democratic vice presidential candidate Geraldine Ferraro was publicly criticized by newly appointed New York Archbishop John O'Connor and other bishops for her position on abortion policy. In response to these attacks, an ad hoc Committee of Concerned Catholics published a full-page advertisement in the *New York Times* on 7 October 1984. Entitled "A Catholic Statement on Pluralism and Abortion," the statement describes a diversity of opinion on abortion within the Church and the theological community, decries clerical attacks on political candidates over the issue, and calls for dialogue on the issue.[21]

This public statement drew an immediate reaction from the Vatican and triggered a series of repressive actions by Church-related agencies against the ad's signers, particularly those signers who were members of religious communities. Twenty-four women religious (including Maureen Fiedler) resisted the Vatican's demand that they publicly retract the statement or face dismissal from their congregations. From 1984 through 1988, the Vatican Congregation for Religious and Secular Institutes reached individual settlements with most of the sisters.

Like all who faced Church sanctions because they signed this "Catholic Statement on Pluralism and Abortion," Fiedler found the ensuing controversy to be a wrenching experience. She signed the statement for two reasons: her experiences listening to women's stories about their reproductive lives and her outrage at the anti-Ferraro actions of certain archbishops. She realized that involuntarily pregnant women "found no help or comfort in abstract legal codes written by men; they sought moral guidelines growing from their loving, lived relational experiences as women, that recognized women's right to be adult moral decision makers in matters of reproduction." But the Church hierarchy's conduct was the last straw:

> It was the action of Archbishops John O'Connor of New York and Bernard Law of Boston that finally propelled me to act. They chose to attack a woman in whom we all took great pride: Vice-Presidential candidate Geraldine Ferraro. I was outraged that leaders of my church would vilify the first woman to run on a national party ticket for her views on abortion—as if this were the only issue on the political spectrum—especially since Catholic male politicians with precisely the same views had never been so criticized. I was scandalized that Catholics were, in essence, being instructed how to vote. I was sick at heart that all this was interpreted as an implicit endorsement of a President who is not only antichoice, but antilife in the deepest sense of that word because his policies threaten the poor of our world and the very survival of our planet.[22]

Fiedler wrote extensively about the Vatican congregation's treatment of the twenty-four sisters who signed the ad. She addressed a 1985 National Organization for Women meeting and a 1987 Woman Church Conference in Cincinnati. She analyzed internal Church politics and discussed the rights of canonical religious to dissent. She also analyzed the political lessons learned from this distressing experience of clerical repression.

She argued that, by standards of contemporary protest, the "Catholic Statement on Pluralism and Abortion" was mild in the extreme: "Columnist Ellen Goodman said it was like the American colonists asking King George III if they could please discuss the matter of tea!" Fiedler defended the signers' exercise of "a human and Christian right to speak their consciences in a responsible public way." She said that the Vatican's response to the ad "exhibited all the characteristics of a centralized authoritarian structure threatened by a public exposure that it was losing control—not only of the 'masses'— but of its 'professional' workers, i.e., priests, nuns, brothers, theologians." In her judgment, the Vatican's behavior "was a raw and arrogant exercise of patriarchal power of the worst kind: a 'case study' in how not to run a church."[23]

In asking the twenty-four sisters to publicly disavow their statement or be dismissed from their communities, the Vatican placed these women in an agonizing dilemma and caused painful soul searching by the nuns themselves and by fellow members of their religious communities. Fiedler herself "muddled through months of this painful struggle and ultimately made a compromise settlement with Rome that I now deeply regret."[24] Sixteen years later, I asked her what she had learned from this controversy and whether she still regretted "having settled" with the Vatican. She commented, "I think I was correct in what I learned from that experience. It is not a good idea to make a deal with the Vatican. The mistake I made was *not* in signing the ad; the mistake was in acquiescing to any kind of a statement at Rome's behest—no matter how vaguely I thought it could be interpreted, which is what I thought at the time. They're not to be trusted."

Fiedler worries about the long-term chilling effects of the "Vatican 24" controversy. The right of priests, nuns, and laity to dissent is at stake. In the aftermath of the Vatican's reaction, members of religious communities developed an aversion to signing public statements on *any* issue, even relatively "safe" ones like nuclear disarmament. Does all this really matter? Would these voices make any difference? According to Fiedler,

> I submit that it *does* matter, especially in a church where right-wing Catholics speak out regularly, complaining loudly about the [Charles] Currans, [Archbishop Raymond] Hunthausens, feminist nuns, liberation theologians and so-called 'abuses' arising from 'misinterpretations' of Vatican II. When those of us who love Vatican II are silent, when we permit fear to keep us from protesting injustices, when we think that the Spirit will work without our response, the church is the poorer for it—and so are we. When progressive voices are hushed and timid, church leaders and the people generally hear only the voices of reaction and regulation.[25]

Sixteen years later, I also asked Fiedler about the abortion issue, which was, after all, the subject of the *New York Times* ad. Specifically, I asked, "Do you disagree with the Church's teaching on the immorality of abortion, or is your main difference of opinion with the fact that the Church tries to translate this moral teaching into law and public policy?" Fiedler replied, "This is the toughest issue for me and always has been. I would call myself both pro-life and pro-choice because I believe very deeply in the sanctity of life." She explained,

> First of all, I would say about the bishops what I would say about anyone: they have a right to lobby for their point of view. I don't agree with it, but they have a right to lobby. Abortion must remain legal, for a whole lot of reasons. First, history shows that women will have them whether it's legal or illegal, moral or immoral, available or unavailable. They will find a way to do it. And if it is not legal, they will die. That

is just a fact. So you will lose women as well as fetuses, the unborn. . . . Secondly, it is not respectful of the fact that many other religious denominations do not agree with us [Catholics] on this matter. And to try to put into public law in a pluralistic country what is the position of a handful of religions, no matter how powerful, in a country that has to respect minorities of any description—this is highly problematic. For those reasons, I think it has to remain legal.

From a moral perspective, this is a very serious issue. I would never try to decide for somebody else when it is moral or immoral. What I believe most deeply is that the agent of decision making is determined by subsidiarity, the one who is closest to the situation, which is the woman in this case. The principle of subsidiarity is an ancient Catholic principle. In a good, intact, egalitarian marriage, a woman ought to consult her husband. If she has been raped or he has gone off, that's a different story. But a woman's moral agency and her moral adulthood have to be respected. I think the role of theologians or pastoral people is to counsel her and to make sure that she understands what her choices are, what the ramifications are, what the theology is. Ultimately, the decision is hers. And I think there are times when it can be a moral choice, but I would not want to say what those are for somebody else. Clinton's phrase about making abortion "safe, legal, and rare" is probably a pretty good standard.

BROADCAST JOURNALISM AND *FAITH MATTERS*

Much of Fiedler's time and energies in the 1990s have been taken up with writing for broadcast and for publication. In the mid-1990s, she became a frequent commentator on NPR. She has addressed a wide range of issues—from prayer in public schools and the death penalty to academic freedom, taxes, raising the speed limit, and the 1996 government shutdown. Her commentary on a 1995 Vatican statement against women's ordination is instructive. She argued that the Vatican's action would not silence advocates of women priests "because this Church policy touches everyone, not just Catholics." She then reminded listeners of the connection between church polity and U.S. politics:

> When the leaders of a church not only practice discrimination but justify it theologically, they bless the sin of sexism. They harm not only Catholic women but women in general. Vatican refusal to treat women as equals gives cover to employers who deny women equal pay, to navy admirals who think of women as property, to husbands who beat their wives, to politicians who wink at sexual harassment, and even to men who commit rape or incest. Refusing to ordain women sends a message that male domination is the way God wants it. Gender discrimination is holy and blessed.
>
> When I was in Catholic school, we called this "bad example." That's why Catholics won't be—and shouldn't be—silent on this issue. As our 1971 Bishops' Synod said, "A church that preaches justice to others must first be just in its own life."[26]

In 1999, Fiedler's radio work shifted from NPR commentator to host of the weekly talk radio show *Faith Matters*. Begun in November 1999, the show is heard in four radio markets and is featured nationwide on the Internet. *Faith Matters* is one hour in length and consists of interviews with one or more guests followed by a "call-in" period. It is a live talk radio show whose purpose is public education for social and religious justice nationwide.

Hosted by Fiedler and produced by Linda Rabben, who is Jewish, *Faith Matters* is explicitly interfaith, welcoming listeners and speakers of many faith traditions and many religious viewpoints. It is consciously designed as an alternative to the programming of Evangelical Protestants such as Jerry Falwell and conservative Catholic broadcasters such as Mother Angelica and Catholic Family Radio. Evangelical Christian programs are heard regularly on 1,616 radio stations in the United States. Mother Angelica, an abbess in Birmingham, Alabama, runs the Eternal Word Television Network, which reaches millions worldwide over satellite television and appeals primarily to an audience of traditionalist Catholics. The Catholic Family Radio Network, headquartered in Los Angeles, was founded by a group of wealthy Catholic businesspeople to broadcast a conservative Catholic spin on politics and the news.[27]

Faith Matters is intended to balance the collective weight of such Religious Right programming. Fiedler emphasizes the interfaith character of the show. She also argues, first, that some of the most creative work in spirituality, theology, and ethics is taking place at the intersection of belief systems. And, second, she contends that in a world in which denominational loyalties are often entwined with racial, ethnic, or nationality groups, interfaith dialogue is integral to work for peace, justice, and racial/ethnic harmony worldwide. *Faith Matters* includes this work as part of its mission on the airwaves.

Indeed, Fiedler claims that *Faith Matters* is the only religious radio program on the national scene that provides informed, interactive, interfaith conversation on the key religious and ethical issues of our time. A glance at some of the show's topics and guests conveys the breadth and range of the programming. For example, there are timely programs linked to major religious holy days or secular holidays with discussions of the spiritual legacy of Dr. King for January 15, Martin Luther King Day—or programs on Hanukkah, Christmas, and Kwanzaa for December. Other shows have discussed Islam, Buddhism, or Jewish–Christian relations in an educational effort to teach listeners about the major world religions. A third type of show discusses key issues in U.S. politics and culture, such as "Religion in the Presidential Campaign" or "Moral Perspectives on the Death Penalty." There are interviews with authors of new books on religion and society, such as Jonathan Kozol's *Ordinary Resurrections*, John Cornwell's *Hitler's Pope*, or Garry Wills's *Papal Sin*. Some shows feature interviews with experts, for example, "The Role of Religion in the Middle East Crisis" or "Religion and Globalization." Other programs interview prominent clergy, such as Catholic Bishop Thomas Gumbleton; Episcopal Bishop John Shelby Spong; Bishop Vashti McKenzie, the first woman bishop in the African Methodist Episcopal Church; and Rabbi Barry Freundel, Senator Joseph Lieberman's rabbi in Washington. There are discussions of religion and moral issues, on shows such as "Racism and Sexism in the Churches" or "Controversial Topics in Bioethics." Finally, *Faith Matters* features discussions of feminist issues, with shows such as "The Gender of God," "The Experience of Ordained Women in Churches and Synagogues," "International Family Planning," "Women's Spirituality," and "Motherhood in Judeo-Christian Theology" (aired on Mother's Day). This is an extraordinary range of programming for a new radio show.

Faith Matters is also irenic in its choice of guests, who come from many faith traditions: Baptist, Catholic, Episcopalian, Methodist, Presbyterian, Jewish (Orthodox and Reform), Muslim, Coptic Orthodox, Bahai, and Native American. Fiedler tries hard for gender and issue balance in guest selection and discussion on controversial topics. In keeping with the show's purpose— to dialogue in a spirit of religious tolerance—conservative and traditional guests and viewpoints are welcome and are treated respectfully. *Faith Matters* also gets conservative callers, and Fiedler notes that listeners include Evangelicals, Muslims, African Americans, Jews, and Christians of all types.

Fiedler emphasizes that *Faith Matters* is a nonprofit organization under the IRS code and is therefore nonpartisan. The show does not take partisan stands or advocate for pending legislation. However, Fiedler has noted that "we are very political in the broad sense of the term because we deal on many shows with the intersection of secular politics and ecclesial politics."

After the show's first year on the airwaves, Fiedler is taking stock of its achievements. The program has been well received in the cities where it is broadcast. The *Denver Post* even ran a major article on the show. *Faith Matters* is therefore seeking to expand its broadcast area in both large and small markets. Plans include enhanced webcasting for Internet listeners, a marketing campaign to secure "free clearances" (free rather than paid airtime), and satellite radio, which promises instant broadcasting nationwide once it is fully developed. *Faith Matters* has also secured sponsors and underwriters such as Crossroad Publishing and Call to Action. The show ultimately aims to become self-sufficient with funds from advertising and underwriting, but that takes at least three years. In the meantime, the show is heavily dependent on fund-raising; *Faith Matters* receives support from religious communities in addition to individual contributors, including some Catholic bishops.

Long-range plans for *Faith Matters* include running a two-hour show or a Monday-to-Friday daily program. Fiedler has an Interfaith Advisory Board of religious leaders who suggest topics and guests and offer critique and suggestions for improvement. Together, the host, the producer, and the board seek to have real cultural impact. The goal is to amplify a powerful nationwide voice for religious tolerance, interfaith dialogue, and social justice.

CONCLUSION

Maureen Fiedler is a progressive Catholic and a dedicated nun in a hierarchically structured, patriarchal church. She is intelligent, courageous, and blessed with a delightful sense of humor, bordering on the mildly outrageous. She cares passionately about social justice yet is shrewdly realistic when analyzing possibilities for successful social reform. She knows full well that politics, whether in church or state, is the art of the possible.

A coherent worldview underlies her work for gender equality and social justice. Fiedler insists that *politics* is not a dirty word and that contemporary spirituality must be politically conscious. Religion and politics are intertwined—always have been, always will be. She agrees with the Religious Right on that point and strongly defends the right of all believing citizens to contribute their views to the policy process. "All" means everybody: Pat Robertson, Jesse Jackson, Mother Angelica, James Dobson, Catholic bishops, Mormons, Muslims, Jews, Native Americans. Governmental power should be used to alleviate the condition of the least advantaged in society. This includes women, the poorest of the poor in many parts of the world, and the objects of discrimination and exploitation even in the affluent West. The Christian Gospels mandate this preferential option for the poor and the vulnerable, as do the documents of Vatican II and recent papal encyclicals. Finally, the Roman Catholic Church must lead the way by seeking internal justice in its own community. It should be leading the struggle against sexism and racism, not impeding it.

Although the road of a progressive, feminist nun is not an easy one to travel in the contemporary Catholic Church, Fiedler will not give up. When asked why she refuses to leave a church that is so unjust to women, she gave three reasons. First, she does not believe that gender discrimination in church and society accords with the teachings of the Christian Gospels. Second, she believes that her Christian duty is to struggle for reform of the Church rather than to abandon it. Finally, she believes that the Church is a sacred community far wider in membership than a few men at the top of the ecclesiastical structure. As she put it, "This Church is *my* church as much as it is anyone else's. It is a believing community which I love deeply, and I claim my right as a member of that community to participate in and develop the life of that community as a feminist, pro-choice, Catholic woman. I love my church, and I speak and act out of that love."

To summarize, Maureen Fiedler is an unusual religious leader primarily because, as a woman, she is ineligible for clerical status in her denomination. Gender bars Fiedler from priesthood and episcopal office. Yet Fiedler clearly is a religious leader and influential political activist. Her life's work, as described here and as most recently exemplified in the radio ministry of *Faith Matters*, is to advance social justice and gender equality in church and society. Fiedler's religious activism illustrates how religious conviction and political action can work together to promote the common good. Her work shows that religious leadership is not necessarily a function of clerical status.

NOTES

1. Mary Ewens, "Political Activity of American Sisters before 1970," in *Between God and Caesar: Priests, Sisters and Political Office in the United States*, ed. Madonna Kolbenschlag (New York: Paulist Press, 1985), 41–59.

2. *Pierce v. Society of Sisters* 268 U.S. 510 (1925), in Ewens, "Political Activity of American Sisters before 1970," 47.

3. Ewens, "Political Activity of American Sisters before 1970," 45–48. See also Jo Ann McNamara, *Sisters in Arms: Catholic Nuns through Two Millennia* (Cambridge, Mass.: Harvard University Press, 1996), 578, 591, 615.

4. For example, Geraldine Ferraro, the first woman to run for high national office on a major party ticket, was a graduate of Marymount-Manhattan College in New York City.

5. Nancy Sylvester, "Post–Vatican II Sisters and Political Ministry," in *Between God and Caesar: Priests, Sisters and Political Office in the United States*, ed. Madonna Kolbenschlag (New York: Paulist Press, 1985), 60–73.

6. Annual Report of the Quixote Center, December 1999. The Quixote Center can be contacted at P.O. Box 5206, Hyattsville, Md. 20782; 301-699-0042; http://www.quixote.org.

7. Maureen Fiedler and Linda Rabben, eds., *Rome Has Spoken: A Guide to Forgotten Papal Statements, and How They Have Changed through the Centuries* (New York: The Crossroad Publishing Co., 1998).

8. Sister Maureen Fiedler, S.L., interview by the author, the Quixote Center, Brentwood, Md., 7 April 2000. Unless otherwise indicated, all quotes of Fiedler are from this interview.

9. In the Roman Catholic tradition, nuns or sisters take vows of poverty, chastity, and obedience within a religious community following the charisma or vision of the community's founder as interpreted over the years. Nuns or sisters are nonordained and are therefore, strictly speaking, laywomen. The distinction is made between nuns—cloistered, living a life of prayer within a monastery—and sisters—engaged in active ministry, serving in a variety of professions within the institutional Church and in secular society. Within religious communities, these distinctions are important, but it is common to see the terms *woman religious*, *nun*, and *sister* used interchangeably, as I do throughout this essay.

10. Mary F. Katzenstein, *Faithful and Fearless: Moving Feminist Protest in the Church and Military* (Princeton: Princeton University Press, 1998), 107.

11. "Stand Up for Women," flier distributed on the occasion of Pope John Paul II's address to women religious, Washington, D.C., 7 October 1979, courtesy of Maureen Fiedler.

12. McNamara, *Sisters in Arms*, 633.

13. This is an excerpt from the exhibit narrative:

> Early on the morning of October 7, 1979, the National Shrine experienced what was described as its "finest hour" as the 263rd successor to the Apostle Peter ascended its granite stairs and entered the Great Upper Church.... The thousands who had assembled to welcome the Holy Father cheered wildly and shouted, "Long Live the Pope-John Paul II, we love you." ... At the main doors, the women religious of the Shrine staff presented the Pope with a bouquet of flowers.

There is no mention of the protest or of Theresa Kane's statement.

14. In 1977, a *Vatican Declaration on the Question of the Admission of Women to the Ministerial Priesthood* argued that the exclusion of women from priestly ministry in the Roman Catholic Church should continue. For a concise summary of the arguments against women's ordination, see Mary Jo Weaver, *New Catholic Women: A Contemporary Challenge to Traditional Religious Authority* (San Francisco: Harper and Row, 1985), 114.

15. Katzenstein, *Faithful and Fearless*, 108.

16. Maureen Fiedler and Dolly Pomerleau, *Are Catholics Ready? An Exploration of the Views of "Emerging Catholics" on Women in Ministry* (Mt. Rainier, Md.: Quixote Center, 1978), 88. See also Maureen Fiedler and Dolly Pomerleau, "American Catholics and the Ordination of Women," *America* 138, no. 1 (14 January 1978): 11–14.

17. Sonia Johnson headed Mormons for the ERA in the late 1970s and early 1980s. See "Savage Misogyny: Mormon Excommunication of Sonia Johnson for ERA Activities," *Time* 114 (17 December 1979): 80.

18. The fasters included Zoe Ann Ananda (of Newport Beach, Calif.), Dina Bachelor (Los Angeles, Calif.), Mary Barnes (Raleigh, N.C.), Mary Ann Beall (Falls Church, Va.), Sonia Johnson (Sterling, Va.), Shirley Wallace (Ft. Collins, Colo.), and Maureen Fiedler, RSM (Washington, D.C.). Fiedler and Beall both kept day-by-day records of the fast activities. These journals are now historic documents and should be placed in archives and published.

19. Fiedler and Pomerleau, *Are Catholics Ready?* 78. See also Elizabeth Alexander and Maureen Fiedler, "The Equal Rights Amendment and Abortion: Separate and Distinct," *America* 142 (12 April 1980): 314–18. Alexander cofounded Catholics Act for ERA and served as a legal consultant to the organization.

20. Jane Mansbridge, *Why We Lost the ERA* (Chicago: University of Chicago Press, 1986), 14–19. In their *America* article "The Equal Rights Amendment and Abortion," Alexander and Fiedler give a carefully reasoned argument that one can be prolife and pro-ERA.

21. For an analysis of this controversy, see Mary Segers, "Ferraro, the Bishops, and the 1984 Election," in *Shaping New Vision: Gender and Values in American Culture*, ed. C. W. Atkinson, C. H. Buchanan, and M. R. Miles, the Harvard Women's Studies in Religion Series (Ann Arbor: UMI Research Press, 1987), 143–67.

22. Maureen Fiedler, "Sounding the Feminist Trumpet at the 'Walls of Jericho,'" address to the National Organization for Women, Washington, D.C., 10 July 1985.

23. Maureen Fiedler, "Claiming Our Power as Women in the Midst of Political Struggle" (address at the Woman Church Conference, Cincinnati, October 1987), in *Church Polity and American Politics: Issues in Contemporary American Catholicism*, ed. Mary Segers (New York: Garland Publishing, 1990), 303–12.

24. Fiedler, "Claiming Our Power as Women in the Midst of Political Struggle," 307.

25. Maureen Fiedler, "The Right to Dissent and Canonical Status: Must We Now Choose?" unpublished manuscript, February 1987.

26. Maureen Fiedler, on *All Things Considered*, National Public Radio, 20 November 1995.

27. Laurie Goodstein, "Catholics Contest Evangelicals' Radio Dominance," *New York Times*, 15 August 1999: 1.

10

Father J. Bryan Hehir: Priest, Policy Analyst, and Theologian of Dialogue

William J. Gould

For the past three decades Father J. Bryan Hehir has been one of the most important and influential voices within U.S. Catholicism. A priest of the Archdiocese of Boston, Father Hehir has long enjoyed distinction as a scholar and teacher in the academic world. Currently, Hehir serves both as chair of the Executive Committee of Harvard Divinity School and as professor of practice in religion and society at the same institution. Prior to coming to Harvard, Hehir held teaching appointments at St. John's Seminary, Boston, and Georgetown University. He has also authored articles and reviews for a wide range of publications, including *Foreign Policy, Social Research, The Review of Politics,* the *New York Times Book Review, Commonweal,* and *America*. In addition, he is a fellow of the American Academy of Arts and Sciences, a member of the Council on Foreign Relations, and an active participant in the Catholic Theological Society of America. He is also the recipient of many academic honors including a MacArthur Fellowship and honorary degrees from twenty-five institutions.

Yet, for all of his prominence as a scholar, Hehir is even better known for his work as an adviser and policy analyst at the U.S. Catholic Conference (USCC), where he worked from 1973 to 1992. During that period, Hehir worked regularly at the intersection of policy initiation, formulation, and implementation, exerting enormous influence on the policy agenda that the American bishops pursued. Widely credited with being the principal author of the bishops' famous pastoral letter on nuclear weapons, *The Challenge of Peace: God's Promise and Our Response*, issued in 1983, Hehir also played a major role in initiating, formulating, and implementing the policy proposals advanced by the hierarchy on Central America, the economy, and abortion.

And his influence even encompassed shaping the overarching direction of the bishops' social policy agenda throughout the 1970s and 1980s.

Accordingly, this essay will examine Father Hehir's contributions as a policy analyst for the U.S. hierarchy and as a public theologian. It is based in part on personal interviews with Hehir himself and with some longtime observers of his work. After briefly summarizing his career and the theological vision that animates his work, I will focus mainly on his key role at the USCC. The central claim here will be that, above and beyond his input on any particular issue, Hehir is largely responsible for the broadening of the bishops' pro-life agenda. Taking it from what was once a rather narrow focus on abortion to the wide-ranging consistent ethic of life that the bishops now propose, Hehir has shifted and enhanced the standing and credibility of the Church in public policy discussions. This essay will conclude with a brief assessment of his contribution to the public voice of modern U.S. Catholicism.

AN OVERVIEW OF FATHER HEHIR'S CAREER

Born 22 August 1940 and ordained in 1966, Hehir has said, "I have lived my priesthood overwhelmingly at the intersection of the Church and the political arena and the Church and the academic arena."[1] This pattern has proved most appropriate given his lifelong interest in politics; in fact, "being engaged with the world has been a major emphasis all my life. I wanted to go into politics before I went into the ministry. I was sure I wanted to study diplomacy before I knew I wanted to study theology."[2] Eventually, however, Hehir decided to become a priest. Given his strong intellectual bent, it is curious that he chose to become a diocesan priest rather than a member of the Jesuits or another academically oriented religious order. He explained his decision in this way:

> On the whole, I think the dominant thing was I really was not drawn to the sort of communal life of religious communities. If I was going to be a priest . . . the structure of life of a secular priest appealed to me more directly than the structure of life of a community. Now you probably could distinguish the structure of life from the activity. Obviously, the activity of Dominicans and Jesuits in academic life, that appealed to me greatly, . . . but I guess, while there was no certainty about what I would do since I would be under the direction of the bishop, I thought—and all my teachers in the seminary at the time encouraged me to think—that you could incorporate serious academic work, serious intellectual work, in the framework of a diocesan priest.[3]

In addition, the diocesan priesthood also afforded him more of an opportunity to be involved in the application of Church teaching to policy than a purely academic life devoted exclusively to teaching and writing likely would have.

Hehir came under the influence of many Catholic thinkers while in the seminary, but "the dominant figure" was the Jesuit, John Courtney Murray. Credited by many with having demonstrated the compatibility of Catholicism and U.S. democracy, Murray is also widely regarded as the principal architect of the Second Vatican Council's *Declaration on Religious Liberty*.[4] Murray influenced Hehir in two important ways. The first was in his choice of graduate study. Before graduate school, Hehir asked Murray how to "prepare to do both ethics and international relations," and Murray told him, "Go someplace where you get the international relations first because your theology will be too rigid if you form it all ahead of time. Get immersed in the fabric of the problem. Then work your way through it. But don't go to a place that will teach you more and more about less and less. Go to a place that has a broad-based conception of international relations and social science."[5] In addition, Murray was also the principal methodological influence on Hehir's thinking:

> Murray's method has always made the most sense to me: to take the world on its own ground, with all its complexity, and respect people who help you understand the world in its empirical density. The content of his theology and the meaning of his life remain an abiding reality for me. He once said that to be a theologian in the Catholic tradition is to stand on the growing edge of tradition, the place where the tradition encounters the rest of reality; the more you understand the center of the tradition, the better you stand creatively at the growing edge.[6]

And so, in keeping with Murray's advice, after receiving his M.A. degree from St. John's, Hehir went on to doctoral studies at Harvard in 1967, pursuing a course of study that combined theology and international relations courses (in fact, half of his courses at Harvard were in political science). At Harvard, Hehir's teachers included Raymond Aron, Hedley Bull, Henry Kissinger, and, most important of all, Stanley Hoffman, whom Hehir calls "the best teacher I ever saw in action"[7]—and with whom, years later, he would team teach courses at Harvard in international relations.[8]

While still pursuing his doctorate at Harvard, from which he would receive a Th.D. in applied theology in 1977, Hehir was offered a job as a policy analyst for the U.S. Catholic Conference (USCC) in Washington, D.C. And so, in 1973, Hehir came to Washington to work at the USCC, where he would remain for the next twenty years. Significantly, he also kept a foot in the academic world during this period, teaching for several years at St. John's Seminary and then from 1983 to 1992 at Georgetown. The job suited him perfectly because the conference "provided an institutional structure and place for work that I was already doing. So, in one sense, it was like not breaking stride at all to walk into that position from what I was already working on."[9] And "given the fact that that structure was designed to help the Church deal with its public policy position relating to secular democratic society in the midst of world politics and a very interesting domestic situation, it was ideally suited for me."[10]

At the USCC, Hehir served as a staff policy analyst in a variety of positions. Initially, he served as director of the Office of International Affairs, which focused on foreign policy issues. Then he became secretary of the Department of Social Development and World Peace, concerned with matters of both foreign and domestic policy. Finally, he served as counselor for Social Policy, where he was able to offer counsel to the bishops on a broad range of areas without having to manage a staff.

Hehir was thus able to play a key role as an adviser to the American bishops on matters of public policy, including the bishops' views on U.S. policy in Central America and American defense policy. In particular, Hehir is generally credited with being the principal influence on the bishops' much discussed 1983 pastoral letter on war and peace, *The Challenge of Peace*. He also served as an adviser to the 1986 economics pastoral, *Economic Justice for All: Catholic Social Teaching and the U.S. Economy*. By that time, he was in charge of the social policy division and, thus, responsible for representing both letters once they got adopted. Moreover, partly because of his role on the pastoral letter and partly because of his prominence as a scholar in the academic world, he began to gain increasing public visibility in the early 1980s. For example, in 1981, he started writing a regular column for *Commonweal* called "Worldwatch," and in 1983 he was the subject of a profile in the *Washington Post Magazine*.[11]

In 1992, Hehir returned to his diocese at the request of Cardinal Law to become pastor of St. Paul's Church in Cambridge, Massachusetts, a parish that ministers to, among others, the Catholic faculty and students at Harvard. Then, in January 1993, Hehir returned to Harvard as the Catholic chaplain. In 1996, he stepped down as pastor of St. Paul's, though he continues to live at the parish and still occasionally says Mass there and as Catholic chaplain at Harvard. He did this in order to take up two new positions: professor of practice in religion and society at Harvard and counselor to Catholic Relief Services in Baltimore, for which he does policy analysis. Then in 1999 he became chair of the Executive Committee at Harvard Divinity School. As chair of the Executive Committee, he is the de facto dean of the Divinity School. Because the position includes large administrative responsibilities, he is assisted as chair by a group of associate deans. As if all this were not enough, Hehir makes his busy life even busier by accepting a large number of speaking engagements, making numerous presentations, writing various conference papers and book chapters, and so on. And of course he continues his work on the Church and international relations, much of which is taken up now with thinking through the applications of a just war ethic in a post–Cold War world, for example, the right to rescue and the crisis in Kosovo.

BACKGROUND: THE IMPORTANCE OF VATICAN II FOR HEHIR'S THOUGHT AND WORK

Father Hehir's theological vision and the methodological approach he has adopted in pursuit of it are deeply influenced by the teachings of the Second Vatican Council (1962–65) inaugurated by Pope John XXIII. After looking on the modern world with deep suspicion for centuries, the Church finally began to adopt a more positive posture toward it at Vatican II. *The Pastoral Constitution on the Church in the Modern World*, or *Gaudium et Spes*, was particularly important in this regard for its nuanced assessment of the strengths and weaknesses of modern life and for its desire to engage the world in dialogue.[12] Not surprisingly, Hehir said he was deeply influenced by the document: "The published document of the Church that most . . . animates my work and symbolically represents it is *Gaudium et Spes* of Vatican II."[13] In fact, "*Gaudium et Spes* is a kind of programmatic document about the Church committing itself to engagement with the world, service to the world. . . . I really see my role as one personal contribution to trying to live out the expectations of that text."[14]

And what are they? Essentially, *Gaudium et Spes* calls for the Church to assume a new posture toward the world, one that seeks to engage the world in a spirit of dialogue and service. Moreover, this dialogue between Church and world is not undertaken in the spirit of a teacher toward a pupil. On the contrary, it is understood to be reciprocal in nature, undertaken in the spirit of what Hehir calls "confident modesty," that is, in the conviction that the Church has something both to teach the world and to learn from it.[15] Indeed, a central theme of *Gaudium et Spes* is acknowledgment of the proper and legitimate autonomy of the world. This involves "clear recognition of the intrinsic value of secular institutions and secular disciplines," including acceptance of "the secular character of the state," "respect for the established methods of research in various fields of knowledge," and the "recognition that effective dialogue means speaking in terms which secular audiences can grasp."[16] Furthermore, in choosing to engage the world, the Church is also committing itself to serve the world as an integral part of its spiritual mission and ministry. It seeks to engage the world so that it can penetrate it with Gospel values—to work with it in solidarity with all of humanity. It does this especially with the poor and oppressed in order to build a more just world—a world renewed and transformed in the light of the Gospel vision.

It is precisely the document's emphasis on respectful engagement with the world and its need of transformation that animates Hehir's vocation as a social ethicist—a vocation he once described in the following way: "First of all, to understand the world in all its complexity; second, to respect it in its secularity; third, to be restless about its infirmities and limitations; and fourth, to feel driven to lay hands on it, which is what Catholic social ethics calls the Church to do—to lay hands on a world you respect but are not ready to accept in its present form."[17] Of course, once the socially oriented agenda proposed by *Gaudium et Spes* has been set forth, the question remains: How is the Church to go about pursuing this agenda? More specifically, how is the local Church, in this case, the Church in the United States, to go about pursuing this agenda? For Hehir, the answer to this question calls for the Church in the United States to be a "public church," that is, one that "accepts social responsibility for the common good and envisions its teaching role as a participation in the wider societal debate."[18] By adopting the model of a public church, the U.S. Church will be able to engage in dialogue with the larger American society in a spirit of "confident modesty," contributing its insights to American society and also learning from it. Furthermore, in addressing the larger public, which, after all, is predominantly non-Catholic, "its public voice ought to be expressed in terms that a wider pluralistic society can understand and make sense of."[19] Accordingly, Hehir believes that the Church ought to rely mainly on a philosophical, natural law–style of discourse in the tradition of John Courtney Murray and exemplified by John XXIII's encyclical *Pacem in Terris* when it addresses the wider society on issues of public debate.[20] He said, "If *Gaudium et Spes* is the theologically symbolic document for my work, *Pacem in Terris* is the philosophically symbolic document for my work—*Pacem in Terris* is the best of Catholic social thought."[21] Moreover, in fidelity to *Gaudium et Spes*, "when the Church engages the world, you've got to marry your theology to a philosophy with some empirical grounding."[22] If the Church is to engage the larger society effectively, in particular if it is to be credible when it makes policy recommendations concerning complex and controversial areas like foreign policy, weapons systems, and the economy, then it must familiarize itself, as thoroughly as possible, with the relevant data from the appropriate academic disciplines before it does so. This is partly how a teaching Church also becomes a learning Church.

HEHIR AND THE U.S. CATHOLIC CONFERENCE

Hehir's career and theological vision underlie his role as a religious/political leader. Because his principal accomplishment in this regard has come from his work as an adviser to the bishops, this section will concentrate on his efforts in this area.

To appreciate the impact of his role at the National Conference of Catholic Bishops (NCCB) in the USCC, it is necessary to understand the nature of that organization. The Second Vatican Council, recognizing the necessity for local Catholic institutions to be better equipped to address the particular needs of their respective areas, called for the formation of national and regional Episcopal conferences. In accordance with this directive, the NCCB was established in 1966 and headquartered in Washington, D.C. Membership in the conference was required of all U.S. bishops, as was financial support from every diocese. Meetings of the entire body are held twice a year, and the bishops elect a president of the conference for a term of three years. The NCCB is thus "a canonical body created by the highest [C]hurch authority and instituted by universal [C]hurch law."[23] Consequently, the conference was authorized to "exercise legitimate authority of its own, separate and apart from the authority of individual bishops."[24] This meant that it was now possible for the American hierarchy to present its views on matters of national significance, including issues of public policy, with an unprecedented degree of unity and cohesion.[25]

In order to assist the NCCB in its work, the USCC was also established to serve as the NCCB's administrative arm and secretariat. The USCC provides the bureaucratic staff necessary to help formulate and carry out the bishops' policy agenda, issuing statements concerning the bishops' views on matters of public policy, giving testimony at congressional hearings, and lobbying members of Congress and other public officials regarding areas of concern to the bishops. Headed by a general secretary, who is appointed by the president of the NCCB, the USCC is divided into several departments, including the Department of International Affairs and the Department of Social Development, each of which focuses on a different aspect of the bishops' agenda. In addition, oversight of each department is provided by a departmental committee chaired by a bishop, who serves for a term of three years.

Even if viewed in isolation, the establishment of the NCCB/USCC represented a very important development for U.S. Catholicism. But its establishment did not occur in a vacuum. On the contrary, it coincided with a number of related developments that, taken together, furnished the American hierarchy with an unparalleled opportunity to exercise national leadership. Its formation occurred in the wake of Vatican II and the council's call for increased Church activism. And this activist spirit was widely shared within the hierarchy at the time, particularly among many of its newer, up-and-coming members. These younger, progressive bishops were sometimes referred to as "Jadot bishops" because they were appointed by the Vatican at the recommendation of Jean Jadot, the Vatican's apostolic delegate to the United States. They included Bishop James Rausch, Archbishop John Roach of Minneapolis–St. Paul, and Archbishop Joseph Bernardin of Cincinnati (later cardinal archbishop of Chicago) all of whom would play a substantial role at the conference. In addition, the U.S. Catholic laity, on whose support the bishops would have to rely if their activist leadership was to have its full impact, were increasingly entering the mainstream of American life. This was true not only in politics, following John Kennedy's election to the presidency in 1960, but in virtually every sphere of life as America's Catholics reached levels of education, income, and occupational status that put them squarely in the middle class. To a large extent, then, the American Catholic Church that emerged in the aftermath of Vatican II was a Church that had come of age. It was a confident Church much surer of its position in U.S. society and more willing than it had traditionally been to voice criticism of America's failings; in short, it was a Church finally prepared to assume a position of major national leadership.

And so when Hehir arrived at the Catholic Conference in 1973, he did so at a time of unprecedented activism among the U.S. hierarchy. How, then, did he contribute to the conference's work, and how influential a role did he play there? Hehir's own assessment of his role at the USCC is characteristically modest, as befits a man who thought of himself not as a leader but as someone "accepting assignments and fulfilling them."[26] Speaking of the various positions he held at the USCC, all of which took the form in one way or another of policy analyst, he offered the following comment:

> The function of those positions is analytic advice to the bishops. So that you identify the areas to see whether they want to address them; if they want to address them, you work yourself and with others in drawing up policy positions that will seek to address them, and then you put them before them to see whether they want to adopt them. If they adopt them, then you inherit the responsibility of articulating those positions and engaging them and relating them to various publics, which I always felt meant relating them to the academic world, to the think tank world, to the official policy framework of Congress and the administration, and to the general public.[27]

To most observers, Hehir's assessment of his work substantially understates the importance of the role he played at the USCC during his years there. For example, conservative critics like Brian Benestad and George Weigel, who believe that the USCC's policy statements during this period reflect a notably liberal or even left-wing bent, charge that conference staff in general and Hehir in particular went beyond policy analysis and engaged instead in policy formation. More specifically, they charge that Hehir and other USCC staffers were leading the bishops to adopt a left-wing political agenda on a whole range of foreign policy issues.[28] But it is not simply conservative critics who attribute a major role to Hehir at the USCC. On the contrary, virtually everyone familiar with the conference's work during this period, including those highly sympathetic to the USCC's policy agenda, credits him with major influence.[29]

In order to assess Hehir's role, then, it is important to know more about the way policies were formulated and priorities were determined at the USCC at the time he was there and the kind of interaction that occurred between the bishops and their staffs in this process. In considering this matter, it is important to note at the outset that those who serve as staff for the USCC share a strong sense of their limited role and are quite "conscientious" about this. Consequently, though the bishops may defer to staff in small matters, when it comes to major statements and policies, bishops lead and the staffs follow.[30]

Furthermore, as Thomas Quigley, a policy adviser in the Department of Social Development and World Peace, has pointed out, much of the conference's policy agenda in the 1970s and 1980s was shaped by external developments. Therefore, the bishops were forced to respond, quite apart from the views staff members may have held on such matters.[31] For example, the enormous attention the bishops devoted to the issue of abortion during this period was a direct response to the Supreme Court's decision in *Roe v. Wade* in 1973 and would not otherwise have received so much prominence. Similarly, the bishops' heavy focus on Latin and Central America in the 1970s and 1980s resulted from reports from Church missionaries serving in the region about monstrous human rights abuses. They made public the plight of immigrants from the region seeking sanctuary in ordinary parishes around the country and the Reagan administration's policy of support for the Contras in Nicaragua.[32]

Even so, it must also be acknowledged that decisions about policy priorities were not guided by external developments alone and that it was certainly possible for conference staff to exert considerable influence regarding which issues should be given priority and, once that was decided, how they should be formulated and implemented. For example, the major pastoral letters of the 1980s, *The Challenge of Peace* and *Economic Justice for All*, though written partly in response to the policies of the Reagan administration, arose chiefly from a "proactive" orientation to address large questions of fundamental importance to the nation. Similarly, the bishops' response to the abortion issue, though engendered initially by *Roe v. Wade*, evolved considerably over the years. Some critics saw it as an almost single-minded opposition in the years immediately following *Roe v. Wade* to the broad-based "consistent ethic or seamless garment" approach to all life proposed by Cardinal Bernardin in the 1980s. And Hehir played a substantial role in shaping the bishops' thinking and implementation in all of these areas.

How, then, was Hehir able to have such an impact at the USCC, and what form did this take? The answer to the first part of this question is that Hehir possessed qualities that made him enormously valuable, if not indispensable, to the bishops as they sought to fashion and promote their policy agenda. In the first place, as a man of very considerable intellect, he was an invaluable resource for the bishops. His formidable mastery of the issues they were interested in pursuing and his ability to provide them with a conceptual framework within which to understand and relate these issues proved vitally important to their efforts to formulate a policy agenda. Second, his manifest desire to carry out his assignments at the USCC without publicity or public recognition reassured the bishops. In addition, the fact that Hehir is a diocesan priest rather than a member of a religious order such as the Jesuits or Dominicans, and that he is a deeply pastoral priest, also tended to convince them that he was a priest essentially like themselves. This in turn made it possible for him to form bonds of trust and friendship with bishops like Cardinal Bernardin as well as USCC staff.[33] Finally, partly by virtue of his close association with Harvard, Hehir had access to elite secular circles, which enabled him to bring the bishops and leading secular intellectuals into unaccustomed contact with each other.

Consequently, it was not long after he began working at the USCC that his considerable gifts came to be widely recognized at the conference. For example, if the USCC were asked, as it frequently was, to give congressional testimony on an issue such as arms control, Hehir would often be the person to draft it; sometimes he would also be the one to deliver it on the Hill as well. Similarly, bishops preparing to give major speeches would often seek Hehir's counsel; indeed, he would often write their speeches himself. John Langan, a professor of Catholic social thought at Georgetown University, remembered Hehir telling him in one instance that he had to write speeches for Cardinals Law, O'Connor, and Bernardin all in the same weekend![34] Hehir also made a favorable impression at USCC staff meetings, where he would rarely be the first to speak; once he did so, however, the clarity of his thought and the cogency of his analysis would tend to shape the subsequent discussion of the matter under consideration.[35]

Over time Hehir's talents also began to receive recognition outside the conference—so much so that by the early 1980s, if not before, he had become something of a public figure, albeit a reluctant one. There were two principal reasons for this development. The first was that though he served on the staff of the USCC, the conference permitted him to express his own views in articles and public lectures. The second was that once a major policy position was decided on by the USCC, Hehir would accept virtually any opportunity to deliver an address or lecture promoting that policy position. As he himself put it,

> The conference was very good about this. I always had a certain degree of an independent existence apart from being a staff analyst. That partly came from the fact that I was in academic life to some degree. So there were certain numbers of possi-

bilities, and invitations, and writing that just went along with it that developed a distinct place for me as me. In other words, the conference allowed me to publish my own views. Secondly . . . , I worked at the intersection of academic and public policy institutions, government agencies. . . . And my view always was that you should try to give the bishops' views, once they had adopted them, maximum impact in the field, so I took all invitations and opportunities, and I suppose after a while you get a certain visibility that comes from that.[36]

The upshot of all of this was that Hehir came to enjoy a unique status at the USCC; quite simply, he was in a class by himself. For within the conference he was such a trusted and respected a figure, someone whose judgment was so heavily relied on by both bishops and staff, that his voice necessarily carried enormous weight in their counsels. And of course his growing recognition and prestige (though unsought) in the larger world served only to add to his stature within the conference. Consequently, he was able to play a substantial, decisive, even architectonic role in shaping the hierarchy's public policy agenda from the late 1970s through the 1980s. This is not to suggest or imply that Hehir told the bishops specifically what to think about particular policy matters or that he persuaded them to adopt positions to which they were really opposed. Rather, he was able to exercise so much influence because, to a very large extent, he provided the intellectual framework within which they came to understand and evaluate major policy questions. After extensive exposure to Hehir's policy framework, the bishops came increasingly to embrace it as their own, which in turn frequently led them to embrace his particular policy recommendations. In addition, he was also able to wield considerable influence because of his ability to work effectively with people of different points of view and to gain the trust and confidence even of bishops who disagreed with him on some issues. The fact, referred to earlier, that he was entrusted with writing speeches on the same weekend for Cardinal Bernardin, who was generally viewed as an ecclesiastical progressive, and Cardinals Law and O'Connor, generally thought of as being conservative, is one small indication of his ability in this regard.

But granting that Hehir exercised considerable influence, in what way did he help to shape the bishops' policy agenda? Or, put another way, how much of a difference did his presence at the USCC make to the bishops' policy agenda? The answer, it seems clear, is that his presence made a very considerable difference. For it was largely through his efforts that the conference's policy agenda evolved. It changed from what was widely perceived to be an almost exclusive focus on opposition to abortion to a wide-ranging agenda in which abortion concerns were situated within a broader pro-life framework. This is sometimes referred to as "the consistent ethic of life"—in which opposition to abortion is linked to the defense and promotion of human life in every phase of its existence, from the womb to old age and all the intervening phases. Such efforts were necessary because shortly after *Roe v. Wade* a major rift developed within the U.S. hierarchy. It was split over whether the fight against abortion ought to serve as the principal, overarching focal point of its agenda or whether the issue should be addressed in conjunction with other threats to life and human well-being such as poverty and nuclear war. This disagreement continued throughout the 1970s and 1980s, with "conservative" bishops like Cardinal Law, Cardinal O'Connor, and Bishop James McHugh of Camden supporting the former approach and progressives like Cardinal Bernardin embracing the latter posture.

As one would expect, Hehir sided with the progressive camp. He did so for two main reasons. First, he believed that the abortion issue, for all of its importance, did not exhaust the riches of Church social teaching and that there were many other grave threats to life and human well-being to which that teaching had something significant to contribute. Second, he also believed that the credibility and effectiveness of the Church's teaching on abortion would actually be enhanced, rather than diminished, by placing it in the context of a broader social agenda.

By placing so much emphasis on abortion, the bishops often created the impression that they were embracing the conservative political agenda of the Republican Party when, in fact, their agenda differed significantly from that of the GOP in several respects. In short, the hierarchy's seemingly exclusive focus on abortion was both distorting the true character of the bishops' social agenda and opening them to charges of partisanship at the same time.[37]

BROADENING THE BISHOPS' AGENDA

Accordingly, Hehir worked with sympathetic members of the hierarchy, particularly Cardinal Bernardin, to fashion a broader political and social agenda for the conference to pursue. He also worked to give this broadened agenda as large a public profile as possible so that the general public would realize that Catholic social teaching encompasses a good deal more than opposition to abortion. These efforts bore considerable fruit, giving rise to the three most ambitious, highly publicized policy initiatives undertaken by the bishops in the 1980s or since. Two major pastoral letters, *The Challenge of Peace* and *Economic Justice for All*, and Cardinal Bernardin's systematic articulation of "the consistent ethic of life," also known as the "seamless garment," emerged.[38]

The first of these initiatives, and the one with which Hehir's name is most prominently associated, is, of course, *The Challenge of Peace* issued by the

NCCB in 1983. *The Challenge of Peace* represents the American bishops' contribution to Church teaching on the challenges posed by modern war. The context out of which the letter arose reflected the teaching of Vatican II regarding war, recent debates within the Church about the viability of just war theory in a nuclear age,[39] and the urgent need felt by many progressive bishops to expand the social agenda beyond abortion.

To begin with, Vatican II had called for "an evaluation of war in an entirely new attitude," but it had also implicitly reaffirmed the just war position by reasserting the traditional right of states to legitimate defense.[40] Nevertheless, severe limitations were placed on the acceptable use of force. In particular, the council condemned weapons "which can inflict massive and indiscriminate destruction, thus going far beyond the bounds of legitimate defense."[41] In addition, it also "set forth a justification for a nonviolent posture as a mode of discipleship, including the right of conscientious objection," thereby establishing, "alongside the just-war position, an option of Catholic pacifism."[42]

One of the notable effects of the council document, then, was to legitimize the position of Catholic pacifism, exemplified by figures like Dorothy Day and Gordon Zahn—a position that traditionally had occupied a rather peripheral place within Catholicism.[43] This gave rise to a vigorous debate within Catholic circles regarding the respective merits of the just war and pacifist positions. With the freedom to write and lecture permitted him by the conference, Hehir became a prominent figure in this debate, in which he carved out a distinct position of his own.[44] Rejecting the absolute pacifist position but extremely skeptical that the use of nuclear weapons, once actually introduced into a conflict, could be kept within reasonable bounds, Hehir called for a version of nuclear pacifism. His interpretation distinguishes sharply between the possession of nuclear weapons, on the one hand, and their use, on the other. In this view, both the use of nuclear weapons and the intent to use them are categorically rejected, but their possession on an interim basis was tolerable because the deterrent, by preserving "peace of a sort," would also protect the human values that such peace makes possible. Acceptance of the deterrent is conditioned, however, on serious negotiations to achieve major bilateral reductions of nuclear arms. Finally, Hehir steadfastly opposed the introduction of any weapons system, for example, MIRVed missiles, the MX missile, the neutron bomb, and so forth, that might have a destabilizing effect on the balance of terror built into Mutual Assured Destruction by making nuclear war seem feasible or winnable and thereby making it more likely.

Largely as a result of this debate about the morality of modern war, an increasing number of bishops began to draw a connection between opposition to abortion and the need for greater efforts toward arms control and disarmament.[45]

This was especially true among those in the hierarchy who believed that the prominence given to the Church's stance on abortion was obscuring its teaching on other important matters. And so, issues of war and peace began to receive more attention from the hierarchy. Many individual bishops began to speak out on the arms race in their own dioceses, and a number of important statements on defense policy were issued by the NCCB/USCC. For example, Cardinal Krol gave his now famous testimony in support of Salt II ratification in 1979.[46]

Clearly, in this context there was already considerable sentiment within the hierarchy for some sort of major pastoral statement on the nuclear issue. Such sentiment grew even greater when, in early November 1980, the hawkish Ronald Reagan was elected president. Consequently, when Auxiliary Bishop Francis P. Murphy of Baltimore requested at the November 1980 Annual Meeting of the NCCB that the conference produce a summary statement of Catholic teaching on war and peace, his suggestion was enthusiastically accepted. Archbishop John Roach, the new NCCB president, appointed a special ad hoc committee of bishops, headed by then Archbishop Bernardin, to write it. The committee also included then Bishop John O'Connor, head of the military chaplaincy, and prominent peace bishop Thomas Gumbleton. Father Hehir, meanwhile, was chosen as the staff director for the project.

It would be an exaggeration to say that Hehir was responsible for the bishops' decision to produce the pastoral letter, for the decision to do so was plainly the result of many factors. But it is nonetheless true that he contributed substantially to the context that made that decision not just possible but likely. Moreover, the role he played in the subsequent conceptualization and drafting of the letter was even greater. The task confronting the Bernardin committee as it set about its work was a formidable one. The desire of the committee, of course, was to produce a major contribution to the public policy debate on nuclear weapons. It wanted to write something that would inevitably prove highly controversial, not least because the letter would almost certainly voice major criticisms of U.S. defense policy in the past and probably even more of the hawkish incoming Reagan administration. At the same time, the committee wished to avoid doing anything that would create a crisis of conscience among American military personnel, a large number of whom were Catholic.[47] Furthermore, whatever the committee finally settled on, it had to be something to which both the peace bishop, Gumbleton, and the firm defender of traditional just war theory, Bishop O'Connor, could agree. Accordingly, the committee decided to move forward somewhat cautiously. In the spirit of *Gaudium et Spes*, and very much in keeping with Hehir's methodological approach concerning the Church–world relationship, it was decided that before the committee spoke, it would listen. Consequently, most of the first year of its work was devoted to holding hearings to which a wide range of experts, including ethicists, arms control experts, former secretaries of defense, and others were invited to offer their insights and expertise. In addition, representatives of the Reagan administration also participated.

Because the committee conceived of the American Catholic Church as a public church, it understood the letter's intended audience to be both the Catholic community *and* the wider society. Consequently, the language of the letter employs a mix of philosophical and theological categories. The sections of the letter in which theological and scriptural languages predominate are intended mainly for the community of faith. And the more policy-oriented parts of the letter, which employ a more philosophical language and rely heavily on empirical analysis, are addressed primarily, but not exclusively, to the larger society, especially the policy community.

Once the committee began to write, it issued a series of drafts, which were the subject of considerable media coverage. Published in hopes of generating comment and discussion, they aroused not just discussion but considerable controversy both within the Catholic community and in the larger society. The drafts were a particular source of concern, if not consternation, to the Reagan administration. It was troubled by the critique of administration policies and the bishops' endorsement of a nuclear freeze—so troubled, in fact, that it lobbied vigorously, though ultimately unsuccessfully, to get the committee to alter the language of the document.[48] Major criticisms were also voiced by Catholic conservatives such as Michael Novak and William F. Buckley, who issued a conservative counterpastoral of their own in response to the bishops' effort.[49] In addition, the French and German bishops' conferences, believing that the pastoral might weaken the credibility of the U.S. deterrent in Europe, voiced reservations about the letter to the Vatican.[50] This led to a meeting at the Vatican in January 1983 of Cardinal Bernardin, Archbishop Roach, Monsignor Daniel Hoye, and Hehir, representing the USCC, and officials from the Vatican and the European hierarchies. Concerns were voiced at the meeting about the specificity of the letter's policy recommendations, although the basic content of the letter does not appear to have been altered as a result. A far more significant result of the Europeans' complaints was a change in the Vatican's attitude toward the bishops' conference. Troubled by what had occurred in this instance, the Vatican decided to downgrade the role of such conferences in the future.[51]

During the course of creating the different drafts, Hehir did the bulk of the drafting, although others were also much involved in the process. As Hehir himself put it, "I wrote a lot in the war and peace letter. I didn't write it all. There were other contributions. Cardinal O'Connor wrote large sections of it,

Tom Gumbleton wrote sections of it. I in the end had to edit things and put them all together, and I wrote some of it myself—its drafts."[52]

Furthermore, as the Bernardin committee continued to discuss and reflect on its work, Hehir played a crucially important role in giving it direction. He was able to supply the conceptual framework in terms of which the discussions took place. This enabled him to define the relevant issues for the rest of the committee's members. And, of course, to define the issues is largely to determine the outcome.[53] In addition, Hehir's capacity to work well with and to gain the confidence of those of a differing point of view also proved significant.[54]

As the letter was being written nearly two decades after the appearance of Vatican II's *Gaudium et Spes* and was being issued by the Catholic hierarchy in one of the two nuclear superpowers, it was decided that the pastoral should not confine itself to repeating or reaffirming previous Church teaching on war and peace but, rather, should also seek to apply moral principles to specific cases.[55] Accordingly, in addition to restating universal moral principles on noncombatant immunity, the document also offers a number of quite specific policy recommendations in the form of "prudential judgments." These were rooted in a careful analysis of the relevant empirical data about which, however, reasonable people of good will might nonetheless differ. These included support for a "no first use" policy, that is, rejection of the idea that the initiation of nuclear war, no matter how restricted in scale, can never be justified given the destructive power of nuclear weapons and the enormous difficulty of keeping such weapons under reasonable controls. In a similar vein, the letter all but absolutely rules out trying to fight a limited nuclear war for essentially the same reasons. As the letter puts it, "The issue at stake is the *real* as opposed to the *theoretical* possibility of a 'limited nuclear exchange.'"[56] Even so, the document does not rule out in principle all possible uses of nuclear weapons or conclude that their use would be intrinsically evil; instead, it leaves open what Hehir has called "a centimeter of ambiguity" regarding their possible use. Furthermore, the letter proposes "a strictly conditioned moral acceptance of nuclear deterrence."[57] This conditioned acceptance is premised on two things. First, deterrence can be accepted not as a long-term solution but only as a step toward some better kind of system of national and international security. Second, that deterrence, as long as it remains in place, must be restricted to its most basic task—deterring nuclear war; consequently, any sort of alteration in a nation's deterrence posture that might increase the likelihood of war must be rejected.

In May 1983, a final version of the pastoral letter was voted on by the American bishops and adopted with their overwhelming approval. In reading over the final version of the letter, it is easy to see the close parallel between the letter's analysis of the nuclear issue and its prescriptions, on the one hand, and the positions expressed by Hehir in his published writings on the subject from the 1970s, on the other. Both seek to "to carve out some middle ground" between proponents of pacifism and those defenders of the just war ethic who believe that the use of nuclear weapons, once they are actually introduced into a conflict, can be kept sufficiently limited to meet rigorous *jus in bello* criteria.[58] To a very considerable extent, then, *The Challenge of Peace* would seem to be Hehir's document. Does this demonstrate the truth of charges leveled by critics such as George Weigel that the letter is really unduly reflective of Hehir's views? Hehir has replied,

> That's a mistake. There is no question that if you have staff analysts, that's going to input. There's no way to deny that. In the end, staff analysts can be accepted, rejected, modified. Kennedy put it well after the Cuban missile crisis—he said advisers come and go, but the people who make the decisions, they have to stay around and accept the responsibility. That was always my view of how we were related to the bishops. You put positions up, you advocate them as vigorously as you could; you listened to what they then wanted and thought and tried to meet their needs, and once they adopted them represented them.
>
> But if they didn't adopt something that was my position on a given issue, I would not represent the position as their position, and I'd write a piece and put my name on it, but that piece was only significant or insignificant as other people gave it credence. So, to say that you didn't have any influence on what the bishops did when you're a staff analyst would seem to be kind of foolish; to say that what the bishops did was your piece and not theirs misses the point that I think it's commonly understood that when an institutional body votes on something, it becomes their document.[59]

Shortly after the pastoral on war and peace had been issued, and no doubt trying to take advantage of the momentum it had generated within the hierarchy, Cardinal Bernardin undertook another major initiative intended to broaden the bishops' pro-life agenda beyond abortion. On 6 December 1983, he delivered a lecture at Fordham University entitled "The Consistent Ethic of Life: An American-Catholic Dialogue." In it, he argued that the contemporary world confronts us with a whole range of threats to human life and well-being for which it is necessary to formulate a consistent and comprehensive response. By way of illustration, he linked the bishops' opposition to abortion to their recent statement on nuclear weapons and went on to draw a further connection with their rejection of capital punishment.[60] Without equating them, he suggested that the bishops' stands on all three issues reflected a commitment to the support and defense of human life—what he called "a consistent ethic of life." Bernardin would deliver several more addresses in this vein over the course of the next few years, expanding the range of issues encompassed within this "consistent life ethic" or "seamless garment" theory. He included opposition to euthanasia and pornography as well as support for greater governmental efforts to fight poverty and provide health care to the poor. The result of his effort was quite novel: an expansive vision of what it means to be truly pro-life and a broad social agenda that cuts across the dominant ideological stances of the Right and the Left on the U.S. political spectrum.

As one would expect, in undertaking this initiative Bernardin received the invaluable assistance of Bryan Hehir. Indeed, it is fair to say that this initiative was chiefly the product of their long collaboration. After working together over the years, the two men had become close friends. According to John Langan, who knew both men well, it is impossible to say which of them actually came up with the idea of the consistent ethic, though the basic substance of the idea was something they had long shared. What is clear, however, is that it was Hehir who was responsible for developing the idea in a systematic fashion.[61] The addresses that Bernardin gave on the subject were thus largely Hehir's work and heavily reflect his thinking. For although it is true that abortion, war, the death penalty, and so on are all life-related issues, the logical connection among them is far from strict. For example, according to Church teaching, abortion entails the taking of an innocent human life; the death penalty, on the other hand, involves the execution by the state of someone guilty of a capital crime. It is not self-evident that opposition to the one should automatically demand opposition to the other. Accordingly, it was necessary that Bernardin receive assistance in order to formulate his conception of the consistent ethic in a rigorous and systematic fashion. Hehir supplied this.

Predictably, Bernardin's initiative proved controversial. Leading opponents of abortion within the hierarchy such as O'Connor and Law feared it would weaken the bishops' commitment to fight abortion. They also feared that pro-choice Catholic politicians would point to their support for other elements of the Church's social agenda as a way of deflecting criticism of their pro-choice position—a fear that, as it turned out, proved well founded. Nevertheless, Bernardin's effort bore some fruit. Building on the work of the peace pastoral, this proposal for a more extensive prolife agenda further challenged the false perception that the Catholic Church was a single-issue church concerned only with well-being of life within the womb. And, in fact, despite the controversy it initially generated, the "consistent ethic of life" has increasingly become the framework within which the American hierarchy, without in any way diluting its opposition to abortion, advances its pro-life agenda.[62]

Finally, brief mention must be made of Hehir's important role in the pastoral letter *Economic Justice for All*, adopted by the bishops in 1986. At the same meeting in which the bishops approved the suggestion to issue the peace pastoral, it was also decided to issue one on Marxism. After Bishop Peter Rozazza of Hartford suggested that the proposed statement also include commentary on the problems associated with capitalism, it was decided that the bishops should also issue a pastoral on capitalism—the document that would eventually become *Economic Justice for All*. Once again, an ad hoc committee was formed that included Hehir, headed this time by Archbishop Rembert Weakland of Milwaukee. Although Hehir was far less involved with this letter than with *The Challenge of Peace*—he did not, for example, draft any of the document—Thomas Quigley nonetheless said he considers him "as responsible as any one person for the document."[63] According to Quigley, it was Hehir who was most responsible for the decision to shift the focus of the letter from capitalism abstractly understood to an examination of contemporary American economic life and institutions in the light of Catholic social teaching.

The production of the letter followed the same pattern adopted for the peace pastoral: holding hearings and issuing a series of widely publicized drafts. Although it did not succeed in generating as much attention as its predecessor,[64] this was not for want of advancing controversial proposals. At a time when Reaganomics was at its height and cuts in federal spending were very much in vogue, the bishops called for an expanded federal role in the economy and greater spending on the needs of the poor. Indeed, at the heart of the letter is its insistence on "the preferential option for the poor," that is, the conviction that "the way society responds to the needs of the poor through its public policies is the litmus test of justice and injustice."[65]

Reflecting on the impact of these three initiatives, it must be acknowledged that their direct effect on public policy proved quite minimal. Although the peace pastoral caused the Reagan administration considerable consternation and doubtless further enhanced the stature of the nuclear freeze movement, it did not substantially alter the direction of U.S. defense policy. The impact of the economics pastoral on Reagan administration economic policies, meanwhile, was utterly negligible. And Cardinal Bernardin's proposed "consistent ethic of life" has not yet succeeded in either diminishing public support for abortion and capital punishment or increasing public support for guaranteed health care for children and the poor. Still less has it given rise to a potential third force in American politics composed of people, at once culturally conservative but economically progressive, who are disaffected with the two currently dominant political alternatives.

Similarly, in spite of having engendered some vigorous discussion among Catholic intellectuals, these initiatives do not appear to have made much of an impact on the attitudes of U.S. Catholics as a whole. This is especially true in the case of younger Catholics, that is, Catholics born after the Second Vatican Council, who are less likely than either older or middle-aged Catholics to have even heard of, much less read, the pastoral letters on war and peace or the economy.[66] But this should not really come as a surprise because, for almost three decades now, the American hierarchy has condemned abortion without having succeeded in convincing a majority of its flock that the practice should be made illegal.[67]

But in matters of this kind there is more than one way to measure success. After all, when issuing their statements, the bishops presumably did not naively assume that either the secular world or the Catholic community would automatically adopt their proposals. Hehir certainly realized this when he worked as a policy analyst at the USCC; he doubtless knew that many, probably most, of the policy recommendations proposed by the bishops would not be adopted. But that was not the only reason for making such recommendations; they were also made so that the Church's perspective could become part of the policy discussion and perhaps over time help to shape that discussion. For example, the pastoral letter on war and peace, according to Hehir, sought to engage the interests of strategists in the ethical concerns being voiced by the Church: "People who aren't necessarily skilled in theology or ethics could read the document and feel that what they knew about the problem was reflected in the document, and then they could go beyond that to look at the normative side."[68] And to a significant extent he still believes that the letter succeeded in this regard by bringing "the normative discussion into direct dialogue and living contact with the empirical literature, so that . . . political scientists . . . felt that the letter was written with at least a grasp on the nature of the strategic literature."[69]

In assessing what the USCC accomplished in the decades he served there, Hehir thus spoke in fairly modest terms. His approach is essentially that of an "incrementalist": someone who measures success in terms of small, gradual, steps. From this point of view, the purpose of the bishops' initiatives was less about achieving certain policy objectives, although that would have been extremely desirable, than that of bringing the Church into the policy debate. Their aim was to make the Church's voice heard in the hope that over time it might move the discussion in a new, more positive direction. Viewed in this light, the initiatives that Hehir played a key role in advancing a greater achievement than may appear at first glance. For the two pastoral letters and the "consistent ethic of life," by publicizing Catholicism's rich, broad social vision, did a great deal to alter the misperception that the Catholic Church is a single-issue church engaged in an unholy alliance with the political Right. Instead, many in the policy community and the academic world began to recognize what they should have known all along: that Catholicism is the repository of a long, complex, and extremely distinguished tradition of moral reasoning that has much to offer our pluralistic society. This did not mean, of course, that they were necessarily converted to the Church's point of view on particular questions. But before people can be persuaded of something, especially something they are not otherwise inclined to accept, they must respect the institution proposing a particular point of view. In the past three decades, in no small part as a result of Hehir's work, the Church has gained greater credibility as a participant in the ongoing dialogue of the academic and policy worlds. Whether that enhanced credibility will translate over time into policy achievements remains to be seen, but the possibility that it might should not be dismissed.

J. BRYAN HEHIR: THEOLOGIAN OF DIALOGUE

In 1992, after twenty years of service there, Hehir left the USCC. Even if he had remained, however, it is unlikely that he could have continued to exert the kind of influence he once did. By the time of his departure, the NCCB/USCC was no longer as important a source of national Catholic leadership as it had once been. One of the reasons for this was the end of the Cold War; in its absence, many of the issues that had once energized the conference, for example, arms control, Central America, and so on, had lost much of their salience. In addition, the days of the Jadot bishops—the progressive bishops committed to an activist Church—are over. Indeed, given the widespread ignorance of many Catholics, especially younger Catholics, about even the rudiments of their faith, a number of bishops have concluded that rather than devote energy and resources to ambitious projects like pastoral letters on political questions, they should instead focus much more on education and catechesis.[70] But most important of all, the Vatican has decided under this pontificate to downgrade the importance and influence of bishops' conferences, partly as a result of the controversy engendered in Europe over the peace pastoral.[71] Leadership in the American hierarchy has thus become more dispersed than it was in the 1970s and 1980s, and the hierarchy's capacity for collective action is far less. To a large extent, then, the important role Hehir was able to play at the USCC was a reflection not just of his talent but of his timing.

Of course, the fact that Hehir is no longer associated with the USCC does not mean that he has ceased to be an influential figure. It does mean, though, that he now exercises influence in a somewhat different way. For he is now much more fully a part of the academic world than he used to be. Significantly, though, he has not chosen to take advantage of his current academic setting to pursue a life devoted chiefly to scholarly writing and research. He is not, for example, at work on some "big book" or major scholarly treatise. No doubt this partly reflects the substantial administrative responsibilities he has to perform as dean at Harvard Divinity School. But it is also a reflection of the fact that he has always been "more drawn to the intersection of normative discourse and policy" than to developing normative discourse in the abstract,[72] a fact reflected in his current work at Catholic Relief Services, for example.

Accordingly, Hehir now exercises influence chiefly as a public theologian. He makes regular appearances on the Public Broadcasting Station, appearing, for example, on *The NewsHour with Jim Lehrer* to talk about the relevance of the just war ethic to Kosovo or on *Fred Friendly's Great Discussions* program. Winifred Gallagher interviewed him for her book about spiritual searching when she needed to find a major representative of the Catholic tradition.[73] He meets twice a year with U.S. military leaders at the Kennedy School of Government at Harvard to discuss the morality of war. In a way, he performs a role somewhat akin to that of his old mentor, John Courtney Murray. Although Hehir's stature is different, still, there is truth to Church–state expert Father Richard McBrien's contention that "Bryan Hehir is the clearest and most faithful interpreter of Murray today" and that "the Catholic theologian most faithful to Murray's vision today is J. Bryan Hehir."[74] If by "being faithful to Murray" one means being faithful to his method but not necessarily his views on particular issues, then McBrien may well be correct, for Hehir does retain Murray's use of a natural law ethic and his commitment to dialogue with the secular world. Indeed, he is fundamentally a theologian of dialogue with the world, a dialogue undertaken in a spirit of "confident modesty." And this commitment to dialogue shapes and informs everything he does.

In a related vein, Hehir's career as an academic reflects a similar pattern. Many of the social scientists with whom he works are secular people, "doubtful about the whole enterprise of belief," but he is nonetheless able to find common ground with them, to identify shared concerns. Moreover, Hehir, who always wears a Roman collar, serves for them as a living representative of the Catholic Church on earth. And so, in addition to his achievements at the USCC, perhaps part of Hehir's importance and influence for U.S. Catholicism is that, at least to a certain extent, he is the successor to Murray as America's leading Catholic theologian of dialogue with the world.

NOTES

1. Father J. Bryan Hehir, interview by the author, 16 December 1999; herein referred to as "the 1999 Hehir interview."
2. J. Bryan Hehir, "Catholic Theology at Its Best," *Harvard Divinity Bulletin* 27, nos. 2–3 (1998): 13.

3. Father J. Bryan Hehir, interview by the author, 21 June 2000; herein referred to as "the 2000 Hehir interview."

4. John Courtney Murray's book, *We Hold These Truths: Catholic Reflections on the American Proposition* (New York: Sheed and Ward, 1960), seeks to show that Catholicism and U.S. democracy are fully compatible. Published in 1960 when John Kennedy was running for president, the book is thought by some to have helped Kennedy get elected. *The Declaration on Religious Liberty*, meanwhile, is the document issued at Vatican II in which the Church finally acknowledges religious freedom as a civil right. The document may be found in Walter M. Abbott, S.J., *The Documents of Vatican II* (New York: Herder and Herder, 1966).

5. The 2000 Hehir interview.

6. The 2000 Hehir interview.

7. The 2000 Hehir interview.

8. To form some idea of Hehir's respect and admiration for Stanley Hoffman's insights as a theorist of international relations, see his discussion of Hoffman's important book *Duties beyond Borders: On the Limits and Possibilities of Ethical International Politics* (Syracuse: Syracuse University Press, 1981) in "Moral Choice and World Politics," *Commonweal* (18 December 1981): 713, 730.

9. The 1999 Hehir interview.

10. The 1999 Hehir interview.

11. See Charlotte Hays, "The Voice in the Bishops' Ear," the *Washington Post Magazine* (3 April 1983): 6–7, 11–12.

12. *The Pastoral Constitution on the Church in the Modern World* may be found in *Catholic Social Thought: The Documentary Heritage*, eds. David J. O'Brien and Thomas A. Shannon (Maryknoll, N.Y.: Orbis Books, 1992).

13. The 1999 Hehir interview.

14. The 1999 Hehir interview. He even noted, "In one sense, you can think of my whole priesthood as trying to work out that document."

15. The 2000 Hehir interview. He went on:

> The business about "confident modesty" was my attempt to summarize what I thought was the spirit of *Gaudium et Spes*, and I think *Gaudium et Spes* is a good guide here. It talks about the need to acknowledge the legitimate autonomy of the secular disciplines, and, to my mind, that simply means trying to understand their rules, their procedures, and what they say about problems—not going to get a normative out of the empirical but to understand the empirical in depth.

16. J. Bryan Hehir, *The Church in the World: Responding to the Call of the Council*, the Marianist Award Lecture (Dayton, Ohio: University of Dayton Press, 1995), 20.

17. Hehir, "Catholic Theology at Its Best," 13.

18. J. Bryan Hehir, "Church-State and Church-World: The Ecclesiological Implications," *Proceedings of the Catholic Theological Society of America* 41 (1986): 64; see also J. Bryan Hehir, "A Public Church," *Origins* 14, no. 3 (31 May 1984): 40–43. The term *public church* comes from the book *The Public Church: Mainline, Evangelical, Catholic* (New York: Crossroad, 1981) by the distinguished Lutheran theologian, Martin Marty. The idea of a public church is intended to form a conscious contrast to a sectarian understanding, which tends to conceive of the "church" as a small community of committed Christians living quite intentionally apart from what they regard as a corrupt outside world.

19. The 2000 Hehir interview.

20. See J. Bryan Hehir, "The Perennial Need for Philosophical Discourse," in "Theology and Philosophy in Public: A Symposium on John Courtney Murray's Unfinished Agenda," theme issue, ed. David Hollenbach, S.J., *Theological Studies* 40, no. 4 (December 1979): 710–13.

21. The 1999 Hehir interview.

22. The 1999 Hehir interview.

23. See Timothy A. Byrnes, *Catholic Bishops in American Politics* (Princeton: Princeton University Press, 1991), 49.

24. Byrnes, *Catholic Bishops in American Politics*, 49.

25. The NCCB thus represented a major departure from the form of national organization that preceded it, the old National Catholic Welfare Conference (NCWC). The NCWC, unlike the NCCB, lacked the canonical status to exercise authority over individual bishops and enjoyed only lukewarm support from the dioceses around the country. During the period prior to the council, most bishops were preoccupied with local affairs, and national leadership on the part of the national hierarchy, to the extent that it existed at all, tended to come from a few leading prelates from major archdioceses, for example, Cardinal Spellman of New York. For a helpful discussion of the role played by the NCWC, see Byrnes, *Catholic Bishops in American Politics*, 25–34.

26. The 1999 Hehir interview.

27. The 1999 Hehir interview.

28. See J. Brian Benestad, *The Pursuit of a Just Social Order* (Washington, D.C.: Ethics and Public Policy Center, 1981), 22–23, 30–32, 49–52, 54, 98, 105; and George Weigel, *Tranquillitas Odinis: The Present Failure and Future Promise of American Catholic Thought on War and Peace* (New York: Oxford University Press, 1987), 314–24.

29. Regarding Hehir's influence on USCC policy, I interviewed Thomas Quigley, a longtime USCC policy adviser in the Department of Social Development and World Peace; Peter Steinfels, religion writer and columnist for the *New York Times* and former editor of *Commonweal*; and John Langan, S.J., Joseph Cardinal Bernardin Professor of Catholic Social Thought, Kennedy Institute, Georgetown University, who was an adviser to the bishops on *The Challenge of Peace*.

30. Peter Steinfels, interview by the author, 2 December 2000; herein referred to as "the Steinfels interview." Certainly, this is his view.

31. Thomas Quigley, interview by the author, USCC, 2 January 2001; herein referred to as "the Quigley interview."

32. In fact, in some cases the bishops' interest in the region took on a very personal character. For example, two of the four churchwomen brutally murdered in El Salvador had been sent there as missionaries by Cardinal Hickey when he was archbishop of Cleveland. Not surprisingly, then, Hickey was a major supporter of the USCC's concern for human rights in Central America.

33. Much of what is said here regarding Hehir's ability to win the trust and confidence of the bishops is from John Langan, interview by the author, 11 December 2000; herein referred to as "the Langan interview."

34. The Langan interview.

35. The Quigley interview.

36. The 1999 Hehir interview.

37. For example, during the course of the presidential election of 1976, Archbishop Bernardin, who was president of the NCCB at the time, appeared to endorse the Republican candidate, Gerald Ford, and to do so exclusively on the basis of Ford's stance on abortion. Then, in the 1984 election, Cardinal O'Connor generated enormous controversy when he criticized the Democratic Party's vice presidential nominee, Geraldine Ferraro, a Roman Catholic, for her prochoice position on abortion. See Byrnes, *Catholic Bishops in American Politics*, 72–81, 118–25. For a church whose social teaching encompasses teachings on a broad range of questions and which wished to avoid even the appearance of political partisanship, this was an unacceptable situation.

38. For example, Quigley says that by virtue of his "unparalleled" role in their conceptualization, the two pastoral letters are more Hehir's work than anyone else's.

39. The traditional framework within Catholic theology for consideration of questions relating to war and peace has been just war theory, which sets forth the criteria for the conditions under which a country may legitimately resort to force (*jus ad bellum*) and the limits that must be observed in the use of force once hostilities have begun (*jus in bello*).

40. *Gaudium et Spes*, in O'Brien and Shannon, *Catholic Social Thought: The Documentary Heritage*, paragraph 80.

41. *Gaudium et Spes*, paragraph 80.

42. J. Bryan Hehir, "Reflections on Recent Teaching," in *Nuclear Disarmament: Key Statements of Popes, Bishops, Councils, and Churches*, ed. Robert Hyer (New York: Paulist, 1982), 6.

43. For a notable discussion of pacifism's increasing acceptance in Catholic thinking alongside the just war tradition, see J. Bryan Hehir, "The Just War Ethic and Catholic Theology: Dynamics of Change and Continuity," in *War or Peace? The Search for New Answers*, ed. Thomas A. Shannon (Maryknoll, N.Y.: Orbis), 15–39.

44. Hehir's views in this area may be found in Robert A. Gessert and J. Bryan Hehir, *The New Nuclear Debate* (New York: Council on Religion and International Affairs, 1976), 35–76, 89–95. A summary of Hehir's position may also be found in William A. Au, *The Cross, the Flag, and the Bomb: American Catholics Debate War and Peace, 1960–1983* (Westport, Conn.: Greenwood Press, 1985), 191–93.

45. According to Hehir, the bishops' "interest in the abortion issue and the whole way they developed that in terms of right to life had a lot to do with pushing them toward the nuclear question, particularly since people began to argue that the nuclear question was such an enormous threat to life" (quoted in Byrnes, *Catholic Bishops in American Politics*, 98–99).

46. Not surprisingly, the influence of Hehir's thinking on deterrence is quite evident in statements issued by the bishops' conference during this period. For example, Cardinal Krol's testimony before the U.S. Senate Foreign Relations Committee on behalf of Salt II (which was written largely by Hehir) offers a conditioned acceptance of the possession of the nuclear deterrent (conditioned on serious arms control negotiations) while utterly rejecting both the use of and the intent to use nuclear weapons. See Cardinal John Krol, "Testimony on Salt II," *Origins* 9 (1979): 197. In a related vein, see the comments of Archbishop John R. Quinn of San Francisco, "Remarks as President of the NCCB on President Carter's Decision to Defer Production of Neutron Warheads," in *Nuclear Disarmament: Key Statements of Popes, Bishops, Councils, and Churches*, ed. Robert Hyer (New York: Paulist, 1982), 195–196, in which Quinn, following Hehir, rejects the neutron bomb because of its potentially destabilizing impact on the balance of power.

47. For this reason, Cardinal Bernardin decided to rule out from the outset the possibility that the committee would recommend unilateral nuclear disarmament. That possibility was taken off the table right from the beginning (see the Langan interview).

48. In particular, the Reagan administration, with the active support of Bishop O'Connor, sought a change in the wording regarding the letter's stance toward a nuclear freeze. The second draft of the pastoral called for "a halt" to the testing, production, and deployment of new strategic weapons. As a result of O'Connor's efforts, the word *curb* was inserted in place of *halt* in the third draft. This "victory" proved short lived, however, because in the final version of the letter ultimately approved by the bishops, the word *halt* was reinserted. See Byrnes, *Catholic Bishops in American Politics*, 110.

49. See Michael Novak, "Moral Clarity in the Nuclear Age," *National Review* 35 (1 April 1983): 354–92.

50. Both episcopates also went on to issue pastoral letters of their own, which adopted a far more sympathetic view of the existing deterrent.

51. The Langan interview.

52. The 1999 Hehir interview.

53. Hehir's ability to define the issues is remarked on by committee members Thomas Gumbleton and Edward Doherty in Jim Castelli, *The Bishops and the Bomb: Waging Peace in a Nuclear Age* (Garden City, N.Y.: Doubleday, 1983), 84. See also Weigel, *Tranquillitas Odinis*, 266.

54. For example, the fact that Hehir was able to gain the respect and support of Georgetown professor William O'Brien, one of the leading proponents of the just war position, enhanced his standing in the eyes of fellow committee member Cardinal O'Connor because O'Connor held O'Brien in such high regard.

55. This insistence on the importance of going beyond generalities and applying Church teaching to specific cases is very much in keeping with Hehir's methodological approach. See J. Bryan Hehir, "The Consistent Ethic: Public Policy Implications," in *Consistent Ethic of Life*, Joseph Cardinal Bernardin (Kansas City, Mo.: Sheed and Ward, 1988), 230–31.

56. O'Brien and Shannon, *Catholic Social Thought*, 526.

57. O'Brien and Shannon, *Catholic Social Thought*, 533.

58. The 1999 Hehir interview.

59. The 1999 Hehir interview.

60. See Joseph Cardinal Bernardin, *Consistent Ethic of Life* (Kansas City, Mo.: Sheed and Ward, 1988), 1–11. This volume also contains the other addresses by Bernardin in support of the consistent ethic of life as well as an essay on its public policy implications by Hehir (218–36).

61. The Langan interview.

62. A recent piece by Cardinal Law, who long opposed the seamless garment approach, is illustrative of this; whatever his reservations in the past, he clearly seems to have embraced it now. See Bernard Cardinal Law, "Defining the Roman Catholic Advocacy of Life," *Boston Globe* (13 February 2000): E5.

63. The Quigley interview.

64. It did manage to generate another conservative Catholic "counterpastoral" from Michael Novak, however. See *Toward the Future: Catholic Social Teaching and the U.S. Economy* (New York: American Catholic Committee, 1984).

65. O'Brien and Shannon, *Catholic Social Thought*, 607.

66. Peter Steinfels, "The Pollsters Look at U.S. Catholics," *Commonweal* (13 September 1996): 16–19.

67. In fact, according to Andrew Greeley, in *The Catholic Myth* (New York: Scribner's, 1990), 97, Catholic and Protestant attitudes toward abortion are basically the same.

68. The 2000 Hehir interview.

69. The 2000 Hehir interview.

70. The Steinfels interview.

71. In a related vein, questions have also been raised about the teaching authority of such conferences, especially in relation to political matters. See Avery Dulles, "What Is the Doctrinal Authority of a Bishops' Conference?" *Origins* 14, no. 32 (24 January 1985): 528–34.

72. The 2000 Hehir interview.

73. Winifred Gallagher, *Working on God* (New York: Vintage, 1999), 213–17.

74. See Father Richard McBrien, *Caesar's Coin* (New York: Macmillan, 1987), 285, 244.

Epilogue

Jo Renee Formicola and Hubert Morken

Each of the individuals profiled in this book is meeting the challenges of the twenty-first century in special ways: through communications, technology, protest, education, innovations, and most importantly, a specific faith. As religious leaders, with distinct motivations and agendas, they are also working to solve the complex public problems in U.S. society with both spiritual solutions and political expertise. And now, as a recognition and complement to their effective efforts and programs, government is moving in a new direction as well—*closer*! For example, within two weeks of taking office, President George W. Bush issued an executive order creating the White House Office of Faith-Based and Community Initiatives under the leadership of Dr. John DiIulio Jr., a political scientist at the University of Pennsylvania well known for advocating close working relationships between government and religious institutions. DiIulio, a Democrat, had earlier condemned the Supreme Court decision opening the door for George Bush to become president. But overlooking such criticism, and by making this a nonpartisan appointment, the new chief executive made it clear that a Bush/DiIulio consensus vision of public support for faith-based charitable and social efforts would become a priority at the highest levels of the federal government.

In a second executive order, the president also created five complementary centers to clear away bureaucratic barriers for faith-based programs in major government agencies. Located in the Departments of Justice, Housing and Urban Development, Health and Human Services, Labor, and Education, these offices are designed "to ensure greater cooperation between the government and the independent sector."[1] Viewed together, then, the two executive orders have the effect of creating a new infrastructure to accomplish this goal. And, in a larger sense, this generation of spiritual and political leaders also has the opportunity to improve and even transform the relationship between church and state, for the betterment of U.S. society and its diverse peoples.

Religious institution–government collaboration on the delivery of charitable and social services centers on a number of Bush assumptions. First, it is based on his belief that "compassion is the work of a nation, not just a government,"[2] that is, that public issues are everyone's concern and business. Second, it is grounded in the confidence that it is possible to encourage faith-based programs without changing the mission of the agencies involved.[3] The president recognizes that it is possible for those organizations to be fully religious without compromising the nation's commitment to pluralism. Third, the chief executive maintains that although government may encourage a different way to use "proven" means to "change and save lives," that "government will never be replaced by charities and community groups" in its obligation to serve those in need.[4] Fourth, he holds that government will not discriminate against faith-based groups that might compete with secular ones for charitable funds.[5] According to him, there will be a level playing field, for all nonprofit as well as private associations, including religious ones. Fifth, George W. Bush believes that both large and small religious organizations provide a variety of charitable and social services and, therefore, that all, regardless of size, must be eligible to receive help from the government.[6] And, finally, he maintains that faith-based and community groups will always have a place at the table of Bush deliberations.[7] He has promised that his administration will host discussions on public matters without imposing government policy solutions on the participants. To no one's surprise, then, religious leaders such as the Reverend Floyd Flake, Rabbi Daniel Lapin, and others were waiting in the wings to cooperate when the president's plan was unveiled.[8]

It was the Charitable Choice provision of the Personal Responsibility and Work Reconciliation Act of 1996, spearheaded by Evangelical Senators Dan Coats and John Ashcroft, that opened the door for greater collaboration on the delivery of social services between the government and faith-based organizations. And now President Bush's executive actions propel him through this portal. In his view, the notion of total separation between church and state must give way to the possibility of partnerships wherein both their responsibilities intersect, particularly in the areas of social and charitable work. If successful collaborations are forged, this will help to create what students of the law call a "zone of accommodation" between religion and government, what approving politicians say is cooperation for the "common good," and what supportive scholars, such as ourselves, sometimes refer to as "prophetic politics."

A MODEL FOR RELIGIOUS LEADERSHIP

Based on a biblical paradigm, "prophetic politics" is grounded on the assumption that religion has an integral role to play in the life of individuals and the advancement of society. Scholars of this kind of thinking,[9] particularly Neal Riemer in his seminal work *The Future of the Democratic Revolution: Toward a More Prophetic Politics*,[10] lay out the framework for a relationship between religion and government that takes into account biblical traditions, constitutional limitations, Enlightenment concerns, and contemporary needs.

According to such proponents, prophetic politics must, first, be motivated by the moral imperative, that is, it must challenge the existing political process to choose and implement an order of values higher than those of the national interest or personal aggrandizement. Thus, prophetic politics is about religious leaders motivating others, including the government, to work toward social justice, equality, peace, and ecological sustenance. It is concerned with the common good of advancing what Riemer calls the needs of the "least free" and by acting as what the Catholic Church calls "the voice of the voiceless."

Second, prophetic politics is about religious leaders acting as moral critics of political actors and as the conscience of public policies. It encourages scrutiny of the political process and its leadership and functions in this capacity with the legitimacy of a higher, divine authority. Therefore, the religious leader who follows prophetic politics must at the deepest levels of motivation and thought be committed to universal values as well as nonpartisan views in order to be objective in the public debate.

Finally, prophetic politics is also predicated on the notion that its practitioners will seek creative solutions, that is, breakthroughs, in the social and political processes to solve problems, to reconcile divisions, and to advance the common good. Such solutions must be ethical as well as prudential, carrying society beyond the ordinary liberal democratic politics toward a higher level of constitutional behavior.[11]

This model, then, is the antithesis of class warfare. It is not to be confused with liberation theology, which accepts a Marxist ideology and methodology to support religious involvement in the transformation of society. For, although prophetic politics must always, by definition, be dissatisfied with the status quo and the plight of the "least free," it must also apply the best of longstanding moral traditions to ensure a higher level of constitutional progress for the future. Therefore, prophetic politics leaves the egalitarian Left, the accommodating political center, and the conservative Right stymied because it represents a paradigm *of its own*. It is a unique model that seeks genuine social transformation and advancement based on transcendent values.

Religious leaders within this model of higher order politics, then, have the opportunity to use their special position within society to see problems through a moral, rather than a personal or self-concerned, prism. Their vantage point opens a vast arena for problem solving, a myriad of possibilities for new ideas based on proven principles of social justice and legitimate jurisdiction—whereby there is distinct yet shared responsibility for improving public life. It provides a framework for questioning and overcoming the grip of bureaucratic inertia, the control of special interests, and the stalemates of partisan politics.

The kind of religious leadership that we support is similar to the Riemer conception of prophetic politics. It is a model in which ministers, priests, nuns, and others work for value-based policies and programs. Their moral imperatives, however, must be all embracing, encompassing higher order principles designed to reconcile individuals and groups within society without requiring them to be of one religion. As the Declaration of Independence recognizes, such pursuits must be beyond the confessional boundaries of any particular faith, no matter how true, and be based on commonly recognized human rights grounded in creation. To fall short of such aspirations could lead to dogmatism and divisiveness, to serious rifts in society, or, even worse, to general indifference to right and wrong, cultural malaise, and chaos.

We would be remiss if we did not point out the obvious in this book, that religious leaders, even those most intelligent, clear thinking, pure, and unselfish by any measure, disagree on what principles should unite the nation. For example, Michael Farris, Benjamin Chavis-Muhammed, Al Sharpton, and Daniel Lapin pursue divergent, even contradictory policies—indicting public schools, Jews, whites, and secular liberals—as each pursues, with zeal, a specific agenda.

They have legitimate concerns, but when do they cross beyond the line of acceptable politics—beyond what the public should tolerate? The issue here is not the strength of their convictions or even their divisive impact on society, for conflict is inevitable in public life. We do well to remember that the Civil War, faced by Abraham Lincoln in 1860, split the heart of the nation in a search for a common principle bigger than hearth and home. But we must ask, "Can the vision and dedication of a leader grounded in moral principles always rise above the passions of the political moment?" And we must answer no. We do not expect perfection even of the greatest statesperson. However, we are convinced that committed religious leaders, particularly those rising to the level of *prophetic leaders*, as Riemer would call them, can help to accomplish the goals envisioned by President George W. Bush. They can be true to their own missions and have a major role to play in finding solutions to festering problems in U.S. society today. As authors, we encourage them to pursue the highest order of change for the good of all.

What characteristics, then, do these religious leaders possess in common that have the potential to raise them to a prophetic level that in turn would help America? All of them are committed to a "faith-based" vision for the future that is more just and better for the people they serve. They are all superior communicators of that vision. At their best they function as organizers and change agents, challengers of injustice, opponents of existing power structures, and people dedicated to universal, moral principles. They are apostles of discontent, participants in a great tradition that looks back to Moses, David, Elijah, Jesus, and Muhammad for inspiration. "Who is my neighbor?" is the haunting refrain of their battle song, calling them to care. Yet each reflects and interacts with this biblical tradition in a distinctive way.

First, these leaders are visionaries. Floyd Flake, for example, is a prominent spokesman on behalf of faith-based initiatives, backing active cooperation with government. When the existing public schools in New York City were unable to meet the needs of the underserved, he refused to turn a blind eye. Leaving Congress, he returned to work for change from his home base, a local congregation of 10,000 strong.

T. D. Jakes preaches to 85,000 women at a time and holds similar meetings for men and for pastors, weeping with them, laughing with them, understanding them, teaching and encouraging them, equipping them, and fighting for their empowerment. He uses church meetings, conferences, video, television, plays, film, and the written word, having published over twenty-five books, to bring his message to an expanding multiracial audience, inside and outside of prisons.

Al Sharpton, on the other hand, takes pride in "being in your face" and "in your neighborhood." He calls this transformational leadership. Even when he is functioning at his abrasive best, Sharpton will not let racism or indifference sleep undisturbed. He defends his community. He prods bureaucracies and the public. These are his great positive contributions.

Dallin Oaks has a sacred commitment to the eternity of the family, a doctrine others do not share. But he finds common ground on social issues, working through his writings to stabilize the erosion of family values within society. We must, he says, shore up traditional marriage and parenting to protect and preserve the legitimacy of marriage during a period of stress, when some question the very nature of what a family is.

Benjamin Chavis-Muhammed embraced the challenge of bringing one million black men to Washington, D.C., to motivate them and to demonstrate their commitment to work and family values. His personal story includes changing his name, religion, and political positions while strengthening his commitment to be involved as an activist.

Daniel Lapin also sees a role for faith-based organizations in changing the future. Disagreeing emphatically with Senator Joseph Lieberman, he links Jewish values to conservative politics and policy positions. However, like Lieberman, he opposes a politics based on religious affiliation alone, looking for commitments that unite diverse groups who agree on basics.

Ron Sider combines theological conviction and political action, calling for a proper stewardship of the earth. He places ecology within the central concerns of Mennonites and other religious denominations, linking them to the environmental movement.

Michael Farris makes a singular contribution to the home school movement, defending the rights of all parents, regardless of religious affiliation, to educate their children at home. He is active in legal defense work, lobbying, and education, including founding a college.

Maureen Fielder, as an active Catholic feminist, stands up to the Vatican as well as the U.S. government on matters of gender equality. This is a difficult role for a nun, who is required to submit to the authority of the Church. While she does, nevertheless, disagree with the views of her superiors, she has become a dissenter as well as a visionary.

J. Bryan Hehir has taken on the U.S. political and religious leadership on matters of missiles and nuclear weapons, economic and social justice, and the advancement of human rights in Latin America, Asia, and Africa. His has been a ministry for peace and life, engaging in contentious disputes and opposing political regimes. The point to be made here is not to endorse Hehir's policy positions—we may well differ with them—but to say that his presence, and that of the others named above, is invaluable to intelligent discourse on difficult issues.

Second, all of the religious leaders studied in this volume have, or have developed, platforms by which to spread their ideas beyond their immediate home audiences. Whether they operate in established organizations or create new structures, most of these religious leaders are "entrepreneurial" in their methods. They have adopted new means or adapted old ways, expanding religious influence to break the inertia of the status quo.

Flake uses his various positions in New York to advance school choice and quality education for the poor and minorities in the inner city. Because he is the senior minister of the influential Allen African Methodist Episcopal Church, directs a complex of community organizations, has a political base in the state, and holds various positions on corporate boards of trustees, he has clout. As a result, he has been able to create a network of interested parties to forge charter school legislation in New York and on a national level. Flake has created a new kind of public education reform that may become the model for America.

Jakes, like Flake, is the founder of several nonprofit and for-profit corporations. His publishing and television contracts give him first a national and then a worldwide reach, to Europe, Africa, and South America. His cooperation with state and local authorities gives him access to prisons. His faith-based efforts in Dallas bring him into contact with local governments. Jakes runs conferences to teach entrepreneurial start-up skills to women, and he plans to set up a business incubator as well. Bringing hope especially to women and prisoners and mobilizing the whole community of faith, Jakes is creating and testing new programs to bring some of the most forgotten people into the American dream.

Sharpton travels weekly from church to church and has his own radio show as well. He has established the National Action Network and the Madison Avenue Initiative, both of which are located in the Empire State Building in New York City and provide his platform for racial justice. Through the organizations and with them, he is willing to take on major corporations and Wall Street, challenging them to spread around the wealth in the United States. Coca-Cola, Burger King, A&P, and other companies have been targeted by his followers to provide better pay and working conditions for the working poor. City, state, federal, and even foreign governments have also been castigated by Sharpton for their persistent roles in institutionalizing discrimination.

Oaks, in contrast, represents Mormons in his public role. He is involved in writing, in testifying before Congress, and in litigation. He makes use of the already in place, mature, well-developed Church of Jesus Christ of Latter-day Saints (LDS) organizational structure. His is a position of resistance to perceived injustice, rather than one of partisan political involvement. His platform is focused on the family, and, as part of the hierarchy of the Mormon Church, his influence is considerable both within and outside its walls.

Lapin has founded Toward Tradition and has a weekly radio talk show to get out his message. He speaks at numerous conferences, writes, and issues frequent press releases. His is a communications platform for prophetic change.

Chavis-Muhammed has been active in all kinds of protest for racial justice during his adult life. Using his leadership positions in college, in prison, and in various civil rights organizations, he has continuously worked to create awareness about discrimination. Now, as a leader and spokesman in the Nation of Islam, he has been able to bring together Muslims, Christians, and secular groups, sponsoring massive rallies and community activities for needed changes in the black community.

Farris is the founder of the Home School Legal Defense Association and is able to use it to promote the interests of home schooling families through litigation and education. Currently, he is also laboring to establish Patrick Henry College on the borders of Washington, D.C., to educate the children of home schoolers. It is his aim to teach them about government, law, and the classics of Western culture and civilization. At the same time, he will be able to influence the curriculum and ideas of its students, presenting to them his vision for educational reform in the United States.

Sider founded both Evangelicals for Social Action and the Evangelical Environmental Network. Both are intended to advance ecological concerns, but each is a means by which he can reach beyond the Mennonite audience as well. His extensive writings also target a broader audience.

Fiedler has as her vehicle *Faith Matters*, a growing radio program in the Midwest. Through her communications platform, Fielder is able to discuss current issues of church and state and provide an alternative to the major Catholic television network in the United States.

Hehir, long active within Catholic organizational structures, has shaped how the Church has developed and implemented policy on public issues for the last quarter of a century. Today, he still affects policy through his academic positions, particularly as a professor of practice in religion and society at Harvard and a member of the Council on Foreign Relations. Hehir's influence is academic—the kind that is sought when think tanks and brain trusts are tapped for solutions to complex social problems.

Third, most of the religious leaders profiled here are also coalition builders, aware that they must join with others to leverage change. In the United States no religious group has the power to impose its views on law and policy making, nor would this be considered appropriate or legitimate. Indeed, most of the faith-based groups have learned from experience to form majorities or a consensus using various forms of persuasion.

Flake has been successful in bringing together segments of the business, political, and religious communities to work together to find new and better ways to deliver educational opportunities to those most in need. Jakes is doing the same thing on behalf of the poor in South Dallas. He also hosts conferences that bring together interested pastors from many denominations, establishing common ground. Sharpton, ever the lightening rod for controversy, nevertheless brings a variety of groups together, such as the National Action Network, its affiliates in a variety of cities, and the Rainbow/Push Coalition and Wall Street organizations, to solve the problem he addresses. Oaks and the LDS cooperate with other religious groups, such as the Evangelicals, in controversies related to religious liberty and family policy. Lapin is a controversialist, engaging in polemics, but he is also a bridge builder who argues for cooperation between Christians and Jews on the basis of common principles. Chavis-Muhammed, as already noted, links with Christian groups in an effort to have more influence on matters of concern to the African American and other minority communities. He created an alliance between the National Association for the Advancement of Colored People and the Nation of Islam and eventually between the followers of Farrakhan and those of Sharpton. Farris represents home schoolers—some of whom are liberal. However, he also fights for a conservative social agenda that brings him into contact with the larger conservative movement. Sider as a Mennonite has sought common cause with Evangelicals who share his theology and with nonreligious groups who favor his liberal-progressive policies. Fielder joins with other women's rights groups to stand together for equality in every respect for women. Hehir, as a staff member of Catholic policy organizations, has had the ability to bring together diverse members of the hierarchy and others outside the Catholic Church to embrace his positions on peace, human rights, and social justice.

Fourth, many of the religious leaders studied here are highly politicized; and all are deeply involved in public life. Some, such as Flake, have already held high political office. As a former congressman, Flake is keenly aware of the nature of politics and how to play the game successfully. His political contacts and skills are invaluable in this attempt to bring school choice to the public agenda.

Others have run for political office in the past. Sharpton and Farris have done so unsuccessfully, but each recognizes the importance of politics to his mission. Each has learned and grown by the experience, and Sharpton contends that he may even run for president in 2004.

Oaks, Chavis-Muhammed, Sider, Fiedler, and Hehir have lobbied for issues. They realize that cooperation with those in political power is a means to advance their specific agendas. Jakes, at this early stage of his ministry, by conviction and calling is less political. However, Jakes, Lapin, and Flake are already on the Bush list of influential religious leaders—people who are critical to the success of his faith-based collaborative efforts to provide social services.

The new chief executive is open to consider their ideas and those of other religious leaders. However, the dynamic tension that currently exists between church and state in America must be respected, appreciated, and closely guarded in order to protect the freedom of religion and the independence of the government in the United States. Working together in new ways will require considerable innovation, patience, and restraint on both sides of the potentially formidable alliance for faith-based initiatives.

THE CURRENT DYNAMIC TENSION BETWEEN CHURCH AND STATE IN AMERICA

The history of the relationship between religion and civil government in the United States, granting each its due, has been predicated on a Constitution based on inalienable rights, particularly religious liberty, and the nonestablishment of religion. James Madison and Thomas Jefferson, among others, knew that there must be line of separation between church and state. By working to forbid the establishment of a national church, they protected religious freedom. Thus, the First Amendment, as promulgated by the Founding Fathers, emerged as a principle with two aspects to it, in which the first, the freedom of religious exercise, must be understood and practiced in relation to the second, the denial of a governmental right to establish an official religion.

That equilibrium has been maintained by a variety of presidential, legislative, and judicial means throughout U.S. history. The Supreme Court, particularly, has struggled to interpret and apply the First Amendment, particularly in the twentieth century, by enlarging individual religious freedom and then by confining what it believes is government's potential to found a religion of its own.

Religious education is one area where the Court has acted conspicuously, providing major implications for public policy today. In 1925, in *Pierce v. Society of Sisters*,[12] the Supreme Court allowed Catholics to send their children to schools other than public ones, thus recognizing the right of parents to choose what kind of education they might want for their offspring. Freedom of religion with regard to education has been institutionalized since then to include the right of the state to use public funds for textbooks, testing, diagnostic services, guidance fees, computers, and remedial education. These are considered "child benefits," that is, rights that every child has in any school, including parochial schools. Free exercise has also been recognized as a legitimate criterion in challenges to employee performance, university funding for denominational journals, the use of public meeting places for religious discussions, and tax deductions for certain educational expenses in church-run schools.

At the same time, the Court has also defined government's role with regard to the establishment clause of the Constitution. In *Everson v. Board of Education* in 1947,[13] it narrowly held that public monies could be spent to transport Catholic students to a parochial high school because their town did not have one, but it also severely limited the government's involvement with religion. It maintained that the state could not favor one religion over another religion over nonreligion, influence an individual to go to church or not attend church, or force a belief or disbelief. It forbade government taxation for religious purposes or institutions and denied the state the right to be involved in the affairs of religious organizations and vice versa. It was no surprise, then, that in 1963 the Supreme Court outlawed the use of the Lord's prayer, Bible reading, or any prayer written by school authorities in public schools.

In 1971, under pressure to clarify its church–state stance, the Supreme Court, in *Lemon v. Kurtzman*,[14] put a test in place to determine if a particular law violated the principle of separation. At that time the Court required that three questions be answered to satisfy the separation criteria: Does a particular piece of legislation hinder or advance religion? Does it serve a secular, legislative purpose? Does it have a neutral effect?

Thus, *Pierce, Everson*, and *Lemon* set out judicial standards to guide the limited interactions between religious and political institutions in the United States. Within this context, then, the election of George W. Bush and his outreach to religious groups are extraordinary. The new president, by calling together influential religious leaders and challenging to them to work more closely with government on social and charitable programs, could usher in an unprecedented era of cooperation not seen in recent U.S. history. More broadly, his actions also represent the possibility of a major change in the understanding of, as well as, the actual relationship between church and state in America, a relationship crafted by centuries of judicial compromises and efforts to maintain the dynamic tension between both institutions.

The individuals profiled in *Religious Leaders and Faith-Based Politics* give us pause, then, because they represent the kinds of leaders that George W. Bush is seeking to work with now and into the near future. What might be extrapolated about the kind of leaders they are and the tenuous new relationship in the making?

First, new and independent individuals characterize the American religious leadership today, and they will be the kinds of persons who will transform the president's vision of faith-based collaboration with the government into reality. The spectrum of players is diverse and is made up of individuals who not only understand the political process in America but also know how to use its mechanisms to advance various social and charitable policies. In this book, Mormons, Evangelicals, Catholics, Mennonites, black Muslims, Pentecostals, and Methodists have been profiled to give an overview of what is going on in the religious leadership community at present. They are all well educated, grounded in their religious convictions, and committed to specific political matters. Many have advanced degrees. They know the extent, responsibility, and power of their positions.

Prominent among these leaders now are black American ministers: religious leaders of congregations that number in the thousands; financial controllers of church holdings that include old age homes, schools, rental properties, media outlets, and commercial real estate; and social activists who work to bring meaningful economic change within their communities. They have filled the void left by many social institutions and agencies that have opted to place their emphasis on suburban needs since the volatile civil rights movement in the 1960s. They educate those who are the poorest and are condemned to the worst schools and work with those who suffer the worst of crime and its effects.

The social model that is emerging among these black ministers is a paradigm based on entrepreneurship—one that empowers individuals, churches, and new for-profit and nonprofit organizations. It is the continuation and the expansion of Marcus Garvey's United Negro Movement Association, and Jesse Jackson's Operation Breadbasket of the 1970s and his Rainbow Coalition, which is working with Wall Street today. This progression is best seen in the ministry of T. D. Jakes. Equipped with new technologies and a masterful use of them, Jakes uses Christian and secular media outlets, television, publishing, music, and drama to impact millions of followers. Locally he is active in multiple dimensions of community development. Religiously, he is helping to energize thousands of churches and is starting hundreds more. Jakes's ministry, like that of the Reverend Floyd Flake, points to the fact that there is more going on within religious institutions than meets the eye. Powerful new social movements of this magnitude in America—in time—have always influenced politics and changed culture, often for the better. The first and second Great Awakenings in the 1700s and 1800s come to mind, laying the foundations for independence from England, the Civil War, and the end of slavery.

Second, the largest religious minority in the United States, represented by the Catholic Church, will mostly likely participate in the Bush administration's faith-based collaborative efforts. It has been less involved in the political process than it was during the volatile 1960s and 1970s because of a confluence of events that began in the early 1980s, prompting Linda Chavez, the former head of the Office of Public Liaison in the Reagan White House, to refer to the Catholic Church at the time as an organization that had the "body of a lion and the voice of a mouse."[15]

In the aftermath of Vatican II in the late 1960s, the Catholic Church was involved in politics throughout the world—an activism that was curtailed, however, by the accession of a new pope, John Paul II, in 1979. One of the pontiff's first acts, as head of a hierarchical organization in which he exercises dominant power, was to remind prelates in Latin America and the rest of the world forcefully that they were preachers and pastors, not politicians.[16] Leadership transitions then began to occur. Most of the social justice and liberation theology advocates of the post–Vatican II years in the United States were replaced, retired, demoted, or disciplined by the pope. Their replacements constitute a new generation of leaders, appointed to the hierarchy to deal with other issues on the conservative Vatican agenda.

This has sorely affected the U.S. Catholic religious establishment. By the 1970s the National Conference of Catholic Bishops/U.S. Catholic Conference (NCCB/USCC) was involved in trying to prevent the use and threat of nuclear weapons, lobbying for human rights in the Southern Hemisphere, protesting against *Roe v. Wade*, and defending the weak in economic matters. But in 1984, when John Cardinal O'Connor publicly challenged Catholic politicians such as Geraldine Ferraro, Mario Cuomo, and Edward Kennedy for their stands on abortion, the NCCB/USCC clarified the conditions under which Church leaders could be involved in politics. It stated that they could not take positions for or against particular parties or individual candidates and could not work to form a voting bloc or preempt the duties of individuals to decide whom they would support for public office.[17] A Church divided began to have less political influence among its adherents and in the nation. At about the same time, a group of individuals also brought suit against the Catholic Church, arguing that it was acting as a political, special interest group and should, therefore, lose its tax-exempt status. The Church won the *Abortion Mobilization Rights* case on a technicality,[18] but as a result the suit forced the NCCB/USCC to reconsider its activities in the political sphere and to pull back rather than risk its financial autonomy.

Catholic political involvement and its broad agenda in the United States have, therefore, changed in the last quarter of a century. Under Vatican direction, the Catholic Church in America has lost much of its domestic focus. Apart from the abortion issue, it has become more internationally concerned with human rights—defined as fetal, civil, social, and economic rights—and, more specifically, Third World development and debt forgiveness in light of post–Cold War change.

Nevertheless, Catholic religious leadership has already begun to respond favorably to the new administration's vision for collaboration in social and charitable work, a phenomenon that might also reignite the Church's involvement in the U.S. political process. Within days of the unveiling of the president's faith-based initiative plans, members of the Catholic hierarchy and clergy met with George W. Bush at the White House to begin to reestablish ties on matters of charitable and social services.[19] This is because of the fact that the Catholic Church is one of the major suppliers of health care and social services in the United States. Its vast network of hospitals, hospices, soup kitchens, and orphanages, along with its major social assistance agency, Catholic Charities, suggests that no plan for government–religious cooperation in this area can be successful without Catholic participation. Furthermore, Catholic coffers are becoming depleted—by a parochial educational system that is increasingly hard-pressed to work with the urban underserved and by activities to support a variety of prolife endeavors in the United States.[20] Charity is also expensive, often because of the high costs of professional salaries. As a result, it is safe to assume that the Catholic hierarchy will reconsider its domestic agenda in the very near future, as well as its *means* to institute new charitable programs. Should collaboration with the government occur, Catholics will have the opportunity to play a leading role in advancing social justice in America, an opening they cannot and do not want to miss.

As this situation shows, religious participation in politics ebbs and flows depending on circumstances, issues, perceived threats, resources, and leadership. It would not be surprising to see many other religious groups in America become more involved as well, given the direction of the present Bush administration.

Evangelicals, for example, have ready access to the Congress and White House today because they continue to vote in large numbers for Republicans and have leaders, such as Wheaton College graduate Speaker Dennis Hastert, representing their interests. The rise of conservative Protestant influence is much studied. Functioning as outsiders in the 1960s and 1970s, they gained some influence, first with born-again President Jimmy Carter and then with Ronald Reagan. The Reverend Jerry Falwell and his Moral Majority led this early reengagement with politics. But, disappointed with the policies of both Carter and Reagan on social issues, Evangelicals subsequently shifted their efforts into state and local politics and, through the efforts of Dr. James Dobson, the Reverend D. James Kennedy, and the Reverend Pat Robertson, have found much success. The political work of the Christian Right moved with considerable strength into precincts, candidate recruitment in elections, and voter registration.[21] The first Bush administration brought pro-life leader Kay Coles James into prominence, and Evangelicals were heavily represented at the Republican National Conventions in 1996 and 2000. At a more substantive policy level, Senator Daniel Coats and former Senator and current Attorney General John Ashcroft, both Evangelicals, have worked to make the government friendly to faith-based initiatives. As former governor, George W. Bush embraced this model in Texas and, in the wake of welfare reform, as president is now seeking to see it implemented at federal and state levels. Evangelical leaders, and others, will be at his side helping to make it happen.

WHAT MIGHT A FUTURE WITH GREATER RELIGIOUS/GOVERNMENT PARTICIPATION BE LIKE?

There are both unprecedented opportunities and pitfalls for religious leaders and faith-based organizations today. On the positive side, new technologies beckon. Government is cooperative. Young ministers and prelates are coming of age. Creativity in religious communities is unleashed. The poor are empowered. On the negative side, there is the possibility of losing religious distinctiveness and secularization, a potential for the abandonment of religious identity by faith-based organizations. Government cooperation could lead to government intrusion in religious matters. And state collaboration could end in decreasing public financial support or the state's abrogation of its social responsibilities. We believe, however, that even with these caveats there are still major problems in the body politic that can be overcome by the mutual efforts of faith-based organizations and their leaders and government officials for the common good. As President George W. Bush has said, "There are still deep needs and real suffering in the shadow of America's affluence, problems like addiction and abandonment and gang violence, domestic violence, mental illness and homelessness. We are called by conscience to respond."[22]

Although the new political milieu has the potential to replace the old way of providing social and charitable services with a collaborative one, we believe that the innovative religious leaders of today have an opportunity to take social justice and the general welfare in America to a new, *prophetic* level. The individuals profiled in this book, by and large, assure us of their commitments to a higher order of values, to a public scrutiny dedicated to the poor and underserved, and their desire to search for creative breakthroughs for the "least free." As a group of disparate individuals with different perspectives, they, each in a striking manner, give us a glimpse of the beginnings of the future. They strikingly characterize it as one that will be mutated by significant political, economic, and cultural differences. We believe that some of these changes can already be seen and that the very nature of change itself is changing. Taking on a paradigm of its own, it is a by-product of *prophetic politics*.

First, there is a new locus of change. Younger individuals with charisma and political expertise are replacing or overshadowing the traditional and mainstream religious leadership as the United States becomes more religiously diverse and technologically sophisticated. For example, T. D. Jakes is already exerting considerable influence on traditional African American denominations and on the white Charismatic and Pentecostal church communities—and beyond. It is difficult to find old-line leadership in the denominations with similar reach, for inflexible hierarchies and interests limit them.

Catholics and Episcopalians, for example, are at a disadvantage in the present environment and will have to reconsider the roles of the laity if they intend to pursue the Bush faith-based agenda. This is particularly true with regard to women and nuns, as Segers points out in her chapter on Sister Maureen Fiedler. Mainline churches will have to give greater respect to them and provide women with opportunities to fill new positions in delivering social and charitable services if they want to be major players in the collaboration between government and faith-based groups.

Second, the type of change that is occurring will be *strategic*. It will be indicative of a different kind of church–state relationship from top to bottom. Old models will have to be abandoned, and new paradigms, developed. Incremental change will no longer suffice to transform society. Not only do people expect religion and politics to work for them, they demand that it produce results quickly. Slow growth by itself is no longer acceptable. This places considerable pressure on religious leaders who must either meet this expectation or lose followers, that is, market share, and politicians who must solve problems or face being turned out of office. Old institutions that appear to be failing, be they local schools or local churches, are in jeopardy—as are old answers. When new leaders demonstrate that people working together can accomplish much and break new ground, the inertia of the past no longer seems inevitable but, in fact, foolish.

Churches will have to reach beyond denominational lines to ensure the success of future government–religious social and charitable initiatives. And they will also have to embrace the most needy already in their pews to break racial barriers and eliminate class divisions. Therefore, the type of change that religious leaders and their organizations will have to pursue must be a *strategic* one capable of transforming old relationships and forging new ones among religious leaders, as well as community and political leaders, and the public at large. Today's parish walls are porous—people flow in and out. Dogmatic concerns, efforts to preserve the purity and integrity of the faith, and proselytizing through evangelism, although admirable in themselves, will not alone solve the problems of America's complex society in the future. Religious leaders must now reach beyond these commitments to incorporate a civic vision in their ministry, to communicate with public officials and strangers alike, working with government to alleviate suffering and to raise up a new generation of productive citizens.

This broadening of perspective, which applies to religion, must also apply to politics. When city officials choose to relate to church leaders on common projects by bridging old barriers, they will begin to discover new resources. When people cooperate in politics across confessional lines, their strength will increase. City planning boards and zoning commissions may consider how best to enhance the spiritual experience of neighborhoods, assisting churches and their related programs. Mayors may grant access to pastors, who are major players in providing essential services. A new civic vision must include religion—and religion must have a civic vision as well.

Third, change is being created by new technologies. The technologies—for example, the Internet—include obvious ways to reach the public, not only in homes and schools but also in prisons and halfway houses. Religious leaders are now in the business of making movies, producing videos, and writing books. New structures also demonstrate their worth—from home schooling to church-encouraged entrepreneurial start-ups. New strategies, noted but barely touched on in this book, are equipping the laity for service—at home and in the community. People are encouraged to bring their talents to church, not just their problems, with the expectation that individual gifts with the help of others can be released and expanded in ways never done before. The list of activity groupings in a modern congregation—mobilizing resources—is astounding. Church, rather than being boring, is becoming a place to expect the unexpected.

What kind of future, then, can be anticipated in an America that sees collaboration between faith-based organizations and government? Most likely, it will be one characterized by a younger generation of religious leaders, less encumbered by hierarchy, with outreach to all, using innovative techniques, structures, and strategies to accomplish much in a short time. Although this all sounds trouble free, it is not. Challenges abound and include the following questions.

What dangers exist if religious leaders degenerate to the level of politicians dominated by ambition and greed? Politics and involvement with those in power always have the potential to corrupt the unwary. What will happen if certain religious groups strive to gain power or benefits? For example, the Mormons in Utah recently were accused of trying to control the press in Salt Lake City.[23] Orthodox Jews in New York who voted for Al Gore and Hillary Clinton allegedly did so to secure the pardon of religious felons imprisoned for fraud. The potential for mischief by the religious involved in politics is enormous—and always will be. For example, Evangelicals have had their own sets of vulnerabilities related to racism, and Catholics have sought to preserve their institutional interests. No one is exempt from the temptations of power or the need for scrutiny. There is only one standard for public rectitude.

Will a cozy relationship between government and religious groups result in an intrusion into or stifling of religious freedom and values? Will the necessary and clear distinctions in law between church and state be erased? A series of cases during the past twenty-five years suggests that this is, indeed, a persistent possibility. In 1979, Georgetown University in Washington, D.C., denied funds to a gay student organization on the basis of the fact that active homosexuality was forbidden within the teachings of the Catholic Church.[24] The students brought suit against the university and, in a decision by the highest appellate court in the District of Columbia, won the right to funding. The court reasoned that the government had a compelling interest to protect human rights and maintained that the university had to provide monies to the gay students or lose its ability to sell bonds or receive federal monies for student tuition loans. The Supreme Court was also as decisive in its decision in the *Bob Jones University* case,[25] holding that a compelling state interest to eliminate discrimination superseded the university's right to oppose interracial dating. In each case the university sought to maintain a religious rule for faith and practice but was required to abandon it for the implementation of state interests. Indeed, religious groups do have something to fear from the government and must weigh carefully the benefits that can be derived from faith-based activities carried out in collaboration with, and under the aegis of, civil authorities.

Are religious leaders playing roles that should really be handled by civil servants, that is, delivering goods and services to the poor and educating children? Or is the government usurping a legitimate role of private entities, including churches? At one time, in centuries past, church and private agencies, exclusively, managed schools and took care of the poor. In fact, churches should ask why the government wants to rely on religious groups for the implementation of social and charitable works. Are they ready to give these roles back to religious institutions? Or is there a legitimate and safe way to share social obligations? What is clear today is that government, by itself, is unable to solve the myriad social problems that exist. In fact, it may even exacerbate them. Defining jurisdiction—who is responsible for what service, who pays the cost, and who manages the program—is not easy in the modern context, in which government is presumed to be provider of first and last resort and yet in many instances is failing in its efforts.

Is it time to reassert a religious responsibility for the charitable needs of those least favored by circumstance? Should government increase its labors, reduce them, or delegate them? Pope John Paul II has continuously told the Catholic clergy that they are priests and pastors, not politicians. He has argued in his eighteen encyclicals that individuals must have the freedom to choose their futures and the paths to their own destinies. He has also maintained that government has the responsibility to help individuals achieve their potential and to provide those structures, such as authentic democracy and capitalism regulated by a rule of law, to make such success possible.[26] Therefore, he urges the Church to stand up for the alienated and marginalized in communities where hope is lost. What does he say on this difficult matter of jurisdiction, which has such obvious public policy implications? Clearly, he supports individual initiative and the mission of the Church to provide charitable and social services, as well as government help when persons, families, communities, and even nations cannot help themselves. Therefore, to him, the narrow definition of function—excluding priests from government service—does not contradict the Church's theological conviction and historic commitment to the poor. Although by itself this ruling on vocation says nothing about the jurisdiction of the government and the church, it is important to ask if the Catholic Church will respond to the Bush outreach as a historic opportunity to partner with government in a new way. Scholars such as Marvin Olasky, a Bush adviser, and John DiIulio see this as a creative opening, an invitation, in effect, to all religious groups to be involved in public life. But we contend that to be prophetic in the end, faith-based initiatives must also lead to a rebirth of voluntary charitable acts by citizens across the nation.

These questions of religion exercising undue influence, of government money and regulations undermining religious programs, and of the confusion of distinct roles for church and state should and do give us pause. We believe that all parties should proceed with caution because these problems will have to be sorted out step by step by religious leaders, politicians, and citizens. However, we also think that this collaboration is a fortuitous way to achieve *prophetic politics*—an opportunity to advance a higher order of values, embodied in social justice, through faith-based and government efforts within the constitutional processes of the United States.

Church and state must work together where this is lawful, without one co-opting the other, for the good of all. The future of a religious–civil partnership, to advance the general welfare and fulfill the needs of the "least free," is promising. Faith-based initiatives, then, as in the past, will provide the impetus to create positive public policies in America for the alienated and underserved. And with the additional assistance of government in the near future, they hold out the possibility of developing creative social and economic breakthroughs to implement them as well.

NOTES

1. George W. Bush, "On the Creation of a White House Office for Faith Based and Community Groups," *New York Times*, 30 January 2001: A18.

2. Bush, "On the Creation of a White House Office for Faith Based and Community Groups," A18.

3. Bush, "On the Creation of a White House Office for Faith Based and Community Groups," A18.

4. Bush, "On the Creation of a White House Office for Faith Based and Community Groups," A18.

5. Bush, "On the Creation of a White House Office for Faith Based and Community Groups," A18.

6. Bush, "On the Creation of a White House Office for Faith Based and Community Groups," A18.

7. Bush, "On the Creation of a White House Office for Faith Based and Community Groups," A18.

8. Bush, "On the Creation of a White House Office for Faith Based and Community Groups," A18.

9. See, for example, Hubert Morken, "Prophetic Politics: Three Models," *The Drew Gateway* (1984): 25–41; James E. Wood, ed., "Public Religion vis-á-vis Religion's Public Role," *Journal of Church and State* 41 (Winter 1999): 51–75; Robin Lovin, ed., *Religion*

and American Public Life: Interpretations and Explorations (New York: Paulist Press, 1986); and James Darsey, *The Prophetic Tradition and Radical Rhetoric in America* (New York: New York University Press, 1997).

10. Neal Riemer, *The Future of the Democratic Revolution: Toward a More Prophetic Politics* (New York: Praeger, 1984).

11. Riemer, *The Future of the Democratic Revolution*, 136.

12. *Pierce v. Society of Sisters*, 268 U.S. 510 (1925).

13. *Everson v. Board of Education*, 330 U.S. 1 (1947).

14. *Lemon v. Kurtzman*, 403 U.S. 602 (1971).

15. Linda Chavez, discussion with Jo Renee Formicola, the White House, Washington, D.C., 1982.

16. Pope John Paul II, "Opening Address," Puebla, Mexico, 28 January 1979; and Pope John Paul II, "Be Pastors, Not Politicians" (papal address given at Kinshasa, Zaire, 4 May 1980), published in *The Pope and Revolution*, ed. Quentin Quade (Washington, D.C.: Ethics and Public Policy Center, 1982), parts 2 and 4. For a deeper discussion, see Jo Renee Formicola, *Pope John Paul II: Prophetic Politician for Change* (Washington, D.C.: Georgetown University Press, in press).

17. National Conference of Catholic Bishops, "Statement by Bishops on Church Role in Politics," *New York Times*, 14 October 1984: 30.

18. *Abortion Rights Mobilization v. USCC and NCCB*, 87-416 Sup. Ct. (1987).

19. The meeting was actually held on 31 January 2001, two weeks after the president took office. See Press Secretary of the White House, press release, 31 January 2001, available at http://www.whitehouse.gov. At that gathering the president revealed that although he had discussed initiatives earlier about mentoring and after-school programs, he wanted to add another component to the discussion: a reform of the tax code that would allow nonitemizers to deduct charitable giving off their incomes. This, George Bush believed, would give people a greater incentive to donate to their churches.

20. See Hubert Morken and Jo Renee Formicola, *The Politics of School Choice* (Lanham, Md.: Rowman and Littlefield, 1999).

21. See papers presented by Hubert Morken on Evangelical politics in the United States: "Public Secondary Education: Equal Access and the Clash over Student Religious Expression," paper presented at a meeting of the American Political Science Association, 1989; "Religious Lobbying at the State Level: Case Studies in a Continuing Role for the New Christian Right," paper presented at a meeting of the American Political Science Association, 1990; "Herbert W. Titus and Phillip E. Johnson, the Children of Liberalism: Religious Conversion, Law, and Politics," paper presented at a meeting of the American Political Science Association, 1991; "The Evangelical Legal Response to the ACLU: Religion, Politics, and the First Amendment," paper presented at a meeting of the American Political Science Association, 1992; "The San Diego Model: Religious-Identity Concealment as Political Strategy," paper presented at a meeting of the American Political Science Association, 1993; "No Special Rights: The Thinking behind Colorado's Amendment #2 Strategy," paper presented at a meeting of the American Political Science Association, 1994.

22. Bush, "On the Creation of a White House Office for Faith Based and Community Groups," A18.

23. Felicity Barringer, "Of Church, State and Journalism in Salt Lake City," *New York Times*, 7 January 2001: section 3, 1 and 13.

24. For a deeper discussion of the case, see Jo Renee Formicola, "The Gays, the Government and Georgetown," in *Church Polity and American Politics*, ed. Mary Segers (New York: Garland Publishing, 1990), 233–49.

25. *U.S. v. Bob Jones University*, 461 U.S. (1983).

26. See, particularly, Pope John Paul II, *Sollicitudo Rei Socialis* (Boston: Daughters of St. Paul, 1987); and Pope John Paul II, *Centesimus Annus* (Boston: Daughters of St. Paul, 1991).

Bibliography

Abbott, Walter M., S.J. *The Documents of Vatican II*. New York: Herder and Herder, 1966.
Abortion Rights Mobilization v. USCC and NCCB, 87-416 Sup. Ct. (1987).
"Al Sharpton Sues RNC for $30 Million." Available at http://www.courttv.com.
Alexander, Elizabeth, and Maureen Fielder. "The Equal Rights Amendment and Abortion: Separate and Distinct." *America* 142, no. 2 (12 April 1980): 314–18.
Allen, Mike. "An 'Unscary Mike' Offered to Voters." *Richmond Times-Dispatch*, 29 August 1993: B1.
———. "Farris Positions: Extremist or in Sync?" *Richmond Times-Dispatch*, 29 August 1993: B5.
American Catholic Committee. *Toward the Future: Catholic Social Teaching and the U.S. Economy*. New York: American Catholic Committee, 1984.
Anderson, Lavina Fielding. "Dallin H. Oaks: The Disciplined Edge." *Ensign* 11, no. 4 (April 1981): 32–37.
Armstrong, Virginia C., and Michael Farris. *The Christian World View of Law*. Sunnyvale, Calif.: Coalition on Revival, Inc., 1986.
Arrington, Leonard J. *Great Basin Kingdom: An Economic History of the Latter-day Saints, 1830–1900* (Lincoln: University of Nebraska Press, 1958).
Arrington, Leonard J., and Davis Bitton. *The Mormon Experience: A History of the Latter-day Saints*. New York: Vintage Press, 1980.
Au, William A. *The Cross, the Flag, and the Bomb: American Catholics Debate War and Peace, 1960–1983*. Westport, Conn.: Greenwood Press, 1985.
Auping, John. *Religion and Social Justice: The Case of Christianity and the Abolition of Slavery in America*. Mexico City: Universidad Iberoamericana, 1994.
Baer, Hans, and Merrill Singer. *African-American Religion in the Twentieth Century: Varieties of Protest and Accommodation*. Knoxville: University of Tennessee Press, 1992.
Baker, Peter. "Farris Asserts His Religious Tolerance." *Washington Post*, 18 October 1993: B3.
Barringer, Felicity. "Of Church, State and Journalism in Salt Lake City." *New York Times*, 7 January 2001: section 3, 1 and 13.

Barstow, David. "The 2000 Campaign: The Arizona Senator; McCain Denounces Political Tactics of Christian Right." *New York Times*, 29 February 2000: A1.

Bass, Jack, and Walter DeVries. *The Transformation of Southern Politics*. New York: Basic Books, 1976.

Bates, Stephen. *Battleground*. New York: Henry Holt and Co., 1994.

———. "Christian Crossover." *Washington City Paper*, 30 July 1993: 22.

Benestad, J. Brian. *The Pursuit of a Just Social Order*. Washington, D.C.: Ethics and Public Policy Center, 1981.

Bernardin, Joseph Cardinal. *Consistent Ethic of Life*. Kansas City, Mo.: Sheed and Ward, 1988.

Billingsley, Lloyd. *The Generation That Knew Not Josef*. Portland, Oreg.: Multnomah Press, 1985.

Billy Graham Evangelical Association. *The Prodigal*. Videocassette. Minneapolis, Minn.: World Wide Pictures, 1983.

Blackstock, Nelson. *COINTELPRO: The FBI's Secret War on Political Freedom*. New York: Vintage Books, 1975.

Blake, John. "Amazing Jakes." *Atlanta Journal-Constitution*, 31 July 1999.

Bloom, Harold. *The American Religion: The Emergence of the Post-Christian Nation*. New York: Simon and Schuster, 1992.

Bositis, David A. "Blacks and the 1996 Elections: A Preliminary Analysis." Paper prepared for the Joint Center for Political and Economic Studies, Washington, D.C., 1996.

Broadway, Bill. "Tending God's Garden—Evangelical Group Embraces Environment." *Washington Post*, 17 February 1996: C8.

Bush, George W. "On the Creation of a White House Office for Faith Based and Community Groups." *New York Times*, 30 January 2001: A18.

Bush, Rod. *We Are Not What We Seem: Black Nationalism and Class Struggle in the American Century*. New York: New York University Press, 1999.

Bushman, Richard L. *Joseph Smith and the Beginnings of Mormonism*. Urbana: University of Illinois Press, 1984.

Byrnes, Timothy A. *Catholic Bishops in American Politics*. Princeton: Princeton University Press, 1991.

Camporreales, Hans. "Elder Oaks Talks to Judges." *Deseret News*, 17 July 2000, available at http://www.desnews.com, accessed 19 July 2000.

Carmichael, Stokely, and Charles V. Hamilton. *Black Power*. New York: Vintage Books, 1967.

Carmines, Edward, and James Stimson. *Issue Evolution*. Princeton: Princeton University Press, 1989.

Castelli, Jim. *The Bishops and the Bomb: Waging Peace in a Nuclear Age*. Garden City, N.Y.: Doubleday, 1983.

Charter Schools Institute of the State University of New York, http://www.newyorkcharters.org.

Chavis, Benjamin. *Psalms from Prison*. New York: The Pilgrim Press, 1983.

Childs, John Brown. *The Political Black Minister: A Study in Afro-American Politics and Religion*. Boston: G. K. Hall, 1980.

Chilton, David. *Productive Christians in an Age of Guilt Manipulators: A Biblical Response to Ronald J. Sider*. Tyler, Texas: Institute for Christian Economics, 1985.

Christianity Today, http://www.christianitytoday.com/ct/current/0221/0221c.html.

Church Educational System. *Church History in the Fulness of Times.* Salt Lake City: LDS Church, 1989.
Church of God in Christ. "The Story of Our Church." Available at http://www.cogic.org.
Church of Latter-day Saints, http://www.lds.org.
Churchill, Ward, and Jim Vander Wall. *Agents of Repression.* Boston: South End Press, 1990.
———. *The COINTELPRO Papers.* Boston: South End Press, 1990.
Cleage, Albert, Jr. *Black Christian Nationalism.* New York: William Morrow and Co., Inc., 1972.
———. *The Black Messiah.* New York: William Morrow and Co., Inc., 1968.
Coalition on Revival. *A Manifesto for the Christian Church.* Sunnyvale, Calif.: Coalition on Revival, Inc., 4 July 1986.
Cone, James H. *Black Theology and Black Power.* New York: Seabury, 1969.
———. *A Black Theology of Liberation.* Maryknoll, N.Y.: Orbis, 1986.
———. *Malcolm, Martin and America: A Dream or a Nightmare?* Maryknoll, N.Y.: Orbis Books, 1991.
Cross, Theodore, and Robert Bruce Slater. "The 1996 Elections: The Real Victor Was Black Voter Apathy." *Journal of Blacks in Higher Education* (Winter 1996): 120–27.
Cruse, Harold. *The Crisis of the Negro Intellectual.* New York: William Morrow, 1967.
Darsey, James. *The Prophetic Tradition and Radical Rhetoric in America.* New York: New York University Press, 1997.
Dawson, Michael C. *Behind the Mule: Race and Class in African-American Politics.* Princeton: Princeton University Press, 1993.
Dulles, Avery. "What Is the Doctrinal Authority of a Bishops' Conference?" *Origins* 14, no. 32 (24 January 1985): 528–34.
Egan, Timothy. "Timothy Leary Meets the Moral Majority." *Seattle Post-Intelligencer,* 16 April 1981: A2.
Elvin, John. "Political Faith." Insight on the News, *Washington Times,* 4 September 2000: 10.
The Empire Foundation and the Lehrman Institute. *Students at Risk: New Yorkers on Education.* New Rochelle, N.Y.: Lehrman Institute, 1995.
Evangelical Environmental Network. Private files, Wynnewood, Pa.; and http://www.esa-online.org/een, http://www.creationcare.org.
Evangelicals for Social Action. Papers, collection 37, Billy Graham Center Archives, Wheaton College, Ill; and http://www.esa-online.org.
"Evangelicals on Justice: Socially Speaking. . . ." *Christianity Today,* 21 December 1973: 38–39.
Everson v. Board of Education, 330 U.S. 1 (1947).
Ewens, Mary. "Political Activity of American Sisters before 1970." In B*etween God and Caesar: Priests, Sisters and Political Office in the United States,* ed. Madonna Kolbenschlag, 41–59. New York: Paulist Press, 1985.
Farris, Michael P. "Conservative Forum." *Human Events,* 22 April 1994.
———. *Constitutional Law for Christian Students.* Paeonian Springs, Va.: Home School Legal Defense Association, 1990.
———. "Fundamentalists Often Targets of Bigotry." *USA Today,* 11 August 1986: A8.
———. *The Home Court Reporter.* November 1991.
———. *Home Schooling and the Law.* Paeonian Springs, Va.: Home Legal Defense Association, 1990.

———. *The Home Schooling Father*. Hamilton, Va.: Michael P. Farris, 1992.
———. *Michael Farris in His Own Words*. Washington, D.C.: People for the American Way, 1993.
———. "People and Events." *Church and State* (April 1988): 14.
———. "Remarks to the Virginia Beach City Republican Committee Meeting." 12 April 1993.
———. *Where Do I Draw the Line?* Minneapolis: Bethany House Publishing, 1992.
Fenton Communications. "Evangelicals Kick Off Million-Dollar Campaign to Protect Endangered Species." Press release, 31 January 1996.
———. "The Truth about the Textbook Controversy." "Farris for Lt. Governor" press release, 1 May 1993.
Feuer, Alan. "Asking How Sharpton Pays for Those Suits." *New York Times*, 21 December 2000: B1, B6.
Fielder, Maureen. "Claiming Our Power as Women in the Midst of Political Struggle." In *Church Polity and American Politics: Issues in Contemporary American Catholicism*, ed. Mary Segers, 195–96. New York: Garland Publishing, 1990.
———. "The Right to Dissent and Canonical Status: Must We Now Choose?" Unpublished manuscript, February 1987.
———. "Sounding the Feminist Trumpet at the 'Walls of Jericho.'" Address to the National Organization for Women, Washington, D.C., 10 July 1985.
———, and Dolly Pomerleau. "American Catholics and the Ordination of Women." *America* 138, no. 1 (14 January 1978): 11–14.
———, and Dolly Pomerleau. *Are Catholics Ready? An Exploration of the Views of 'Emerging Catholics' on Women in Ministry*. Mt. Ranier, Md.: Quixote Center, 1978.
———, and Linda Rabben, eds. *Rome Has Spoken: A Guide to Forgotten Papal Statements, and How They Have Changed through the Centuries*. New York: The Crossroad Publishing Co., 1998.
Firmage, Edwin B. "Restoring the Church: Zion in the Nineteenth and Twenty-first Centuries." In *The Wilderness of Faith*, ed. John Sillito, 1–13. Salt Lake City: Signature Books, 1991.
Fiske, Warren. "Lt. Governor Hopeful Distances Himself from 'Hyperbole' of Past." *Virginia Pilot and Ledger-Star*, 5 September 1993: A3.
Flake, Floyd, and Donna Marie Williams. *The Way of the Bootstrapper: Nine Action Steps for Achieving Your Dreams*. New York: HarperCollins, 1999.
Formicola, Jo Renee. "The Gays, the Government and Georgetown." In *Church Polity and American Politics: Issues in Contemporary American Catholicism*, ed. Mary Segers, 233–49. New York: Garland Publishing, 1990.
———. *Pope John Paul II: Prophetic Politician for Change*. Washington, D.C.: Georgetown University Press, in press.
Fowler, Robert Booth. *A New Engagement: Evangelical Political Thought, 1966–1976*. Grand Rapids, Mich.: Eerdmans, 1982.
———. *The Greening of Protestant Thought*. Chapel Hill: University of North Carolina Press, 1995.
———, and Allen D. Hertzke. *Religion and Politics in America*. New York: Westview Press, 1995.
———, Allen D. Hertzke, and Laura R. Olson. *Religion and Politics in America: Faith, Culture, and Strategic Choices*. 2nd ed. Boulder: Westview Press, 1999.

Franklin, John Hope. *From Slavery to Freedom*. New York: Alfred A. Knopf, 1967.
――. *The Free Negro in North Carolina 1790–1860*. Chapel Hill: University of North Carolina Press, 1995.
Gallagher, Winifred. *Working on God*. New York: Vintage, 1999.
Gardell, Mattias. *In the Name of Elijah Muhammad: Louis Farrakhan and the Nation of Islam*. Durham: Duke University Press, 1996.
Gay, Craig M. *With Liberty and Justice for Whom? The Recent Evangelical Debate over Capitalism*. Grand Rapids, Mich.: Eerdmans, 1991.
Genovese, Eugene. *Roll, Jordan, Roll*. New York: Vintage Books, 1974.
Gessert, Robert A., and J. Bryan Hehir. *The New Nuclear Debate*. New York: Council on Religion and International Affairs, 1976.
Glennon, Fred. "Blessed Be the Ties that Bind? The Challenge of Charitable Choice to Moral Obligation." *Journal of Church and State* 42, no. 4 (Autumn 2000): 825–43.
Glick, Brian. *War at Home: Covert Action against U.S. Activists and What We Can Do About It*. Boston: South End Press, 1989.
Goodstein, Laurie. "Catholics Contest Evangelical's Radio Dominance." *New York Times*, 15 August 1999: 1.
Gordon, Eugene. "A New Religion for the Negro." In *A Documentary History of the Negro People in the United States*, vol. 3, ed. Herbert Aptheker, 572–79. New York: Citadel Press, 1972.
Greeley, Andrew. *The Catholic Myth*. New York: Scribner's, 1990.
Hadden, Jeffrey K., Anson Shupe, James Hawdon, and Kenneth Martin. "Why Jerry Falwell Killed the Moral Majority." In *The God Pumpers: Religion in the Electronic Age*, eds. Marshall W. Fishwick and Ray B. Browne, 101–15. Bowling Green, Ohio: Bowling Green State University Popular Press, 1987.
Hamilton, Charles V. *The Black Preacher*. New York: William Morrow, 1972.
Harris, Fredrick. *Something Within: Religion in Afro-American Political Activism*. New York: Oxford University Press, 1999.
Harris, Teresa. "Holding Up the Stones." *Gospel Today* 10, no. 1 (January 1999): 25–28.
Hartocollis, Anemona. "Religious Leaders Plan Schools with Public Funds in New York." *New York Times*, 29 December 1998: A1.
Hays, Charlotte. "The Voice in the Bishops' Ear." *Washington Post Magazine*, 3 April 1983: 6–7, 11–12.
Hehir, J. Bryan. "Catholic Theology at Its Best." *Harvard Divinity Bulletin* 27, nos. 2–3 (1998): 13.
――. "The Church in the World: Responding to the Call of the Council." The Marianist Award Lecture. Dayton, Ohio: University of Dayton Press, 1995.
――. "Church–State and Church–World: The Ecclesiological Implications." *Proceedings of the Catholic Theological Society of America* 41 (1986): 54–74.
――. "The Consistent Ethic: Public Policy Implications." In *Consistent Ethic of Life*, Joseph Cardinal Bernardin, 230–31. Kansas City, Mo.: Sheed and Ward, 1988.
――. "The Just War Ethic and Catholic Theology: Dynamics of Change and Continuity." In *War or Peace? The Search for New Answers*, ed. Thomas A. Shannon, 15–39. Maryknoll, N.Y.: Orbis, 1980.
――. "Moral Choice and World Politics." *Commonweal* (18 December 1981): 713, 730.
――. "The Perennial Need for Philosophical Discourse." In "Theology and Philosophy in Public: A Symposium on John Courtney Murray's Unfinished Agenda," theme

issue, ed. David Hollenbach, S.J., *Theological Studies* 40, no. 4 (December 1979): 710–13.

———. "A Public Church." *Origins* 14, no. 3 (31 May 1984): 40–43.

———. "Reflections on Recent Teaching." In *Nuclear Disarmament: Key Statements of Popes, Bishops, Councils, and Churches*, ed. Robert Hyer. New York: Paulist, 1982.

Henig, Jeffrey, Richard Hula, Marion Orr, and Desiree Pedescleaux. *The Color of School Reform*. Princeton: Princeton University Press, 1999.

Hill, Marvin S. *Quest for Refuge: The Mormon Flight from American Pluralism*. Salt Lake City: Signature Books, 1989.

Hinckley, Gordon B. "The Family: A Proclamation to the World." *Ensign* 25, no. 11 (November 1995): 102.

Hoffman, Stanley. *Duties beyond Borders: On the Limits and Possibilities of Ethical International Politics*. Syracuse: Syracuse University Press, 1981.

Horsch, James E., ed. *Mennonite Directory 1999*. Scottdale, Pa.: Herald Press, 1999.

Howard Center. "A Call from the Families of the World." 17–20 May 1998, available at http://www.worldcongress.org/call99, accessed 8 August 2000.

Hunter, James Davison. *Culture Wars: The Struggle to Define America*. New York: Basic Books, 1992.

Hutchinson, Earl Ofari. "The Criminalization of Black Men." In *MultiAmerica*, ed. Ishmael Reed, 417–24. New York: Penguin Books, 1997.

Jakes, T. D. *The Great Investment: Faith, Family, and Finance*. New York: G. P. Putnam's Sons, 2000.

———. *Maximize the Moment*. New York: G. P. Putnam's Sons, 1999.

———. *Woman, Thou Art Loosed! Healing the Wounds of the Past*. Tulsa: Albury Publishing, 1996.

John Paul II. "Be Pastors, Not Politicians" (papal address given at Kinshasa, Zaire, 4 May 1980). In *The Pope and Revolution*, ed. Quentin Quade, 101–07. Washington, D.C.: Ethics and Public Policy Center, 1982.

———. *Centesimus Annus*. Boston: Daughters of St. Paul, 1991.

———. "Opening Address." Puebla, Mexico, 28 January 1979.

———. *Sollicitudo Rei Socialis*. Boston: Daughters of St. Paul, 1987.

Jones, Jeffrey McClain. "Ronald Sider and Radical Evangelical Political Theology." Ph.D. dissertation, Northwestern University and Garrett-Evangelical Theological Seminary, 1990.

Katzenstein, Mary F. *Faithful and Fearless: Moving Feminist Protest in the Church and Military*. Princeton: Princeton University Press, 1998.

Key, V. O., Jr. *Southern Politics in State and Nation*. New York: Alfred A. Knopf, 1949.

Klinghoffer, David. *The Lord Will Gather Me In: My Journey to Jewish Orthodoxy*. New York: The Free Press, 1999.

Krol, Cardinal John. "Testimony on Salt II," *Origins* 9 (1979): 197–98.

Kurlander, Gabrielle, and Jacqueline Salit, eds. *Independent Black Leadership in America*. New York: Castillo International Publications, 1990.

LaHaye, Tim F., and Jerry B. Jenkins. *The Indwelling: The Beast Takes Possession*. Wheaton, Ill.: Tyndale House, 2000.

Lapin, Daniel. *America's Real War*. Sisters, Oreg.: Multnomah Publishers, 1999.

———. "Does God Command Environmental Extremism?" Available at http://www.towardtradition.org.

———, and Michael Medved. Personal audiotape. Address at the Jewish Policy Center Conference, Philadelphia, 9 August 2000.
Law, Bernard Cardinal. "Defining the Roman Catholic Advocacy of Life." *Boston Globe*, 13 February 2000: E5.
Layton, Mike. "State Moral Majority Chief Talks about Sex." *Seattle Post-Intelligencer*, 15 February 1981: A2.
Lecky, Robert S., and H. Eliot Wright, eds. *Black Manifesto: Religion, Racism, and Reparations*. New York: Sheed and Ward, 1969.
Lemon v. Kurtzman, 403 U.S. 602 (1971).
LeQuire, Stan. "A Ministry of Madness." Unpublished manuscript, Eastern Baptist Theological Seminary, Wynnewood, Pa., 2000.
Lincoln, C. Eric. *The Black Church since Frazier*. New York: Schocken Books, 1974.
———, and Lawrence H. Mamiya. *The Black Church in the African American Experience*. Durham: Duke University Press, 1990.
Lloyd, R. Scott. "Looking Forward to Congress of Families." *Deseret News*, 28 November 1998, available at http://www.desnews.com, accessed 8 August 2000.
Lovin, Robin, ed. *Religion and American Public Life: Interpretations and Explorations*. New York: Paulist Press, 1986.
Lynch, James R. "Christian Peacemaking Teams: Opportunities for Active Peacemaking." In *Sustaining Peace Witness in the Twenty-first Century: Papers from the 1997 Quaker Peace Roundtable*, ed. Chuck Fager, 263–304. Wallingford, Pa.: Pendle Hill Issues Program, 1997.
Magida, Arthur J. *Prophet of Rage: A Life of Louis Farrakhan*. New York: Basic Books, 1996.
The Manhattan Institute, http://www.manhattan-institute.org.
Mansbridge, Jane. *Why We Lost the ERA*. Chicago: University of Chicago Press, 1986.
Marable, Manning. *Black American Politics: From the Washington Marches to Jesse Jackson*. London: Verso, 1985.
———. "Black Fundamentalism and Conservative Black Nationalism." *Race and Class* 39, no. 4 (April-June 1998): 1–22.
———. "Black Politics after the March." *New Statesman and Society* 8, no. 376 (October 1995): 14–17.
———. "Reaganism, Racism, and Reaction: Black Political Realignment in the 1980s." *The Black Scholar* 13, no. 6 (1982): 2–15.
Marty, Martin. *The Public Church: Mainline, Evangelical, Catholic*. New York: Crossroad, 1981.
McAdam, Doug. *Political Process and Development of Black Insurgency, 1930–1970*. Chicago: University of Chicago Press, 1982.
McBrien, Richard. *Caesar's Coin: Religion and Politics in America*. New York: Macmillan, 1987.
McClain, Paula D., and Joseph Stewart. *"Can We All Get Along?" Racial and Ethnic Minorities in American Politics*. 2nd ed. New York: Westview Press, 1998.
McCormick, Joseph P., II, and Sekou Franklin. "Expressions of Racial Consciousness in the African-American Community: Data from the Million Man March." Paper presented at the Annual Meeting of the American Political Science Association, Boston, September 1998.
McDonnell, Lorraine M., and Richard F. Elmore. *Alternative Policy Instruments*. Santa Monica: Center for Policy Research in Education, the Rand Corporation, 1987.

McDougall, Harold. *Black Baltimore*. Philadelphia: Temple University Press, 1993.
McIntyre, Michael. "Religionists on the Campaign Trail." *The Christian Century*, 27 December 1972: 1319–22.
McMurrin, Sterling M. *The Theological Foundations of the Mormon Religion*. Salt Lake City: University of Utah Press, 1965.
McNamara, Jo Ann. *Sisters in Arms: Catholic Nuns through Two Millennia*. Cambridge, Mass.: Harvard University Press, 1996.
Milbank, Dana. "Bush to Host Black Ministers." *Washington Post*, Federal Page, The Transition, 19 December 2000: A1.
———, and Hamil R. Harris. "Bush, Religious Leaders Meet." *Washington Post*, 21 December 2000: A6.
Mill, John Stuart. *On Liberty*. 1859.
Million Family March. *The National Agenda: Public Policy Issues, Analyses, and Programmatic Plan of Action 2000–2008*. Washington, D.C.: Million Man March, Inc., 2000.
Miller, Lisa. "Grammy Nomination, Book Deal, TV Spots—A Holy Empire Is Born." *Wall Street Journal*, 21 August 1998.
Mohler, R. Albert, Jr. "Against an Immoral Tide." *New York Times*, Opinion, 19 June 2000.
Morken, Hubert. "The Evangelical Legal Response to the ACLU: Religion, Politics, and the First Amendment." Paper presented at a meeting of the American Political Science Association, 1992.
———. "Herbert W. Titus and Phillip E. Johnson, the Children of Liberalism: Religious Conversion, Law, and Politics." Paper presented at a meeting of the American Political Science Association, 1991.
———. "No Special Rights: The Thinking behind Colorado's Amendment #2 Strategy." Paper presented at a meeting of the American Political Science Association, 1994.
———. "Prophetic Politics: Three Models." *The Drew Gateway* (1984): 25–41.
———. "Public Secondary Education: Equal Access and the Clash over Student Religious Expression." Paper presented at a meeting of the American Political Science Association, 1989.
———. "Religious Lobbying at the State Level: Case Studies in a Continuing Role for the New Christian Right." Paper presented at a meeting of the American Political Science Association, 1990.
———. "The San Diego Model: Religious-Identity Concealment as Political Strategy." Paper presented at a meeting of the American Political Science Association, 1993.
———, and Jo Renee Formicola. *The Politics of School Choice*. Lanham, Md.: Rowman and Littlefield, 1999.
Morris, Lorenzo. "The Million Man March and Presidential Politics." Paper presented at the Annual Meeting of the National Conference of Black Political Scientists, Savannah, Ga., March 1996.
Mozert v. Hawkins Country Board of Education, 582 F. Supp. 201, 201 E.D. Tenn. (1984).
Murray, John Courtney. *We Hold These Truths: Catholic Reflections on the American Proposition*. New York: Sheed and Ward, 1960.
Myerson, Michael. *Nothing Could Be Finer*. New York: International Publishers, 1978.
Nash, Ronald H. *Why the Left Is Not Right: The Religious Left—Who They Are and What They Believe*. Grand Rapids, Mich.: Zondervan, 1996.

Nathan, Richard P., Julian Chow, and Michael L. Owens. "The Flipside of the Underclass." *Rockefeller Institute Bulletin* (Winter 1995): 14–22.
National Conference of Catholic Bishops. "Statement by Bishops on Church Role in Politics." *New York Times*, 14 October 1984: 30.
New York Charter School Resource Center, http://www.nycharterschools.org.
New York State Education Department. "New York City Public Schools 1998–1999 Annual District Report for District 29." Available at http://www.emsc.nysed.gov/repcrd2000.
New York State Education Department, http://www.emsc.nysed.gov.
Niebuhr, Gustav, and Laurie Goodstein. "New Wave of Evangelists Vying for National Pulpit." *New York Times*, 1 January 1999.
Novak, Michael. "Moral Clarity in the Nuclear Age." *National Review* 35 (1 April 1983): 354–92.
Oaks, Dallin H. "Abortion and Due Process." *Child and Family* 9, no. 4 (1970): 343–48.
———. "Antidotes for the School Prayer Cases." *The Improvement Era* 66 (December 1963): 1048–50, 1134–36.
———. "The Divinely Inspired Constitution." *Ensign* 22, no. 2 (February 1992): 68–74.
———. "The Family in Today's World." *Utah Parent Teacher* (May–June 1972): 8–11.
———. "Free Agency and Freedom." In *The Book of Mormon: Second Nephi, The Doctrinal Structure*, ed. Monte S. Nyman and Charles D. Tate Jr., 1–17. Provo: Religious Studies Center, Brigham Young University, 1989.
———. "Introduction." In *The Wall between Church and State*, ed. Dallin H. Oaks, 1–16. Chicago: University of Chicago Press, 1963.
———. "Judicial Activism." *Harvard Journal of Law and Public Policy* 7, no. 1 (1984): 1–11.
———. "On Learning and Becoming." In *On Becoming a Disciple-Scholar*, ed. Henry B. Eyring, 91–101. Salt Lake City: Bookcraft, 1995.
———. "Religion and Law in the Eighties." In *Belief, Faith and Reason*, ed. John A. Howard, 109–26. Belfast: Christian Journals, 1981.
———. "Religion in Public Life." *Ensign* 20, no. 7 (July 1990): 7–13.
———. "Religious Values and Public Policy." *Ensign* 22, no. 10 (October 1992): 60–64.
———. "Rights and Responsibilities." *Mercer Law Review* 36 (1985): 427–42.
———. "Same-Gender Attraction." *Ensign* 25, no. 10 (October 1995): 6–14.
———. "Separation, Accommodation, and the Future of Church and State." *DePaul Law Review* 35, no. 1 (Fall 1985): 1–22.
———. "Some Responsibilities of Citizenship." In *The Spirit of America*, 105–23. Salt Lake City: Bookcraft, 1998.
———. "Statement on the Religious Freedom Restoration Act." Testimony before the Committee on the Judiciary, U.S. Senate, on S. 2969 (18 September 1992): 30–40.
———. "Statement on the Religious Freedom Restoration Act." Testimony before the Subcommittee on Civil and Constitutional Rights of the Committee on the Judiciary, U.S. House of Representatives, on H.R. 2797 (13 May 1992): 23–32.
———. "Statement on the Religious Liberty Protection Act." Testimony before the Committee on the Judiciary, U.S. Senate, on S. 2148 (23 June 1998): 6–17.
———. "Weightier Matters." Devotional address at Brigham Young University, 9 February 1999. Available at http://speeches.byu.edu/devo/98–99/OaksW99.html, accessed 10 July 2000.

———. "World Peace." *Ensign* 20, no. 5 (May 1990): 71–73.
———, and Joseph I. Bentley. "Joseph Smith and Legal Process: In the Wake of the Steamboat *Nauvoo*." *Brigham Young University Law Review*, no. 3 (1976): 735–82.
———, and Marvin S. Hill. *Carthage Conspiracy: The Trial of the Accused Assassins of Joseph Smith*. Urbana: University of Illinois Press, 1975.
———, and Lance B. Wickman. "The Missionary Work of the Church of Jesus Christ of Latter-day Saints." In *Sharing the Book: Perspectives on the Rights and Wrongs of Proselytism*, ed. John Witte Jr. and Richard C. Martin, 247–75. Maryknoll, N.Y.: Orbis Books, 1999.
O'Brien, David J., and Thomas A. Shannon, eds. *Catholic Social Thought: The Documentary Heritage*. Maryknoll, N.Y.: Orbis Books, 1992.
O'Dea, Thomas F. *The Mormons*. Chicago: University of Chicago Press, 1957.
Ostrom, Carol M. "Conservative Christians Fear 'Humanistic' Takeover." *Seattle Times*, 9 April 1983.
Owens, Michael Leo. "Local Party Failure and Alternative, Black Church-Based Nonparty Organizations." *Western Journal of Black Studies* 21, no. 3 (1997): 162–72.
Ozard, Dwight. "*Rich Christians in an Age of Hunger:* An Introduction." *Prism* (published by Evangelicals for Social Action) (May–June 1997): 8–9.
Patrick Henry College, http://www.phc.edu.
Persons, Georgia. *Dilemmas of Black Politics*. New York: HarperCollins, 1993.
Pierce v. Society of Sisters, 268 U.S. 510 (1925).
Pierce, Neal R. *The Border South States*. New York: Norton, 1975.
Pohlmann, Marcus D. *Black Politics in Conservative America*. 2nd ed. New York: Longman, 1999.
Pottenger, John R. "Mormonism and the American Industrial State." *International Journal of Social Economics* 14, no. 2 (1987): 25–38.
Press Secretary of the White House. Press release, 31 January 2001, available at http://www.whitehouse.gov.
Public Agenda. *On Thin Ice: How Advocates and Opponents Could Misread the Public's Views on Vouchers and Charter Schools*. New York: Public Agenda, 1999.
Pruzan, Adam. "Senator Lieberman and Torah Values." Toward Tradition, press release, 6 October 2000.
Quinn, Archbishop John R. "Remarks as President of the NCCB on President Carter's Decision to Defer Production of Neutron Warheads." In *Nuclear Disarmament: Key Statements of Popes, Bishops, Councils, and Churches*, ed. Robert Hyer, 195–96. New York: Paulist, 1982.
Quixote Center, http://www.quixote.org.
Rabkin, Jeremy. "The Culture War That Isn't." *Policy Review*, no. 96 (August and September 1999): 3–19.
Raboteau, Albert. *Slave Religion: The "Invisible Institution" in the Antebellum South*. New York: Oxford University Press, 1978.
Reed, Adolph, Jr. "Black Politics Gone Haywire." *The Progressive* 59, no. 12: 20–23.
Religious New Service. "Evangelicals Back Up Endangered Species." *Cleveland Plain Dealer*, 5 February 1996.
Riemer, Neal. *The Future of the Democratic Revolution: Toward a More Prophetic Politics*. New York: Praeger, 1984.
"Ronald J[ames] Sider." *Contemporary Authors Online*. Farmington Hills, Mich.: The Gale Group, 1999.

Rosin, Hanna. "Force for Change: Preaching Phenom Stops by Washington." *Washington Post*, 11 September 1999.

Rozell, Mark J., and Clyde Wilcox. Second Coming: *The New Christian Right in Virginia Politics*. Baltimore: Johns Hopkins University Press, 1996.

Salem, D'Jamila. "Stronger Endangered Species Law Urged—Coalition of Evangelicals Opens Campaign to Keep Congress from Weakening Statute. Ads Will Highlight Biblical Teachings." *Los Angeles Times*, 1 February 1996.

Salisbury, Robert H. "Political Movements in American Politics: An Essay on Concept and Analysis." *National Political Science Review* 1 (1989): 15–30.

Sanders, Deion. *Power, Money and Sex*. Dallas: Word Books, 1998.

"Savage Misogyny: Mormon Excommunication of Sonia Johnson for ERA Activities." *Time* 114 (17 December 1979): 80.

Sawyer, Mary R. *Black Ecumenism*. Valley Forge, Pa.: Trinity Press International, 1994.

Schneider, John. *Godly Materialism: Rethinking Money and Possessions*. Downers Grove, Ill.: InterVarsity Press, 1994.

Seabrook, the Honorable Lawrence. New York State Senate, testimony given at Citicorp Foundation on Public Charter Schools, New York, 20 November 1997.

Segers, Mary. "Ferraro, the Bishops, and the 1984 Election." In *Shaping New Vision: Gender and Values in American Culture*, eds. C. W. Atkinson, C. H. Buchanan, and M. R. Miles, 143–67. The Harvard Women's Studies in Religion Series. Ann Arbor: UMI Research Press, 1987.

———, ed. *Church Polity and American Politics: Issues in Contemporary American Catholicism*. New York: Garland Publishing, 1990.

Sharpton, Al, and Anthony Walton. *Go Tell Pharaoh*. New York: Doubleday, 1996.

Shipps, Jan. *Mormonism: The Story of a New Religious Tradition*. Urbana: University of Illinois Press, 1985.

Sider, Ronald J. *Christ and Violence*. Scottdale, Pa.: Herald Press, 1979.

———. *Completely Pro-Life*. Downers Grove, Ill.: InterVarsity Press, 1987.

———. "Curriculum Vitae, Ronald J. Sider." Photocopy, Eastern Baptist Theological Seminary, Wynnewood, Pa., 2000.

———. *Just Generosity: A New Vision for Overcoming Poverty in America*. Grand Rapids, Mich.: Baker Books, 1999.

———. *Living like Jesus: Eleven Essentials for Growing a Genuine Faith*. Grand Rapids, Mich.: Baker Books, 1999.

———. "Message from an Evangelical—The Place of Humans in the Garden of God." *Amicus Journal* (published by the National Resource Defense Council) (Spring 1995): 14.

———. "Redeeming the Environmentalists." *Christianity Today*, 21 June 1993: 26–29.

———. *Rich Christians in an Age of Hunger*. 4th ed. Dallas: Word Publishing, 1997.

———. "*Rich Christians in an Age of Hunger*—Revisited." *Christian Scholar's Review* 26, no. 3 (Spring 1997): 322–35.

———. "They're Still Hungry; We're Still Rich." *Prism* (published by Evangelicals for Social Action) (May–June 1997): 34.

———, and Richard K. Taylor. *Nuclear Holocaust and Christian Hope*. Downers Grove, Ill.: InterVarsity Press, 1982.

Skinner, Andrew C., and Robert L. Millet. *C. S. Lewis: The Man and His Message*. Salt Lake City: Bookcraft, 1999.

Smith, Robert C. *We Have No Leaders: African-Americans in the Post–Civil Rights Era*. Albany: State University of New York Press, 1996.

Steinfels, Peter. "The Pollsters Look at U.S. Catholics." *Commonweal* (13 September 1996): 16–19.
Sum, Andrew, and Neal Fogg. "The Changing Economic Fortunes of Young Black Men in America." *The Black Scholar* 21, no. 1 (January–March 1990): 47–55.
Sylvester, Nancy. "Post–Vatican II Sisters and Political Ministry." In *Between God and Caesar: Priests, Sisters and Political Office in the United States*, ed. Madonna Kolbenschlag, 60–73. New York: Paulist Press, 1985.
Taylor, James Lance. "Black Politics in Transition: From Protest to Politics to Political Neutrality?" Ph.D. dissertation, University of Southern California, 1999.
Tate, Katherine. *From Protest to Politics: The New Black Voters in American Elections.* New York: Russell Sage Foundation, 1993.
Thomas, Cal, and Ed Dobson. *Blinded by Might.* Grand Rapids, Mich.: Zondervan Publishing House, 1999.
"Ticket to Ride." *Richmond Times-Dispatch*, 28 February 1993: F6.
Toussaint, Pamela Ann. "Concord Baptist Church: Taking Care of Business in Bed-Stuy." In *Signs of Hope in the City: Ministries of Community Renewal*, eds. Robert D. Carle and Louis A. DeCaro Jr., 68. Valley Forge, Pa.: Judson Press, 1999.
Toward Tradition, http://www.towardtradition.org.
———. "President-Elect Bush Seeks Advice from Rabbi Daniel Lapin on Role of Faith in Public Affairs." Press release, 20 December 2000.
———. "Rabbi Lapin Tells Opening Congressional Bi-Partisan Opening Ceremony, Pray for Unity but Pursue Principle." Press release, Mercer Island, Wash., 8 January 1999.
U.S. Department of Justice, Bureau of Prisons. "National Prisoner Statistics Bulletin Number 46—Capital Punishment 1930–1970."
U.S. v. Bob Jones University, 461 U.S. (1983).
Van Wagoner, Richard S. *Mormon Polygamy: A History.* Salt Lake City: Signature Books, 1992.
Vest, Jason. "Mike Farris, for God's Sake." *Washington Post*, 5 August 1993: C6.
Walker, David. *Appeal to the Coloured Citizens of the World.* New York: Black Basic Press, 1993.
Walker, Jack. *Mobilizing Interest Groups in America.* Ann Arbor: University of Michigan Press, 1991.
Walton, Hanes, Jr. *African American Power and Politics: The Political Context Variable.* New York: Columbia University Press, 1997.
Weaver, Mary Jo. *New Catholic Women: A Contemporary Challenge to Traditional Religious Authority.* San Francisco: Harper and Row, 1985.
Weber, Max. *The Protestant Ethic and the Spirit of Capitalism.* 1904–05.
Weigand, Stephen. "Claiming the Moral Ground in Politics—Lapin among Clergy Who Met with President-Elect Bush." *Mercer Island Reporter*, 4 January 2001, available at http://www.mi-reporter.com/sited/story/html/40517.
Weigel, George. *Tranquillitas Ordinis: The Present Failure and Future Promise of American Catholic Thought on War and Peace.* New York: Oxford University Press, 1987.
West, Cornel. *Race Matters.* New York: Beacon Press, 1993.
Wildavsky, Aaron. *Assimilation versus Separation: Joseph the Administrator and the Politics of Religion in Biblical Israel.* New Brunswick, N.J.: Transaction Books, 1993.

———. *The Rise of Radical Egalitarianism*. Washington, D.C.: American University Press, 1991.

Wilhoit, Francis M. *The Politics of Southern Resistance*. New York: George Braziller, Inc., 1973.

Williamsburg Charter. In *Articles of Faith, Articles of Peace, the Religious Liberty Clauses and the American Public Philosophy*, ed. James Davison Hunter and Os Guiness, 127–45. Washington, D.C.: Brookings Books, 1990.

Wilmore, Gayraud S. *Black Religion and Black Radicalism: An Examination of the Black Experience in Religion*. Garden City, N.Y.: Anchor Press, 1972.

Winn, Kenneth H. *Exiles in a Land of Liberty: Mormons in America, 1830–1846*. Chapel Hill: University of North Carolina Press, 1989.

Witham, Larry. "The Churches Debate Role in Gay Unions." *Washington Times*, 19 June 2000.

Witte, John, Jr. *Religion and the American Constitutional Experiment: Essential Rights and Liberties*. Boulder: Westview Press, 2000.

Wood, James E. "Public Religion vis-à-vis Religion's Public Role." *Journal of Church and State* 41 (Winter 1999): 51–75.

Workman, Dave. "Moral Majority Changes Name, Methods." *Spokesman-Review*, 8 September 1982.

INTERVIEWS

Elder Dallin H. Oaks with John R. Pottenger, 14 July 2000.
Elder David Yeazell with Hubert Morken, Dallas, 10–11 August 2000.
Elder Nathaniel Tate with Hubert Morken, Dallas, 10–11 August 2000.
Elder Pat Martin with Hubert Morken, Dallas, 10–11 August 2000.
Elder Shawn Wood with Hubert Morken, Dallas, 10–11 August 2000.
Elder Silas Wheeler with Hubert Morken, Dallas, 10–11 August 2000.
Elder Stephen Sledge with Hubert Morken, Dallas, 10–11 August 2000.
Elder William Blue with Hubert Morken, Dallas, 10–11 August 2000.
Father J. Bryan Hehir with William J. Gould, 16 December 1999 and 21 June 2000.
John Langan with William J. Gould, 11 December 2000.
Michael Farris with Mark Rozell, 12 August 1994 and 29 November 2000.
Mr. Curtis Wallace, Esq., with Hubert Morken, Dallas, 10–11 August 2000.
Mr. Jim Ball with Joel Fetzer, Washington, D.C., 30 August 2000.
Mr. Stan LeQuire with Gretchen Carnes, Wynnewood, Pa., 8 August 2000.
Pastor Lawrence Robinson with Hubert Morken, Dallas, 10–11 August 2000.
Peter Steinfels with William J. Gould, 2 December 2000.
Rabbi Daniel Lapin with Hubert Morken, Mercer Island, Wash., 19 May 2000.
Sister Maureen Fiedler, S.L., with Mary Segers, Brentwood, Md., 7 April 2000.
The Reverend Al Sharpton with Jo Renee Formicola, New York, 14 June 2000.
The Reverend Benjamin Chavis-Muhammed with James Lance Taylor, conversations between 1996 and 2000.

The Reverend Floyd Flake with Michael Leo Owens, Queens, N.Y., 5 June 2000.
The Reverend Ronald Sider with Gretchen Carnes, Grand Rapids, Mich., 24 June 2000.
The Reverend Ronald Sider with Joel Fetzer, Germantown, Pa., 28 May 2000 and 9 November 2000.
The Reverend T. D. Jakes with Hubert Morken, Atlanta, 25 July 2000 and 10–11 August 2000.
Thomas Quigley with William J. Gould, USCC, 2 January 2001.

Index

Abbyssian Baptist Church, 54
Abernathy, Reverend David Ralph, 56, 122, 124
abortion, 83, 108, 216, 237
Abzug, Bella, 123
ACLU (American Civil Liberties Union), 81, 142–43, 244n21
Acton Institute, 89
ADL (Anti-Defamation League), 107, 128–29
affirmative action, 125
Africa, 32, 44, 98, 100, 230–31
African Americans, 65–66, 128; church attendance patterns, 43; "criminalization" of, 139n54; electoral politics, 13–14, 46, 61–62; Gospel, views of, 32; and school reform, 20; voting patterns, 25
African Congregation of the Black Messiah, 121
African Methodist Episcopal Church, 192
African National Congress. *See* ANC
Afro-Christian churches, 4–7, 13, 29, 34, 55–56, 66
Afro-Christian religious leaders, 15, 17, 29–30, 235–36; black Christian nationalism, 119–20; black radical Christian preachers, 128; definition of, 21
Alcohol, Tobacco, and Firearms Division. *See* U.S. Treasury Department
Alexander, John, 160

Allen African Methodist Episcopal (AME) Church, 1–2, 4–8, 16, 23n22, 230
Allen Christian School, 8–9, 20
Allen, Jeanne, 10
American Bar Foundation, 72
American Catholic Church. *See* Roman Catholic Church
American Catholicism. *See* Catholics and Catholicism
American Civil Liberties Union. *See* ACLU
American Jewish Committee. *See* Jews
American Methodist Episcopal (AME) Church, 1, 4–8, 16, 21n3, 56
American Methodist Episcopal (AME) Zion Church, 21n3, 56
American Missionary Association, 136n29
anabaptists, 159–60
ANC (African National Congress), 125
Anderson, Lavina Fielding, 72–73
Anti-Defamation League. *See* ADL
anti-Semitism, 90, 107, 128, 138n44, 140n60
apartheid, 125, 142
Arizona, 65, 195n16
Armstrong, Virginia C., 148
Aron, Raymond, 199
Ashcroft, John, 67, 226, 238
Asia, 230
Atlanta Coalition, 124, 140n62
Audubon Society, 167
Azusa Conference, 28

261

Baer, Hans, 5
Bahai, 192
Bakewell, Danny, 128, 139n58
Baldwin, James, 122
Ball, Jim, 165, 168
Baptists, 21n3, 57, 91, 141–57; National Baptist Convention USA, Inc., 21n3, 56, 124; Progressive National Baptist Convention, Inc., 21n3, 56; Southern Baptist Convention, 93–94
Barstow, David, 69n33
Bass, Jack, 118
Bauman Foundation, 162
Beall, Mary Ann, 186
Benestad, Brian, 204, 220n28
Bennett, William, 10
Benton, Marc G., 94
Bernardin, Archbishop Joseph, 203, 205–8, 210–15, 220n29, 222n47
BET (Black Entertainment Television), 16, 28, 39
Bethel African Methodist Episcopal Church, 21n3
Bethlehem Presbyterian Church, 94
Beyer, Donald, 152
bible, 36, 78, 92, 96, 104, 107, 111, 147, 162, 164
Bill of Rights, 75–76, 144, 150. *See also* U.S. Constitution; First Amendment
Bill of Rights Legal Foundation, 142
Billy Graham Center Archives, 172n18, 173n33
Billy Graham Evangelistic Association, 163
Black Christian nationalism. *See* Afro-Christian religious leaders
Black Christian Pan-Africanist Church, 120
Black Church. *See* Afro-Christian churches
Black Muslims. *See* Islam, Nation of
"Black Nation Israel," 136n24
black nationalism, 119, 123, 129–30, 135n17, 140n65
Black Panthers, 119–20
Black Power, 116, 119–20, 135n20, 135n23
black radical Christian preachers. *See* Afro-Christian religious leaders
Black Youth Building a Black Community (BYBBC), 121
Blacks. *See* African Americans
Blackwell, Kenneth, 11
Blake, Reverend Charles, 89

Bloom, Harold, 73
Blue, Reverend William, 43
Bob Jones University, 161, 241
Book of Doctrine. See Doctrine, Book of
Book of Mormon. See Mormon, Book of
Bork, Robert, 142
Boston University, 4
Boy Scouts of America v. Dale, 82
Bradley, Bill, 17, 61
Bradley, Tom, 138n44, 138n46
Brawley, Tawana, 59, 66–67
Brigham Young University (BYU), 72–73, 82, 95
Brotherhood Crusade, 139n58
Brown, H. Rap, 120
Brown, James, 54–55
Brown vs. Board of Education, 18, 117–18, 134n12
Buchanan, James, 74
Buchanan, Patrick, 152
Buckley, William F., 211
Buddhism, 191
Bull, Hedley, 199
Bush (George H. W.) administration, 142
Bush, George W., 68; administration, 110, 225, 236; and Christian right, 17; on compassion, 226; on faith-based initiatives, 89, 92, 225, 236, 238–39, 243n1–8; and religious leaders, reaching out to, 25–27, 29, 46, 89–90, 110, 233
Butts, Calvin, 6, 56
BYBBC. *See* Black Youth Building a Black Community
BYU. *See* Brigham Young University

California, 80, 97–98, 100, 102
Calvin College, 161
Campolo, Tony, 160
Canaan Baptist Church of Christ, 18
Canada, 159
Carmichael, Stokely, 119–21
Carmines, Edward, 125
Carter, Jimmy, 90, 221n46, 238
Castro, Fidel, 53, 64
Catholic Family Radio Network. *See* Catholics and Catholicism
Catholic Relief Services, 200
Catholic Statement on Pluralism and Abortion. *See* Roman Catholic Church

Catholics and Catholicism, 81, 95; American Catholicism, 198–223; Catholic Family Radio Network, 191; Catholic social justice lobby, first, 177; Catholic Statement on Pluralism and Abortion, 187–88; Catholics Speak Out (CSO), 178; Catholics Act for ERA, 175, 184; Committee of Concerned Catholics, 187; LCWR (Leadership Conference of Women Religious), 182–83; reform movements, 175, 177–78; social ethics, 202; Women's Ordination Conference (WOC), 183. *See also* Roman Catholic Church; Sisters, orders of
Cato, Gavin, 60
CBN (Christian Broadcasting Network), 95–96
Center for Education Reform, 10, 23n45
Central America, 200, 205, 217
charter schools, 3, 8–11, 21, 22n14, 23n46, 24n59; Public Charter School Program, 19
Charter Schools Institute of the State University of New York, 24n59
Chavez, Linda, 67, 236, 244n15
Chavis, John, 117
Chavis–Farrakhan Alliance, 127
Chavis–Farrakhan–Shapton Alliance, 128–33
Chavis-Muhammed, Reverend Benjamin F., 115–40, 228, 231; black nationalism, 119, 123; Million Man March, 115–17, 122–27, 229
Children's Scholarship Fund, 10, 23n44
Chilton, David, 163
Christ, Jesus, 13, 32, 106, 153
Christian Broadcasting Network. *See* CBN
Christian Coalition, 69n33, 78, 104, 110
Christian Environmental Council. *See* EEN
Christian Methodist Episcopal, 21n3
Christian right, 17, 238; boycott activities, 144–45; Jews, coalitions with, 91, 95–97, 103–4; political tactics, 69n33, 151–54, 244n21. *See also* Moral Majority
Christianity Today, 161
Church of Jesus Christ of Latter-Day Saints (LDS), 71–87, 186, 231. *See also* Latter-Day Saints; Brigham Young University
civil rights, 54, 116–17, 124, 162. *See also* religious liberty
Civil War, 55, 91, 228, 236

Clay Academy, 44
Cleage, Minister Albert, Jr., 119–20
Cleaver, Eldridge, 121
Clinton, Bill, 89, 111, 139n58, 190
Clinton, Hillary Rodham, 61, 67, 241
Coalition on Revival, 148, 156n41–42
Coats, Dan, 226, 238
COGIC. *See* Pentecostal Church of God in Christ
COINTELPRO (Counter Intelligence Program), 117–18, 133n7
Cold War, end of, 217
Colorado, 177, 244n21
Committee of Concerned Catholics. *See* Catholics and Catholicism
"common good," 226–27
Concerned Women for America, 141
Concord Baptist Church of Christ, 5, 23n27
Congress of Racial Equality (CORE), 119, 135n20
Congressional Black Caucus, 128–29
Connecticut, 160
conservatives, 65, 211, 216. *See also* Christian right
constitutions, 72, 75–76. *See also* Bill of Rights; First Amendment
Conyers, John, 122
Coptic Orthodox, 192
CORE. *See* Congress of Racial Equality
Cornwell, John, 191
"Creation Care." *See* EEN
CRIS (Vatican Congregation for Religious and Secular Institutes). *See* Roman Catholic Church
Crouch, Paul, 28
Crow, Jim. *See* Jim Crow period
CSO (Catholics Speak Out). *See* Catholics and Catholicism
Cuba, 213
Cuban missile crisis, 213
culture wars, 93–98
Cuomo, Mario, 59, 237
Czech Republic, 82

D'Amato, Alfonse, 7
Daughtry, Herbert, 6
Davis, Angela, 121–22
Day, Dorothy, 209
death penalty. *See* capital punishment

Declaration of Independence, 107, 147–48, 228
Democratic National Convention, 116
Democratic Party, 15, 61, 103, 107, 118
Democrats, 7–8, 10–11, 25, 46, 90, 97, 143, 187
Department of Education. *See* U.S. Department of Education
Department of Health and Human Services. *See* U.S. Department of Health and Human Services
Department of Housing and Urban Development. *See* U.S. Department of Housing and Urban Development
Department of Justice. *See* U.S. Department of Justice.
Department of Labor. *See* U.S. Department of Labor
developing nations. *See* Third World
DeVries, Walter, 118
Diallo, Amadou, 60–61
Diaspora Jewry. *See* Jews
DiIulio, John, Jr., 225, 242–43
Dinkins, David, 69n35, 138n44–45
Diocese. *See* Roman Catholic Church
discursive politics, 182
District of Columbia. *See* Washington, D.C.
Dobson, Dr. James, 104, 238
Dobson, Reverend Ed, 96
Doctrine, Book of, 86n24
Dominicans. *See* Roman Catholic Church
Dorismond, Patrick, 61
Drexel, Mother Katharine, 177
Du Bois, W. E. B., 119, 133n5
Dulles, Avery, 223

economic development, 15, 40, 43, 132, 139n58
economic justice, 162–65, 200
Edison Charter Schools (ECS), 3, 18–19, 21, 24n55
Edison Project, 24n55
Edmunds Act, 74
Edmunds–Tucker Act, 74
Education Week, 149
EEN (Evangelical Environmental Network), 163–70, 174n50, 232; "Creation Care," 164, 167; Christian Environmental Council, 166, 174n56; on deforestation, 164; work with, Endangered Species Act, 165–68, 174n54, 57, 72; on environmental justice, 168–69; on global warming, 168; "Noah Congregations," 168; "takings" legislation, 169
Egypt, 37
Eisemann, Rabbi Moshe M., 104
Elijah Muhammad. *See* Muhammad, Elijah
Elmore, Richard, 22n14
Emerge, 17
Employment Division v. Smith, 79–80
Endangered Species Act, 165–68
Endangered Species Recovery Act. *See* ESRA
England. *See* Great Britain
environmental politics, 108, 113n33; environmental racism, 115, 124. *See also* EEN
Episcopalians, 117, 239
Equal Rights Amendment (ERA), 75, 175, 184–87, 195n17
ESA (Evangelicals for Social Action), 159, 161–64, 168, 170, 172n13, 172n17–19, 172n21–23, 172n25; "Chicago Declaration of Evangelical Social Concern," 161–62
Escobar, Samuel, 161
ESRA (Endangered Species Recovery Act), 166
Eternal Word Television Network, 176, 191
Europe, 231, 119
Evangelicals, 160
Everson v. Board of Education, 234–35

faith-based initiatives, 89, 92, 225, 236, 238–39, 243n1–8
Falwell, Jerry, 69n33, 142, 155n2, 238
Farmer, James, 123
Farrakhan, Minister Louis, 69n33, 115–17, 123–25, 127, 140n60, 233; Chavis–Farrakhan–Shapton Alliance, 128–33
Farris, Michael, 141–57, 228, 231–32
FBI. *See* U.S. Federal Bureau of Investigation
Federal Bureau of Investigation. *See* U.S. Federal Bureau of Investigation
feminism, 147; awakening, personal, 180–81; theories of, 180–81. *See also* women's rights

Index

Feminists: religious feminism, 175–96, 230. *See also* National Organization for Women
Ferraro, Geraldine, 187–88, 194n21, 221n37
Fiedler, Sister Maureen, 175–96, 230; gender equity and equality, 182–84
Fiorenza, Bishop Joseph, 89
First African Methodist Episcopal Church, 139n58
First Amendment, 76, 144, 234. *See also* Bill of Rights; U.S. Constitution
First Great Awakening, 236
Flake, Floyd H., 1–24, 89, 226, 229–30, 232–33, 236; as electioneer, 14–15; as charter school reformer, 1–3, 8–25; as civic educator, 16–17; as founder of Allen School, 9; as lobbyist, 12–14; and New York Charter Schools Act, 8, 11
Flanigan, Peter, 10
Florida, 43
Focus on the Family, 96
Fogg, Neal, 127
Fordham University, 213
Forstman, Ted, 10
Foxman, Abraham, 128–29
Frank, Anne, 144–45, 152
Franklin, John Hope, 117, 134n10
Franklin, Sekou, 128
Freundel, Rabbi Barry, 192
Friedberg, Susan, 101
Friendly, Fred, 218
Fulani, Lenora, 128

Gallagher, Winifred, 218, 224n73
Gallup organization, 175
Garvey, Marcus, 119, 133n5, 236
Gaudium et Spes. *See Pastoral Constitution on the Church in the Modern World*
gays, 93–94. *See also* homosexuality
gender equity and equality, 182–84
Genovese, Eugene, 68n6
George III, King, 188
Georgetown University, 175, 220n29, 241
Georgia, 26–27, 63, 118, 124
Giuliani, Rudolph, 15, 138n45
Godly Materialism, 163
Goetz, Bernhard, 58
Goldsmith, Judy, 123
Goldsmith, Stephen, 89

Goldwater, Barry, 81
Goodman, Ellen, 188
GOP. *See* Republican Party
Gordon, Eugene, 68n5
Gore, Al, 17, 27, 46, 61, 67, 89, 108, 241
Gospel principles, 176, 177, 180–82, 193. *See also* bible
G. P. Putnam's Sons, 40
graduated tithe, 162–63
Graham, Billy, 26, 48, 163
Grant, Jim, 137n32
Great Britain, 29, 99–100
Greater Northeast Baptist Church, 11
Greeley, Andrew, 223n67
Green, Roger, 11
Greene, Jay, 24n49
Gregory Congregational Church, 121
Griffith, Michael, 59
Grimstead, Jay, 148
Gumbleton, Bishop Thomas, 192, 210, 212

Haiti, 178
Hampton, Fred, 121
Harris, Frederick, 56
Harvard University, 24n49; Harvard Divinity School, 200, 218; Kennedy School of Government, 218
Hasidic. *See* Jews, Orthodox
Hastert, Dennis, 238
Hatfield, Mark, 161
Hawaii, 75
Hawkins, Yousif, 60
Hehir, Father J. Bryan, 197–223, 230, 232
Height, Dorothy, 131
Hemings, Sally, 27
Henig, Jeffrey, 1
Henry, Carl F. H., 161
Henry, Paul, 161
Hildebrand, Richard Allen, 4
Hindus, 91
Hirsh, Rabbi Samson Raphael, 101
Hispanics. *See* Latinos
Hoffman, Stanley, 199, 219n8
Holocaust, 93
Home School Legal Defense Association (HSLDA), 141, 148–49, 231
home schooling, 141, 146, 148–50, 154
homosexuality, 82, 108, 245n25
Hooks, Benjamin, 123–24

Hoover, J. Edgar, 118, 136n30
House. *See* U.S. House
Howard Center for Family, Religion, and Society, 81–82
Hoye, Monsignor Daniel, 211
HSLDA. *See* Home School Legal Defense Association
HUD. *See* U.S. Department of Housing and Urban Development
human rights, 76, 84, 177, 188, 230, 236. *See also* civil rights
humanism, 145–46
humanitarian aid, 175
Hunter, James Davidson, 94–95

Illinois, 74, 82, 175–76, 185; Illinois Constitutional Convention, 72; Illinois Supreme Court, 72
incrementalist, 216
In-Service Ministerial Training Program, 120
InterVarsity Christian Fellowship, 160–63
Iowa, 150
Ireland, Patricia, 185
Islam, Nation of, 69n33, 115–17, 123–25, 127, 129, 140n62, 233. *See also* Muslims
Israel, 38, 103, 162

Jackson, Michael, 54
Jackson, Reverend Jesse, 67, 129; political endorsements of, 90–91; presidential candidacy, 122, 124; recruiting efforts, 54; work with, Rainbow/Push Coalition, 63–64, 128, 236
Jadot, Jean, 203
Jakes, Bishop T. D., 25–52, 229, 231–32, 236, 239; The Potter's House, 29, 37, 40–43, 44, 46–47; T. D. Jakes Enterprises, 27, 45–46; T. D. Jakes Ministries, 29, 43; teachings, synopsis of, 33–34
Jakes, Ernest, 28
Jakes, Odith, 28
Jakes, Serita, 41
James, Kay Coles, 238
Jamison, T. J., 56
JDL (Jewish Defense League). *See* Jews
Jefferson, Thomas, 27, 234
Jenkins, Jerry B., 96
Jesuits. *See* Roman Catholic Church
Jesus Christ. *See* Christ, Jesus

Jewish Defense League. *See* Jews
Jews, 67; American Jewish Committee, 105; Christians, relations with, 91–112, 232; Diaspora Jewry, 105; Jewish Defense League (JDL), 129; Orthodox, 60, 89–113; Palestinian Jewry, 128; Reformed, 94; Union of Orthodox Rabbis, 108; Zionism, 105. *See also* Rabbis; anti-Semitism
John XXIII, Pope, 180, 201–2
John Paul II, Pope, 177, 182, 236, 242, 24n16, 245n24
Johnson, Sonia, 185, 195n17
Jones, Bob, 241

Kane, Sister Theresa, 182–83
Karenga, Ron Maulana, 131
Katzenstein, Mary F., 182
Kean College, 129, 140n60
Kennedy, D. James, 238
Kennedy, Edward, 237
Kennedy, John F., 90, 204, 213, 219n4
Kerem College, 100
Key, V. O., 117–18
Kilberg, Bobbie, 151
King, Don, 54–55
King, Larry, 46
King, Martin Luther, Jr., 119–20; Martin Luther King Jr. Afro-American Center, 4
King, Rodney, 126, 138n46
King, Scott, 123–24, 128
Kirk, Ron, 27
Kissinger, Henry, 199
Klinghoffer, David, 101–2
Klinsky, Steven, 10
Koch, Edward I., 7
Kosovo, 200, 218
Kozodoy, Neal, 106
Kozol, Jonathan, 191
Kurlander, Gabrielle, 128

Lahaye, Tim F., 96
Langan, John, 206
Lapin Marine Enterprises, 99
Lapin, Rabbi Abraham Hyam, 98
Lapin, Rabbi Berel, 98
Lapin, Rabbi Daniel, 89–113, 228, 230, 232; Christians, relations with, 91–112; Republicans, relations with, 97, 103; Torah, views on, 100–2, 105–6, 109;

"Toward Tradition," 89, 91, 99, 103–4, 108, 111, 231
Lapin, Rabbi Eliyahu (Elya), 98–99
LaRouche, Lyndon, 129
Latin America, 205, 230, 236
Latinos, 13–14, 17, 20, 43
Latter-Day Saints, 71–87, 92, 195n17. *See also* Church of Jesus Christ of Latter-Day Saints; Brigham Young University
Law, Cardinal Bernard, 188, 206–8, 222n62
LCWR (Leadership Conference of Women Religious). *See* Catholics and Catholicism
LDS Church. *See* Church of Jesus Christ of Latter-Day Saints
LDS. *See* Church of Jesus Christ of Latter-Day Saints
Leary, Timothy, 143
Lebanon, 93
the Left. *See* liberalism
Lehrer, Jim, 218
Lemon v. Kurtzman, 234–35
LeQuire, Stan, 165, 168
lesbians. *See* homosexuality
Lewinsky, Monica, 90
Lewis, C. S., 95
Lewis, John, 123
liberalism, 92, 108, 111, 123, 159–74, 204
liberals, 10, 67, 103
Lieberman, Joseph, 90–92, 107, 192, 230
Lincoln, Abraham, 90, 107, 228
Lincoln, C. Eric, 4
Lincoln University, 4
Lithuania, 98
Little, Malcolm. *See* Malcolm X
Little Sisters of the Poor. *See* Sisters, orders of
Loretto, Sisters of. *See* Sisters, orders of
Louima, Abner, 60
Luce Foundation, 162

MacArthur Fellowship, 197
Maddox, Alton, 59
Madhubuti, Haki, 131
Madison Avenue Initiative, 63, 231
Madison, James, 234
Madison, Project (PAC), 141, 153
Malcolm X, 116, 119–20, 123, 125
Mamiya, Lawrence, 4
Mandela, Nelson, 64, 125

Manhattan Institute for Policy Research, 3, 22n19, 24n49
March on Washington, 129–30
marriage, same-sex, 80
Martin Luther King Jr. Afro-American Center. *See* King, Martin Luther, Jr.
Martin, Pat, 41–42
Maryland, 100
Mason, C. Vernon, 59
Mason, Charles Harrison, 57
materialism, 161, 163, 165, 168, 173n38
McCain, John, 65, 69n33
McCormick, Joseph P., II, 128
McDonnell, Lorraine, 22n14
McDougall, Harold, 22n3
McGovern, George, 121, 160; support from, Evangelicals for McGovern, 160
McHugh, Bishop James, 208
McKenzie, Bishop Vashti, 192
MEDC (Metroplex Economic Development Corporation), 40, 43–44
Medicaid, 7
Medicare, 7
Medved, Michael, 100, 110
Mennonites, 159–74, 230, 233
Messiah College, 160
Methodists, 5, 91. *See also* A.M.E. American Methodist Episcopal (AME) Church
Metro Kids Church, 42
Metroplex Economic Development Corporation. *See* MEDC
Mexican-American War, 74
MFM (Million Family March), 116, 132
Mfume, Kweisi, 129
Michigan, 72, 119, 150, 161
Middle East, 44, 192
Miller, James, 152
Miller, Rabbi Avigdor, 104
Miller, William, 81
Million Family March. *See* MFM
Million Family March Economic Development Fund, 132
Million Man March. *See* MMM
Million Mom March, 131
Million Woman's March, 131
Million Youth March, 131
Missionary Training Center, 73
Mississippi, 57, 68n9, 134n14, 134n16
Missouri, 74

MMM (Million Man March/Day of Absence), 115–17, 122–27, 129–32
Mohler, R. Albert, Jr., 94
Mollenkott, Virginia Ramey, 181
Monsma, Stephen, 160
Moon, Sung Yung, 131
Moral Majority, 141–43, 238. *See also* Christian Right
Morken, Hubert, 243n9
Mormon, Book of, 73, 86n24
Mormons. *See* Latter-Day Saints
Morrill Law. *See* Anti-Bigamy Act
Moss, Reverend Marlon, 11, 21n3
Mozert v. Hawkins County Board of Education, 141, 144–45, 152
Muhammad, Elijah, 119, 123, 127, 132
Muhammad, Khallid, 116, 129, 140n60
Muhammad, Wallace, 123
Murphy, Bishop Francis P., 210
Murray, John Courtney, 199, 202, 218, 219n4, 220n20
Muslims, 91. *See also* Islam, Nation of
Myerson, Michael, 118

NAACP (National Association for the Advancement of Colored People), 115, 117, 120, 124–25, 128–29, 135n20, 140n63, 232–33
NAALS (National African American Leadership Summit), 124, 128
NAN (National Action Network). *See* Shapton, Reverend Al
Nation of Islam. *See* Islam, Nation of
National Action Network (NAN). *See* Shapton, Reverend Al
National African American Leadership Summit. *See* NAALS
National Alliance Against Racist and Political Repression, 122, 137n37
National Association for the Advancement of Colored People. *See* NAACP
National Baptist Convention of America. *See* Baptists
National Black Independent Political Party, 124
National Catholic Welfare Conference. *See* Roman Catholic Church
National Center for Home Education, 149
National Conference of Catholic Bishops. *See* Roman Catholic Church

National Council of Black (formerly Negro) Churchman, 135n23
National Council of Negro Women, 131
National Education Association (NEA), 150
National Missionary Baptist Convention of America, 21n3
National Organization for Women (NOW), 188, 195n22
National Public Radio (NPR), 190–91
National Youth Movement. *See* Sharpton, Reverend Al
Native Americans, 176, 192–93
NCCB (National Conference of Catholic Bishops). *See* Roman Catholic Church
NCWC. *See* Roman Catholic Church
NEA. *See* National Education Association
Nelson, Limerick, 60
Nevada, 184
"New Evangelicalism," 161
New Jersey, 19
New Mexico, 134n11, 177
New York (state), 1–24, 71, 150, 230; New York State Assembly Education Committee, 12; New York State Charter School Resource Center, 24n59; New York State Charter School Stimulus Fund, 19; New York State Education Department, 20–21, 24n59; New York State United Teachers, 13
New York Charter Schools Act, 8, 11, 20; New York Charters Schools Law, 12
New York City, 1–8, 14–16, 18, 22n15, 53–69, 99, 116, 125–28, 132, 138n45, 229; New York City Police Department, 60–61
New York Democratic Presidential Primary, 17; *New York Post*, 3, 16
New York Stock Exchange, 65
New York University, 132n2, 244n9
New York Times, 16, 30, 50n8, 81, 183, 189, 244n17
Newton, Huey P., 121
Nicaragua, 178
Nicaraguan Cultural Alliance, 178
Nicholson, Jim, 65–66
Nigeria, 29
Nixon, Richard M., 121, 166; administration, 121
"Noah Congregations." *See* EEN
North Carolina, 116–22

North Dakota, 150
Northern Virginia Community College, 144
Novak, Michael, 211, 223n64
NOW. *See* National Organization for Women
NPR. *See* National Public Radio

Oaks, Elder Dallin H., 71–87, 229, 231
O'Brien, William, 222n54
O'Connor, Archbishop John, 187–88, 206–8, 210–11, 214, 221n37, 222n48
Office of Faith-Based and Community Initiatives, 225
Office of Public Liaison, 236
Ohio, 11, 74, 83; United Technological Seminary, 4
Oklahoma, 28, 184
Olasky, Marvin, 242–43
Oliver, James, 47
Operation Breadbasket, 54, 236
Oral Roberts University, 29. *See also* Roberts, Oral
Oregon, 176
Orthodox Jews. *See* Jews

Pacific Jewish Center (PJC), 98, 100–1
Pagones, Steven, 59, 67
Palestinian Jewry. *See* Jews
pan-African, 64, 120, 133n5
papal encyclicals. *See* Roman Catholic Church
Parker, Charles, 137n32
parochial schools, 177, 234, 237. *See also* private schools
The Pastoral Constitution on the Church in the Modern World, or *Gaudium et Spes*, 177, 181, 201–2, 210, 212, 219n12, 219n15–16
Pataki, George, 8, 15, 19
Pater Alliance, 43
Patrick Henry College, 153, 157n63, 231
Paul VI, Pope, 180
Pearson, Bishop Carlton, 28
Pennsylvania, 18–19, 150
Pentecostal Churches, 4–8; Pentecostal Church of God in Christ (COGIC), 56–57. *See also* Sharpton, Reverend Al
Perkins, John, 162
Personal Responsibility and Work Reconciliation Act of 1996, 226
Pew Charitable Trusts, 162, 164

Pierce v. Society of Sisters, 177, 234–35
PJC. *See* Pacific Jewish Center
plural marriage. *See* polygamy
Pohlmann, Marcus D., 126
Poland, 93
Poland Act, 74
polygamy, 71, 73–74
Pombo, Richard, 166
Pomerleau, Dolly, 184
Pornography, 103, 142, 148, 214
post-Cold War politics, 200, 237. *See also* Cold War, end of
The Potter's House. *See* Jakes, Bishop T. D.
poverty, 5, 33, 40, 43, 45, 84, 123, 162–65, 169–71, 208, 214
Powell, Adam Clayton, 54, 56, 133n5
Pratt, Geronimo, 121
Presbyterians, 94, 136n29
Princeton University, 117
private schools. 146. *See also* parochial schools
profitability, 35
Progressive National Baptist Convention, Inc. *See* Baptists
"Promise Keepers," 131
Proposition #22, 80
Proposition #187, 64, 125
protestants, 94, 95, 105, 159, 180, 191, 238
Provo Temple, 73
Public Charter School Program. *See* charter schools
public education. *See* education, public
Puerto Rican Nationalist Party, 122

Quakers, 186
Quigley, Thomas, 205, 215
Quinn, Archbishop John R., 221n46, 221n46
Quixote Center, 178–79, 183–84
Quorum of Twelve Apostles, 72

Rabben, Linda, 191, 194n6
Rabbis, 89–113. *See also* Jews
Rabkin, Jeremy, 95–96
Raboteau, Albert, 68n6
racial justice, 116, 120, 135n20, 137n40, 231
racism, 55, 58, 65. *See also* anti-Semitism
Rainbow/Push Coalition (RPC), 63–65, 128, 236
Rather, Dan, 111
Rausch, Bishop James, 203

Reagan, Ronald, 55, 210, 238;
    administration, 123, 125, 127, 142,
    210–11, 215, 222n48, 236
Reaganomics, 215
Reddy, T. J., 137n32
Reformed Jews. *See* Jews
Rehnquist, William, 81
Reid, Reverend Frank, 21n3
Religious Freedom Restoration Act. *See*
    RFRA
religious liberty, 74–78
Religious Liberty Protection Act, 80
Republican National Committee, 65–66, 185
Republican National Conventions, 116, 150, 238
Republican Party, 150–53, 185, 208
Republicans, 7–8, 46, 150; on education, 11;
    Christian right, relations with, 141–44;
    clergy endorsements of, 14–15; clergy
    influence of, 25; Rabbi Daniel Lapin,
    relations with, 97, 103
Reynolds v. the United States, 74
RFRA (Religious Freedom Restoration Act),
    79, 87n44
Rhenquist, William, 121
Ridge, Tom, 18
Riemer, Neal, 227–28
Rivers, Reverend Eugene, 89
Roach, Archbishop John, 203, 211
Roberts, Oral, 29, 48. *See also* Oral Roberts
    University
Robertson, Reverend Pat, 27, 69n33, 90,
    95–96, 104, 238
Robinson, Pastor Lawrence, 40–41,
    51n49–50
Roe v. Wade, 187, 205, 208, 236
Roman Catholic Church, 93, 227; American
    Catholic Church, 202–23, 236–37, 239;
    charities, 47, 237; diocese, 198, 200, 203,
    206, 210, 220n25; Dominicans, 198, 206;
    in Hawaii, 75; Jesuits, 198, 206; NCCB
    (National Conference of Catholic
    Bishops), 89, 186, 202–3, 208–10, 217,
    220n25, 236–37, 244n17–18; National
    Catholic Welfare Conference (NCWC),
    220n25; papal encyclicals, 178, 180–81,
    202; pastoral letters, 199–202, 205,
    208–10, 212, 214–15, 244n17; Second
    Vatican Council, 177–78, 181–82, 199,
    203, 215; U.S. Catholic Conference
    (USCC), 197–200, 202–8, 210–11,
    216–18, 220n29, 244n18; Vatican II, 177,
    182, 189, 201, 204, 209, 212, 219n4,
    236; "Vatican 24," 187, 189; Vatican, on
    bishops conference, 211, 217; Vatican
    Congregation for Religious and Secular
    Institutes (CRIS), 188; Vatican Council,
    177; Vatican, on women issues, 188–89.
    See also Catholics and Catholicism;
    Sisters, orders of
Rome, 177
Rome Has Spoke, 178
Rosenbaum, Yankel, 60
Rozazza, Bisop Peter, 215
RPC. *See* Rainbow/Push Coalition
Ruderman, Rabbi Jacob, 99

Salit, Jacqueline, 128
same-sex marriage. *See* marriage, same-sex
Sanders, Reverend Cheryl, 89
Sanders, Deion, 30
Sanders, Steven, 12
Santa Fe Independent Schools v. Jane Doe,
    81
Schatz, Eunice, 161
Schlafly, Phyllis, 186–87
Schneider, John, 163
scholarships, 3, 9–10, 15, 23n13, 24n49
school choice, 10, 24n49, 244n20. *See also*
    charter schools
School Choice Scholarship Program, 10
school prayer, 77–78, 81
school reform, 1–25; urban, 1
school vouchers. *See* vouchers, school
SCLC. *See* Southern Christian Leadership
    Conference
Seabrook, Lawrence, 11, 23n46
Second Great Awakening, 71, 236
Second Vatican Council. *See* Roman
    Catholic Church
sectarian schools, 20
secular humanism, 145–46. *See also* African
    Congregation of the Black Messiah;
    Muslims
Segale, Sister Blandina, 177
Senate. *See* U.S. Senate
Shakur, Assata, 121
Sharpton, Reverend Al, 6, 53–69, 123,
    228–29, 233; Chavis–Farrakhan–Shapton
    Alliance, 128–33; National Action

Network (NAN), 6, 63–64, 67, 231;
National Youth Movement, 54;
Pentecostal Church of God in Christ, 57;
Rainbow/Push Coalition (RPC), 63–65
Shipps, Jan, 71
Sider, Arbutus, 160
Sider, Ron, 159–74, 230–31, 233;
Evangelicals for Social Action, 161–63,
232. *See also* EEN
Sierra Club, 167
Silver, Sheldon, 12
Simpson, O. J., 125, 129
Singer, Merrill, 5
Sirico, Reverend Robert, 89
Sisters, orders of: Little Sisters of the Poor,
176; Sisters of the Blessed Sacrament,
177; Sisters of the Holy Names of Jesus
and Mary, 176; Sisters of Loretto, 175,
179; Sisters of Mercy, 179, 183
Sisulu Children's Charter School, 18
slavery, 36, 55, 134n13, 236
Smeal, Ellie, 185
Smedes, Lewis, 160
Smith, Joseph, 73–76, 86n24
social justice, 177–78, 180, 228
Soledad Brothers, 122
South Africa, 29, 98–100, 125, 142, 145
South America, 43, 231
South Carolina, 150
Southern Baptist Convention. *See* Baptists
Southern Baptist Theological Seminary, 94
Southern Christian Leadership Conference
(SCLC), 120, 122, 135n20
Spong, Bishop John Shelby, 192
Standard Achievement Test, 146
Stansel, Mary, 140n63
Starr, Ken, 111
stewardship, 164, 230
Stimson, James, 125
Stolper, Rabbi Pinchas, 104
Suiter, Phil, 152, 155n21
Sum, Andrew, 127
Supreme Court, U.S. *See* U.S. Supreme
Court
Switzerland, 82

"takings" legislation. *See* EEN
Tate, Nathaniel L., 43
Taylor, Reverend Gardner C., 5
TBN (Trinity Broadcasting Network), 28, 39

T. D. Jakes Enterprises. *See* Jakes, Bishop
T. D.
T. D. Jakes Ministries. *See* Jakes, Bishop
T. D.
Tennessee, 141, 144
Texas, 27, 29, 40–45, 63, 118, 231, 238
Third World, 169–70, 237
Thomas, Cal, 96
Thomas, Clarence, 64, 108
Time, 17
Tocqueville, Alexis de, 100
Torah, 100–2, 105–6, 109
Toward Tradition. *See* Lapin, Rabbi Daniel
Trinity Broadcasting Network. *See* TBN
Truman, Harry S., 118
Tyndale House, 96

UCC (United Church of Christ), 115,
119–21, 135n23, 136n29, 137n40
Unification Church, 131
Union of Orthodox Congregations, 104
Union of Orthodox Rabbis. *See* Jews
United Church of Christ. *See* UCC
United Hebrew Congregations of South
Africa, 99
United Negro Movement Association, 236
U.S. Catholic Conference. *See* Roman
Catholic Church
U.S. Congress, 46, 79–80, 98, 111, 165–68,
176, 203, 238
U.S. Constitution, 75–76. *See also* Bill of
Rights; First Amendment
U.S. Department of Education, 10, 225
U.S. Department of Health and Human
Services, 225
U.S. Department of Housing and Urban
Development, 7, 225
U.S. Department of Justice, 72, 225
U.S. Department of Labor, 225
U.S. Federal Bureau of Investigation (FBI),
117, 133n7, 136n30
U.S. House, 7, 13, 87n44
U.S. News and World Report, 17
U.S. Senate, 80, 221n46, 226
U.S. Supreme Court, 72, 121, 142, 148, 187;
U.S. Supreme Court Decisions: First
Amendment issues, 234; gay leaders,
rejected by Boy Scouts of America, 82;
polygamy, 74; racial discrimination, 241;
religious liberty, 79–80; school

desegregation, 117; school prayer, 77, 81; schools, parochial, rights of, 176–77, 234–35
U.S. Treasury Department: Alcohol, Tobacco, and Firearms Division, 117
United Theological Seminary, 4
University of Chicago, 72
University of Michigan Law School, 72
University of North Carolina at Charlotte, 116–19
University of Pennsylvania, 225
urban school reform. *See* school reform, urban
USCC (U.S. Catholic Conference). *See* Roman Catholic Church
Utah, 73–74, 241; Utah Supreme Court, 73

Vatican II. *See* Roman Catholic Church
Vatican Congregation for Religious and Secular Institutes. *See* Roman Catholic Church
Vatican Council. *See* Roman Catholic Church
Vermont, 94
Virginia, 144, 152–53
Vitteritti, Joseph, 1
Volpe, Justin, 60
vouchers, school, 2, 8, 10, 13, 22n13, 90

Walker, David, 133n10
Walker, Reverend Dr. Wyatt Tee, 11, 18
Wall Street, 232, 236. *See also* New York Stock Exchange
Wall Street Journal, 16, 50n8
Wallace, Curtis, 45
Wallace Muhammad. *See* Muhammad, Wallace
Walton, John, 10
Warner, John, 152
Warren, Earl, 72
Washington (state), 91, 104, 141–42, 144; Washington State Moral Majority, 141–42
Washington, D.C., 176–78, 182, 241
Washington, George, 90
Washington Post, 50n8, 65, 131, 200
Waterloo Lutheran University, 160

Watts, J. C., 11
Weigel, George, 204, 220n28
Weinberg, Rabbi Matis, 100
welfare programs, 61, 243
welfare reform, 20, 61, 68n22, 103, 108, 142, 238
West, Cornel, 126
West Virginia, 26, 28, 40–41
Weyrich, Paul, 96
Wheaton College, 238
Wheeler, Silas, 44
White House Office of Faith-Based and Community Initiatives, 225
Whittle, Chris, 24n55
Whittle Communications, 24n55
Wilberforce University, 4
Wildavsky, Aaron, 93
Wilderness Society, 167
Williamsburg Charter, 76, 86n29
Wills, Garry, 191
Wilmore, Gayraud, 5
Winfrey, Oprah, 39
WOC (Women's Ordination Conference). *See* Catholics and Catholicism
Woman Church Conference, 188
Women's Ordination Conference. *See* Catholics and Catholicism
women's rights, 176. *See also* feminism
World Bank, 53
World Congress of Families, 82
World Family Policy Center, 82
World Vision, 164
World War I, 55

Xavier University, 177

Yale University, 160; Law School, 100
Yard, Molly, 185
Yeshiva College of South Africa, 99–100
Young, Andrew, 124, 128, 140n62
Young, Brigham, 74
Young, Don, 166
Young-Pombo Bill, 166, 168, 170

Zahn, Gordon, 209
Zaire, 74

About the Contributors

Gretchen S. Carnes is a Ph.D. candidate in political science at Pennsylvania State University and holds an M.A. in political science from Central Michigan University. Her publications and research examine lobbyists in Michigan, immigration in rural areas, and the tactics of religious interest groups.

Joel Fetzer is an assistant professor of politics at Pepperdine University, where he specializes in European and American politics, immigration politics, and religion and politics. He is the author of *Selective Prosecution of Religiously Motivated Offenders in America* and the forthcoming *Public Attitudes toward Immigration in the United States, France and Germany*.

Jo Renee Formicola is a professor of political science at Seton Hall University. She is the author of *The Catholic Church and Human Rights* and the forthcoming *John Paul, Prophetic Politician*. She is also the coauthor of *The Politics of School Choice* and the coeditor of *Everson Revisited*, both with Hubert Morken. She has published a significant number of articles and chapters in books on religion and politics.

William J. Gould is a member of the administration of Fordham University in New York. A specialist in political theory, he concentrates on Catholic politics and has been a contributor to Catholic journals. He is currently preparing a manuscript on John Courtney Murray for publication.

Hubert Morken is a retired professor of government, active for many years in the Religion and Politics Section of the American Political Science Association. His research and writing focus on political activism and religion in the

United States. He is the author of *Pat Robertson*, coauthor of *The Politics of School Choice*, and coeditor of *Everson Revisited* with Jo Renee Formicola.

Michael Leo Owens, a 2000–01 Ford Foundation Fellow, is a visiting assistant professor in the Department of Political Science and scholar in residence at the Office for University–Community Partnerships at Emory University. His research interests are urban politics, public policy implementation, community development, and religion and politics. He previously conducted urban public policy research at the Rockefeller Institute of Government at the State University of New York.

John R. Pottenger is an associate professor of political science at the University of Alabama in Huntsville, where he teaches courses in classical, modern, and contemporary political philosophy. He is the author of *The Political Theory of Liberation Theology* and numerous articles on political theology, moral philosophy, and social theory.

Mark Rozell is an associate professor of politics at the Catholic University of America, teaching in the areas of Congress and the relationship between the media and the government. His writings include a variety of articles in those areas as well as two books: *Second Coming: The New Christian Right in Virginia Politics* and a coedited volume titled *Prayer in the Precincts*.

Mary Segers is a professor of political science at Rutgers University in Newark. She is the coauthor of *A Wall of Separation: The Role of Religion in American Public Life* with Ted Jelen and coeditor of *Abortion Politics in the American States* and *The Catholic Church and Abortion Politics: A View from the States* with Timothy Byrnes. She also coauthored *Elusive Equality: Liberalism, Affirmative Action and Social Change in America* with James Foster and edited *Church Polity and American Politics: Issues in Contemporary Catholicism*. She is currently editing a volume tentatively titled *Religion and Liberal Democracy: An American Perspective*.

James Lance Taylor is an assistant professor of politics at the University of San Francisco and has taught religious, racial, and urban politics. His research emphasizes black politics in transition.